SHAKESPEAREAN ARRIVALS

In this distinctive study, Nicholas Luke explores the abiding power of Shakespeare's tragedies by suggesting an innovative new model of his character creation. Rather than treating characters as presupposed beings, Luke shows how they arrive as something more than functional dramatis personae – how they come to life as 'subjects' – through Shakespeare's orchestration of transformational dramatic events. Moving beyond dominant critical modes, Luke combines compelling close readings of *Romeo and Juliet, Othello, Hamlet, Macbeth* and *King Lear* with an accessible analysis of thinkers such as Badiou, Žižek, Bergson, Whitehead and Latour, and the 'adventist' Christian tradition flowing from Saint Paul through Luther to Kierkegaard. Representing a significant intervention into the way we encounter Shakespeare's tragic figures, the book argues for a subjectivity which is not singular or abiding, but perilous and leaping.

NICHOLAS LUKE is an Australian Rhodes Scholar with degrees in Law and the Arts. He is a Research Fellow at the University of Queensland Node of the Australian Research Council Centre of Excellence for the History of Emotions (Europe 1100–1800).

SHAKESPEAREAN ARRIVALS

The Birth of Character

NICHOLAS LUKE

The University of Queensland

CAMBRIDGE
UNIVERSITY PRESS

CAMBRIDGE
UNIVERSITY PRESS

University Printing House, Cambridge CB2 8BS, United Kingdom

One Liberty Plaza, 20th Floor, New York, NY 10006, USA

477 Williamstown Road, Port Melbourne, VIC 3207, Australia

314-321, 3rd Floor, Plot 3, Splendor Forum, Jasola District Centre, New Delhi - 110025, India

103 Penang Road, #05-06/07, Visioncrest Commercial, Singapore 238467

Cambridge University Press is part of the University of Cambridge.

It furthers the University's mission by disseminating knowledge in the pursuit of
education, learning and research at the highest international levels of excellence.

www.cambridge.org
Information on this title: www.cambridge.org/9781108433822
DOI: 10.1017/9781108380881

First published 2018
First paperback edition 2022

A catalogue record for this publication is available from the British Library

Library of Congress Cataloging in Publication data
NAMES: Luke, Nicholas, 1982– author.
TITLE: Shakespearean arrivals : the birth of character / Nicholas Luke.
DESCRIPTION: Cambridge ; New York, NY : Cambridge University Press, 2018. | Includes index.
IDENTIFIERS: LCCN 2017036756 | ISBN 9781108422154
SUBJECTS: LCSH: Shakespeare, William, 1564–1616 – Characters. | Shakespeare, William,
1564–1616 – Tragedies. | Characters and characteristics in literature.
CLASSIFICATION: LCC PR2989 .L85 2018 | DDC 822.3/3–dc23
LC record available at https://lccn.loc.gov/2017036756

ISBN 978-1-108-42215-4 Hardback
ISBN 978-1-108-43382-2 Paperback

Contents

Acknowledgements   *page* vi

Introduction   1

1   Thinking Arrivals: Rupture, Event, Subject   13

2   The Subject of Love in *Romeo and Juliet*   38

3   Love's Late Arrival: Wonder and Terror in *Othello*'s
     'High-Wrought Flood'   71

4   The Ghostly Event(s) of *Hamlet*   103

5   *Macbeth*: The Arrival of Evil   141

6   The Cordelia Event: Seizing the Vanished in *King Lear*   173

Afterword   205

Notes   208
Works Cited   242
Index   249

Acknowledgements

Whom to thank is the easy part. First and foremost, I thank Simon Palfrey, who guided my doctoral studies with patience, warmth and intellectual vigour. But that is only part of the story, for while this book began its life as a thesis, it has since undergone many and substantial changes. Long after I left Oxford, and far beyond the call of duty, Simon continued to bounce around ideas with generosity and insight. His feel for Shakespeare's language is inspiring, and his insights are doubtless scattered throughout this book – I only hope I offered a couple in return.

I also thank my doctoral examiners, John Gillies and Laurie Maguire, who gave invaluable feedback and encouragement; Adelaide Luke, Ann Luke and Joanna Ward, who provided much needed editorial assistance at various crucial stages; Sarah Stanton and the team at Cambridge University Press, who were a pleasure to deal with; and my first reader at Cambridge University Press, who gave two wonderfully detailed and insightful reports. My thanks go further back too: to Ruth Blair at the University of Queensland, who in many ways set me on my path in literary studies. And thanks end, as they often do, at the very beginning: I'm profoundly grateful to my parents, Don and Ann Luke, first for bribing me to read (the bribes soon weren't needed), but most of all for the many early forums for love and exegesis.

But the end is not the end and my thanks go forward too: to my daughter Ella and most of all my wife Adelaide. I'm not sure you'd classify love as an existential project in world creation, but you make me see it feelingly. For that, and for everything, I thank and love you.

Introduction

How do you say something new about Shakespeare? No doubt all Shakespeare scholars have been asked the question at some point, or even asked it themselves. And what is 'new' in any event? We know that nothing is wholly new, that nothing comes of nothing. Contexts and critical histories fill our minds. Indeed, the new often seems to be little more than a reaction against the old: character critics against old historicists, New Critics against character critics, various postmodern theorists and New Historicists against New Critics and character critics. And on it goes, as new old historicists return to dominate the critical landscape. The actions and reactions of criticism often seem to say more about us, and our academies, than they do about Shakespeare. That is perhaps no great cause for alarm. It is unavoidable that we encounter Shakespeare through the prism of our present concerns, and this is particularly the case in an academic industry that demands constant newness to justify the next paper, the next publication, the next position.

Looking back, it seems clear that this book began in another of these reactions: the ill-defined reactions of a frustrated postgraduate student, uprooted from encouraging Queensland to challenging Oxford. Placed in a foreign environment, a reaction was only natural. Mine was against both the historicist norm and the postmodern scorn for 'character'. It seemed to me that these critics had placed their contextual, linguistic and ideological constructions above the imaginative responses of audiences, readers, directors and actors through the centuries. It seemed as if the heart had been stripped out of the plays, as if the fact that emotional engagement is insufficient for scholarly study had caused critics to reject it entirely. 'If it is not enough, it is nothing!' they seemed to cry, like so many disappointed Lears. Another overreaction – as was mine. For even as I reacted against the more extreme reaction against character and subjectivity, I began to realise that the movement to re-theorise and reinvigorate the human 'subject' and Shakespeare's 'character' had already begun. The reaction was already bubbling away. Character, in particular, did not need my help: 'Character has [already] made a comeback.'[1]

Time passed, as it does, and things changed. I experienced my own arrivals – a daughter born surprisingly early – and perhaps I changed too. But still I felt there was something different about Shakespeare's major characters, only it was something that could not be captured in terms of traditional character. All plays have characters and some even have strong, 'believable' or original ones. All audiences react to characters in some way and some even bring them 'to life' through their imaginative investments and responses (including to the actors' own imaginative responses). Character, I realised, was too general a concept to explain Shakespeare's ongoing newness. But if not character, what? What was it about the plays that made certain Shakespearean characters seem different: to seem as if they were *more* than characters? Something must happen to them, I reasoned, for they do not start out being more than characters. The name 'Juliet' does not pre-empt or contain the extraordinary and singular entity that emerges in the following scenes, any more than her first line, 'How now! Who calls?' (I.iii.5).[2]

So something must happen. A lover's voice from the dark. A ghost on the ramparts. Weird figures on the stormy road. Slowly, a thought formed: what if, in the most basic sense, it is the new that happens to these characters? And the question prompted a reappraisal. What if, rather than desperately trying to say something new about Shakespeare – or to rehabilitate his character and distinguish it from its antecedents – I looked at how the new comes about and operates in Shakespeare's plays? Of course, there are always new interpretations of Shakespeare and this is yet another, but the new also lies at the heart of Shakespeare's dramaturgy. The great tragedies seem to engender it, or spring from it, like Macbeth on the road – a kind of dark Saint Paul – at once confronted by its radical intrusion and transformed by the confrontation. When I looked again, it seemed that it was this rupturing newness, and not Macbeth's ('ambitious') character, that was driving the action and, indeed, driving Macbeth. 'Macbeth' only seemed to come about after, as an effect of the newness – as if drawn from the weird sisters' cauldron. It seemed as if the weird sisters were given the dramatic and imaginative force to convulse the dead world of Duncan's Scotland and thereby conjure the new mode of being that is Macbeth's imaginative subjectivity.

But again, what is the new? Is it the next page of the history, the next link in the chain, or is it the break that unbinds the chain, shuts the book and begins again? For there are many 'news': there is the new product, the new invention, the new dawn, the new breath, the new man. We must anatomize the new. In the Early Modern period, no thinker exemplifies newness more clearly than Montaigne. His new essay form surveys the era's novelties and, in doing so, helps create a new means of representing the self. Montaigne is his subject and, in subjecting himself to a multitude of assays, he builds a remarkably vivid, compelling and at times touching portrait of a mind at work. It is a mind filled with diversity: with generosity and scorn, wonder and disdain; with Falstaff and Hamlet, Miranda and Prospero. Of course, comparison between Shakespeare and Montaigne is almost a given, and for good reason. Reading the essays, the Shakespeare scholar is constantly struck by resemblances, whether it be Montaigne's Hamlet-like distrust of show, his Iago-like insistence that he is not what he is, or his Lear-like recognition of the need for divesting and unlearning. But is Montaigne's self-portraiture commensurate to Shakespeare's creations?

It is here worth looking at two distinct types of newness that are apparent in Montaigne. The first is what we might call the newness of diversity: 'No quality is so universall in this surface of things, as variety and diversity.'[3] In turning his mind to novel customs, occurrences, and discoveries, Montaigne envisages a multi-layered, world-spreading diversity. As he writes of the law: even 'a hundred thousand kinds of particular cases ... hath no proportion, with the infinite diversity of humane accidents'.[4] For Montaigne, inconstancy is the end result of this type of newness, and this inconstancy undercuts the idea of a stable determining 'character'. The human mind is simply too variable and dependent on circumstance: 'If I speake diversly of my selfe, it is because I looke diversly upon my selfe. All contrarieties are found in her.'[5] Montaigne thus splinters the unity of the self in a strikingly modern manner.

Although in one sense Montaigne revels in the newness of diversity, in another his essays are an extended effort to rise above its 'infinit confusion of opinions'.[6] Here enters the second type of newness in the *Essays*: the process of writing that allows Montaigne to, in part, escape this infinite diversity. The process is productive of Montaigne's self and perhaps of a new form of representing selfhood.[7] Montaigne *becomes* a subject – the subject of his essays – through the action of testing, assaying, essaying and self-reflecting that is embodied in the essays themselves: 'I have no more made my booke, then my booke hath made me.'[8] Despite the inconstancy, the custom and the contradiction, for his readers he does emerge as something singular: as Montaigne. In Chapter 1, I therefore discuss how critics have turned to Montaigne as an important Early Modern thinker of 'process', who stresses that one only *becomes* one's self. Furthermore, such a constructed self connects with recent critical attempts to chart a course between the inward-looking and allegedly essentialist understandings of character put forward by Romantic and Bradleian criticism, and the endless diversity of context, discourse and ideology on the other. The subject may not be natural or pre-existing but that does not mean that it cannot *come to be*.

There is, however, a seismic rift between the way in which Montaigne comes to be and the way Shakespeare's major tragic characters 'arrive' as something more than characters. Throughout this book I therefore use Montaigne as an important point of contrast that throws the explosiveness of Shakespeare's creations into relief. To understand this distinction, we must examine how Montaigne establishes an alternative to the limitless diversity of human customs. After showing how custom infiltrates our deepest selves, Montaigne's 'Of Custome' offers something of a way out. Briefly put, we need not thoughtlessly follow our inherited structures and beliefs if we assay them and thereby ourselves: the 'man of understanding' may follow the 'common guise' at the level of appearances, but 'inwardly' he 'retire[s] his minde from the common presse' and possesses 'liberty and power to judge freely of all things'.[9] Montaigne's exceptionalist formulation foreshadows both Hamlet's famed interiority and Iago's dark workshop of inwardness. But it also foreshadows modern capitalist forms of interiority more generally, in which a space is created inside the mind for judgement and freedom – a space for the individual – even as the individual seems almost powerless in the outward world, where it must follow the 'common presse' of consumption.

The final chapter of the third book, appropriately titled 'Of Experience', is a fitting end to Montaigne's *Essays*, concluding in a glorious tribute to the greatness of ordinary life. For all of Montaigne's wide-ranging diversity, there is a charming modesty to this conclusion, in which he celebrates a life of congenial isolation. The voyaging mind tests itself in the world's infinite confusion of opinions, but it does not advance too far into this chaos. It constructs its home and there retires. To some extent, Montaigne emerges as an exception to custom – emerges as Montaigne – precisely by retiring from the world. It is here that the gulf between his essays and Shakespeare's drama begins to yawn. In the chapter 'Of Solitarinesse', Montaigne praises the 'man that is able [to] have wives, children, goods, and chiefly health, but not so tie himself unto them, that his felicitie depend on them':

> We should reserve a store-house for our selves, what need soever chance; altogether ours, and wholy free, wherein we may hoard up and establish our true libertie . . . there to discourse, to meditate and laugh, as, without wife,

without children, and goods, without traine, or servants; that if by any occasion they be lost, it seeme not strange to us to passe it over.[10]

How far we are from Juliet! How far from her violent commitment. How far from Othello and his violent despair. Or from Macbeth's rapture at the words of the weird sisters. Or Hamlet's cursed inability to let go of the ghost – or further still from his rash violence in Act V. There is no retiring for Shakespeare's great tragic characters. There is no modesty. No home. Lear may attempt to retire but he ends up plunging into the storm. Hamlet may long to retire but he ends up plunging into providential action, plunging in the rapier. Montaigne charts a course that is simply not open to Shakespeare's Prince. His selfhood is a slowly drawn portrait: its form emerges gradually as it is placed in manifold scenes and settings, from ancient Greece to far-flung lands only just discovered. And a rich and compelling painting it is. Indeed, more than a painting, for we feel we have seen his mind at work. But that is not Shakespeare or even Hamlet. For Shakespeare's tragic characters, there is no next essay; there is only now, only this world. And it is this violent attachment to their world, to their present moment, in which they must arrive and act, that divides Shakespeare's subjects from Montaigne.[11]

There is, then, an existential urgency in Shakespeare that is not present in Montaigne: the present, the moment, the urgency of now. And not just as a political slogan but a matter of life and death, of becoming what we will forever be. One might respond: well, that's drama; dramatic characters must act and become themselves in the two hours' traffic of the stage. And that's true too, but there is something more at play, something beyond saying 'it's a play'. There are many plays, but not many stage such radical transitions as Hamlet's movement from withdrawal to readiness. Or Romeo's from Petrarchan parrot to committed lover. Or Othello's from sure-footed warrior to crumbling husband. This is not to simply say that Shakespeare's characters change; rather, that through Shakespeare's staging of the radical intrusion of the new they become something other than what they were. They become 'themselves'. Or at least the selves we know. They arrive as 'subjects'.

What, though, does it mean to say that they arrive? First, and most fundamentally, it means that they were not. The change that takes place is more than one of circumstance or knowledge. It is not the old Grecian *peripeteia* but a *creation*. Far from being 'already there' as presupposed entities, I show how they are born before our eyes. It is this radical sense of creation that I believe distinguishes Shakespeare. In examining the emergence of Shakespeare's major tragic characters, the following chapters will show a persistent sense of something coming from nothing, or at least of the coming of something that is nothing like what went before. And this radical form of creation is an irrevocable departure from Montaigne's portraiture. Metaphysically, which is to say dramatically, the world(s) works differently in Shakespeare; things come to be in a different way. The new arrives like a thunderbolt.

The term 'arrival' is vital because it signals a break from traditional notions of character. Seen as a process of arriving as much as a product that arrives, I reach a different understanding of both 'what' and 'where' these characters are. Although Shakespeare's arrivals may be metaphysical, involving the emergence of new subjects and new worlds, their basis always lies in dramatic process. More specifically, the sense of radical creation is the product of a particular type of dramatic motion: an intrusive happening that, following Alain Badiou, I call an 'event'. The following chapters therefore show how Shakespeare's important tragic characters burst excessively from fissures within the play-text and the play-world that configure new forms of language, structure and action. They arrive through dramatic events that rupture the pre-existing 'situation' of both narrative and dramatic structure and thereby prompt them to become something more than functional dramatis personae. The result is a sharp reversal of Bradley's Hegelian notion of a defining character. Action does not come from 'within' character; rather, action reconfigures characters and creates 'subjects'. The subject, here, is not an individual or a settled substance but a diffused dramatic process of arriving. It is not synonymous with character but is something that may (or may not) emerge from these events. We are thus looking at a supra-individual process that builds something more than a character's words or deeds. The point is not an obvious one, for it goes against the search for origins that permeates historicist, cultural and linguistic criticisms, as well as the 'essentialism' of humanist thought. It rejects the search for some extant 'thing' – whether it is language, historical context, culture or spirit – that underpins the subject, and instead looks to its 'becoming': how characters *become* something more than a role or a mouthpiece for cultural and ideological discourses.

It is here worth making a further note about the terminology. There are two reasons why I make the somewhat unusual distinction between 'character' and 'subject'. The first relates to the philosophy of Badiou, which suggests that the subject only emerges through an event and is thus distinct from the individual. But this ties into a second, more fundamental, reason that drew me to Badiou in the first place: there is something of a terminological and conceptual deadlock when it comes to discussing the creation of dramatic character. Is it a name, a role or a virtual person? Is it something that is already there or something that happens? For instance, Bert O. States speaks quite reasonably of 'a single character-entity that will convincingly support a particular range of behavioral acts conditioned by the needs of the plot and idea'.[12] He calls this the character 'container' or 'character base' and argues that it can 'be found in characters of most, if not all, plays from the Greek to the modern period'.[13] For my purposes, the concept of the character-base is too general to help explore what Shakespeare *does* with it, but that does not mean that, in one sense at least, States isn't right that 'character is what is always all there'.[14] For character *has* to always be there: it is what ties together certain actions and utterances in one name, one actor's role, one virtual life. When character is seen as a role, or character-base or even as 'the organizing principle of Shakespeare's plays',[15] it is hard to disagree that the character at the play's end is (necessarily) the same as the character at the play's beginning. States thus points to a terminological difficulty for those – like me – who claim that character is *not* always 'all there'.[16] It is for this reason that I have split the subject from the character. Character, in a functional sense, may always be there, but the 'subject' is not. The split allows an exploration of what Shakespeare does with this base: of what is born *from* character or into what character is born. The character remains the bedrock, but the rising volcanic island of the subject – for as long as it lasts – alters its co-ordinates, its cartography and its language. In short, in becoming a subject, the character relates to, and communes with, its world in a different manner.

The emergence of the new is a difficult thing to map, however. It involves the borderlands between something and nothing, form and form-lessness, borderlands where language begins to break down. Such phrases are evocative of Shakespeare and the clash between Lear and Cordelia, but how does something arrive? Is it possible for something to come from nothing after all? The answers must depend on what counts for nothing and what counts for something. Relevant to these fundamental yet per-plexing questions is the work of Badiou, whose thought is outlined in Chapter 1. Badiou's notion of the 'event' is precisely an examination of these treacherous borderlands. It is critical to my project because it departs from Montaigne at a similar point to Shakespeare: how the new arrives. Badiou's first axiom, like Montaigne's, is multiplicity. For both, the world's 'infinite diversity'[17] (Badiou would say 'infinite multiplicities'[18]) precludes any easy notion of an essential or natural self. And for both, the task of thought is to reach something that lies beyond this inconstancy and diversity. But whereas, for Montaigne, this infinite diversity precludes any radical commitment or revolutionary moment, Badiou's response is quite the opposite: the genuinely new and singular can only emerge through a (revolutionary) rupture of a given multiplicity. In other words, something beyond multiplicity – some 'one' or 'truth' – *can* arrive, albeit through a rare and seemingly miraculous happening. That is Badiou's event. It is not another of Montaigne's 'infinite diversity of humane accidents' but the interruption of this multiplicity, its violent rupture.

The effects of this interruption are profound. Badiou takes up 'adventist' thinkers, such as Saint Paul, in the context of mathematical 'set theory' to show how it is possible for things – above all the 'subject' – to emerge from 'nothing'. Nothing, here, means that which is not presented within a given situation and is, therefore, unthinkable from that situation's perspective. Badiou's event is a dysfunction, or rupture, of a situation's constitutive structure, through which that situation's 'void' – its unknown or unspoken truth – suddenly intrudes as an uncontrollable but creative excess. It is an almost miraculous happening that makes the invisible visible. As with Saint Paul's own transformation, such a rupturing event may cause what previously counted for nothing to suddenly become everything. Saint Paul is a hero for Badiou because, unlike Montaigne, he makes the critical move from the diversity of custom to the radically transformative event that breaks down established differences ('there is neither Jew nor Greek, there is neither bond nor free, there is neither male nor female') in the creation of a new 'truth' ('for ye are all one in Christ Jesus': Galatians 3:26–28).[19] As with Paul's Damascus happening, the result of the event is the birth of a 'new man' (Ephesians 4:24). Put in Badiou's terms, the 'subject' is not a pre-existing entity but is what emerges in fidelity to such a rupture or 'truth-event'. It is what grasps such an event and sets it to work inside the situation. Badiou's subject is not natural, then, but irruptive, breaking into a situation from its 'void'.

Badiou's thought is complex and challenging, but I believe it helps to articulate something complex and challenging in Shakespeare: the dynamic and evental process by which character arrives as something more than character, of how, in a flash, Romeo and Juliet arrive as something other than they were. From the love of *Romeo and Juliet*, to the ghost of *Hamlet*, the weird sisters of *Macbeth* and the 'Nothing' of *King Lear*, Shakespeare founds his plays around gaps, breaks, scandalous intrusions, that irrupt into an existing structure. The generators of these events are found equally in the happenings of plot and in changes of poetic intensity and form. The following chapters show how, in the wake of such happenings, characters confront their changed selves through asides, mid-line shifts and soliloquies, thereby becoming a new 'subject'. The subject, then, does not 'belong' to the character; rather, the movement between character and subject is an event for us, the audience. Such a subject is unstable and precarious but also explosive and creative. Characters may arrive as subjects unexpectedly, almost unprepared for, but they need not arrive at all and, even when they do, they may also fade, retreat or flicker uncertainly.

Some might object that using Badiou to help articulate Shakespeare's dramatic technique is anachronistic, but there are, I think, two counter-points. The first is that this is how history works: that it is, to some extent, anachronistic. History, as Nietzsche writes, is 'untimely', 'acting on our time and, let us hope, for the benefit of a time to come'.[20] It is belated. The following chapters show how events such as Hamlet's voyage strike after the fact to transform the subject and its present. In short, different aspects of the past, and of Shakespeare, arrive at different times. Or, as Benjamin puts it, we should 'grasp[] the constellation' that our era forms with an earlier one.[21] The second, and not unrelated, point is that Badiou taps into a tradition that pre-exists Shakespeare – what I call Christianity's 'adventist' tradition – and which Shakespeare himself belatedly translated into drama. As we shall see, Christian notions of advent and rebirth provide something of a historical model for the immediacy and irruptiveness of Shakespeare's arrivals.

Recognising that Shakespeare's subjects are produced by what happens to them as much as by what they say or do, or that these things are indeed inseparable, forces us to recognise their provisional status: that they rely on something other and alien. Badiou may be chief amongst the thinkers I employ, but he is also part of a long religious and philosophical tradition, from Saint Paul to Luther, Soren Kierkegaard to Slavoj Žižek, which stresses that the genuine subject only arrives through an alien and excessive happening. The subject is, in these terms, not reducible to its cultural and linguistic circumstances but is precisely what *exceeds* these circumstances. Also important is the process-orientated philosophy of Henri Bergson, Alfred North Whitehead and more recently Bruno Latour, which stresses that an entity is not a stable substance but a process of becoming. What unites the thinkers I employ is the insistence that the subject *comes to be*. Together, I use them to establish a more creative alternative to the deadlock between the impossible fullness of the humanist subject and the empty, or even non-existent, postmodern subject.

By stressing the irruptive nature of subjectivity, I hope to get closer to basic questions of passionate emotion – of how the plays embody the passions – that lie outside contemporary criticism's desire for objective scholarship and nameable continuums. It is perhaps closer to what drama does than what we are used to saying about it. My focus on the excessive break is more commensurate with the constant newness and surprise in Shakespeare than the strict thinking of context and causal connection, more commensurate with what Hazlitt describes as the 'whirling rapidity' of Shakespeare's 'imagination' and 'language', with all its 'sudden transitions and elliptical expressions'.[22] My approach is thus removed from historicist criticism, which focuses on historical context and progression rather than the exceptional moment that interrupts this linearity and establishes a new paradigm. Scrupulous historicism is necessarily involved with nameable continuums. It maps literature onto these continuums or nominated histories, which therefore come to structure and 'explain' the work. Shakespeare's drama, however, produces configurations that surpass context and, indeed, the very idea of causal progression. It reflects Nietzsche's claim that we 'need history', and literature, 'for the sake of life and action'.[23] The love of Romeo and Juliet or the 'Nothing' (F.I.i.85) of Cordelia come from somewhere else, somewhere beyond their contextual horizons, even as they arise in plays that are conditioned by their historical moment and are part of our cultural history. As T. S. Eliot puts it:

> [T]here is, in all great poetry, something which must remain unaccountable however complete might be our knowledge of the poet, and that that is what matters most. When the poem has been made, something new has happened, something that cannot be wholly explained by anything that went before. That, I believe, is what we mean by 'creation'.[24]

After theorising the notions of 'arrival', 'event' and 'subject' in Chapter 1, I put them into action by analysing the creation of the joint-subject 'Romeo and Juliet'. The event of love ruptures the 'situation' of Verona – structured by Petrarchan cliché and the opposition of Montague and Capulet – and gives rise to new modes of speech, dramatic form and metaphysics that constitute the lovers' emergence as a 'new baptized' (II.i.92) subject. Chapter 2 thereby provides a (comparatively) straightforward introduction to Shakespeare's arrivals, which I go on to complicate. Chapter 3, for instance, addresses *Othello* as a dark twin to *Romeo and Juliet*. I develop a novel account of Othello's tragic trajectory, showing how Desdemona's love is the central event of the play, which halts Othello's closed narrative and opens up the space for the new, vulnerable Othello subject – ruptured and shaken by events rather than 'all-in-all sufficient' (IV.i.262) – that arrives belatedly in Cyprus. Iago, here, operates as a force for the 'situation', ensnaring Othello by opening a terrifying abyss between the alien event and the stability of his romantic story. Shakespeare's 'arrivals' are thus neither final nor necessarily positive but are precarious and unstable, both always threatening and under threat.

Chapter 4 analyses how Shakespeare calibrates Hamlet's interiority on the obscure borders of representation. Rather than one event of arrival, however, *Hamlet* has two: the intrusive ghost of Act I and the mysterious voyage of Act V. First, Hamlet mirrors the ghost in being divided between a restrictive command to revenge, which follows the circular violence of the 'situation', and a spectral excess that arrives from the situation's void. Second, the nebulousness of his never-present voyage to England brings about a new Hamlet who shares porously with his environs. The almost religious 'beyondness' and blurred temporalities of Hamlet's absent voyage contrast with the material presence of the graveyard and complicate both Badiou's truth-events and critical notions of 'immanence'.

Chapter 5 turns further to the dark side of arrivals, showing how Shakespeare's dramaturgy animates even the most bloody and tortured subject. The spectral intrusion of the weird sisters conjures Macbeth's imaginative consciousness from the cyclical and subject-less situation of Duncan's Scotland. However, the imaginative (the void) comes to take over the whole of the waking mind, so that 'nothing is / But what is not' (I.iii.140–41). That Macbeth comes alive through an openness that ultimately closes him from life makes *Macbeth* something of a problem play for this book and raises difficult questions of Badiou's categories of 'evil'. Finally, Chapter 6 approaches *King Lear* through the prism of the 'Cordelia event'. Opposing bleak postmodern readings, I show how Cordelia's silent love, expressed as 'Nothing', not only breaks down the 'mechanistic' calculability of Lear's love-test – its creative impetus also spreads throughout the play, unleashing the explosive energies of the situation's void and cueing the unexpected arrival of France (and Poor Tom). In *Lear*, however, the energy does not attach to one character – Cordelia and France disappear – but disperses, almost prefiguring the diffused subjectivity of *The Tempest*'s isle. The 'Cordelia event' vanishes into the situation as a haunting excess that is resurrected in various subject 'points'.

From this brief account, I hope it is clear that not all Shakespearean characters arrive as subjects. Of course, all characters do make an entrance, arrive on stage and come before the audience through their actions, words and movements. While such basic dramatic facts are fundamental to how character is built, they do not necessitate the sort of 'events' that found Shakespeare's major tragic subjects. Shakespeare's characters do not necessarily arrive; and, when they do, it is not a matter of once-and-for-all arrivals, of coming to their final modes of being. Character is not a given but is produced anew in specific dramatic moments. As such, character can undergo 'multiple births'.[25] It may arrive as a subject, like the transformed Othello in Cyprus, only to self-destruct or disintegrate. It may arrive only to arrive again, but differently, like Hamlet from his voyage to England. It is never simply 'there' but is perilous, evental and leaping.

CHAPTER I

Thinking Arrivals
Rupture, Event, Subject

Although this book largely rests upon its account of the arrivals of Shakespeare's major tragic characters, it first needs to address some basic questions: what is the nature of these arrivals? How do we talk about them? And how do they fit within existing Shakespeare criticism? To do so, this chapter looks to various critics and thinkers who develop ideas of becoming, transformation and creativity. It finds some commonalities between them, but it does not seek to synthesise these ideas. Indeed, the differences between them will become important in my analysis of the plays, helping to reveal varying and even conflicting aspects of Shakespeare's methods of representing the new. In what follows, I first look to Hegel and A. C. Bradley, who both raise and contain the question of arrivals. Second, I look to various process-oriented thinkers who stress *becoming* over substance. Third, Montaigne's writings about religion lead me to identify an alternative Christian (Pauline) tradition of thinking about the subject: what I call the 'evental' or 'adventist' tradition. Finally, I turn to Badiou, who takes up elements of this tradition in his theory of the evental subject.

At times this discussion might seem to involve a strange brew of disparate theoretical models. I shall endeavour to explain why this is so. When it comes to Shakespeare's drama, all these models are, to some extent, approximations or even metaphors. For instance, I turn to Badiou, not as a rigid framework into which Shakespeare's characters must be squeezed but as an opening to another way of speaking about their arrivals. In other words, the theories put forward provide divergent, differently accented theories of how the new comes about. None fits Shakespeare perfectly. Indeed, to risk stating the obvious, the failure to fit within any one theory is fundamental to poetic literature. Whether we think of it in terms of Kant's free play of the faculties or Derrida's textual play, literature holds or creates a surplus that cannot fit within any one concept. And this is doubly so when we are thinking about how literature *creates* the new. Furthermore, the theories I examine are themselves trying to get at something that is not fully articulable: the way something that was not passes into being, a sort of crossing of the threshold, a non-causal link, a movement from one language to another, a joyous or monstrous birth. As Derrida puts it, we tend to 'turn our eyes away when faced by the as yet unnameable which is proclaiming itself'.[1] Derrida is not, by and large, a thinker of the new. The Derridean event is largely deferred and unknowable, almost messianic. And yet, at times, this may be just the sort of model to help articulate a particular theatrical moment. For instance, I turn to Derrida's future-to-come in the context of Hamlet's mysterious voyage to England. So, there are many theories or metaphors of the new, and one theory may be more germane to one moment in a play, a different theory to the next. In this chapter, I set out the thinkers that I find most consistently useful in constructing a model of Shakespeare's arrivals. However, in the chapters that follow, I also note the limits of this model and point to moments in the plays when philosophical categories break down.

Departures: Bradley and Hegel

The most famous twentieth-century account of Shakespearean character is Bradley's *Shakespearean Tragedy*.[2] And yet, for more than eighty years, we have been told to look somewhat condescendingly at Bradley.[3] There are, of course, good reasons why Shakespeare criticism has moved on, and it is certainly not my intention to turn the clock back a century. I do, however, identify an element in Bradley that should be salvaged. In sum, I seek to acknowledge an important debt and also draw a sharp distinction between his 'characters' and my 'arrivals'. Although Bradley's strategy of bringing 'a vivid and intent imagination' to Shakespeare's plays (rather than approaching them through 'literary history and the like'[4]) might seem old-fashioned, it is not a simple celebration of character. In fact, Bradley's approach involves a sophisticated questioning of character's difficult and *mysterious* relationship with the dramatic action that I seek to follow. We are not, Bradley tells us, dealing with 'the close and unbroken connection of character, will, deed and catastrophe', in which 'the individual . . . fail[s] to conform to . . . the moral order and draw[s] his just doom on his own head'.[5] Things are not that simple. Rather, there is a 'profound sense of sadness and mystery'[6] as these characters we cherish destroy themselves. We might trace this complexity back to Hegel, Bradley's major philosophical influence. Hegel's dialectic famously destabilises our thinking of the subject by defining it by its 'other'. As T. M. Knox observes in his preface to Hegel's *Aesthetics*, 'the one essential route to man's knowledge of himself as spirit is through his knowledge of what is *other* than his true self.'[7] The result is a dynamic and complex relationship between subject, other, and action. While Badiou's relation to Hegel is complicated and evolving,[8] we will see that Badiou is (as his translator Alberto Toscano notes) also 'a thinker of division'.[9] Badiou's event divides both the 'situation' and the subject it initiates.

In Hegel, we can best see this sense of division in *The Phenomenology of Mind*: 'Nothing has a spirit self-established and indwelling within it; rather, each is outside itself in what is alien to it.'[10] The Hegelian movement of confronting otherness (and strangeness) gives a foretaste of the 'alien', excessive and formative events that I seek to pinpoint in Shakespeare. Spirit or mind, as Hegel continues, 'externalizes itself, and then comes back to itself from this state of estrangement'.[11] We will see this sort of 'astonishing'[12] revelation through 'estrangement' at key moments in Shakespeare's tragedies, whether it is Othello confronting an otherness within himself upon arriving in Cyprus, or Hamlet becoming 'himself' by confronting the ghost. Needless to say, such alienation is both rich in dramatic potential and ripe for tragic twists. For one thing, Shakespeare's characters do not necessarily return to 'themselves', or 'transcend[] this otherness',[13] as Hegel dictates. For another, in Shakespeare we are dealing less with a revelation of what was already there than the arrival of something that was not. Such alienations also link to the 'astonishing' power of Hegel's 'Understanding', which works through a dismembering 'action' of 'break[ing] up an idea' and 'separating [its] elements'.[14] Because '[w]hat is "familiarly known" is not properly known', the drive to understand an 'idea' involves 'doing away with its character of familiarity'.[15] As such, I look not to the old, familiar, self-enclosed concept of character but seek to dismember it: to look at the elements of its arrival, at how it is produced. Moreover, I argue that Shakespeare himself creates his characters by staging dramatic breaks of situation and form.

In Bradley, the alienating aspect of Hegel's thought is most evident in the mysterious coming together of character, action and fate at the hero's tragic end. It leads to an explosive breakdown between self and action, as thought strikes something other and becomes other to itself:

> Everywhere, in this tragic world, man's thought, translated into act, is transformed into the opposite of itself. His act, the movement of a few ounces of matter in a moment of time, becomes a monstrous flood which spreads over a kingdom.[16]

Bradley may be discussing the hero's unwitting self-destruction, but we can draw something from this – in particular the frighteningly gratuitous power of action and events – and apply it to the constructive events that *found* Shakespeare's tragic subjects. In the arrivals that I trace, dramatic events seem to unleash a 'monstrous flood' that precedes any intention or agent. These are the moments of 'birth-time', of 'qualitative change', as 'the sunrise, which, in a flash and at a single stroke, brings to view the form and structure of the new world'.[17]

Such an expansion of Bradley's 'monstrous flood' is supported by States's view that Shakespeare employs a 'transformational', as opposed to a '*disposi-tional*', 'method of characterization'.[18] However, States's view that 'character will always be itself … [and] will rarely, if ever, surprise us',[19] leads to something of a definitional tangle when it comes to Shakespeare's 'transfor-mational' method. Although the character's 'behavior … may be "warped" out of its normal disposition by the pressures of the situation', for States this does '*not* [mean] that the character changes in nature'.[20] But if we separate the character-base from the living subject it may become, we can acknowl-edge that the 'pressures of the situation' may in fact produce subjects. Indeed, States points in this direction when he writes that '[u]nlike Marlowe's heroes of the massive appetite, who seem to be born with motives in full flight, Shakespeare's tend … to have motives thrust upon them'.[21] There is a 'lightninglike speed' in which '[m]etaphysical forces like the Witches … "rap" the hero and ionize his world into a metaphysical field'.[22] I will argue, these sorts of ionising events unleash a violent but creative torrent that, in a sense, *is* the subject.

In Bradley, however, the torrential aspect of dramatic character and action is ultimately sidelined. Viewing the tragedy as 'pre-eminently the story of one person, the "hero"',[23] Bradley contains this explosive power within the individual. He fails to see how this 'monstrous flood' may, in fact, *create* the 'hero': how this excess produces something that is more than 'one person'. In large part, this failure stems from Bradley's emphasis on the totalising end of Hegel's dialectic: on how 'otherness' is ultimately 'transcend[ed]'.[24] It is this aspect of Hegel that Bradley stresses when he concludes that Shakespeare's tragedies involve an overarching spiritual order that violently 'casts' the tragic hero 'out' to restore its unity.[25] The result is that he explains away the tragedy's 'division or conflict'[26] (the driving force of the play) as a *corruption* of this spirit. Shakespeare's 'alien' and electrifying dramatic happenings are moralised and normalised in his contention that 'the main source of the convulsion which produces suffer-ing and death is never good: good contributes to this convulsion only from its tragic implication with its opposite in one and the same character'.[27] The thrust of this book, in contrast, is that the plays' 'convulsions' are not corruptions but creative events that give rise to Shakespeare's subjects. So whereas Bradley concludes that 'Iago is the main source of the convulsions in *Othello*',[28] I show that Iago's power arises only because Desdemona's love has already convulsed Othello's monumental self-sufficiency. Far from being 'evil', the convulsion is an almost miraculous moment that allows him to arrive as a subject, however briefly.

In contrast, Hegel's totalising leads to the idea that material action is merely an expression of character's inwardness: it is 'characteristic of the living subject . . . to act . . . because this ideal has to carry out and bring to fruition what is implicit in it'.[29] Badiou decries this type of reasoning as 'Hegelian circularity',[30] which 'basically claims that what is attained in a dialectical move is nothing more than what was already there from the very immediate beginning'.[31] For Hegel's tragic hero, action merely 'reveal[s]' the 'true kernel of his disposition and capacity':[32] 'So, for example, Macbeth's character is determined by his passion of ambition.'[33] We thus reach the derided notion of pre-existing character, albeit after a process that is far more fruitful than its result: 'calamities and catastrophe follow inevitably from the deeds of men, and . . . the main source of these deeds is character.'[34] For Bradley, '[t]he centre of the tragedy, therefore, may be said with equal truth to lie in action issuing from character, or in character issuing in action'.[35] The movement here is all one way: action issues 'from' character, and character issues 'in' action, but action does nothing to character.

A similar tendency is evident in two recent revivals of Bradley. Peter Holbrook champions Bradley as part of his broader celebration of the 'I am that I am' ethos that he finds in Shakespeare's work.[36] Although I very much share Holbrook's interest in the becoming of the self – including the creative and sometimes morally troubling way that it may break from social convention – my analysis charts an almost diametrically opposed course. Whereas Holbrook focuses on the individual who finds a 'true self' that 'was always there',[37] I focus on the event that divides the character from itself and turns it into what it was not. Lorna Hutson has sought to rejuvenate Bradley's 'quasi-forensic inquiry'[38] into motivation in a very different way. In short, the inferential reasoning demanded by Renaissance legal training authorises 'an appreciation of Shakespeare . . . that . . . suggest[s] that characters have "prehistories" and "normal lives"'.[39] Of course, Hutson's point is that these prehistories are not pre-existing but are created by the quasi-legal processes of inference and rhetoric ingrained in Shakespeare's drama. Nonetheless, I show that Shakespeare's dramatic events often interrupt, and even shatter, this sense of a character's pre-existing life. Rather than constructing character and motivation through novelistic inference,[40] I look to moments in which inference, causation and motivation are swept away in the evental flood.

The ultimate problem with Bradley's approach is that it places character prior to the dramatic action and events through which it arrives. Treating character as the plays' 'prime mover' prevents him from grasping the dramatic origins of the mysterious and 'monstrous' action that he rightly highlights. It causes him to apologise for events of insanity, the supernatural or accident, because they threaten character's agency. It is, however, precisely these events that make Shakespeare's characters something extraordinary and rupturing. Bradley stresses that the supernatural does not destroy agency,[41] and I do not disagree, but he does not address how its intrusion may impel an emergent agency. Bradley stresses that too much 'accident' may break 'the causal connection of character, deed, and catastrophe',[42] but he does not address how it may *cause* a new subject to leap into existence, as when Hamlet returns from his encounter with the pirates, or when Othello arrives belatedly in Cyprus after the storm. Of course, we need go no further than Aristotle to see that Bradley's is not the only vision of tragic character: 'tragedy is a *mimesis* not of people but of their actions and life.'[43] The idea of 'arrivals' stems from a similar recognition: action does not come from within character but produces character. As a dramatic construct, there is no 'within' from which action can stem. I therefore seek to reverse the trajectory of Bradley's understanding of character and, in so doing, to revitalise his interest in the mysterious relationship between action and character.

Movements: Process Philosophy

The term 'arrival' suggests both that Shakespeare's subjects must arrive and, in its verb form, that they are sustained by an ongoing action or process of arriving. The first, and broadest, theoretical underpinning for this position is the 'process philosophy' that was developed by the likes of Alfred North Whitehead and Henri Bergson. It may be less dramatic, and more general, than Badiou's event, but it is nonetheless important to my analysis of the plays. In this sense, my project is very much in line with recent critical movements to turn to ideas of process, flux and becoming in the analysis of Shakespeare.[44]

Central to process philosophy is the rejection of the Cartesian separation of the thinking mind and the external mechanical universe. As Bruno Latour explains, Descartes's division led him to search 'for absolute certainty from a brain-in-a-vat, a certainty that was not needed when the brain (or the mind) was firmly attached to its body and the body thoroughly involved in its normal ecology'.[45] Descartes's subject–object divide casts a long shadow. Although Hegel's dialectic to some extent breaks down this opposition, the totalising impulse of his thought maintains a fundamental division between self-consciousness and the 'alien world'.[46] Michael Inwood describes this as Hegel's 'metaphysical (and aesthetic) xenophobia',[47] by which the alien other is annulled and made part of self-consciousness. 'Postmodernism', meanwhile, also 'inherited … the disconnected mind-in-the-vat's quest for absolute truth', with the difference that 'it has *stopped* believing it is possible to carry out this implausible program successfully'.[48]

If the subject arrives through an action or process, however, the great divide between subject and world begins to break down. The result is not the subject's disintegration into linguistic superstructure, but its entanglement in its world. The subject does not lose its reality in this entanglement but gains layers of reality. In contrast to the way the modern 'settlement' attempts to 'construct a tiny footbridge over th[e] chasm' 'between words and the world', Latour outlines 'an entirely different phenomenon: circulating reference'.[49] Latour bases this idea on scientific practice. He focuses not on 'the resulting abstraction' that graces the scientific report, but on the process by which things become words, so that the 'immense abyss separating things and words … [is] … distributed to many smaller gaps'.[50] Focusing on process allows Latour to develop a 'positive meaning of relativism', which 'define[s] existence not as an all-or-nothing concept but as a gradient'.[51] The concept is important for analysing the 'unreal' world of drama because it permits its constructions and affects a reality, despite its fictionality. Dramatic characters – these strangely real unreal people – need not be labelled essence or illusion, everything or nothing, but may be given a reality that circulates elusively between the drama, its events, its characters and its spectators.[52] They arrive not as Hegel's absolute spirit but as relative subjects, subject to the drama. And yet they do arrive.

Latour is writing in the tradition of Bergson and Whitehead, for whom the basic building blocks of existence are not 'substances' – independent and static in the Cartesian sense – but processes and occasions. Whitehead offers a 'direct denial of the Cartesian doctrine, "… an existent thing which requires nothing but itself in order to exist"'.[53] Rather, an 'entity, in virtue of being *what* it is, is also *where* it is'.[54] An entity is never 'just its static self' – an independent substance – for its 'very essence … is *process*'.[55] Being is therefore 'immanent': 'the essence of being is to be implicated in causal action on other beings'.[56] Michael Witmore places Shakespeare in the company of Bergson and Whitehead because of 'his refusal to make the being of a particular thing – whether we are talking about a thinking person, a perception, or a phenomenal attribute – a property of a single body and thus a purely local "possession"'.[57] The 'identity' of things is, rather, 'immanent to – or better, intertwined with – the situation or process in which they came to exist'.[58] For Witmore, therefore, 'events . . . are the most basic units of any theatrical experience'.[59] Not only is 'occasion', in all its corporeality and contingency, 'the fundamental metaphysical building block' of theatre, it is what brings about 'the immanence of theatrical personhood as it coalesces on stage'.[60]

Bergson is also relevant in this regard because he critiques the 'mechanical explanation' of nature that 'regard[s] the future and the past as calculable functions of the present' and thus 'claim[s] that *all is given*'.[61] Against this 'finalism', which is 'reluctant to see . . . an unforeseeable creation of form',[62] Bergson opposes evolutionary life, which, like art, creates something that did not previously exist:

> The finished portrait is explained by the features of the model, by the nature of the artist, by the colours spread out on the palette; but, even with the knowledge of what explains it, no one, not even the artist, could have foreseen exactly what the portrait would be.[63]

Similarly, I seek to examine how the processes of Shakespeare's drama, full of sudden interruptions and poetic shifts, create something unforeseen. To co-opt Latour's words about the scientific 'experiment', Shakespeare's drama is not a 'zero-sum game' that can be 'accounted for by a list of the elements that entered the situation *before* its conclusion', but '*an event*'[64] that produces new entities.

Observing the processual nature of Shakespeare's characters is not a recent phenomenon. Hazlitt pointed in this direction long ago, writing that while '[i]n Chaucer we perceive a fixed essence of character', in Shakespeare 'there is a continual composition and decomposition of its elements, a fermentation of every particle in the whole mass'.[65] As an admirer of Montaigne, it is perhaps no surprise that Hazlitt envisages a character that is subject to what is outside it – that is changing, mutating, not at one with itself. It is unpredictable and evental: 'Till the experiment is tried, we do not know the result, the turn which the character will take in its new circumstances.'[66] Character is thus not a calculable result of its context but emerges in the dramatic moment: 'every instant teems with fate.'[67] And it is this teeming creation, decomposition and recomposition that underpins my understanding of Shakespeare's arrivals.

Much more recently, Philip Davis has captured this aspect of Shakespeare by taking up both process philosophy and Hazlitt's 'whirling rapidity'[68] in his work on Shakespeare's vital, 'morphological'[69] linguistic experiments. As Davis suggests, John Florio's Montaigne would have given Shakespeare 'his own sense of process philosophy'.[70] And this connects with Holbrook's idea that Montaigne (who in this was 'soulmates' with Shakespeare[71]) 'repeatedly insists upon the preeminent importance of th[e] project of becoming oneself'.[72] The two differ, however, on the origins of this becoming. Holbrook's emphasis tends to be on becoming, or accepting, who we already are: 'For Montaigne the raw material for unity of character was *always there*.'[73] Holbrook thus speaks of a 'master-form' or 'essence' that one has to 'find', 'discover' and 'embrace' to become one's true self.[74] Davis offers a sharp alternative: 'Mind, like character itself, is not there to begin with in Shakespeare; it is dramatically *thought into being* on the stage.'[75] In his earlier book, *Sudden Shakespeare*, Davis stresses the rapid, unconditioned way in which Shakespearean character springs into being. He argues that 'character', in the traditional sense of 'fixed and ready-made people', simply 'does not exist in Shakespeare'.[76] The master-form is not already there. Rather, '[c]haracter is what *happens*'.[77] 'Shakespeare's people' only 'discover how much they indeed have in them' by 'dangerously giving themselves'.[78] Davis's work thus both anticipates and complements my account of how Shakespeare's subjects give themselves, suddenly and transformatively, to events.

Simon Palfrey is another recent critic who contends that character is something that happens: 'Characters' births are on-going and *evental*, their "composition" ensuing from all sorts of theatrical moments and materials.'[79] The result is that '[e]very word, or cue-space, or costume . . . might be a subject-altering or subject-making event, or a fold of one'.[80] For Palfrey, however, character is not the primary focus. Rather, he seeks to examine the manifold – indeed seemingly infinite – 'points of life' in Shakespeare's plays.[81] He calls these points 'formactions': 'the active forms of play-worlds, their working parts and craft materials', which include everything from 'cues' to 'metaphors', 'scene breaks' to 'onstage silence'.[82] Whereas Palfrey looks to the endless (possible) worlds that are conjured by the smallest details of Shakespeare's plays, my project is much more limited: it looks at the emergence of one particular type of character-sized life. In their very different ways, Davis and Palfrey take the micro approach to Shakespeare's life and suddenness, whereas I try to build these micro-elements into a macro-structure of how Shakespeare's tragic subjects come to be. Moreover, my Badiouan understanding of the event is far more specific than the ordinary 'occasions' and endless 'happenings' that constitute Whitehead's immanent reality; the creative vitality of Bergson; the formactions of Palfrey; or, indeed, the 'verbal chemistry' that Davis's linguistically sudden Shakespeare employs to create 'infinite variety out of a finite matrix'.[83] Not just any type of happening founds a subject. It is an event that intrudes into a situation, breaks its structures and introduces an unseen excess.

In this I also depart from the broader return to character.[84] For instance, while Yachnin and Slights' collection valuably explores how character is created through the coming together of actors, texts and audiences, it tends to conclude with a general affirmation of the 'basic processual, collaborative nature of character' as 'something actively being made by actors and audience-members'.[85] These collaborative processes are, of course, foundational to Shakespeare's construction of character. However, they are also very general processes that do not specifically address the ongoing newness of Shakespeare's characters. I argue that Shakespeare's evental process supplements this foundation. Character, in the event, becomes something else; it becomes a different sort of construct. As such, my approach is deliberately partial. It does not seek to capture all of Shakespearean 'character', let alone 'Shakespeare', but to highlight an evental aspect of Shakespeare's dramaturgy that has often been overlooked: how something excessive arrives *from* the character-container.

As such, my approach does nothing to dismiss either theatrical or phenomenological understandings of character. We might return, here, to the name 'Juliet'. I earlier stated, obviously enough, that the name does not contain the extraordinary being that emerges, but this does not mean that the name is unimportant. Indeed, Thomasson shows that part of the reality of fictional characters stems from their textual 'naming', which 'serves as a kind of indexical reference to the character', 'by means of which that very fictional object can be baptized by author or readers'.[86] Shakespeare necessarily begins with a named role, or dramatis persona, or character-base. But then something happens: something happens whereby character becomes more than a role or 'indexical reference'. What I argue, in essence, is that Shakespeare's major tragic characters must undergo some sort of 're-baptism'. If the first mention of Romeo by Lady Montague baptises 'Romeo' – calling him into existence as an 'abstract artifact'[87] – we await a second, evental, baptism ('Call me but love and I'll be new baptized' (II.i.92)) in which he truly arrives as part of the new subject 'Romeo and Juliet'. The following chapters thus trace the coming-to-life of the name: how, in response to an event, Shakespeare's character is not only altered from its original co-ordinates, it comes to speak – dare I say think – its own alteration, its distance from its base.[88] What we have, then, is almost a meta-character: a baptism within a baptism, a birth within a birth. Character, as subject, is born again.

Arrivals: Events and Subjects

The critical turn to ideas of 'process' is composed of a broad church of dynamic movements, Deleuzian assemblages, becoming and immanence.[89] As I have noted, I broadly join with its examination of how Shakespeare's linguistic and dramatic processes create worlds and characters before our eyes and ears.[90] However, I also offer an important correction, or caveat. The focus on process and immanence sometimes threatens to become a description of the 'way of all things'. The world is flowing. Nothing is fixed: '*All* things *always* change.'[91] We have a sort of universalised Heraclitus or Lucretius. Witmore, for instance, speaks of a 'certain creativity at the heart of being, one whose signature or trademark is the singular novelty of each new occasion'.[92] And Palfrey writes that '[t]here are points of life everywhere'[93] in Shakespeare and follows Leibniz's claim that 'substance is change'.[94] While I largely agree with these sentiments, Shakespeare's drama also suggests something else: the exceptional moment as well as the universal flow. Process and flux may be integral to 'being' (and to Shakespeare), but there is also a form of *discontinuity* – of rupture and event – that threatens to be effaced by such semi-structural or vitalist interpretations. Relevant, here, is Badiou's critique of Bergson and Deleuze. He argues that they treat Life or Being as one vitalist Whole in which '"All" *is* grace'.[95] But, for Badiou, 'to say that all is grace' (or change) 'means precisely that we are never ever accorded any grace' (or genuine change).[96] 'But this is not correct', for '[grace] *does* occur', only it occurs 'by interruption or by supplement'.[97]

We can think of this distinction another way. Richard Shoaf's Lucretian focus on 'swerving' atoms emphasises 'turbulence' as *the* quality of life – '[a]ll vitality is turbulent'[98] – but turbulence can be a slight bump *en route* or it can alter the course, divert the flight, send it back or send it down. In other words, even if there is constant change and motion, not all change is equal. Some motion may not amount to anything, as we will see with the upheavals of Duncan's Scotland in I.ii. In Badiou's terms, one might say that such inconsequential motions are contained within a 'situation'. The atoms may be constantly swerving, but they are swerving within a sealed cylinder. But there are also changes that crack the cylinder and send the atoms swerving for real – that, suddenly, release a different kind of movement. We see this with the weird sisters: they unseam the situation so that atoms swerve from its void in unforeseen directions, creating dark new configurations. It is with these sorts of unstructural, indeed, de-structuring, changes that this book deals. This is not to deny the broader arguments for Shakespeare's processual, fluxional, dynamic language. Indeed, the ideas may be complementary: Shakespeare's language may produce endless swerves, but I look to how some of these become events. As such, while I unashamedly focus on large transformative happenings, I also look to how these arise from, or are manifest in, the smallest levels of detail: in shifts in language or regard or in seemingly peripheral scenic devices. The micro and macro often merge.

To articulate the nature of these events, I return to the fundamental divide between Shakespeare and Montaigne. Although Davis notes the importance of Montaigne as a processual influence on Shakespeare, he also shows that Montaigne's 'gradual accretion of an implicit autobiography'[99] and his desire for an 'essentially *un*dramatic time and space in which to pause and be free' are 'radically unlike tragic Shakespeare'.[100] Davis accounts for this difference through his account of Shakespeare's cognitive and linguistic processes: of how Shakespeare's lightning-fast metaphor involves a 'primal life-thinking';[101] of how Shakespeare's 'quasi-neurological language affect[s] movements of [the] brain at a level anterior to mental conceptualization'.[102] My account is quite different. Above all, I argue that Montaigne's essayistic self-reflections are incommensurate to the violent and terrifying intrusion of newness in Shakespeare.

Part of the difference stems from the dramatic form itself. For instance, in Chapter 2, we will see the peril that exists in the 'part' of Juliet: how the part's speech-closing half-lines, such as 'Take all myself' (II.i.91), cue an unknown speaker and refuse to tell the actor from where, or even if, a response will come. Palfrey and Stern's analysis of actors' parts is relevant to this study because it shows that this sort of risk was integral to Shakespeare's play-texts. The fact that actors were given only their own lines, rather than the whole play, resulted not only in 'every subject assum[ing] his own existence as the predicate of all else',[103] but also in clashes with other part-texts. The part may be the actor's 'founding possession', but this possession is far from stable, for the actor must encounter the unknown of other parts in the 'urgent immediacy' of 'the event of performance'.[104] Palfrey and Stern thus argue that Shakespeare used the discrepancies between the incomplete part-texts to make his actors feel something of the 'character's similar experiential peril'.[105] We might say that a character arrives as a 'subject' for the actor – claiming its own dramatic and 'ontological integrity'[106] – through the textual events and ruptures, convergences and disjunctions, that occur when discontinuous part-texts collide.

There is, then, a critical distinction between Montaigne's solitary, calm and 'gradual accretion' of self and the social, dynamic and often sudden irruptions of selfhood in Shakespeare's plays. The life and death 'immediacy' of 'the event of performance' simply cannot be captured by Montaigne's wide-angle portraiture. Whereas Montaigne 'assays' the subject by 'tast[ing]' his self from all angles – 'I uncessantly consider, controle and taste my selfe'[107] – Shakespeare assays the subject by putting his characters on trial and in peril. There is no next essay for Shakespeare's characters. The play's tumult is their sole world and foundation, in which they arrive and perish. So although Montaigne paints a compelling picture of a subject-in-motion, his emphasis is not on how the subject can be irrevocably made or unmade by intrusive events. Montaigne may have influenced Hazlitt, but Hazlitt's idea that the tragic action 'depends upon the turn of a thought' – that '[a] word, a look, blows the spark of jealousy into a flame; and the explosion is immediate and terrible as a volcano'[108] – captures an eruptive power that is qualitatively different to Montaigne's slow, diary-like accretion of selfhood. Whereas 'the variation within the personality that Montaigne found … [entailed] a horizontal multiplicity of expression', it 'precluded transformation'.[109] But transformation is precisely how Shakespeare's subjects arrive. The present moment in Shakespeare is far more efficacious – and terrifying – than Montaigne allows. Things change in an instant and they change forever. In a glance, Juliet is no longer the old Juliet. In a word, Macbeth is transported from Glamis. Old worlds perish and new worlds spring into being. There is no path back. There is no next time. There is often no judgement. The difference from Montaigne, as we shall see, is as much metaphysical as dramatic, as much substance as form. It is, indeed, the very heart of what 'arrival' means.

The Pauline Event

The metaphysical rift between Shakespeare and Montaigne is perhaps best delineated in religious terms. Whatever he actually believed,[110] Montaigne draws a strict opposition between faith and the infinite diversity of human opinion. His trials of judgement are '[a] matter of opinion, and not of faith. What I discourse according to my selfe, not what I beleeve according unto God.'[111] Religion, on the other hand, is something 'setled, concluded, and directed by celestiall ordinance, incapable of any doubt or alteration'.[112]

God-given faith is thus not part of the questionable world. It is not to be tested, tasted or put on trial. And it is therefore detached from the questioning, doubting 'Montaigne' who emerges in the essays. So although Montaigne refers to faith as an absolute, it does not enter the frame of his self-portraiture. One might be tempted to say something similar of Shakespeare. Critics have been tantalised by the question of Shakespeare's faith because the plays do not declare it. But that is to talk of Shakespeare the man (about whose beliefs I have no beliefs) rather than the subjects that arrive in his plays. I look to moments in which the absolute enters the frame of the plays and inspires a leap into the unknown. The faith here is hardly a personal Christian faith, however. It is perhaps better conceived as an imaginative faith that an absolute moment – of love or magic or providence – may come to transform a life. Such leaps are central to the way that Shakespeare constructs his major tragic figures. Whether it is Juliet, communing with a voice that comes from the darkness before she leaps into love, or Macbeth, communicating with the forces of darkness before he leaps into 'what is not', the 'beyond' enters the frame of the plays and radically reconfigures their existing parameters. Indeed, it is my argument that these characters arrive as 'subjects' *through* such leaps.

If there is one word that describes the gulf between Montaigne's essays and Shakespeare's drama, then, it is surely 'advent'. There is a critical distinction between the adventist, or evental, Christian tradition, as founded by Saint Paul, and Montaigne's severed absolute. Starobinski notes that, for Montaigne, 'the truth of things is out of reach': 'Truth dwells with God ... in a beyond that men can only "imagine unimaginable."'[113] Now, it is no great surprise that the divine should be described as cut-off from ordinary, material existence. But there is more than this to the Christian tradition, for there is also sublimation, and there is also advent. Montaigne's separation of divine and human is far removed from this aspect of Christianity, which stresses that the beyond does enter the frame; the divine becomes man; the divine becomes material. Whether it is the sublimation of Christ, or Saul's transformation on the road to Damascus, the divine does not remain 'absolutely and perfectly other'[114] but miraculously enters the ordinary world. As we shall see with Hamlet's rash providence, the 'other' or absolute also enters the frame in Shakespeare, and it does so with transformative power.

I turn to this 'evental' or 'adventist' Christian tradition for three reasons. First, it founds a model of the subject – the subject that is reborn through the irruptive event – that is taken up by the likes of Kierkegaard, Badiou and Žižek.[115] Second, it was a central pillar of Early Modern thought about the subject, and one that, as we will see with Romeo's claim that he will 'be new baptized' (II.i.92) in love, is manifested in Shakespeare's technology of character creation. Again, the point is not that Shakespeare believes in a Christian rebirth but that, as a matter of dramaturgy, it is in operation in the plays. And third, criticism has struggled to address it. Jackson and Marotti note that early modern religion 'resists our alterity criticism', which is primed to recognise and respect 'difference' or 'otherness', with the ironic result that it fails to respect religion's otherness, instead 'transforming religion into politics or culture, and ignoring its alterity'.[116] Badiou reveals how religion may speak to quite the opposite movement: a movement not to explain events by some pre-existing concept but to experience an event's transformative and inexplicable excess. The religious moment is not reducible to the context in which it is placed but may transform its place into alterity by generating new modes of thought and expression.

In large part, this aspect of Christianity stems from Saint Paul. Following Saul's road to Damascus encounter, whereby he breaks out of his inherited signifying practice and becomes Paul the Apostle, founder of the Christian church, there is a Christian tradition that focuses on the birth of a new subject. Paul, who is dead to his old self, commands us to 'put on the new man' (Ephesians 4:24). Doubtless this adventist strand was, and is, often obscured by dogma and custom and habit. Nonetheless, it was always there, waiting to be reborn. Indeed, a millennium and more after Saint Paul, after the collapse of scholasticism, amidst the rise of capitalism, Luther returned to Paul's 'new man': 'But the Spirit, the divine grace, grants strength and power to the heart; indeed, he creates a new man who takes pleasure [in obeying] God's commandments.'[117] Luther here declares the utter centrality of man's transformation by grace. And while this grace becomes part of the subject's interiority, manifest as faith, it also remains unavoidably foreign, coming from the outside as 'a divine work in us which changes us to be born anew of God'.[118] It is an 'alien righteousness', a 'righteousness of another, instilled from without', which comes from Christ and 'works by grace alone' to change us.[119]

The Pauline happening is fundamentally different from Montaigne's ancient religion. For Paul, religion is a response. It is a new way of living, developed in response to an event that intrudes, ruptures and radically transforms. It kills the old law and the old self. It creates a new man. And it happens now, in the life and death urgency of the present moment. As Agamben stresses, the time of the apostle is 'the time of the now'.[120] For Montaigne, faith is not a leap but an inheritance. It is passed down and received as an ancient tradition that continues, sustains and stretches back. Its origins are distant and unrecoverable. It is the old law and the old self. It is already there and in no way creates a new man:

> I am no more upon termes of any great alteration nor to thruste my selfe into a new and un-usuall course, no not toward augmentation: it is no longer time to become other or be transformed ... To conclude, I am ready to finish this man, not to make another.[121]

In short, we have a venerated ancient custom rather than a revolutionary individual experience. For Montaigne, the customary laws of religion should not be easily changed. For Paul and Luther, customary laws and beliefs are razed to the ground. Montaigne's experience of his country's religious conflicts bred a deep distrust of revolutionary change: '*Onely change doth give forme to injustice, and scope to tyranny.*'[122] It may be justifiable to make small improvements but to 'change or remoove the foundations of so vast a frame, belongeth only to them, who instead of purging, deface and in liew of cleansing, scrape out'; them that 'cure diseases by death'.[123] The evental Christian tradition embraces Montaigne's charge. It embraces the death of the old. The new beginning absolutely requires a 'defac[ing]', a 'scrap[ing] out', a razing. It requires the hatred of father and mother, wife and children, brother and sister, and of one's own life (Luke 14:26). It requires a death to be reborn.

We have, then, a distinctive motion or physics of the subject's emergence, which entails the sudden interruption and razing of the old self and its place within the existing codes of communication. The old self is unrecognisable, indeed dead, to the radically new creation that emerges by grace. Žižek thus describes 'the "good news" of Christianity: the miracle of faith is that it IS possible to traverse the fantasy, to undo this founding decision, to start one's life all over again, from zero point – in short, *to change Eternity itself (what we "always-already are")*'.[124] It is this sense of starting over that makes Paul an important thinker for Badiou. Badiou's event also comes as grace, from outside the situation's old law, from its void, to open up a new mode of being. Paul therefore provides a model for how Badiou's 'events' reconfigure the subject. Žižek outlines how 'although Saint Paul's particular message is no longer operative for us':

> the very terms in which he formulates the operative mode of the Christian religion do possess a universal scope as relevant for every Truth-Event: every Truth-Event leads to a kind of 'Resurrection', – through fidelity to it and a labour of Love on its behalf, one enters another dimension.[125]

Christianity's subjective transformation thus need not be limited to religious salvation. It is a model that itself flickers through the millennia, returning in vastly different contexts, and turning to vastly different ends. Even secular philosophy. Even secular drama. The point is not the salvational framework but the sense of the arresting event ripping the subject from its old identity in a moment of transfiguring intensity.

Such thinking also flows into the proto-existentialist work of Kierkegaard, who shows how one can be dead, then alive, and then dead again – how life can be unlived. Kierkegaard is an important thinker of 'arrival' because he stresses how the subject *comes to be*: 'the new is brought about through the leap.'[126] Subjectivity is not natural or essential; it is attained through a great and hazardous movement. There are many that 'take a hand in the game of life as it were, but … never have the experience of staking all upon one throw'.[127] For Kierkegaard, of course, this 'throw' is, like Pascal's wager, rooted in the Christian faith. *Fear and Trembling* celebrates Abraham's suspension of the ethical in his faith that God would achieve the impossible. Greatness, then, is determined 'in proportion to the greatness of what *he loved*' and in 'proportion to his *expectancy*', so that 'he who expected the impossible became greater than all'.[128]

We can now see why the eventual model challenges many existing theories of character. Trevor Ponech, for instance, conceives of character as 'a *public agent-concept*: a certain kind of psychological item standing in a reciprocal, historical relation to a certain vehicle of expression'.[129] But as well as being too broad to get at the particularity of Shakespearean character, such concepts are what Shakespeare's drama regularly breaks down. Apparent 'agent-concepts' suddenly face something other – another agent-concept or an other within themselves – that re-conceptualises them with sudden violence. Hamlet, that most famous agent-concept, meets another, even more obscure and amorphous agent-concept, Providence, on an unseen voyage to England, and he is transformed as both an agent and a concept. Romeo, a byword or agent-concept for a starry-eyed young lover, becomes a different kind of agent and concept through his baptism into the new, joint, agent-concept 'Romeo and Juliet'. Of course, the 'new man' is never entirely new. He has the same body. He exists in the same space. One might be tempted to say that he speaks the same language. But, as Badiou makes clear, language is precisely what *is* changed, however provisionally and incompletely. The event reconfigures one's way of relating to, and speaking about, the world.

Badiou's Evental Subject

In a non-salvational form, Badiou captures something of how Paul's creative grace emerges from 'elsewhere'. He gets at how things come to be. And he thereby provides a language that allows me to get closer to Shakespeare's creativity than historicism's search for explanatory origins or Montaigne's prolonged self-explorations. Because it only emerges through fidelity to a rupturing 'truth-event', Badiou's subject is irruptive, breaking into the situation from the outside and fragmenting its existing parameters:

> Let us say that a *subject*, which goes beyond the animal (although the animal remains its sole foundation) needs something to have happened, something that cannot be reduced to its ordinary inscription in 'what there is'. Let us call this *supplement* an *event*, and let us distinguish multiple-being, where it is not a matter of truth (but only of opinions), from the event, which compels us to decide a *new* way of being.[130]

Unlike Bradley's character, Badiou's subject does not direct what happens but flows from it. And unlike the postmodern or historicist subject, Badiou's subject exceeds its inherited position within culture, language and ideology. It does so because the event itself exceeds the situation, revealing what it has excluded. In short, rather than being constituted by 'what there is', the event 'compels us' to *become* a subject. Badiou names the enacting of this compulsion 'fidelity': 'the decision to relate henceforth to the situation *from the perspective of its evental supplement*'.[131] The subject 'in no way pre-exists the process' of this fidelity; rather, the event and its 'process of truth *induces* a subject'.[132] Indeed, as James Kuzner (who also quotes this passage) points out, 'events produce subjects who in turn cannot fully comprehend what brought them into being'.[133]

It is important to stress that the event is not some mystical or supernatural happening, however, even if it seems as such within a situation. It is 'an *immanent break*', which means that the 'truth proceeds *in* the situation, and nowhere else – there is no heaven of truths'.[134] For Badiou, there are four categories of such breaks: 'political, loving, artistic or scientific'.[135] Within any given situation, the 'event is both *situated* – it is the event of this or that situation – and *supplementary*; thus absolutely detached from, or unrelated to, all the rules of the situation'.[136] It therefore 'enables [a] truth-process ... [that] meant nothing according to the prevailing language and established knowledge of the situation'.[137] As Badiou continues, 'the event names the void inasmuch as it names the not-known of the situation'.[138] For example, 'the emergence of the classical style, with

Haydn . . . was an event' for the musical situation: it authorised 'musical configurations' that were 'not comprehensible within the plenitude achieved by the baroque style; it really was a matter of *something else*'.[139]

Badiou argues that because '[i]nfinite alterity' – or the 'infinite and self-evident multiplicity of human kind' – is 'quite simply *what there is* . . . differences hold no interest for thought'.[140] Given that 'New Historicism', along with other forms of historicist and postmodern criticism, 'organizes itself around a claim to respect alterity, otherness, and difference',[141] the results are potentially profound for literary criticism. As Julián Jiménez Heffernan notes, Badiou 'is radically opposed to the multicultural defence of difference for the sake of difference, to the neo-humanitarian prescription of minority rights and to the ethics of the Other'.[142] That is not to say that differences are non-existent, or even unimportant, but that to point out such diversity is trite. It is obvious that there is endless difference amongst humanity. For Badiou, difference is not an end but a beginning. What matters, ultimately, and what should be the aim of genuine thought, is how we arrive at 'truths' from such cultural and circumstantial differences. So, for Badiou, 'since differences are what there is, and since every truth is the coming-to-be of that which is not yet, so differences are then precisely what truths depose'.[143]

One might here note something of a similarity between Badiou's 'infinite alterity' and Montaigne's 'infinit confusion of opinions'.[144] Because this 'infinit confusion' is brought forth wherever 'medleth' our 'goodly humane reason',[145] it infects thought itself. We cannot escape a 'universall and perpetuall[] disputation, in and concerning the knowledge of things'.[146] Unfashionably for our times, Montaigne, like Badiou, therefore places little value on diversity. The mad multiplications of human fantasy are simply what there are: '*Diversity is the most universall quality.*'[147] There is a further similarity too, for both require faith in something beyond multiplicity, something that cuts through its infinite confusion. Because of 'the imbecilitie of our reasons' and the 'infinite varietie of our opinions', Montaigne writes that a man's duty must not be 'referred to his own judgement'; otherwise, 'we might peradventure forge and devise such duties unto our selves, as would induce us . . . to destroy and devoure one another'.[148] In short, we must humbly submit our defective reason to the 'authority' that 'come[s] to us from heaven' – to ancient faith.[149]

For Badiou, truth must also enter from beyond the infinite alterity of human opinion. There are, however, two fundamental differences. First, whereas Montaigne's detached absolute seems to declare a truth that is beyond this world (or does not exist), Badiou's truths are always truths of this world (of a given situation). The second difference – and one vitally important for drama – is *how* truth enters this world. Whereas, for Montaigne, the truth is what has already been revealed and passed down through the Church, for Badiou the truth enters, and may still enter, through an event. Of course, some events have already happened, and these may still inspire faith in the mode of Montaigne's religious faith or Badiou's faith in Marx's revelations about the capitalist situation. For Badiou, however, events are also *still happening*, still intruding and reconfiguring individuals and worlds in the manner of Paul's conversion. Whether it is the discovery of gravitational waves or the experience of love, things from beyond the frame of our knowledge still cut through infinite alterity and found new subjects and new truths.

We see, then, that Badiou's subject emerges not from the differences in which it is placed (community), or its pre-existing uniqueness (the individual), but from an event that transforms its place. Or, as Badiou puts it, 'the existence of any truth … requires the destitution of established differences and the initiation of a subject divided in itself by the challenge of having nothing but the vanished event to face up to'.[150] Division is not the end of the subject but its beginning:

> [A]n eventual rupture always constitutes its subject in the divided form of a 'not … but', and … *it is precisely this form that bears the universal.* For the 'not' is the potential dissolution of closed particularities (whose name is 'law'), while the 'but' indicates the task, the faithful labor, in which the subjects of the process opened up by the event (whose name is 'grace') are the coworkers.[151]

We have here a two-step process of which most postmodern theory takes only the first: the demystifying 'not'. The absence of the second term, the reconstructive 'but', is why Žižek argues that the 'fundamental lesson of postmodernist politics is that *there is no Event*, that "nothing really happens"'.[152] Against 'this structural scepticism', Badiou 'insist[s] that – to use the term with its full theological weight – *miracles do happen*'.[153] In other words, the subject comes as 'grace'; it 'comes *without being due*'.[154]

The theoretical underpinning of the event is set out in *Being and Event*, which relies on a complex engagement with mathematical 'set theory'. Although I do not have scope to provide a detailed account of Badiou's mathematical reasoning, I believe that what I extract from *Being and Event* – the framework of situation, void and event, through which the new arrives – is the heart of Badiou's thought. It is, moreover, a framework that, in works such as *Saint Paul*, Badiou himself happily applies without the mathematical details. Badiou's thought can be difficult, but I believe it can help us to talk about something that is difficult in Shakespeare: in particular, how his drama is able to open itself to what is 'outside' or 'beyond' its representational structure – to an emergence from the 'void' – and how this openness calls forth a transformational and sometimes terrifying newness. In the remainder of this chapter, I offer a more detailed explanation of Badiou's evental framework, but those eager to get to Shakespeare may want to skip straight to *Romeo and Juliet* and return to this discussion later.

The basic fact that Badiou draws from Cantor's set theory is that being is made up of infinite multiplicities. Set theory posits that 'all is multiple, everything is a set'.[155] A given multiple, therefore, is not 'composed of ones'[156] but more multiples: 'Any multiple is intrinsically multiple of multiples.'[157] This means that the idea of the 'one' is secondary: 'the one is only there as a result.'[158] It comes about *afterwards* as the product of a mathematical 'operation' – the 'count-as-one'[159] – which separates out a consistent multiplicity from the inconsistent multiplicities of Being. Put otherwise, within the pure multiple of Being, there are various situations that each separate out a particular 'one' – what Badiou calls a 'presented mulitiplicity' – from infinite multiplicity.[160] Each 'situation admits its own particular operator of the count-as-one. This is the most general definition of a *structure*; it is what prescribes, for a presented multiple, the regime of its count-as-one.'[161] In other words, the situation is a structure, or organisational principle, that counts and arranges multiplicity. More specifically, the situation's 'count-as-one ... splits the multiple ... into consistency (the composition of ones) and inconsistency (the inertia of the domain)'.[162] By counting a consistent 'one', the structured situation therefore excludes (i.e. does not present) infinite multiplicity (inconsistency) from its presented multiple. There is thus a form of 'statism' to any situation, in that it rests upon a 'regime' that counts what is to 'count' within its domain (to matter, to exist, to be presented). Crucially, however, the regime itself is not counted or presented. In other words, the underlying structure of a situation – its truth– is invisible within the situation.

The result is that a situation's structure always 'leaves a remainder'.[163] The fact that the structure produces, or counts, the 'one' shows that something has not been counted and thus counts as 'nothing' within the situation: what Badiou calls the 'phantom remainder'.[164] The unpresented (this 'nothing') is both the necessity of the regime's count, or structure, to produce the 'one' and also the inconsistent multiples that were not counted or presented. And it is by excluding this 'nothing' that the situation is 'sutured to being': 'I term *void* of a situation this suture to its being. Moreover, I state that every structured presentation unpresents "its" void, in the mode of this non-one which is merely the subtractive face of the count.'[165] As the situation's suture to the infinite multiplicity of being, the void designates the crossroads or stitching between the 'one' that is counted by the situation and the infinite multiplicity that is not counted. In other words, it designates both the 'operation of the count' ('which, as source of the one, is not itself counted') and 'the pure multiple upon which the count operates'.[166] Although it is not counted or presented, the void is nonetheless included in every situation; it is 'a subset of any set'.[167] It is where the presented 'ones' meet the 'non-one[s]' of unpresented multiplicity.

The void is 'outside situations, unpresentable', and therefore 'in excess of being as a thinkable disposition'.[168] It here recalls the 'fearful and mysterious'[169] aspect of Shakespeare's tragedies, highlighted by Bradley. Because the void is a subset of any set, there is always more to the situation than its structure counts, and it is 'literally impossible to assign a "measure" to this superiority in size'.[170] Badiou calls this *the theorem of the point of excess*.[171] Any 'reference to the void' within the situation 'produces an excess over the count-as-one, an irruption of inconsistency'.[172] The word 'excess' here hints at the connection between Badiou's theory of the void and his 'event'. There is always an excess of unpresented multiples over the consistent multiples presented in the situation, and, as we saw, Badiou's event exceeds the existing situation. The event, then, is what causes the void's excess to irrupt *into* the situation's presented structure: 'for the void to become localizable at the level of presentation … a dysfunction of the count is required, which results from an excess-of-one. The event will be this ultra-one of a hazard, on the basis of which the void of a situation is retroactively discernible.'[173] To clarify, the void is always 'there' as the situation's (invisible) suture to the infinite multiplicity of being; it is, in fact, the condition of the situation. It is not *in* the situation, however. It can only enter the situation, and thus become presentable and effectual, through the rupturing event, which involves a breakdown of structure, an irruption of new multiples, and thus an opening to new possibilities.

Badiou's model helps express how, in Shakespeare, the singular arrives through ruptures and intrusions into an existing structure. The 'structure' here is multifaceted. It can be dramatic, poetic, narrative, or metaphysical. Most often these dramatic events serve to transform all these structures simultaneously. As we see in Chapter 5, Macbeth's meeting with the weird sisters ruptures both the historical narrative and the stable language of Duncan's Scotland, thereby releasing a new mode of being and speaking that is Macbeth's imaginative subjectivity. It is Macbeth's exposure to the dark imaginative excess, to the void of 'what is not' (I.iii.141), that brings him to life. We are in a very different dramatic realm to that of Hegel, who views 'the witches [as] only the poetic reflection of [Macbeth's] own fixed will'.[174] Macbeth is already there as a haunted, excessive consciousness for Hegel, rather than emerging from their intrusive appearance. That this is inevitable for Hegel is indicated by Badiou's observation that 'all of Hegel can be found in the following: the "still-more" is immanent to the "already"; everything that is, is already "still-more."'[175] This is 'Hegelian circularity'.[176] Although externality still does something in Hegel, what it does is reveal the true inner reality of the thing, which is 'already' in it. The excess is already in the thing; the subject is already in the character. But the void is not already in the situation even if it is attached to it, and, when it enters via the event, it 'proceeds "explosively", or "everywhere"'.[177]

The subject is central to Badiou because it is only through a subject's 'intervention' that an event, which is outside the situation's 'count', comes to transform the situation. Quite simply, without the 'intervention [that] puts it into circulation within the situation . . . the event does not exist'.[178] The movement between the situation and the unpresented event *is* the subject: 'I will call *subject* the process itself of liaison between the event (thus the intervention) and the procedure of fidelity (thus its operator of connection).'[179] The subject here 'is not a substance'[180] or a psychological entity but a 'generic procedure' that strives towards 'the incorporation of the event into the situation'.[181] The idea fits well with drama because the dramatic subject is never pre-existing. It therefore calls us to examine the dramatic procedures and processes that incorporate the subject. But Badiou's subjective process is not a straightforward one. Because the event is 'undecidable' within the situation, it demands a 'choice'.[182] It requires a Pascalian 'wager'.[183] Badiou therefore stresses Pascal's insistence on 'the doctrine of miracles': existing 'in excess of proof', the 'miracle' is a 'pure event' that breaks down existing laws of causation.[184] It is 'the symbol of an interruption of the law in which the interventional capacity is announced'.[185]

The need for a wager raises a central dilemma with Badiou's thought, which is rich with dramatic potential: how do you identify a genuine event if it is 'in excess of proof? Badiou's answer – that you cannot, that a leap is required – may be philosophically cogent, but, dramatically speaking, it is potentially terrifying. Juliet will take such a plunge into darkness, but the event's unseen, unverifiable, nature is also the dark abyss in which Othello drowns. There is also something mysterious here, for what is it that 'decides' or 'wagers' before the subject comes to be? For Badiou, the event strikes an individual without his or her 'knowledge' or rational choice – like Saul on the road to Damascus – but the subject only arrives through a subsequent re-choosing that sustains the evental rupture. This is Badiou's *fidelity*, which is not a religious faith but the ongoing decision to remain faithful to what has happened. Badiou's subject is never complete, never fully 'here', but continues to arrive in a wager on the undecidable – on a truth that comes from a chance or miracle, and whose trajectory remains unseen. Badiou thus writes of a 'choice' between thinking the subject as 'a structural recurrence ... and a hypothesis of the rarity of the subject, which suspends its occurrence from the event'.[186] For thinkers such as 'Foucault and Lacan as well as Althusser ... [l]anguage is that of which experience is the effect'.[187] For Badiou, however, the subject is not structural but something rare that 'passes in force, at a point where language fails'.[188] Whereas poststructuralism reacts against, and often remains defined by, the classical idea of the subject as 'the point of *departure*', this book follows Badiou's vital claim that 'we can only *arrive* at the subject'.[189]

We can now grasp why Badiou claims that we are 'the contemporaries of a *second epoch* of the doctrine of the Subject'.[190] It is 'no longer the founding subject, centered and reflexive, whose theme runs from Descartes to Hegel and which remains legible in Marx and Freud'.[191] Rather than the opposition between an essential subject and the death of the subject, we have a processual subject, a void subject and a divided subject. Its process is to incorporate an irruptive event into the situation. Its void is the unseen excess that the situation excludes. And its division is the division between the old situation and its new mode of being in 'fidelity'. As such, the evental subject not only breaks with its old situation, the 'subject is equally the process of recomposing, from the point of the interruption, another place and other rules'.[192] It is this dual process of rupture and recomposition that 'guarantees that the subjective process in part escapes repetition'.[193] The subject is a repetition neither of its eternal essence nor of its linguistic or cultural context. Both repetitions efface the subject by making all subjects structurally the same. Badiou, however, stresses that we must 'not giv[e] up on the subjective element':

> Even though the subject is neither a transparency, nor a centre, nor finally a substance, and even though nothing attests to its necessity for the organiza-tion of experience, it nevertheless remains the case that it is the key concept from which it turns out that we can think the decision, ethics, and politics.[194]

It is because it is an exception that transforms existing structures that '[e]very subject is political. This is why there are few subjects and rarely any politics.'[195] It is political because it opens a path of being in the world that did not previously exist. It is political because it reveals what the old situation, the old regime, excluded from presentation. We here approach Benjamin's description of those revolutionary moments that 'make the continuum of history explode'.[196] The subject is not an ideological illusion that shuts down political action; it is precisely what exceeds ideology and enables political action. Badiou therefore attacks the postmodern rejection of the subject as a 'return[] to classicism': to the idea that 'everything has always already begun, and it is vain to imagine that foundations are built on nothing, that one will create a new art, or a new man'.[197] It is to such creations that the following chapters – and Shakespeare's tragedies – constantly turn.

CHAPTER 2

The Subject of Love in Romeo and Juliet

Montaigne takes a wide-angle lens for his portrait of the self: 'to judge a man, we must a long time follow, and very curiously marke his steps; whether constancie doe wholy subsist and continue upon her owne foundation in him.'[1] Shakespeare twists the zoom. Nowhere is this telescopic view more apparent than in *Romeo and Juliet,* in which his famed lovers spend barely twenty-four hours together. Does this mean that what we see is a lightning flash and not a life or subject? It depends, of course, on one's definition of life and subject. Key to my argument that the lovers 'arrive' through the lightning strike of the event, rather than unfold or reveal themselves, is the fact that they are 'not [yet] here' in the opening scenes. 'I am not here', Romeo tells Benvolio, '[t]his is not Romeo; he's some other where' (I.i.190–91). Romeo may be claiming that he has lost himself in his unrequited love for Rosaline, but he is more right than he knows: the 'real' Romeo is indeed 'some other where'. In the opening scenes, Shakespeare places Romeo within a narrowly defined set of parameters, which, following Badiou, we might call Verona's 'situation', with its 'regime' or 'count-as-one'.[2] In this situation, structured by the Montague-Capulet opposition[3] and the Petrarchan model of language and love, Romeo and his initial love-object are manifestly not singular subjects. Both dramatically and metaphysically, Shakespeare's lovers only arrive as 'themselves' through the event of love that punctures this situation and allows them to become 'Romeo and Juliet'.

It is, of course, not new to say that Romeo and Juliet only become themselves through love. Palfrey captures the lovers' initial absence when he writes of how, in the opening scenes, Shakespeare 'engineers highly sophisticated staggered entrances for his main characters, who are given no soliloquies, no easy intimacy with the auditory, and who thus appear without truly *arriving*'.[4] Holbrook, meanwhile, writes that all the 'talk about the "self" in this opening scene . . . amounts to nothing'.[5] The lovers' true arrival waits for the self-creating power of love: 'in order truly to be Romeo, he must part with his name, make himself a new one, baptize himself. Love can do this.'[6] I seek to take this insight further by showing *how* Romeo and Juliet arrive. For Romeo does not 'make himself' a new name, he is remade through an evental process. Various factors have obscured this re-recreation. For one, we have been conditioned by realist art, which creates the impression that we are encountering pre-existing beings whose depths will only be discovered slowly through the narrative. For another, it is difficult to remove Shakespeare's characters from their network of cultural associations. A mythology surrounds them and there is a constant temptation to think of character without looking at the means of its production: Romeo and Juliet are 'lovers'. But how do they become lovers? Perhaps the biggest factor is the continued influence of Hegel's notion that '[a]ction is the clearest *revelation* of the individual'.[7] This influence can be glimpsed in Holbrook's idea of the individual finding its master-form, States's notion of an unchanging character,[8] and Paul Kottman's recent reading of *Romeo and Juliet*.[9] I argue that love, in this play, does not 'find' or 'realise' something that already exists – some already implicit individuality struggling for authenticity or self-realisation – but creates something that was absent.

If phenomenology deals with the general question of how what appears makes a world, I take from Badiou a more particular, and explosive, question: how does what did *not* previously appear in the world suddenly make its entrance? How is it thrown from the dark and onto the stage? For when we enter a play-world, much is treated as pre-existing. The Verona we enter, at the beginning, *appears* to already be in existence (and has a type of existence in that appearance). The social forms, alliances, relationships and languages appear well settled. 'To be a body' may be 'to be tied to a certain world',[10] but this chapter traces what happens when that world is transformed: what happens when a different world is given to an extant body.

The Situation

At the outset, Romeo loves the faceless Rosaline rather than his 'star-crossed lover' (Prologue, 6). Coleridge remarks that 'Romeo became enamoured of the ideal he formed in his own mind, and then ... christened the first real being as that which he desires'.[11] One might question, however, in what sense Rosaline is a 'real being'. Take Romeo's response to Benvolio's (soon fulfilled) promise that Rosaline will be outshone at the Capulets' feast: 'I'll go along, no such sight to be shown, / But to rejoice in splendour of mine own' (I.ii.100–101). The splendour is indeed Romeo's 'own', for it is nothing of Rosaline's. The unseen Rosaline exists only through the words of Romeo and his friends – words that form a pastiche of courtly love poetry. Romeo's 'ideal' is, of course, not really 'his' at all: it is learned by 'rote' (II.ii.88) from Petrarchan rhymes. His early speech is characterised by comically wordy paradox – 'Feather of lead, bright smoke, cold fire, sick health, / Still-waking sleep, that is not what it is!' (I.i.173–74) – that elicits Benvolio's 'laugh' (I.i.176). Shakespeare is of course parodying the 'savage sweetness' of love in *The Canzoniere*.[12] He seems to follow Montaigne in mocking these 'fantasticall, new fangled, Spagniolized, and Petrarchisticall elevations'.[13] But Romeo's absurd oppositions also do something more serious: they suggest an absence of genuine difference. All distinctions collapse into the 'One' of his inward-looking melancholy.

Shakespeare's gentle mockery of Romeo hints, however, that something different is coming.[14] We wait for something real. We wait for something new. The fact that we wait for true love, and that passion will shift radically from one lady to another, is not without its difficulties, however. Rosaline has certainly worried critics. Roland Knowles writes that 'it is difficult to understand how, if Shakespeare had intended to present only a poignant tragedy of ideal love, he chose to emphasize Romeo's first love, Rosaline, who is swiftly passed over in the source'.[15] More specifically, Jonathan Goldberg argues that 'Juliet as replacement object is inserted within a seriality rather than as the locus of uniqueness and singularity'.[16] I want to suggest another possibility. To begin with, the fact that Romeo's first 'love' is so obviously parodic lightens the charge that it undermines his second. While Petrarch and Philip Sidney were mature men who were assailed unexpectedly by love and learned from its long hardships, Romeo is a boy, a figure of fun who burlesques the literary language of older men. But perhaps we can go further. What if the non-seriousness of Romeo's first love reflects Empson's idea that double plots may 'anticipate the parody a hearer might have in mind without losing its dignity'?[17] He gives the example of a 'play of heroic swashbucklers which has a comic cowardly swashbuckler (Parolles), not at all to parody the heroes but to stop you from doing so: "If you want to laugh at this sort of thing laugh now and get it over"'.[18] Romeo's love for Rosaline is not a 'double plot' but it does act as a (sometimes comic) foil to the main plot. In this chapter, I show how Juliet *refuses* to be placed in the sort of 'seriality' that Goldberg (and at times Romeo himself) envisages. The lovers soon enact a different kind of love than that which we (do not) see in the opening scenes.

Although Romeo parodies Petrarchan poetry, there is also something serious at stake. Romeo's solitary idealising operates according to the underlying structures of courtly love poetry, which lock Romeo into a narrow conception of love and selfhood. Juliet, as we shall see, struggles to shake Romeo out of this mode of desire. So although others laugh at Romeo, his Petrarchan mode of desire nonetheless highlights the manner in which love – as a relationship with another – is blocked in the opening scenes. Rosaline is the figure of that blockage – forever unencountered, absent. Romeo's Petrarchan idealising projects fantasies of wholeness onto this never encountered figure. As Žižek writes:

> In Lacanian terms, the difference here is the one between *idealization* and *sublimation*: false idolizing idealizes, it blinds itself to the other's weaknesses – or, rather, it blinds itself to the other *as such*, using the beloved as a blank screen on to which it projects its own phantasmagorical constructions; while true love accepts the beloved the way she or he is, merely putting her/him into the place of the Thing, the unconditional Object.[19]

There is no dramatic interrelation, no encounter of difference, only projections onto a 'blank screen'. As Kottman puts it, 'Rosaline need not take the stage' because 'she is a mere lack, as Romeo says, a "not having"'.[20] In these Lacanian terms, Rosaline is nothing but absence: an absence that Romeo's imaginary idealising projects over and converts into an impossibly full presence. It is a 'love' composed of one.

By establishing a situation in which love does not arrive, Shakespeare sets the scene for a qualitative shift. He sets the scene for what Levinas describes as the 'astonishing or traumatizing' event of 'facing the Other', whereby the subject 'awakens from the egological'.[21] Our anticipation of this 'facing' builds in Juliet's first scene, where she promises to encounter her proposed love-match, Paris, while making no promise as to what it will bring: she will 'look to like, if looking liking move' (I.iii.99). Whether 'looking liking move[s]' is not an egological projection but an unknown, to be discovered in the moment of the encounter, in the 'facing' of the other. It has us looking forward to the mysterious eventuality of love's happening: to what Badiou describes as the 'absolute contingency of the encounter'.[22] The situation awaits the liking-upon-looking or unaccountable 'falling' that will make Romeo and Juliet lovers. Needless to say, it happens at first sight.

The Event of Love

When it comes, however, the explosive moment of love is not strictly locatable. It is in Romeo's 'torches' (I.v.41) speech, but it is also beyond it, for Juliet remains distant, 'enrich[ing] the hand / Of yonder knight'

(I.v.39–40). We still await their encounter. Do they look at one another, these about-to-be lovers, as Romeo crosses the room and Tybalt speaks violently against the Montague who desires the Capulet? Is this where love arrives, in a look, unscripted, while Capulets quarrel about whether they will 'endure' (I.v.73) this 'shame' (I.v.79) to their name? For no sooner has Tybalt finished promising 'gall' (I.v.89) than Romeo is touching Juliet's hand, beginning their sonnet, and promising his 'tender kiss' (I.v.93), and here surely love has arrived – but where? In words? Or in a look? And when?

The point of this perhaps too precise thinking on the event is to suggest that the location of their love-at-first-sight is opaque. It is perhaps an inheritor, or enactor, of the obscure power of Mercutio's poetic excess, which came from 'nothing' (I.iv.96), but nonetheless spilled into the situation with transformative effect: 'This wind you talk of blows us from ourselves' (I.iv.104). The event of love is similarly obscure. It seems to come from nowhere in a double sense. For one thing, Rosaline is forgotten absurdly quickly. We have old Capulet reminiscing and then Romeo's sudden 'O, she doth teach the torches to burn bright!' (I.v.41). For another thing, there is no stage direction or speech that designates precisely where or when 'love' takes place. It haunts the space-time between Romeo's admiring speech (I.v.50) and his touching of her hand (I.v.90) – an interim that is otherwise filled with Tybalt's enraged assertion of the situation-defining feud. So while the event of love occurs as their hands touch and they speak their first words together, it has also already occurred in this anticipated confluence, in the change in poetry, in the coming together of bodies across the stage and, above all, in their first look somewhere amidst it all.

Something thus happens that is amidst speech – between Romeo's 'torches' and their sonnet – but also outside, or between, words. It is desire, bodily attraction, certainly. But it is also something unaccountable: the critical liking-on-looking that Juliet foreshadowed; the 'falling' into love that changes how words work. As Badiou puts it: '[l]ove always starts with an encounter. And I would give this encounter the quasi-metaphysical status of an *event*, namely of something that doesn't enter into the immediate order of things.'[23] The play's central event is, in a sense, indiscernible. It comes from beyond the situation and certainly from beyond Romeo's Petrarchan beginnings. And yet, it immediately transforms the scene and its speech. It does not remain 'beyond' but intrudes violently, altering the situation's structure, interrelations and language at multiple levels. As Juliet cries when she learns Romeo's name: 'too early seen unknown, and known too late!' (I.v.136). Love happens before they know it (or the loved one). Seen unknown, love makes known, but the knowledge is too late for love has arrived and cannot be undone. We have, here, an early glimpse of how Shakespeare uses indistinction and temporal folding in constructing his character-altering 'events'.

Shakespeare's orchestration of the obscure but foundational liking-upon-looking is suggestive of the invisible 'crossing of gazes'[24] that, for Jean-Luc Marion, distinguishes 'love' from the image: 'I see not the visible face of the other, an object still reducible to an image (as the social game and its makeup demands), but the invisible gaze that wells up through the obscurity of the pupils.'[25] The crossing entails an exposure to what is other and unseen; an exposure that was impossible with the unseen and faceless Rosaline. Whereas the idealising projections of courtly love poetry come from within (the male), love here is something alien that comes from without. But while its location may be uncertain, its force is central. We see, for instance, in Zeffirelli's 1968 *Romeo and Juliet*, how love arrives through the crossing of their gazes while dancing, while in Luhrmann's 1996 film their falling into love hinges on their gazes crossing through a fish tank, which precedes Romeo's declaration of her beauty. They look, and love has already burst into their hearts. The 'treasure' of their love is, in Badiou terms, 'nothing but the event as such, which is to say a completely precarious having-taken-place'.[26] In this excessive, diffused event we are far from Shakespeare's source. Arthur Broke's Romeus chooses Iuliet after 'he wayd the bewty of eche dame',[27] signalling a comparative rather than irruptive moment. Here, Iuliet is indeed a 'replacement object' as Goldberg suggests:

> And as out of a planke
>   a nayle a nayle doth drive:
> So novell love out of the minde
>   the auncient love doth rive.[28]

Further, when the lovers do come together they are inarticulate: 'vehement love' Romeo's 'tong dyd stay', while in Juliet's 'mouth, her tong he glewed fast'.[29] Any poetry resides not in the lovers but in the poet. In Shakespeare, however, their first words famously take the form of a sonnet, channelling the energy of their liking-upon-looking into a new mode of speaking that *is* their arrival. We see the effects of the event of love afterwards, in the transformation of both the poetic tradition and the lovers' voices.

It is not that differences (Montague v. Capulet, Romeo's idealising v. Mercutio's excess) are annulled here, but that they are suddenly transformed. The Petrarchan sonnet, parodied in Romeo's opening scenes, fully enters the play only to be turned upside down, so that the poetry of inaccessibility and lack becomes the poetry of intimacy and touch, becomes a mutual back and forth rather than a solitary lament. There is now another voice, an *other*, in the poem. There is an introduction of difference into what was an imaginary oneness. The lady, far from inaccessible, joins the game. And this, as Lloyd Davis notes, moves their interaction 'beyond single-voiced Petrarchism ... which portray[s] the poet by stifling the woman's voice (just as Romeo invokes and silences Rosaline)'.[30] The language may declare her to be a 'dear saint' (I.v.100), but Juliet irrevocably steps off her pedestal, out of fantasy, and down to earth, where she returns her lover's kisses. Juliet thereby alters the very shape of the sonnet. She transforms the *a-b-b-a-a-b-b-a* rhyme scheme of the Petrarchan sonnet into an opportunity for creation and sharing. Romeo begins with an *a-b-a-b* rhyme but, by starting the second quatrain with rhyme 'c', Juliet introduces a new term when she should have repeated the old 'a' rhyme. The conversion of the sonnet into a mutual song is creating something: creating new voices and relations. But it is also an occasion for union. Juliet returns from the differentiating 'c' to share Romeo's rhyme 'b', not only using words ending in 'is' and 'iss', but using exactly the same words as Romeo, which just happen to be a sharing of 'this' and 'kiss'. The Petrarchan mould is thus broken from the inside. Its idealising lament over lack is transformed into the celebratory march toward the sharing of 'this kiss'.

The shape of the sonnet is further breached in the third quatrain, which is split between two voices – a breach that continues into the concluding couplet, which is also split between two, and ends with their consummating kiss. The sense of breach, here, has a metaphysical import. For Badiou, love is a sort of truth experiment: 'What is the world like when it is experienced, developed and lived from the point of view of difference and not identity?', 'when one experiences it from the point of view of two and not one?'[31] Taken in this light, the breach in the sonnet marks the splitting of Romeo's previously solitary worldview; it marks an emergence of difference that is not nullified by paradox (as in Romeo's 'heavy light-ness' (I.i.171)). As Badiou puts it, 'love involves a separation or disjuncture based on the simple difference between two people and their infinite subjectivities'.[32] As such, love always begins with dislocation and differentiation: 'You have *Two*. Love involves Two.'[33] But it also triggers a creation out of this difference: the creation of a new world and a new subject.

Here I both join with and depart from Kottman's reading of Romeo and Juliet's 'love' as a Hegelian 'struggle' whereby each risks his or her own life 'for freedom'.[34] Drawing on Hegel's master–slave dialectic, Kottman stresses the need for the *other* to realise one's self: 'Romeo and Juliet are formed as subjects through acts of mutual self-recognition.'[35] In many ways, this chimes with Badiou's idea of the 'Two'. Indeed, the One becoming Two is not only the most basic feature of love but also of thought. For Hegel, the subject can only think itself through its other. It must split itself between being-for-itself and being-for-another, which, as Badiou writes, 'is proof that in order to think anything at all . . . it must be split in two'.[36] Starobinski notes a similar motion at the heart of Montaigne's *Essays*: Montaigne begins to write because of 'an inexpugnable inner otherness which makes it impossible for the self to feel tranquilly at home and at one with itself'.[37] The introduction of the new voice in the sonnet thus suggests a fundamentally different experience of the world through which it becomes possible to think the 'subject'.

For Kottman, however, love founds the subject by *separating* it. The play tells the 'story of two individuals *who actively claim* their separate individuality, their own freedom, in the only way that they can – through one another'.[38] Part of this seems undeniable. Because it allows us to break from social groupings and risk our being for something else, love provides scope for genuine individual choice and freedom. But questions arise as to the nature of this new individuality. Most pressingly, *from where* do this choice and this new choosing self emerge? I have begun to argue that the lovers arrive from the unaccountable event of liking-upon-looking. For Kottman, however, this is no event: 'Be fitting the spirit of the masque, this is still an anonymous, replaceable desire. Both are probably masked when they meet. Nothing at this point distinguishes Romeo and Juliet's encounter from the seduction of any other Capulet by Benvolio or Mercutio.'[39]

As Kottman notes, this raises an obvious question: 'From what, then, does the ensuing drama between Romeo and Juliet arise?'[40] Kottman's answer is that 'Romeo and Juliet are not satisfied with the "satisfaction" offered by the masque and its anonymity' and so they now 'want to know *whom* it is they desire'.[41] But this does little more than raise further questions: Why? What is the basis of this dissatisfaction if there was no event? And what is this '*whom*'? Kottman's answer is a sort of in-built Hegelian drive to 'self-realization',[42] 'self-individuation',[43] 'self-determining' or 'self-determination'.[44] Although the recognition of the 'other' is necessary for this journey, this other is so quickly transcended and folded inwards that it doesn't seem to do anything *except* reveal the singular self (what Badiou calls the 'founding subject'[45]). According to Kottman, then, mutual recognition does not transform the subject but reveals what is already implicit within it (the drive to 'individual freedom' and 'self-realization'). In a Hegelian circle, the 'struggle for individual freedom'[46] is both the subject's origin and destination.

Like another Hegelian, Bradley, Kottman thus places the self prior to the dramatic events through which it arrives. But if the 'real' Romeo is 'some other where' in his initial Petrarchan hollowness, how can we say that there is a singular selfhood or '*whom*' already in Romeo? Here it is worth returning to Palfrey's claim that the 'staggered entrances' of the opening scenes mean that the lovers 'appear without truly *arriving*':

> Romeo is reported before we meet him, stealing from view, glimpsed askance at dawn in the wood; then he enters, and speaks inept Petrarchan cliché; Juliet is reported in ghostly terms by her father, pre-emptively claimed by Paris, and then enters surrounded and drowned out by her garrulous Nurse and jealous mother.[47]

In short, at the beginning of the play there was no '*whom*' to desire. Shakespeare seems to deliberately call attention to the self's absence. If there is a 'musical key'[48] to the early Romeo, it is flat and hackneyed. The whom that is desired only begins to emerge in the movements and language of desire of the sonnet. The better question is not whom but how: how does a whom arrive? And this is where Badiou's theory becomes relevant to Shakespeare's drama. However things may work in ordinary life, Badiou's focus on the radical split between before and after forces us to think about how these characters are created dramatically. The dramatic subject must arrive, for there is nothing already there. Relevant, here, is a rupturing aspect of Hegel's thought that Kottman neglects: '[mind] only wins to its truth when it finds itself utterly torn asunder.'[49] The breach in the sonnet begins to show how the lovers are dismembered from their old unitary selves by the 'astonishing'[50] confrontation with the other.

The astonishment stems not just from confronting a distinct subjectivity (an 'other'), however, but from joining one's self with it. In other words, while their love involves Two, the two are not merely separate Ones seeking their individual satisfactions. Rather, the Two come together in a new joint poetic construction. They are always separate – they never fuse or synthesise, this is not *Tristan and Isolde* – and yet they are nonetheless held together in a process that is at once poetic and existential. They are not *merely* separate. Kuzner captures the complexity of Badiou's conception of love when he writes: 'Love offers neither an easy communion, in which differences dissolve, nor a simple separation, in which differences are respected and sustained, but creates a "unique Subject."'[51] Or, as Badiou puts it, the 'surprise', or wonder, of the event 'unleashes a process that is basically an experience of getting to know the world'.[52] The world (and the self) is no longer the same but must be learnt again, must be constructed on a new foundation. Hence, for Badiou, love 'is a construction, a life that is being made, no longer from the perspective of One but from the perspective of Two'.[53] Love, here, is not directed towards individual self-fulfilment but to the formation of a joint-subject that aims to inscribe the event's unlocatable excess onto the situation.

In Romeo and Juliet's too brief love this (re)construction is evidenced only in their joint poetic constructions. So let us return to their sonnet. Even if their initial interaction does stem from 'an anonymous, replaceable desire', it very quickly transforms the Petrarchan model of desire and its poetic form. After their kiss, Romeo immediately begins what looks like a new sonnet, with a new *a-b-a-b* rhyme sequence:

ROMEO   Thus from my lips, by thine my sin is purged.
JULIET   Then have my lips the sin that they have took.
ROMEO   Sin from my lips? O trespass sweetly urged!
           Give me my sin again.
JULIET   You kiss by th' book   (I.v.104–7)

Kiernan Ryan argues that Juliet 'sabotages this sonnet . . . by . . . turning its second half back against the speaker in playful mockery of his textbook courtship',[54] and in one sense this is certainly true. Her sportive mockery interrupts Romeo's line and breaks the unity of his conceit. By introducing a note of (joyous) scepticism, it suggests another mind entering the frame. Here, we begin to see how Juliet interrupts 'seriality' and refuses to be a 'replacement object'.[55] Her interjection halts the stream of Romeo's Petrarchan projector and introduces something foreign – introduces a point of difference. And yet, despite all this, Juliet nonetheless *completes* Romeo's rhyme, as her 'kiss by th' book' rhymes with the 'sin' her lips 'have took'. Juliet does not simply 'sabotage' their joint sonnet but completes it by asserting her separate voice – by insisting that *she* is to speak the '*b*' to Romeo's '*a*'. She thereby brings together what is separate. And she also further transforms the sonnet form, breaking down the univocality of the line, just as she has broken down the univocality of the sonnet, quatrain and couplet. We witness smaller and smaller units of shared language – sonnet, quatrain, couplet, line – that dramatise the lovers' movement together, almost becoming one joint-speaker of the event, united in their difference as much as differentiated in their unity. Their joint poetic construction is a response to the event – contingent, opaque, unjustified – but it is also the beginning of the lovers' attempts to recreate the world and its language from the perspective of Two.

Needless to say, we do not see this world come to fruition. Indeed, the second sonnet does not move beyond its first quatrain, as the Nurse intrudes with the names Capulet and Montague. Their creative poetry is hemmed in by the feud, with Tybalt's raging on the one side and their naming on the other. We immediately see that the lovers do not have the power to overturn the existing situation and its names. Indeed, when Tybalt hears Romeo's 'torches' speech he immediately – 'by his voice' – knows him to 'be a Montague': 'Fetch me my rapier, boy' (I.v.51–52). So while love occurs here and begins to create, it occurs within tragic theatre, which dislocates. Badiou gets at this when he writes that although love involves the 'hard work' of 'a construction of eternity within time, of the experience of the Two', 'literature on love contains very little in terms of the experience of its endurance over time'.[56] Theatre captures the 'miraculous encounter',[57] 'the triumph of love, but not its duration'.[58] All of this is true – and particularly true of these star-cross'd lovers – but there is another truth too. For, in the too brief interim of their love, we are also given precious moments – call them instantiations – of a world of Two. The broken sonnet is the first of these, but certainly not the last.

The interim is short, but in it something creative takes place. The liking-upon-looking, the reconfiguration of the sonnet, the coming together of two distinct voices to bear witness to one event, all happens in a space between their names (between Tybalt's hypersensitivity to identity and the Nurse's naming). They are never without names but their language creates a space between names, which *is their space*. The lovers hijack existing linguistic structures and turn them to their purposes, thereby transforming these structures' significance. The creativity of their shared language games has often been overlooked. If Kottman's focus on individual freedom denies their joint poetic creation from one side, the critical preoccupation with discrediting the 'essentialist' subject does so from the other. Catherine Belsey, for instance, inscribes Romeo's initial projections onto the entirety of their relationship: 'Lovers are prone to perceive the imaginary essence of the object of desire, to identify a "self", a presence which subsists beyond the symbolic order.'[59] As the shared sonnet suggests, however, Romeo and Juliet do not attempt to escape the 'symbolic order' but come together through their shared, double-voiced linguistic creations. Moreover, in the 'balcony scene' Juliet battles to escape the idealising impulse of Petrarchan poetry, which projects an 'imaginary essence' onto an unencountered other.

The Work of Love

Thus far we have witnessed the moment of these characters' conception but not their birth as 'Romeo and Juliet'. The remarkable feeling of their first encounter is not a consummation but a new beginning. However, love-at-first-sight is only a beginning, a foundational event, in and through what happens after. As we saw in Chapter 1, an 'event does not exist' without an 'intervention [that] puts it into circulation within the situation'.[60] The lightning strikes at the lovers' first meeting, but they must make it something more than 'the lightening which doth cease to be / Ere one can say it lightens' (II.i.161–62). Key, here, is Badiou's idea of the 'declaration' through which the lovers 'move on from' the 'chance nature of the encounter' and 'embark on a construction of truth'.[61] The 'encounter' only becomes an event 'in so far as [the lovers] retroactively declare it to have been the origin of a life-changing sequence that is not deducible from it'.[62] Without the declaration the lightning vanishes and there is nothing to say it ever was.

It is in the balcony scene, then, that the lovers arrive as the 'subject' of the event of love. They arrive because they seek to live, and speak, in faithfulness to the liking-on-looking of the previous scene. It is, however, an arrival that is as difficult as it is joyous. It raises a linguistic problem: how is this rupturing event to be spoken in the old language? But it is also a dramatic and metaphysical problem. For them, metaphysical: how will they, as separate 'ones', respond to the event? Will they be the same selves or new ones? How are two very different beings to be held together? For us, it raises a dramatic question: are these dramatic entities simply passing through events, or has this happening formed new creations? Is this a new Romeo or the old one? These interrelated questions find their answers in the way Shakespeare stages the aftermath of the event, which is, in the end, the main game of *Romeo and Juliet*.

Romeo begins the balcony scene speaking on the borderlands of the old and the new. Although Romeo is now in his loved one's presence, she is not in his. The results are somewhat misshapen, both glorious and absurd. For instance, T. S. Eliot somewhat humorously notes the ongoing 'artificiality' of Romeo's speech: 'it seems unlikely that a man standing below in the garden, even on a very bright moonlight night, would see the eyes of the lady above flashing so brilliantly as to justify such a comparison [to the stars].'[63] There is thus a less philosophically serious element to all this talk of Two. Put simply, Romeo has no idea what he is doing. He doesn't know how to talk. And perhaps that is inevitable. Perhaps love always involves a blundering coming together of two beings in the dark. Love is not only difficult; it is also notoriously foolish: a blind attempt to navigate a new world, while speaking a new language, without a guide. But while love may be a 'fool's game', it is also a world-creating one. The play may laugh at Romeo's starry-eyed seriousness, but it also thinks seriously, even cosmically, about the nature of love. Eliot's assessment is thus a little too sneering, a little deaf to the way Romeo's passionate sincerity now draws him *towards* communication: 'O, speak again, bright angel' (II.i.68). Romeo here is calling the Two on stage and not merely celebrating a splendour of his own. His desperate desire for communication – 'It is my lady, O, it is my love. / O that she knew she were!' (II.i.52–53) – is worlds away from his solitary idealisation. And this, as Eliot does recognise, is reflected in the poetry: 'Yet one is aware, from the beginning of this scene, that there is a musical pattern coming, as surprising in its kind as that in the early work of Beethoven.'[64] In a sense, this is Romeo's moment of glory. His poetry builds anticipation: 'But soft, what light through yonder window breaks?' (II.i.44). He is on the threshold.

Of course, in the ensuing 'duet', 'it is Juliet's voice that has the leading part'.[65] Whereas Romeo skirts the borders of the old idealising language, Juliet confronts it head on. She is preoccupied, however joyously and naïvely, with the serious dilemma of reconciling an exuberant love that breaks through existing orders – moving beyond essence (whom), social determinism (family), and background (Rosaline) – with the linguistic and social orders that still conspire against them through their names: 'What's Montague? It is nor hand, nor foot, / Nor arm, nor face, nor any other part / Belonging to a man. O, be some other name!' (II.i.82–84). 'In recognising that the name of the rose is arbitrary, Juliet [may] show[] herself a Saussurean *avant la letter*' but, according to Belsey, 'she simply affirms what her own desire dictates' when she draws 'the inference that Romeo can arbitrarily cease to be a Montague'.[66] As Derrida shows in 'Aphorism Countertime', however, Juliet never quite draws this inference. Far from seeking to 'encounter directly, immediately, the rose that exists beyond its name',[67] Derrida shows how 'the most vibrant declaration of their love still calls for the name that it denounces'.[68] Indeed, Juliet incessantly speaks Romeo's name: her 'tongue' is 'hoarse' '[w]ith repetition of [her] Romeo's name. Romeo!' (II.i.207–8). In a very different way to Badiou, Derrida also stresses the uneasy balance between the lovers' separateness and togetherness: the 'name' is what 'separates them' yet also 'tighten[s] their desire with all its aphoristic force'.[69] Separating Romeo from his name is both 'necessary and impossible':

> She knows it: detachable and dissociable, aphoristic though it be, his name is his essence. Inseparable from his being. And in asking him to abandon his name, she is no doubt asking him to live at last, and to live his love (for in order to live oneself truly, it is necessary to elude the law of the name, the familial law made for survival and constantly recalling me to death), but she is *just as much* asking him to die, since his life *is* his name.[70]

If this seems like an eternal deadlock, it is because we have yet to grasp what is little more than a suggestion in Derrida but is central to this chapter: the idea that their separate desires are 'held together . . . in the dislocated now of a love or a promise. A promise in their name, but across and beyond their given name, the promise of another name, its request rather: "O be some other name. . .".'[71] Unlike Derrida's almost Petrarchan deferral of this 'promise', however, we shall see that Shakespeare fulfils it, if only in the briefest dramatic moments.

Shakespeare's dramatic solution to this deadlock not only departs from the refusals of Petrarchan ladies – Juliet freely gives her kisses, unlike the stolen kisses of sonnet sequences such as *Astrophil and Stella* – but also from Broke's poem, in which Iuliet only forsakes her 'father's house' and gives herself to Romeus 'whole to . . . betake' after various reservations and conditions: 'For if you doe intende my honor to defile'; 'But if by wanton love'.[72] In stark contrast, Romeo *overhears* Juliet's unconditional gift of herself. Shakespeare's use of this archetypal dramatic happening stresses its evental nature: that love stems from a happening and not some inner quality. But Juliet's unknowing gift also does something more: it brilliantly bypasses Marcel Mauss's influential idea that gifts are never 'voluntary' but 'are given and reciprocated obligatorily'.[73] Rather than a courtly exchange of vows, Juliet declares her love out into the dark.

Scenically, Shakespeare thereby achieves something profound. As Kottman writes in an earlier reading of the play, 'what radically suspends the tragedy of the name, and its attendant political order, is the *scene itself*'.[74] Following the strangely invisible liking-upon-looking, Juliet now speaks out into the darkness, into the unseen, as she tackles the constraining situation and its names. The fact that the event comes from the darkness marks its 'risky or contingent form'.[75] It prompts a radical decision to commit oneself to the alien event. We see this theatrically too: that Juliet's exposure is reflected in the actor's part. Palfrey and Stern show

how the Juliet part suggestively incorporates 'speech-closing half-line[s]' that cue an unknown speaker, thereby 'encapsulating an existential risk that the actor too must partly share in'.[76] For instance, Juliet's 'Take all myself', which concludes the 'overheard soliloquy' set out later, is 'a leap into the dark', cueing another without knowing whether the ensuing speech 'will be addressed to "Juliet" or not'.[77] The actor must 'commit absolutely to the emotion . . . without quite knowing whether satisfaction will come immediately, soon, or not at all'.[78] Speaking her love without knowledge of Romeo's presence, Juliet expresses herself without coyness or courtly games. Just as the event was a gift, coming without being due, so the incipient subject gives itself to the event. Love is *given* to the dark, to the unseen future, and Juliet is utterly exposed. And so Romeo, longing for communication, gets it without asking, from Juliet, who gives it without knowing:

> Romeo, doff thy name,
> And for thy name – which is no part of thee –
> Take all myself.
> ROMEO   I take thee at thy word.
> Call me but love and I'll be new baptized.
> Henceforth I never will be Romeo.
> JULIET   What man art thou, that thus can bescreen'd in night
> So stumblest on my counsel?   (II.i.89–95)

By giving herself to the darkness, Juliet removes the lovers from the ordinary economies of language and love, where vow is exchanged for vow. In what follows, what is initially an unknown gift becomes a genuine giving because Juliet affirms it afterwards. She affirms this unknown, bescreened 'thou' that emerges from the darkness. It is thus the lovers' great *recognition scene*.

Badiou is helpful here because his 'event', like their love, comes from beyond the existing situation to reconfigure the subject's relation to the world. As Žižek puts it: 'within [the situation's] horizon . . . the Event necessarily appears as *skandalon*, as an undecidable, chaotic intrusion that has no place in the State of the Situation.'[79] There are two breaches going on here. Most obviously, the feud is breached. There is not supposed to be a 'set', or structure, in which Montague belongs to Capulet or vice versa. The love-event thus ruptures the 'State of the Situation' by showing the inconsistency of its defining structure. But there is also a more universal divide that the feud merely accentuates: the divide between one mind and another. As Badiou points out, '*Romeo and Juliet* is clearly the outstanding allegory for this particular disjuncture because this Two belong to enemy camps.'[80] Indeed, the play further highlights the separateness of the lovers through the Petrarchan model of desire, which disconnects the lover from the love-object. As we'll see, however, it is the very separateness of the loved one that breaches the individual's self-unity. Without the blade of difference there would be no cut in the unity of the 'One'. Juliet's giving herself to the dark, to someone unseen and radically separate, cuts into shadowy new horizons beyond the walls of the feud-driven, Petrarchan situation. Ultimately, it opens the possibility of 'some other name' (II.i.84) that holds together what is separate. And, in being grasped by a 'subject' – this 'Romeo and Juliet' – it establishes the possibility of a new 'set', or multiple, in which Montague belongs to Capulet, Capulet to Montague.

The dramatic process by which the lovers arrive is certainly very different from the mode of Elizabethan sonnet sequences. In contrast to the confessional tone of Sidney's *Astrophil and Stella*, in which the poet's muse tells him to 'look in thy heart, and write' (Sonnet I, 14),[81] we do not witness Romeo and Juliet revealing their hearts in an inward-looking manner; we watch them be born onstage through the evental experience of difference – of the alien other. Let us first consider this from Juliet's perspective. Juliet speaks to the dark, and then, without warning, the darkness answers. Without permission, another enters her 'counsel' and intrudes upon her private thought. This is a critical moment of decision: she chooses to understand her overheard declaration not as a (potentially outrageous) violation of privacy but as the foundation of a joint project of reconfiguring the name. She must bid 'farewell' to 'compliment' (II.i.131) (glossed as 'polite convention' in the *The Norton Shakespeare*) and begin to think of, and with, this intrusive other voice.[82] In short, Juliet sees that it is only by giving themselves to the event of love that they will be able to resist the names that seek to conform them. She will give all of herself to transform his name. And Romeo will take it and be changed.

Romeo's idea that he will be 'new baptized' speaks eloquently to this new beginning. It implies both the washing away of the old and the birth of the new. It indicates that this event not only changes these characters; it *recreates* them. The play thereby connects with Badiou's understanding of Saint Paul as a thinker of the event. There is a real sense of overcoming existing identity, circumstance, culture and history in Paul's idea of baptism: 'For as many of you as have been baptized into Christ have put on Christ. There is neither Jew nor Greek, there is neither bond nor free, there is neither male nor female: for ye are all one in Christ Jesus' (Galatians 3:26–28). The happening 'on the road to Damascus' is 'a thunderbolt, a caesura', 'a conscription instituting a new subject'.[83] It is a radical rebirth that is different in kind from Montaigne's essays, which frequently praise 'moderation' and warn against passions that

> rowze our soule farre beyond her ordinary pitch, as stirred up by the discourses, or provoked by the examples of others. But it is a kinde of passion, which urgeth, mooveth, agitateth and in some sorte ravisheth her from out her selfe: for, that gust overblown, and storme past, wee see, it wil unawares unbend and lose it selfe, if not to the lowest pitch, at least to be no more the same she was.[84]

For Saint Paul, Badiou and Romeo and Juliet, it is only by being raised 'farre beyond [one's] ordinary pitch', 'ravishe[d]' by grace, and thereby 'los [ing] [one's] self', so that one is no longer what one was, that it is possible to become a genuine subject. The result is a loss of self but also a paradoxical finding of a self that was *not* already there: 'The Christian subject does not pre-exist the event he declares (Christ's resurrection)' and is thus not a product of the pre-existing 'conditions of his existence or identity'.[85] So while Romeo's extravagant claim that '[h]enceforth [he] never will be Romeo' may be false semantically, for even now he uses his name, it nonetheless speaks to a truth. The old Romeo is dead. The lovers' past relationship with the world – their families, their enemies, their love-objects, their names – is retrospectively changed. And while the old names still operate, and while the names still destroy them, the lovers create the new name of 'Romeo and Juliet', and the old names never mean the same again.

Like Juliet, Romeo experiences his moment of risk in the recognition scene. In stepping from the shadows, he must both expose himself and reveal Juliet's exposure (that he has been watching). He must put himself in her hands: both his immediate safety in the enemy camp and his future self. He throws in his hand and now everything depends on her response to an intruder. As such, Romeo does not say that he is baptised but that he will be – if she allows. His statement is not an immediate performative but a contingent promise: 'Call me but love and I'll be new baptized.' Juliet, of course, *does* call him her love, albeit some eighty-one lines later, but her great declaration of love is not a final statement but another promise of the future. Love is never done but is taken back to 'give it thee again' (II.i.173). The new name 'Romeo and Juliet' is held together by a tenuous membrane – 'and' – that might break at any moment. And yet, this fragility is the very condition of its happening. To break from the 'One' requires a future-oriented trust in what will come from the dark. The self is cut by giving itself to an unknown other. Or, as Derrida puts it, to say 'I love you' necessarily entails 'non-assurance' and 'risk of mis-understanding': it '*gives* without return and without recognition', without being able to 'calculate assured, immediate or full comprehension'.[86] Perhaps most importantly, this risk lies 'in not knowing *who*': 'in not knowing the substantial identity of *who* is, prior to the declaration of love, at the origin of who gives and who receives, *who* is in possession or not of what happens to be offered or requested'.[87] Or again: love is given to the dark.

Here I radically depart from Kottman's understanding of the scene, both dramatically and philosophically. For Kottman, the return of Romeo's words from the darkness enacts 'the audible manifestation of Romeo's uniqueness through his voice'.[88] He therefore concludes that what the scene 'communicates' is Romeo's 'embodied uniqueness' and that what really matters is not 'what [Romeo] says' but 'who is saying it'.[89] We have, here, a sense of a pre-existing, unique identity. Kottman reaches a similar point in his more recent reading when he claims that Romeo and Juliet 'want to know *whom* it is they desire'.[90] The lovers, however, are only 'who' they are because of the event. Their singularity is not pre-existing in voice or body, or Petrarchan parroting, but arises from the uniqueness of the obscure event and the change of language it triggered. Juliet recognises Romeo's voice because she has already shared with it in their joint poetry. Romeo's voice is imprinted, inscribed, on Juliet's mind not because of its structural 'uniqueness' – what Badiou calls the 'infinite and self-evident multiplicity of human kind'[91] – but because of what has happened. The dramatic happening of love is the foundation of their new community of Two.

Both of Kottman's readings rely on notions of individual identity. He writes that Juliet 'seeks through Romeo precisely what she had always sought: the freedom to claim her separation from him as her own'.[92] Identity, here, may be dialectically produced,[93] but it remains identity: separating, individualising, and self-possessing. And identity, according to Badiou, is love's chief enemy when love is understood as 'the birth of a world'[94] or 'an existential project: to construct a world from a decentred point of view other than that of my mere impulse to survive or re-affirm my own identity'.[95] Identity places such love 'under threat'[96] because it challenges the primacy of the event. It suggests that I am who I am before, or independently from, this intrusion of difference. It establishes a self-possession that may refuse to give itself to the future, refuse to be ruptured by the event, and thus seek 'to ward it off'.[97] Love, in contrast, involves a *letting go* of one's self-possessed identity even as one experiences one's separateness. As

Vernon writes of the love-event: 'Nothing within the situation . . . justifies the amorous encounter that explodes our self-sufficient oneness.'[98] This is the importance of Juliet's gift to the darkness: it suggests that who they were before doesn't matter, that what matters is what comes from the dark – who they will become.

It is perhaps because of this peculiar sense of rebirth that Shakespeare stages a discrepancy between the post-evental attitudes of Romeo and Juliet: because the idea that the subject arrives through an event is not an obvious one. They declare their love but this also involves a vigorous debate as to *how* the declaration should be made. Of course, the disagreements stress their separateness. They never stop being individuals with individual interests and desires; indeed, this is what makes love profound, hard and intense. They are never entirely new. They have the same names, bodies and even 'character traits' as before the event. Romeo is still youthful, yearning and hyperbolic. This all continues. And yet it is all transfigured. The 'truth' of love is the never-ending process of mediating these interests and identities by thinking from the perspective of the event. Romeo thereby becomes more than a bundle of traits. The miracle of love is the discontinuity of continuance, the break that separates one from one's old self. Their disagreements show not only how difficult it is to break from the old models but also that the biggest threat is the old language. As we see in Romeo's continued use of the language of courtly love poetry, the temptation is always to project from past experiences, to treat the new event as a continuation of the old, to smooth over the rupture. Hence why Žižek stresses the importance of the evental tradition: 'Against the pagan and/or Gnostic Wisdom which celebrates the (re)discovery of one's true Self . . . Christianity calls upon us to thoroughly reinvent ourselves.'[99] If they are reborn they are reborn not in substance but in language. And so to sustain their rebirth they must alter how they relate to and speak about the world. Juliet, in sum, realises that they must change their 'musical key'.[100]

On one level, of course, the new subject is not sustained. In the end, the old names kill and the new ones are encased in the cold dead weight of gold. Moreover, many have seen a violent death drive in their love. Julia Kristeva contends that 'Juliet's jouissance is often stated through the anticipation – the desire? – of Romeo's death' and links this with 'the intrinsic presence of hatred in amatory feeling itself'.[101] To make death and hatred the play's hidden core, however, Kristeva must abandon all known texts and speculate on what would happen if the lovers 'had escaped their persecutors' and 'experienced' the 'banal, humdrum, lackluster lassitude of . . . normal marriage'.[102] She thereby reduces a notoriously overdetermined ending – with its missing letters, plague, poison and banishment – into an equation of love with death and violence. Ironically, Kristeva is here caught within the metaphysics of finished states. The question of *what* love is underpins her attempts 'to decide if, when speaking of love, we spoke of the same thing':

> [S]uch questioning hints that love would, in any case, be solitary because incommunicable. As if, at the very moment when the individual discovered himself to be intensely true, powerfully subjective, but violently ethical because he would be generously ready to do anything for the other, he also discovered the confines of his condition and the powerlessness of his language.[103]

Kristeva raises an important aporia in the common conception of love as an almost mystical union: that we can never be certain in love, never sure we speak of the same thing. And yet, in many ways this is precisely Juliet's lesson to Romeo. She knows they are irrevocably separate – irrevocably Two – and that she cannot know if Romeo is true. She, like Kristeva, recognises the 'powerlessness of his language', and yet Juliet does not abandon language or remain 'infinitely remote'[104] from her love. Unlike the 'tradition of seeing death as the secret content of desire',[105] Juliet treats love not as a secret essence but as an open process, even though she understands the old model of desire all too well:

> Dost thou love me? I know thou wilt say 'Ay',
> And I will take thy word. Yet if thou swear'st
> Thou mayst prove false. At lovers' perjuries,
> They say, Jove laughs. O gentle Romeo,
> If thou dost love, pronounce it faithfully;
> Or if thou think'st I am too quickly won,
> I'll frown, and be perverse, and say thee nay,
> So thou wilt woo; but else, not for the world. (II.i.132–39).

Juliet's speech raises two problems with Romeo's tendency to name their love using the old language: a problem of knowledge and a problem of desire. The first problem is that of knowledge: 'Dost thou love me?' Juliet here acknowledges the impossibility of knowing the other's love (or the other) through language. As we've seen, love begins from the point of disjuncture: 'the simple difference between two people and their infinite subjectivities'.[106] The gulf separating two minds is, objectively at least, uncrossable. And yet, she will believe Romeo's affirmation even though he 'mayst prove false'. Juliet takes the plunge into love but with open eyes, *knowing the event of love is uncertain*. Such is 'fidelity'.

Here we have a sort of dialectical reversal between weakness and strength. In courtly love poetry, the lady remains strong and aloof (a kind of blank screen) and her servant remains weak and narcissistic (a kind of masochistic projector),[107] but Juliet, in admitting her weakness and lack of knowledge, envisages a different dynamic that escapes this zero-sum game. It suggests Kuzner's idea that 'the new can arrive through humility and disorientation ... and unremitting self-risk'.[108] Juliet's instruction of Romeo, her desire to escape the old oaths and names, is an attempt to conceive such a vulnerable and uncertain love. It is a point lost in Kottman's focus on the uniqueness of Romeo's voice: 'what they say to each other is finally less crucial than the fact that they reveal who they are to one another *in spite of what they say*.'[109] Shakespeare stresses, however, that the lovers are saying very different things. He stages an important, if tender, clash about how the event is to be thought and lived. *What* Juliet says is crucial, for she is trying to develop a new way of living – a new joint-subject – in response to the event of love.

The second problem with Romeo's language is the problem of desire. Juliet grasps how desire may function as lack, forever circling around its unobtained object. She shares Cressida's realisation that '[w]omen are angels, wooing; / Things won are done' (*Troilus*, I.ii.264–65). Juliet thus wishes half-heartedly that she had 'frown[ed]' and been 'perverse', allowing Romeo's desire to circle her – in other words, that she stayed aloof and they did not become 'Two'; that she remained an object of seriality or projection. Of course, Juliet does quite the opposite. She reaffirms her unreserved gift: 'I'll prove more true / Than those that have more cunning to be strange' (II.i.142–43). Romeo then interrupts her probing of love with counterproductive attempts to prove his love by swearing oaths:

<pre>
ROMEO   Lady, by yonder blessèd moon I vow,
        That tips with silver all these fruit-tree tops –
JULIET O swear not by the moon, th'inconstant moon
        That monthly changes in her circled orb,
        Lest that thy love prove likewise variable.
ROMEO   What shall I swear by?
JULIET Do not swear at all,
        Or if thou wilt, swear by thy gracious self,
        And I'll believe thee.
ROMEO   If my heart's dear love –
JULIET Well, do not swear.   (II.i.149–58)
</pre>

The content of the language is again important, here, because Romeo's courtly language reproduces the problem Juliet is trying to avoid. His oaths suggest an absolute knowledge and 'satisfaction' (II.i.168) that is final and named. He suggests a singular self, finding its completion, rather than a mutual work of fidelity. Juliet rejects this model of desire. Whereas Cressida accepts circling desire in her maxim, '[a]chievement is command; ungained, beseech' (I.ii.271), Juliet is convinced that love is different. As Žižek writes, 'desire is always caught in the logic of "this is not that", it thrives in the gap that forever separates the *obtained* satisfaction from the *sought-for* satisfaction' but 'love FULLY ACCEPTS that "this IS that" – that the woman with all her weaknesses and common features IS the Thing I unconditionally love'.[110] By breaking up Romeo's conventional language, Juliet pre-empts Badiou's idea that 'it is only by breaking up all ordinary prose that [poetry] extends the limit of the communicable'.[111] It indicates that love 'shatters our egotistical normalcy' and opens a new path.[112] This is not to say that love is 'unspeakable', but that it enters from the unspeakable void and must *then* be spoken, not as an oath or name that encapsulates its potential but as a process of enacting it within the situation. For Juliet, it is spoken as a love of give-ness that receives as it gives and gives forever:

ROMEO   O, wilt thou leave me so unsatisfied?
JULIET   What satisfaction canst thou have tonight?
ROMEO   Th'exchange of thy love's faithful vow for mine.
JULIET   I gave thee mine before thou didst request it,
        And yet I would it were to give again.
ROMEO   Wouldst thou withdraw it? For what purpose love?
JULIET   But to be frank and give it thee again.
        And yet I wish but for the thing I have.
        My bounty is as boundless as the sea,
        My love as deep. The more I give to thee
        The more I have, for both are infinite.   (II.i.167–77)

Juliet develops her process of boundless giving in response to her concern that their love is '[t]oo like the lightening' (II.i.161). One might even see it as a response to Montaigne's warning against the momentary 'passion' that 'ravisheth [our soule] from out her selfe'.[113] Juliet thinks otherwise. The event may strike like lightning, disappearing with its flash, but, as Badiou puts it, the 'chance' of the encounter 'must turn into a process that can last'.[114] Juliet's process of giving – the beautiful taking back of love only to give it again and go on giving forever – with its rhythms that elongate the shared moment, is provided by Shakespeare as Juliet's means of reworking ordinary language and continuing to inscribe the event after the flash is gone. Like Saint Paul, Romeo and Juliet do not pre-exist the event that they declare but arrive in 'the decision' to 'completely rework [their] ordinary way of "living" [their] situation'.[115] 'Saint Paul for the Church or but also Simon, Bernard or Claire, if they declare themselves to be in love', are names that designate a 'subject' that strives to 'incorporat[e] ... the event into the situation'.[116] Composed of two, and designated 'Romeo and Juliet', the new subject is this work of connecting the event of love to their situation (and thereby transforming Verona and its language). This is not simply 'mutual self-recognition',[117] for the self and the world are no longer what they were. Rather, the lovers are 'incorporated into [a] unique Subject, the Subject of love that views the panorama of the world through the prism of [their] difference'.[118]

Of course, holding another's perspective within one's own is an extremely difficult notion at the best of times, let alone within the brief course of their tragic interim. We do not reach this new world of difference in *Romeo and Juliet*: yet, we are given lightning-flashed glimpses. Moreover, in scripting Juliet's struggle to give birth to a new world, Shakespeare captures something essential about love as an ethical and creative enterprise: how the self is *given over*. And it captures how this involves a struggle to wrench one's self (and another) from the old language, to reach for a poetic process that does not come easily to hand, and to open oneself to the unknown other. In this, Juliet pre-empts something of the rapturous, euphoric daring celebrated by Hélène Cixous: the way '[t]he new love dares for the other', the way the lover 'runs her risks', and thereby moves beyond love-as-hate, '[b]eyond the struggle-to-the-death that's been removed to the bed, beyond the love-battle that claims to represent exchange'.[119] The movement of giving is a movement beyond knowing: 'She gives more, with no assurance that she'll get back even some unexpected profit from what she puts out. She gives that there may be life, thought, transformation. This is an "economy" that can no longer be put in economic terms.'[120]

To break down the logic of the 'One', Cixous turns, like Juliet, to a risky poetic endeavour that is never complete. One is not shut up in one's lack but is exposed to another – gives to another – and thereby creates something. We can glimpse the ongoing risk of this project in Nancy's idea that '[t]he heart ... does not say "*I love*," which is the reflection or the speculation of an ego ... but it says "I love you," a declaration where "I" is posed only to be exposed to "you."'[121] Again we have an experience of the 'Two'. Love is not a 'thing'[122] to be known or named, or a 'satisfaction' to be had, but a process, an address, an offering, in which '[w]hat is offered is the offered being itself'.[123] As such, 'love's name is not "love", which would be a substance or a faculty, but it is this sentence, the "I love you"', which is a 'promise [that] does not anticipate or assure the future'.[124]

Juliet's giving, then, moves beyond the static name to something more alive and processual. In envisaging love as a perpetual motion of giving, Juliet foreshadows Florizel's speech to Perdita in *The Winter's Tale*: 'When you dance, I wish you / A wave o'th' sea, that you might ever do / Nothing but that' (IV.iv.140–42). There is an important difference, however, for whereas Florizel describes the other's motion, Juliet describes *her own*. Moreover, she repeats the motion, the undeserved gift – to 'give it thee again' – in a constant re-choosing. So whereas Florizel's beautiful perpetual wave has an automated and almost static quality ('ever do / Nothing but that'), Juliet's re-giving entails a physics of distinct units. Each gift is a conscious action or commission. Juliet's repeated giving here recalls Kierkegaard's idea that 'repetition' is essential to genuine subjecthood, else we would be either 'a tablet upon which time writes every instant a new inscription' or 'a mere memorial of the past'.[125] There is a repetition that becomes inward and creates the self through a faith that looks forward. Juliet's repetition forms her ceaseless '*work* of love':

> As every true Christian knows, love is the *work* of love – the hard and arduous work of repeated 'uncoupling' in which, again and again, we have to disengage ourselves from the inertia that constrains us to identify with the particular order we were born into . . . Christian 'unplugging' is *not* an inner contemplative stance, but the *active* work of love which necessarily leads to the creation of an *alternative* community.[126]

To remain uncoupled from the inertia of the old language and sustain their '*alternative* community', Juliet must keep giving herself over and over. Kottman steadfastly denies that the lovers form such a joint 'community': they are 'not a united "pair" but two separate individuals'.[127] And, of course, they *do* remain separate individuals. But through their labour they also reconfigure their world and join together what is separate.[128] That is the point of Juliet's giving. Giving is the grace that replaces the old law of desire (the One) and allows them (as Two) to 'inscribe' the 'truth's postevental universality . . . in the world'.[129] The initial event of love arrived like grace – unforeseen, undeserved, excessive – and Juliet's work of fidelity is a process of enshrining that grace by giving more than is due.

It is this possibility of grace that distinguishes *Romeo and Juliet* from the courtly love tradition. Despite the parallels with the fourth song of *Astrophil and Stella*, 'where Astrophil meets Stella in a garden by moonlight',[130] there is a profound divide between the two gardens.

Sidney's forbidden and frustrated desire involves a movement to take consummation – 'Take me to thee, and thee to me' – that repeatedly approaches climax, only to be repeatedly denied. The structure of the song relies on a vision of final 'satisfaction' (per Romeo) that is forever deferred by the beautiful refusal of Petrarchan poetry: 'No, no, no, no, my dear, let be' (*Astrophil*, Fourth Song). While there is mutuality here, it is, ultimately, the shared suffering of their failed encounter: 'I sighed her sighs, and wailed for her woe, / Yet swam in joy, such love in her was seen' (LXXXVII, 10–11). Shakespeare's lovers also long for the night not to end, are hemmed in by iron laws and share something beautiful in failure, but there is something altogether different in their garden scene, for there the opposition between law and love is sublated not sustained. The event comes as grace, or 'miracle', which is 'the symbol of an interruption of the law'.[131] So whereas Sidney's lovers are thwarted by the 'iron laws of duty' (LXXXVII, 4), Juliet institutes a process of giving that suspends the old law.

Not that all is positive and processual. As Kristeva suggests, there is, particularly in Juliet, a fierceness – almost an absolutism – that seems to call forth death, or at least declares her death to all other joys. For instance, Kristeva sees Juliet's great epithalamium as reflecting 'Juliet's unconscious desire to break up Romeo's body'.[132] To some extent, the concept of 'arrivals' is able to rehabilitate this violence as the inherent violence of a new beginning:

> Is not such love one of the greatest pulverizers of social hierarchy? When, in the balcony scene, Romeo and Juliet pathetically proclaim their renunciation and hatred of their own family names (Montague, Capulet), and thus 'unplug' themselves from their particular (family) social substance, do they not provide the supreme example of 'hatred of one's parents' as the direct expression of love?[133]

The 'term "new creation" . . . [reveals] a terrifying *violence* in the subject's arrival: 'that of the *death drive*, of the radical "wiping the slate clean" as the condition of the New Beginning'.[134] Love shatters the self. It is thus fitting that Žižek references Luke 14:26, with its requirement that one 'hates' one's 'own life'. The demands are brutally high. Here we see, with Kristeva, the centrality of violence and hatred to their love. But it is less a structural 'desire as death' than a violent drive to do away with the old name – with one's 'inscription into' the old 'socio-symbolic structure'[135] – for the sake of the new subject. Hence why 'love "is violent, irresponsible, and creative"': it wages an almost inhuman war against the pre-existing self, teaching us 'that the individual as such is something vacuous and insignificant'.[136] But this tearing violence also tries to reconfigure the heavens themselves:

> Give me my Romeo, and when I shall die
> Take him and cut him out in little stars,
> And he will make the face of heaven so fine
> That all the world will be in love with night. (III.ii.21–24)

Juliet both foreshadows their tearing death and looks forward to a subjective sexual encounter that will explode into a new cosmic order. As Badiou writes, the subject's 'courage' in fidelity to the event 'is compensated by the supernumerary emergence of the constellation, which fixes in the sky of Ideas the event's excess-of-one'.[137] So while there is something dark and violent in their exuberant love, death and absolutism are not the most important elements of the play, let alone its true, hidden content. What is most important is the new constellation they create. If their tragic fates are in some sense 'star cross'd' by the overarching power of the situation, what they *become* is not: a new subject.

Of course, some have thought that Romeo and Juliet could have done with some Montaigne-like moderation: 'Wisely and slow; they stumble that run fast' (II.iii.100). But I doubt that is Shakespeare's counsel. Indeed, there are hints that the opposite is true: that the lovers' fatal moment stems not from their violence, but from not being violent enough. From the perspective of the love-event, Romeo's killing of Tybalt, which kick-starts the play's tragic trajectory, is a retreat from the lovers' violent commitment into the passive violence of the name. The incident is quite different in Broke's poem, in which Romeo attempts to break up a bloody fray but is attacked by Tybalt, who 'at Romeus hed, a blow he strake so hard, / That might have clove him to the brayne'.[138] Shakespeare transforms the duel so that 'Romeo is confronted with a highly personal dilemma of having to choose between his love for Juliet and his desire to revenge his friend's death as well as his own slandered reputation'.[139] For the duel-loving Kottman,[140] tellingly, this is not a dilemma at all. Rather, the duel offers the same sort of opportunity for 'self-realization' as love: 'Romeo must accept Tybalt's challenge if he is to reaffirm his own existence: "Either thou, or I, or both" (3.1.131).'[141]

In fact, Romeo does not rush into the duel as a hyped-up Hegelian, driven by a strangely paranoid need to 'reaffirm his own existence'. Rather, he begins by thinking of the duel from the perspective of the Two, from the perspective of Juliet: 'Tybalt, the reason that I have to love thee, / Doth much excuse the appertaining rage / To such a greeting' (III.i.57–59). Mercutio, the cynic of love, dubs this 'calm, dishonourable, vile submission!' (III.i.68). But it is only in his rage after Mercutio's death that Romeo accepts his friend's logic. Holmer argues that '[f]rom the Friar's perspective, Romeo's peaceful offers of conciliatory love to Tybalt would be viewed not as evidence of "vile submission" or "effeminate"'; rather, he 'would approve Romeo's strength to turn the other cheek'.[142] While this may be true, it is hardly the point. In bemoaning how 'sweet Juliet' has 'made [him] effeminate' (III.i.108–9) and instead embracing the logic of the name – revenging Mercutio to restore his 'reputation stained / With Tybalt's slander' (III.i.106–7) – Romeo fails to continue in fidelity to the event. His 'fire-eyed fury' (III.i.119) is not a failure because it is immoral or unchristian, neither of which has played a part in Romeo's arrival, but because it betrays their new name for the sake of the old. There is, doubtless, more than stained reputation at play here: there is intense grief, anger, guilt and shame. Nonetheless, in this moment of stress Romeo returns to the old logic of reputation.[143] In this harsh light,[144] Romeo's duel is the precise opposite of Badiou's 'definition of courage: exile without return, loss of one's name'.[145] In a tragic irony, Romeo is physically exiled because he cannot bear the existential exile from his old self that is decreed by fidelity, because, in 'fire-eyed fury', he tries to recapture his name. He returns to the structural violence of the feud-driven situation and thereby retreats from the event that has violently torn this structure apart.

Interestingly, another book of Kottman's sheds a very different light on Romeo's insistence upon reputation: 'Shakespeare shows worldly rights and entitlements . . . to be precisely that which invariably *blinds* us to the recognition of others.'[146] We can link this back to Badiou, who stresses that the 'difficulties love harbours . . . are internal to the process': 'Selfishness, not any rival, is love's enemy. One could say: my love's main enemy, the one I must defeat, is not the other, it is myself, the "myself" that prefers identity to difference, that prefers to impose its world against the world re-constructed through the filter of difference.'[147]

There is a twin scene for Juliet, though her duel with 'identity' is not physical. When she hears that Romeo has slain Tybalt she turns violently against her lover: 'O serpent heart hid with a flow'ring face!' (III.ii.73). According to Lloyd Davis, this suggests that '[n]ot only can the lovers not escape the eternal feud that frames them, they even play parts in it, responding impulsively, at the threshold of nature and nurture, to news of Mercutio's and Tybalt's deaths'.[148] Juliet is faced with a choice of whether to return to the old name – condemning Romeo for killing a Capulet – or to continue in the thought of Two. For a second, it appears that Juliet will take Othello's path and insist on a true, hidden content beneath the surface of the love-object. It is here, and only here, that Juliet takes up Romeo's extravagant use of Petrarchan paradox: 'Beautiful tyrant, fiend angelical! / Dove-feathered raven, wolvish-ravening lamb!' (III.ii.75–76).[149] In other words, she treats Romeo as an object: as a (beautiful) deceptive mirror. She returns to the logic of the One and the Nurse concurs: 'There's no trust, no faith, no honesty in men' (III.ii.86). But Juliet's duel has a different result. She throws down the feudal sword and returns to the violence of love when she pounces on the Nurse ('Blistered be thy tongue / For such a wish!' (III.ii.90–91)) and rebukes herself: 'O, what a beast was I to chide at him!' (III.ii.95). Shakespeare here changes Broke's scene in one crucial way: whereas Iuliet *knows* that 'Tybalt bears the fault'[150] and Romeus acted in self-defence, Shakespeare's Juliet must take it on faith. In a sense, Romeo does not merit this faith. If we were to weigh the merits, he *has* failed. But, as Badiou writes, '[g]race is the opposite of law insofar as it is what comes *without being due*'.[151] In another sense, then, Juliet's faith saves their love and makes possible their marriage night.

Being Some Other Name

If we take up Derrida's promise of *'another name'* in the dramatic moment rather than his deferred future, we see that Romeo and Juliet do rework their dislocated names into a new joint name. Belsey is thus only partly right that 'the signifier, however arbitrary, is not at the disposal of the subject'.[152] Old names and meanings may not be erased but a new name can nonetheless arise from the event. We can think of this in processual terms. Whitehead describes how '[m]odern physics … abandoned the [Newtonian] doctrine of Simple Location' with the result that a given 'thing' is no longer seen as an 'independent individuality': rather, the 'thing itself is what it does, and what it does is [a] divergent stream of influence'.[153] One of the problems with Romeo's static imagery and final, everlasting oaths is that they envisage the cessation of movement and influence. Arrivals in Shakespeare, however, are an ongoing process. Shakespeare grants the promise of another name not as a final substance or satisfaction but through the creativity of the extended moment. We see this in the back-and-forth motion of Romeo's and Juliet's poetic interactions:

JULIET   I have forgot why I did call thee back.
ROMEO   Let me stand here till thou remember it.
JULIET   I shall forget, to have thee still stand there,
         Rememb'ring how I love thy company.
ROMEO   And I'll still stay, to have thee still forget,
         Forgetting any other home but this.   (II.i.215–20)

The passage contrasts starkly with Romeo's earlier attempts to 'swear' a once-and-for-all oath: 'Lady, by yonder blessèd moon I vow.' There, Romeo turned Juliet back into the 'Lady', 'yonder', suspended in space, to which the 'I' swears. But here they operate as Two. Each line in their interaction involves thinking of the other, entails a movement between 'I' and 'thou'. We have 'I' forgetting why it called 'thee back', 'me' standing until 'thou remember[s] it', and then 'I' forgetting in order to have 'thee still stand[ing] there'. The agency is consistently passed on to the 'thou', to whom the 'I' is consistently made subject. And, indeed, theirs is no 'other home but this' movement, this brief new world.

Here I fully accept that *what* they say is not the most important thing. Juliet forgets why she 'did call [him] back' so that the language has no 'content'. Language is now used in a non-idealist manner, without seeking any final name or satisfaction. What matters is what their speech *does*. Juliet's words have the physical effect of elongating their time together: she has exited and she returns; he moves away and she calls him back to her. The specific signified is forgotten as the lovers use words to take pleasure in each other's presence. The work of love is revealed to be a game of forgetting everything but this moment. Language is used to actively extend their time together by repeating leave-takings: 'To lure this tassle-gentle back again' (II.i.204). As Emrys Jones writes, 'the repeated terms – "stand here", "still stand here", "still stay" – repudiate (or try to) all distracting thoughts of past and future' and thus convey the 'feeling of a prolonged present moment'.[154] Shakespeare thus creates a 'profound sense of occasion', a sense of 'something happening now' that is 'unique, marvellous, and tragically unrepeatable'.[155] It is through such slowed down, loving moments – what we might call the 'long time' of their scenes together, which counterbalances the 'short time' of their tragic end – that their constellation of Two crystallises.

The contrast with Kottman's reading is here at its sharpest. For Kottman, the passage is evidence of the 'self-defeating turn *within* the lovers' freedom', which emerges '[b]ecause nothing external comes between the lovers'[156] and they must therefore script their own separation from each other.[157] Rather than a joyous extension of their time together, Kottman views this moment as two lovers refusing to admit they want to hang up the phone: 'If we are honest with ourselves, is not what every lover wants at such moments, really, to hang up the phone?'[158] In other words, they want to be separate, to reflect alone on their 'self-realization'. Because there is no event or joint process for Kottman, there is nothing to share except the mutual recognition of separateness. The other is a tool or instrument through which one surgically extracts recognition and thereby 'self-realization'. The other becomes an object once more – a phone to be put down – and love comes to seem a lonely thing.

Against this self-enclosing view, I instead make positive use of Kottman's sense of scene: 'the trajectory of the plot is suspended in the balcony scene, whereupon something like an alternative story for the two lovers is presented as an absolute possibility.'[159] Between names, they use language to commune together, to extend their shared scene, and thereby create their community of joint witnesses to the event. It is this alternate community that Romeo betrays in revenging Mercutio. Despite their end, however, Shakespeare's scene opens an alternative mode of existence. Julia Lupton writes that 'Shakespeare allows us to glimpse a possible polity *even where it has no chance of flourishing*'[160] – a sentiment we'll return to throughout this book. For a moment at least, Romeo and Juliet abide in a moment, rather than long for *the* moment. They are able to love not through the prohibition of the name or the sublime failure of the tomb but (to repeat Kristeva's words about 'normal marriage') through the seemingly 'banal, humdrum'[161] back and forth occasioned by Juliet's forgetting. Here Žižek's idea of the 'Sublime' in the everyday is apposite:

> [The] 'sublime' is not the cold elevated figure of the Lady who had to remain beyond our reach – if she were to step down from her pedestal, she would turn into a repulsive hag. 'Sublime' is the magic *combination* of the two dimensions, when the sublime dimension transpires through the utmost common details of everyday shared life.[162]

Romeo and Juliet are never so 'everyday' or 'common', and yet, they do clear small domestic spaces within the overarching violence. There are moments in which they call back, elongate and repeat together rather than rush to their tragic ends. Whether it is Juliet's almost banal forgetting why she called Romeo back or their interplay as they awake on the marriage bed, Shakespeare's dramaturgy creates little shared moments of intensity in which they accept appearance at face value, allowing them to become 'true believers' in their event. To quote Žižek: 'the cynic misses the efficiency/ actuality of the appearance itself, however fleeting, fragile and elusive it is; while the true believer believes in appearances, in the magic dimension that "shines through" an appearance.'[163] The creativity of the moment is what enacts this 'magic dimension'. It is how 'the promise of *another name*'[164] *is lived* through their shared poetry and not simply deferred into the always retreating future. The critical tendency to superimpose prior concepts over the processes of drama, over Juliet's movement of giving, stifles this creativeness. Whether it is the inescapable structure of language, the inescapable coupling of death and desire, or the quasi-Hegelian march to 'self-realization', criticism often overlays analytic structures on the fluid movement of their arrival. Such critics thereby let 'what is *new* in each moment of a history escape',[165] and, in particular, how the dramatic 'moment' creates this 'new' subject of Two: how the lovers use language to create spaces within the feud, in which they can emerge as a new term between 'Montague' and 'Capulet'.

One of the supreme examples of this creativeness occurs in Romeo and Juliet's shifting between the names of the lark and the nightingale. From classical times the nightingale's song was associated with lament; in the Petrarchan tradition it comes to be a solitary lament over lost love: 'and the / nightingale that sweetly in the shadow every night laments and / weeps / burdens our hearts with thoughts of love.'[166] In stark contrast, Romeo and Juliet use the nightingale as a tool for togetherness and play, while Shakespeare uses it to continue his anti-Petrarchan artistry of the moment. As the day breaks on their one night together, Juliet tells Romeo: 'It was the nightingale, and not the lark, / That pierced the fear-full hollow of thine ear' (III.v.2–3). In the touching comic exchange that follows, the bird's significance is open, shifting back and forth. Juliet here uses the nightingale, this signifier of loss, to push back the separating dawn and extend the togetherness of the night; to show it is 'not yet near day' (III.v.1). Romeo, afraid for their safety, takes the literal approach and uses the material evidence – the 'envious streaks' that 'lace the severing clouds in yonder east' (III.v.7–8) – to name the bird as 'the lark' (III.v.6). Juliet, not wanting to part, fights against this dawning of material necessity by interpreting these streaks not as the natural order but as the profoundly singular intrusion of 'some meteor that the sun exhaled' (III.v.13), which would allow Romeo to 'stay yet' (III.v.16). Romeo agrees not to leave but the prospect of his death causes Juliet's urgent reversal. Her rapid, inflamed shift to the lark contradicts Kristeva's idea that she desires Romeo's death. Indeed, she forgoes his presence so that he may live: 'It is the lark that

sings so out of tune, / Straining harsh discords and unpleasing sharps'
(III.v.27–28).

The back-and-forth between the two lovers and the two birds not only
dramatises their desire and concern for each other, it actively extends
their time talking together: 'stay yet'. Ultimately, of course, Juliet returns
to the material and acknowledges the dawn, while the nightingale fades
like their hours of bliss. And yet, the *meanings have been changed*.[167] Their
joint name – their new existence as a divided 'us' – alters the conventional
significance of names: the lark no longer 'makes sweet division', 'for she
divideth *us*' (III.v.29–30, italics mine). Although the 'signifier' may not
be 'at the disposal of the subject',[168] and although the nightingale does
still signify loss – just as Romeo is still 'Romeo' – the nightingale now
signifies something more: those blessed moments of the night in which
killing names are suspended along with civil strife. The nightingale may sing
of loss, but it is a loss that is yet to come – a loss held off by this song of two
and not of one. We have a dramatic moment that is neither idealistically free
of names nor bound in their service but exists in between names, which is
the space for 'us'. We have, in Geoffrey Hill's words, a happening of grace
in which 'grammar and desire are miraculously at one'.[169] They steal a
moment from the dawning of tragic necessity. It is in such fluid moments,
shifting between names, that we glimpse their new world of Two.

By focusing on the lovers' linguistic process, rather than its end result,
we can thus see that the promise of 'some other name' is more than
Derrida's 'promise'. Romeo and Juliet fulfil the 'promise', if only for the
moment, and only through the moment. They do form the new name
'Romeo and Juliet', and they do so through an active process of circulating
between names, between the nightingale and the lark, between the pressing
materiality of the dawn and their dawning as a new subject. The result is
not simply in-between-ness but creativeness. This is not to deny difference,
dislocation and multiplicity. Nor is it to suggest that they 'become one' in a
psychological sense, for their psychological difference is manifest throughout in their constant disagreements. Rather, through their difference and
interplay, the two become a joint 'subject' of the event. Or, in Badiou's
terms, as 'the bearer of a fidelity . . . [they] enter into the composition of *one*
loving subject, who *exceeds* them both'.[170] Together, in their difference, in
their dislocation, in their multiplicity, they declare their baptism. They
join to 'declare' the love-event 'to have been the origin of a life-changing
sequence'.[171]

The tomb of course halts that life-filled sequence. We have known from
the beginning that their love is bound to death. And materialist readings

will thus never be wrong; there will always be much earth and gold to feast upon. But the lovers' end is inevitable in an even more basic sense. Drama, of necessity, radically contracts the interim between life and death. We have hours not years, scenes and moments rather than a long course of marriage. In this sense, the tomb reveals the ghostly existence of play-worlds and characters at large: '*here* before us yet absent'.[172] The spirits always vanish in the end. The curtain always falls. So how can love, in a play, ever endure? If it continues, it continues in an 'elsewhere' evoked here but here not.[173] If it lasts, it lasts in a distant constellation, gleaned but unpeopled. Or else it trails into the black hole of a 'happily ever after'.

And so, the play of love's end must 'stellify' the lovers.[174] For all that their love is too fast, too soon, too late, too rash, too much and too much like the lightning that too soon ceases, there is, as Tony Tanner states, 'another source of light in the play, which is the reverse of transient – the stars'.[175] As much as their mourning families try to contain the lovers' story within the weighty mass of golden statues, the play's history resists this gravity. It constantly leaps from earth to stars as a figure of 'something else': a guiding light, however ill fated, in the utopian dream that in love we become something new; a 'truth' that 'transits from world to world through the centuries', awaiting 'resurrection' in new contexts, through 'new event[s]';[176] a 'feasting presence full of light' (V.iii.86) that illumines even the tomb's 'detestable maw' (V.iii.45). The tomb, then, is not the end. '[P]erishing', as Whitehead stresses, 'is the initiation of becoming'.[177] The tomb, with its lifeless bodies and drawn-out post-mortems, begins this process by which 'Romeo and Juliet' 'perishes into the status of an object for other occasions'.[178] It functions, to appropriate States's words about the 'curtain call', as 'a decompression chamber halfway between the depths of art and the thin air of reality',[179] in which the 'character remains in the actor, like a ghost'.[180] Through it, the love of Romeo and Juliet passes into an afterlife. It is an afterlife encased in the gold of Verona's patriarchy, but it is, more fundamentally, an afterlife whose living (if the stars align) is left to us. It becomes 'an object for other occasions' in future playhouses and, indeed, suburban houses, an opportunity for future 'becoming' for us to grasp in a new falling moment.

CHAPTER 3

Love's Late Arrival: Wonder and Terror in Othello's 'High-Wrought Flood'

Since T. S. Eliot's rather scathing assessment of Othello's final speech – that, essentially, he ignores Desdemona and keeps on telling stories in order to '*cheer*[] *himself up*'[1] – many critics have found it difficult to work out how, or even if, he is a tragic character.[2] Indeed, in a recent 'Iagocentric' reading of the play,[3] Paul Cefalu writes, 'it is open to question whether we can even empathize with a character who, by the end of the play, has so withdrawn into his own narrative fictions that he seems unable to empathize with anyone else'.[4] To some extent, I accept the premises behind these readings: Othello is largely ensconced in his romantic story of himself,[5] often closed off from others and not often self-reflective in the manner of Juliet. Once one accepts these points, accepting the earlier critical praise of Othello as 'a nobly tragic figure'[6] becomes much more difficult. For some, such as Cefalu, the result is that Iago necessarily becomes the play's major point of interest, but I want to suggest another path. In this chapter, I locate the tragic element of Othello not in his noble nature but in something that happens, something that arrives in Cyprus.

I begin by showing how Shakespeare constructs Othello through a peculiarly enclosed way of speaking about, and seeing, the world. But there is also something else to Othello and this comes through Desdemona. To some extent, *Othello* is Desdemona's tragedy. She is given the dramatic impetus to interrupt Othello's self-sustaining tale and propel a new, vulnerable subject into being. *Othello* complicates the dramaturgy of arrivals, however, by upsetting the event's temporality. Despite already being married, love only hits Othello after the fact, upon his arrival in Cyprus. On the foreign isle, the foreignness of love strikes him belatedly and opens the disorienting uncertainty of the subsequent acts. In short, in Cyprus he belatedly experiences love as an *event*, and this opens a new horizon of possibility, opens him to something other than his tale. It is this possibility, soon betrayed but powerfully evoked, that provides Othello with his tragic dimension. And this is true in a double sense. First, in old-fashioned terms, the possibility opened in Cyprus gives us the 'impression of waste' that, for Bradley, is the 'centre of the tragic impression'.[7] Second, in evental terms, Iago would have had no power over Othello without Desdemona's rupture of his tale: there would have been no tragic fall. Iago's role, then, is that of the 'situation'. He reinstates the foundational opposition between Othello and Venice and asserts the 'impossibility' of the event that threatens to dismantle it.

'Were it my cue to fight': Othello's Non-Arrival

The structure of Othello's arrival relies on the solid image of him that is created in the first act. Although, in narrative time, the opening scenes occur after his marriage, dramatically, they seem to happen before he experiences love. His marriage to Desdemona is thus made differently present throughout the drama. In the opening scenes, Shakespeare seems to build a stone-like statue of Othello as he was before marriage. Whereas we awaited Romeo's arrival as he repeated rote-learned rhymes, Othello is immediately present, speaking a distinctive language. His heroic story has already been told, glorious, certain and commanding:

> Let him do his spite.
> My services which I have done the signory
> Shall out-tongue his complaints.   (I.ii.17–19)

Unlike Romeo, Othello already possesses his voice: 'Keep up your bright swords, for the dew will rust 'em' (I.ii.60). In short, he begins with a solid and imposing sense of *identity*. Othello's exceptionalism, his way of setting himself apart from Venice, both creates and is created by a peculiar way of speaking that G. Wilson Knight calls the '*Othello* music', whose 'dominant quality is separation': 'Its thought does not mesh with the reader's' and this 'aloofness is the resultant of an inward aloofness of image from image, word from word'.[8] And this music forms what States calls the 'tonal chord'[9] or 'musical key' that defines the 'character-base'.[10] We see the music's separating quality in Othello's use of 'grand single words . . . with their sharp, clear, consonant sounds, constituting defined aural solids'.[11] The result is not only 'the most Miltonic thing in Shakespeare',[12] it also reflects Othello's self-enclosed, almost transcendent, idea of himself. Bradley describes him as 'colossal', 'towering above his fellows'.[13] He speaks with the cool self-assurance of the mighty, as if the world he strides upon is not that of other men.

My point, I should stress, is not that Othello *is* masterful. To risk sounding overly philosophical, I'm here trying to build a phenomenological rather than ontological picture of Othello. The focus is not on what Othello is but on how he appears to himself through the masterful separateness of the '*Othello* music'. I here depart from Kuzner's impressive recent reading,[14] in which he argues that Othello 'acknowledges his lack of self-sufficiency from the outset'.[15] Formally speaking, this is true enough. As his speech continues, Othello openly acknowledges his dependency: 'I fetch my life and being / From men of royal siege' (I.ii.21–22). And this supports Cefalu's contention that 'Othello's self-definition is determined by his willingness to serve'.[16] But a question arises as to the nature of this service and dependency. For, far from being a straightforward admission of weakness, it is what gives him his commanding voice: 'My services . . . [s]hall out-tongue his complaints.' In fact, his words of seeming dependence are part of the same speech, the same thought, in which he defies the 'magnifico' (I.ii.12): 'Let him do his spite.' In his words of deference and service Othello appears more masterful than his 'noble and approved good masters', more potent than his '[m]ost potent, grave, and reverend signors' (I.iii.76–77). In short, he is not masterful because he is the 'master' but because his self-identity is assured, certain and settled. He may not be the sun but his planetary mass orbits certainly and serenely around these 'men of royal siege'.

Indeed, Othello's 'architectural stateliness of quarried speech'[17] chimes with the 'motionless tranquillity' that, for Hegel, characterises early 'Symbolic' art.[18] Like the 'old temple structures' whose 'absence of situation' gives them their 'character of profound impassive seriousness', Othello's language possesses a 'most peaceful, even motionless but grandiose, sublimity'.[19] Bradley describes this as his 'massive calm'.[20] As Othello continues in the separate block-like clauses of his music:

> Not I. I must be found.
> My parts, my title, and my perfect soul
> Shall manifest me rightly.   (I.ii.30–32)

These solid bricks build a wall that insulates Othello from the outside. They do not reflect back on the speaker but establish it as a self-contained structure in which little compartments of speech form around 'I', 'me' and 'my'. We are far removed from Juliet who, from the start, is questioning, trying to get at something that is not quite within reach: 'What's in a name?' (II.i.85). Othello speaks neither to another nor to another voice within himself. Rather, each clause centres upon, and is defined by,

Othello's simple self-reference – 'I', 'I' / 'My' 'my' 'my' / 'me' – so that there is nothing external to question this 'I'.

There is, of course, a bitter irony to Othello's 'Not I', given his end. 'Even I' might be more appropriate final words as Othello joins the list of Iago's deceived and his nonchalant coolness is incinerated by 'roast[ing]' 'devils' and 'liquid fire' (V.ii.284–87). Knight does not see a connection between the monolithic beauty of Othello's 'in control' speeches and his 'ugly, idiotic' language when 'enduring loss of control'.[21] I argue, however, that the '*Othello* music' not only provides the height from which he falls, it also sets him on his course, sets him up, if you will. The music's architectural quality – Goethe calls architecture 'frozen music' – entails a stasis and a separation that fundamentally conflicts with the evental ruptures and creative processes of Shakespeare's drama. The key feature of Othello's masterful block-like music is his self-certainty. We see this clearly at the end, as a firm selfhood re-emerges through the certainty of his damnation and Desdemona's purity, but it is present from the outset:

> Hold your hands,
> Both you of my inclining and the rest.
> Were it my cue to fight, I should have known it
> Without a prompter. (I.ii.82–85)

Beyond the 'tragic irony' that Othello will soon be prompted by Iago, Othello's speech implies a sort of automatism. Othello claims a oneness with his world that would, if granted, obliterate any possibility of confusion, doubt or subjective decision making. The right course is simply 'known'. This is characteristic of Othello's masterful language of service. He may not command but he *knows* what is commanded (by the state, the world, the universe). So while he may depend on his cues and serve higher powers, he is granted special access to them. If this is a position of weakness, it is the sort of 'weakness' proposed by popes and potentates who 'do but the Lord's bidding' and, in serving, command. Othello is, of course, also claiming the impossible. To grasp this, it is worth turning to early modern actors' cues themselves. Palfrey and Stern show how, in his use of cues:

> Shakespeare can be seen to be purposively scripting cross-purposes, lateral recognitions, and meta-performative surprises ... In the disjunction and discrepancies between play-text and part-text, in the false starts and mistaken attributions that ensue, Shakespeare is often scripting a battle for understanding, definition, and recognition.[22]

It seems fair to say that while actors 'knew their cues' – putting the word(s) preceding their lines to memory – they did not *know* their cues. That is, they did not know where they were coming from. They did not know in advance who was speaking them, thus giving 'the event of performance . . . [an] urgent immediacy'[23] that seems absent in the first-act *Othello*. Moreover, it was not known where the speaker was coming from: the intention, the context, the desire, of this murkily perceived cuer could only have been re-constructed, speculated upon. The 'cue-phrase' thus 'lays extraordinary focus upon the separation of one mind from another' as it may mean different things to its speaker and its recipient.[24] So when Othello claims that he would know *his* cue, he is claiming absolute ownership of something that is not his to possess, for it 'belongs to both' the giver and the taker 'and is a locus of sharing and co-dependence'.[25] He is claiming to know the thoughts of the universe and its playwright.[26] From an actor's perspective, then, to claim to know one's cue was asking for trouble. The actor was subject to Shakespeare's cues – to being played with by Shakespeare – while the character was subjected to Iago's cues. Further still, if Othello were granted his wish, the result would be a character untouched by dramatic events: a character not *subject* to the dramatic world. For the actor, there would be no surprise or transition, only a smooth unflappable surface. Meanwhile, Othello-the-character would somehow channel the world's cues, would always know in advance what to do, and this would always be a confirmation and reiteration of his masterfulness. We are left with an extreme form of Hegel's 'metaphysical (and aesthetic) xenophobia',[27] which wants to banish all foreignness. There is nothing rupturing or creative, dynamic or moving, but an all-enclosing knowledge.

Because what arrives was not here before and may not remain hereafter, the metaphysics of 'arrivals' highlights the fragile creation of the subject. What Othello envisions, in contrast, is the cessation of subjective action. It reflects a desire to have always-already arrived as one's self, for what Badiou refers to as '[t]he identity cult of repetition'.[28] This is particularly evident in the way he sees himself as his story:

> I will a round unvarnished tale deliver
> Of my whole course of love, what drugs, what charms,
> What conjuration and what mighty magic –
> For such proceeding I am charged withal –
> I won his daughter.   (I.iii.90–94)

Although Othello is mocking Brabanzio's allegations here, the speech nonetheless reveals a key feature of Othello's story-telling: it is a story of the past, ending in the block-like 'I won his daughter'. The past tense of 'won' suggests that love is not *present* for Othello, that it is done. Like the fantastical events of his story, the action of love is distanced from the present moment. And while Othello is being ironic when he speaks of the 'mighty magic' that won Desdemona, in the account of their love that follows their wooing does have an automated, almost magical quality, as if there were no choice, agency or even individuals. As Christopher Pye writes, Othello's tale is '[s]elf-consuming, self-producing', 'inscrib[ing] teller and addressee alike'.[29] The centrality of Othello's story certainly raises questions about their love: 'And [Desdemona] bade me, if I had a friend that loved her, / I should but teach him how to tell my story, / And that would woo her' (I.iii.163–65). For one thing, this 'friend' raises the shadow of Cassio. For another, it suggests that the tale, rather than Othello, has won Desdemona, a suggestion reiterated by the Duke: 'I think this tale would win my daughter, too' (I.iii.170). It thereby breaks down our common conception of love, as love for *someone*, hinting that what we love is a story that the love-object is seen to embody. For the self-certain Othello, the absolute centrality of story is not a problem, for *he is* his story and there is no 'friend' who could tell it. Needless to say, however, how Othello sees things is not the final word.

Othello, it should be acknowledged, already places enormous importance on Desdemona. He not only places his life on Desdemona's 'report' (I.iii.117) to the Senate, he famously places his 'life upon her faith' (I.iii.293). Indeed, for Kuzner, 'Othello figures Desdemona as encompassing him completely'.[30] Kuzner sees this as another indication of Othello's 'radical dependency'[31] in the opening scenes, but the key question is for *what* he is dependent on her? The answer seems to be for his being, for his life, in other words, for his identity and story. He is not seeing the world through Two; he has merely placed his world on a different foundation. If he has been encompassed by Desdemona, he has not been ruptured by her. 'He' remains intact. We might put this another way. Rhetorically, Othello compulsively stakes his whole 'life and being' upon something external, whether it is 'men of royal siege' or Desdemona's 'faith'. In the opening scene, however, the external does not intrude or alter his being but confirms and supports: it is the *Logos* that guarantees his stability and certainty as the One.

Although there is an absence of any locatable agency or subjective transformation in the 'magic' story of the lovers' courtship, this is not where Shakespeare's scene ends. As we saw in *Romeo and Juliet*, love only becomes something more than a momentary flash by what comes after, and what comes after in *Othello* comes through Desdemona. Desdemona's performance before the Senate immediately suggests a more active alternative to Othello's story-telling. Indeed, Desdemona follows Juliet in reconstituting her relationship with the world in response to the event. Unlike Othello, 'she' does not remain intact. Brabanzio's entire part seems dedicated to declaring her mutilation: that a 'maiden never bold' who 'Blushed at herself' (I.iii.96) has been 'stol'n' and 'corrupted' (I.iii.60), that magic has 'abused' 'the property of [her] youth and maidhood' (I.i.173–74). According to her family, she has *destroyed* her identity by her 'downright violence and storm of fortunes' (I.iii.248). This is precisely why she is an eventual figure. Like Juliet, she breaks with her father for the love of something that, under the rules of the situation, should be hated. And like Juliet she openly expresses her sexual desire: 'That [she] did love the Moor to live with him' (I.iii.247). Critically, she formulates her love as an active commitment rather than as passive knowledge: 'I saw Othello's visage in his mind, / And to his honours and his valiant parts / Did I my soul and fortunes consecrate' (I.iii.251–53). She sees, she admires, she chooses, and she *consecrates*. Because he views himself as synonymous with his story, Othello's position is altogether more passive: 'My life upon her faith' (I.iii.293).

Of course, the accounts given by Othello and Desdemona are very public performances and critics have long doubted both their veracity and their self-knowledge. Where my approach differs from 'traditional character criticism' is that it focuses not so much on whether Desdemona can 'really know Othello or he her, given that what he presents and she responds to is a performance',[32] but on what arrives through Desdemona's declaration. For Laurie Maguire, Desdemona's desire stems from a self-deceiving category error in which she 'confuses the character and the actor'.[33] For Nicholas Potter, Desdemona is drawn to 'a world outside the world she knows' and takes the sort of 'risks that imaginative people take'.[34] I prefer the latter, but who can say what fantasies first spark desire. What I take from Desdemona's declaration is not a true reflection of past events (that we never see), but how they found what comes after: a new mode of relation between self and world. However her imagination was stoked, Desdemona's declaration of consecration speaks to an eventual understanding of love. She may have initially fallen for a story or an actor – and maybe we all do as lovers – but consecration turns that falling into something else.

It is through Desdemona's consecration that the '[s]elf-consuming' tale becomes an event of love. The OED defines 'consecrate' as '1. make or declare sacred; dedicate formally to a religious or divine purpose. 2. (in Christian belief) make (bread and wine) into the body and blood of Christ.

3. (foll. by *to*) devote (one's life etc.) to (a purpose). 4. ordain (esp. a bishop) to a sacred office'. The 'sacred' element of consecration speaks to a connection to something extraordinary and unaccountable, something outside the rules of the situation, something that should be impossible. Like Badiou's fidelity, then, consecration is a process that connects the situation to its 'void'. The void's excess is not purely transcendent, however, but centres on the 'body and blood', the 'valiant parts', of a living being. Further, the excess is coupled with the dedicatory element of consecration, which speaks to an ongoing commitment. It is, then, a sacred pledge to something more than one's self and one's place.

Given Desdemona's activeness, it seems odd that Othello describes Desdemona's pity, rather than her consecration, as foundational to their love: 'She loved me for the dangers I had passed, / And I loved her that she did pity them' (I.iii.166–67). Pity seems a strangely inadequate foundation for such a transgressive love. 'I don't want your pity' is a common phrase in contemporary film and television, suggesting that something other than 'love' is being offered. Of course, to a great extent, Othello is not a reliable witness to their courtship. The fact that he loves her that she did pity 'them' (the dangers he'd passed) points to a mental deadlock in which he cannot disassociate his self from his story. And yet perhaps Othello gets at something important here, even if he gets the object of Desdemona's pity wrong. Perhaps pity requires a second look. What if the adverse reaction to pity is too modern and too secular? What if pity can be an active love as well as a passive sentimentality? It does seem that pity was far more closely associated with love in Shakespeare's day. Shawn Smith shows how pity was bound up with the courtly love tradition from Chaucer to Sidney, in which pity is a sign of nobility and love.[35] Moreover, the Christian tradition closely associates God's pity for mankind with his love and grace. As the hymnist Isaac Watts wrote:

> Was it for crimes that I had done
> He groaned upon the tree?
> Amazing pity! grace unknown!
> And love beyond degree!
>
> ('Alas! and Did My Saviour Bleed')

The New Testament confirms this confluence of love, pity and grace. In the King James Bible, pity and compassion are used interchangeably in Matthew, as in the parable where a lord forgives his servant's debt, only for the servant not to forgive his own debtors: 'Shouldest not thou also have had compassion on thy fellowservant, even as I had pity on thee?' (Matthew 18:33).[36] Further, whenever Jesus performs miracles of healing they arise from his pity or compassion for the afflicted: 'So Jesus had compassion *on them*, and touched their eyes: and immediately their eyes received sight, and they followed him' (Matthew 20:34). Whatever we call it, compassion or pity, it is intimately linked with grace, forgiveness, healing, new commitment and also neighbourly love: 'Finally, *be ye* all of one mind, having compassion one of another, love as brethren, *be* pitiful, *be* courteous' (1 Peter 3: 8). Pity is not a position of superiority or condescension, then, but an openness of the heart, an empathetic attachment, the *recognition* of an individual or group as 'brethren'. Taken in this light, pity is an integral part of Paul's 'agape', his charity or love. Paul's charity is not our charity – for 'though I bestow all my goods to feed *the poor* . . . and have not charity, it profiteth me nothing' (1 Corinthians 13:3) – just as biblical pity is not our pity. Paul's charity is the human love that inscribes God's grace into everyday life. It transcends self and knowledge: if I 'have not charity, I am nothing' (1 Corinthians 13:2). It sustains all else: charity '[b]eareth all things, believeth all things, hopeth all things, endureth all things' (1 Corinthians 13:7). These words of bearing, believing, hoping and enduring, so apt for Desdemona (and so unapt for Othello), reflect the way her initial pity (*agape*) might lead to consecration. They suggest how the symbolic realm of self-constituting narrative may become a present action of fidelity.

It is important to distinguish Desdemona's commitment from the general Venetian admiration of Othello, which is more a projection of fantasy than a recognition of mutuality. Lodovico is here representative:

> Is this the noble Moor whom our full senate
> Call all-in-all sufficient? Is this the nature
> Whom passion could not shake[?]   (IV.i.261–63)

It is not Desdemona but Venice that equates Othello with his masterful story of himself. It is for Venice that love magically follows the narrative. They bought into the legend, calling him 'all-in-all sufficient'. Othello's story fulfils a longing in Venice as it does in himself: to be so in touch with the world that one knows its cues and enacts them without fear or doubt. Again, we don't need to accept that Othello *is* 'all-in-all sufficient' to see that his story and his language tap into such a longing. He may not be the master, but he is 'in-all' – all circumstances and conditions, even in service – 'sufficient', without doubt or lack. Dramatically speaking, then, Othello does not arrive in or through his story, which is fanciful and far removed from the Othello that appears onstage. There are no 'disastrous chances', 'hair-breadth escapes', 'cannibals' (I.iii.133–43) or other such pitiable and wondrous happenings in Act I; there is only a cool, deferential, but unwaveringly self-assured man with a propensity to romantic story-telling. The Othello of these tales never does arrive. That Othello is a bookend, a point of emergence and departure. Othello arrives out of these stories and departs back into them in his tale of smiting the 'turbaned Turk' (V.ii.362). It is an Othello that is, belatedly, shaken apart by Desdemona.

Because it is based on an action of consecration and not a dream of knowing, Desdemona's love withstands the cracking of Othello's myth of self-certainty, whereas Lodovico must treat it as a failure of knowledge: 'I am sorry that I am deceived in him' (IV.i.279). More fundamentally, while the Venetians treat Othello as synonymous with his tale, Desdemona's pitying consecration produces a subject that exceeds its tale. Prior to Desdemona's intrusion, the granite monolith of Othello's story makes no distinction between the tale's plot and the subject that experiences it, hence his awkward 'She loved me for the dangers I had passed'. To be synonymous with one's tale is to be over and done with, already told, without agency or interrelation. But pity implies something altogether different from Venetian admiration and envy. It asserts not his 'all-in-all sufficiency' but his weakness: that he is to be pitied. It does not even occur to anyone else that Othello could or should be pitied. Pity is not awed or envious; rather, it implies the recognition of another: of *him*.

While it might be a stretch to think that Desdemona pities him because of his story – because it has dominated him and overcome his humanity – it is not a stretch to think that her pity helps produce a vulnerable human presence that Othello's grand story forbids. As Cefalu notes, Desdemona is confronting for Othello because she does not love 'merely his biographical, caricatured military identity, the only identity to which he is accustomed'.[37] We can thus rethink the meaning of Desdemona's consecration to 'Othello's visage in his mind'. It not only 'implies a Pauline indifference to outer marks and signs',[38] it also works in a Pauline fashion to 'put on the new man' (Ephesians 4:24). She sees, perhaps, something in his mind that he sees not: the subject of love. Taken in these terms, Desdemona's pitying love becomes the central event of the play, opening up the space for the Othello subject – ruptured and shaken by love – that arrives in Cyprus.

'[I]t is too much of joy': The Arrival in Cyprus

One of the most striking things about Othello's arrival in Cyprus is its belatedness. Othello arrives after the fact of the Turkish threat, which has already drowned, but also after the arrival of his wife, who was meant to follow him. It is a deliberate departure from Cinthio's tale, in which Disdemona and the Moor arrive together after plain sailing and no Turkish threat. Moreover, the emotional rupture of his love for Desdemona arrives after the fact of their marriage, which again differs from Cinthio, in which they are passionately in love from the outset. We do not see Othello experience Desdemona's love as an emotional event in the first act. Indeed, Othello only once addresses Desdemona directly, in his typical tone of command: 'Come, Desdemona. I have but an hour / Of love, of worldly matter and direction / To spend with thee' (I.iii.297–99). We witness no subjective experience of being transformed by love, no loss of rhetorical control. Othello's arrival in Cyprus is, then, a sort of embodied recognition of an event, love and marriage, which has already taken place – a sort of double take, if you will. We are not simply dealing with punctual happenings but with their retrospective inscription on the living subject.

Othello's involvement in this long scene is very brief, only thirty lines, so how can it mark the arrival of a new subject? As with the arrival of love in *Romeo and Juliet*, Shakespeare primes us through the scenic form, which creates the sense of an emergence from outside the frame:

> Let's to the sea-side, ho! –
> As well to see the vessel that's come in
> As to throw out our eyes for brave Othello,
> Even till we make the main and th'aerial blue
> An indistinct regard.   (II.i.37–41)

Shakespeare's movement to and from the 'indistinct' limits of representation – to the void – is central to this book and particularly the *Hamlet* chapter. Chrisopher Pye makes a similar connection: 'Montano's enjoining our gaze at a point where Othello momentarily disappears recalls the interval during which Hamlet also disappears in the midst of his drama – his transformative sea journey to England – drawing all eyes to him on his return.'[39] For Pye, however, 'Shakespearean tragedy['s] … ability to incorporate its own formal limit and vanishing point' – as (un)seen in Montano's 'indistinct regard' – 'correspond[s] to the aesthetic work's capacity to figure its own illimitability as representational form'.[40] Pye thus contends that '*Othello* exemplifies the emergence of the aesthetic as such'.[41] The 'vanishing point' points not only to the 'self-grounding' or 'autochthonic character of the work' but also of subjectivity.[42] The subject, like the play, is an 'autonomous, self-constituting form'[43] with no grounding but itself.

By concentrating on the subject's arrival, I reach a very different model of Shakespeare's indistinction. In short, drama need not travel with Montano's eyes *towards* vanishing but may emerge, like Othello's ship, *from* the 'vanishing point'. Taken in this way, the moment of 'indistinct regard' is both a vanishing and an emergence, a to-and-fro between drama and its limit, rather than a bleeding into a limitless realm of indistinct aesthetics. It is another of those points, as with *Romeo and Juliet*'s unlocatable event of love, at which Shakespeare structures his arrivals around an obscure gap or break. It is, in short, a marker of the new: by drawing our eyes to the edge of the representational structure, Shakespeare signals the new's intrusion from beyond the situation. Or, as the Third Gentleman responds to Montano: 'Come, let's do so, / For every minute is expectancy / Of more arrivance' (II.i.42–43). In Badiou's terms, we might call the 'seaside' an *'evental site'*, which is 'an entirely abnormal multiple; that is, a multiple such that none of its elements are presented in the situation'.[44] The 'site, itself, is presented' in the situation – here we, the audience, see (or at least hear) the watchers looking out to the indistinct horizon – but what lies 'beneath' it, what belongs to it, is not:[45]

MONTANO   What from the cape can you discern at sea?
RST GENTLEMAN   Nothing at all. It is a high-wrought flood.
                 I cannot 'twixt the heaven and the main
                 Descry a sail.   (II.i.1–4)

From the edge of land 'Nothing' of the event can be discerned, only the chaos of the void's infinite multiplicity. Here Shakespeare's messengers are, like Elsinore's sentinels, looking out over the edge of the representable situation. And, as in *Hamlet*, it is from beyond the situation that the excessive and new arrives: from 'a high-wrought flood' that is not nothing (it is 'high-wrought' after all) but which is indiscernible for those peering outward. Pye follows Montano's eyes out into this void but I follow the as yet undiscerned sail into shore, bearing the new Othello from *outside* the dramatic frame. The eyes are going out, but the ship is coming in, from the unseen. Taken in this light, Othello's journey through the indistinction of the 'high-wrought flood' is a marker of how the event '*is on the edge of the void*, or *foundational*'.[46] Coming from the unseen void, and directed towards an unseen future, the 'intrinsic indiscernibility'[47] of the event severs the self from the situation and forms the subject *on new ground*. The 'vanishing point' is thus not the beginning of a purely aesthetic, self-grounded subject but the emergence of a subject grounded by the indiscernible event. As in *Hamlet*, the voyage beyond representation at once displaces – taking Othello beyond the old situation and old story – and results in a more solid (and actable) sense of place. Othello returns from the limitless sea as a living subject that is irrevocably placed in relation to his wife.

Suddenly, Othello is in a new land, and the rapid shift in location is mirrored by a rapid shift in Othello. The cool self-assurance and closed language that made him seem mighty falters in Desdemona's almost overwhelming presence. Othello's speeches here are hardly as simple as conveying 'the harmonious marriage of true and noble minds'.[48] Rather, Othello is amazed, almost overcome, by a contentedness of which he cannot speak enough:

OTHELLO	O my fair warrior!
DESDEMONA	My dear Othello.
OTHELLO	It gives me wonder great as my content
	To see you here before me. O my soul's joy,
	. . .
	If it were now to die
	'Twere now to be most happy, for I fear
	My soul hath her content so absolute
	That not another comfort like to this
	Succeeds in unknown fate. (II.i.179–90)

Instead of solid blocks centred upon 'I', 'me' and 'my', the wondrous occasion of meeting his wife becomes the centre of everything. His language no longer suggests Hegel's early Symbolic art, with its 'absence of situation', but the gripping presence of the moment: 'To see you here before me'. It is a critical turn for Othello. He turns and, unexpectedly, confrontingly, he sees a 'you', an other, that lies outside his self-constituting tale. He turns and, finally, he sees her standing 'before [him]' in the absolute present of the moment. We are far from the inwardness of 'I must be found'. Othello is now looking outwards to Desdemona, addressing *her* and not an audience. And while this new emotion retains elements of the old grand language – the martial 'barque' climbing 'Olympus-high' (II.i.184–85) – it is transformed by its new direction.

In processual terms, one might say that Othello is no longer a self-enclosing static entity. He is no longer contained by his story because things are happening *now*. He is no longer his own planet, on its own orbit, but is arrested by Desdemona and the occasion. He is thus 'without mastery'[49] in the scene. As Kuzner continues: 'Othello does not try to possess his wife here, does not even try to capture love in a verbal frame.'[50] Rather, he is subjected, and made relative, by and to Desdemona's miraculous presence. And so, in the foreign place of Cyprus, a new foreignness enters Othello. We begin to get a sense of Badiou's idea of love as the 'experience of the world from the perspective of difference'.[51] To 'see you here before me' suggests not only that Desdemona is present before him but also that she is anterior to, the predicate of, this 'me', that she is a foundation '*before* me'. Now we truly see Othello's 'radical dependency'[52] – 'truly', because it now reorients Othello. Desdemona's unexpected appearance on the other side of the storm is the sort of breach of the symbolic that we saw with Romeo's emergence from the darkness, a transformative excess drawn from the indiscernible void of the 'high-wrought flood'. As such, the foreignness that Othello feels intruding upon him (however joyously) is not only that of culture but a metaphysical foreignness, felt as something 'absolute' that ruptures and reorients his very conception of himself in 'wonder', 'joy' and 'fear'. In Badiou's terms, the endless 'repetition' of 'identity' is 'challenged by love of what is different, is unique, is unrepeatable, unstable and foreign'.[53] And we see this in the actor's part too. The fact that Othello is now exposed to the outside, to the alien, is reflected in the cue he gives out at the end of his speech: 'unknown fate'.

Beginning with his seemingly involuntary exclamation, 'O my fair warrior!', Othello's newfound 'wonder' also coincides with a distinct change in address. As well as beginning to address Desdemona, when he speaks of his 'soul's joy' and his 'fear' at his 'absolute' 'content', Othello is starting to address *himself* and his self-estrangement. As with Hegel's Spirit, Othello here becomes an 'other to [him]self'.[54] And as with Hegel's slave, Othello transcends his masterful self precisely because he 'has trembled throughout [his] every fibre, and all that was fixed and steadfast has quaked within [him]'.[55] He is taken aback, not only by encountering Desdemona but also by his own 'joy' and 'wonder', by a foreignness within. As in Romeo and Juliet's liking-upon-looking, wonder comes from beyond the ordinary world to reconfigure the individual's regard and language. Othello here shares something with Levinas's idea that 'consciousness of miracle, or wonder' is what 'ruptures biological consciousness' and marks 'the *beginning* of thought'.[56] And it thus marks how this is a *new* Othello, how it wasn't already there. Shakespeare certainly infuses Desdemona's presence with wondrousness. Her journey to Cyprus is miraculously quick: 'Tempests themselves' let the 'divine Desdemona' 'go safely by'; she 'anticipates our thoughts' (II.i.69–77), arriving before she is due. In sum, Othello's 'wonder' both expresses his astonishment at the event – intrusive and miraculous and unjustified – and simultaneously constitutes his first real self-address, his movement to self-consciousness. An open, self-questioning Othello – suddenly aware of his difference from his old self – emerges from his destabilising confrontation with Desdemona's unaccountable presence.

There is, then, an enormous gulf between Othello's certain knowledge of his cues and the foreign wonder that now erodes his stable state. Othello's arrival, like Romeo and Juliet's, is not a triumph of knowing but an exposure to something alien; an opening to 'unknown fate'. As Luther puts it, through grace an 'alien righteousness . . . is . . . instilled from without'.[57] Here Kuzner's enlightening work on weakness and submission reinforces my concept of arrival. He points to 'a moment' in Shakespeare's 'texts' when characters or readers 'become aware that a frame by which they understand selfhood, ethics or freedom is not the only or the natural one'.[58] Othello, for instance, 'stops assuming . . . that love is self-creation'.[59] And there 'follows a moment' of 'possibility' in which one might alter these 'conceptual frames'.[60] Critically, this involves a 'decision' whether to 'adopt a frame that grants a greater or a lesser degree of control'.[61] Translated into my terms, there comes a decision as to whether to embrace the weakness of abandoning the grand old identity and the conceptual framework it involves: masterfulness, solidity, certainty. We know, of course, that Othello will ultimately demand 'occular proof' (III.iii.365), but here, on the other side of the indistinct voyage, we can nonetheless glimpse something of 'how the new can arrive through humility and disorientation, through waiting and bearing-with, through serious and unremitting self-risk'.[62] We can see that Othello is more than he was, that in this moment he is very far from being 'withdrawn into his own narrative fictions'.[63] In short, we glimpse an Othello who exceeds the closed figure censured by Cefalu, Leavis, and Eliot. We have a tragic glimpse of an Othello who 'might have been': of a vulnerable Othello, subjected to love.

In Žižek's terms, we might say that by placing this moment of exposure after Othello's marriage, Shakespeare extends

> the minimal gap, the delay, which forever separates an event 'in itself' from its symbolic inscription/registration; this gap can be discerned in its different guises from quantum physics (according to which an event 'becomes itself', is fully actualized, only through its registration in its surroundings – that is, the moment its surroundings 'take note' of it) to the procedure of 'double take' in the classic Hollywood comedies.[64]

For Othello, it is only upon seeing Desdemona already in Cyprus ('here before me') that love hits him and prompts this 'double take'. Is this really happening? Could I be this lucky? That she has arrived before me, waiting for me? That she loves me? And this precipitates a further erosion of Othello's self-possessed language:

OTHELLO   Amen to that, sweet powers!
            I cannot speak enough of this content.
            It stops me here, it is too much of joy.
            And this, and this, the greatest discords be
            That e'er our hearts shall make.   (II.i.192–96)

As if for the first time, he feels the excessiveness of love: he 'cannot speak enough' of it, it is 'too much', '[i]t stops [him] here'. It arrests his musical flow and forces him into stilted repetition: 'And this, and this'. He is stopped in his tracks because his tracks are no longer his to make. He never knew! He never knew what another could mean or what joy and love were. Love 'strikes him', in Kuzner's words, 'with the force of something never before seen'.[65] It is not just another adventure added to Othello's narrative; it is the beginning of a reconfiguration of that narrative. The turning wheel of his endless reiterations is knocked from its axis. It is not 'Iago' who 'make[s] discord of the *Othello* music',[66] then, it is the belated love-event that cracks its architectural stability:

                Come, let us to the castle.
    News, friends: our wars are done, the Turks are drowned.
    How does my old acquaintance of this isle? –
    Honey, you shall be well desired in Cyprus,
    I have found great love amongst them. O my sweet,
    I prattle out of fashion, and I dote
    In mine own comforts.   (II.i.198–204)

Othello starts out martial and block-like. He directs the crowd formally ('let us to the castle') before steering his speech to the serious business of the 'Turks'. But despite only finally addressing the military situation here, at the scene's end, he is almost immediately distracted by the thought of Desdemona: 'Honey'. His regard is unstable and jumpy. In the space of six lines it shifts abruptly between the castle, the Turks, old memories, present love and his awareness of his changed language.

The puncturing of Othello's tranquil aloofness by this 'prattl[ing]' marks a deeper change. Present concerns segue easily enough into his old story, into his 'old acquaintance' with the 'isle', but Othello no longer possesses this memory in the same way. It is now turned towards Desdemona and how she will be 'well desired in Cyprus'. It suggests Badiou's idea that, in love, 'we can encounter and experience the world other than through a solitary consciousness'.[67] The meaning of his history is retroactively altered. What matters now is how it relates *to her*. I thus accept Kuzner's words about Othello's dependency, but only now, after Othello has travelled through the void: 'Othello, too, cannot think of himself without also thinking of Desdemona; virtually every thought he has of himself in the play is accompanied – and not just accompanied, but conditioned – by thoughts of her.'[68] We see the change in Othello in the change of tenses. Othello's attempt to move into the past tense of his story – to things 'done', Turks 'drowned' and love 'found' – is interrupted by Desdemona's presence, – 'Honey' – which turns the tale of 'old acquaintance' to the future: Desdemona 'shall be well desired in Cyprus'. No longer self-contained, his story and language now flow into the presence of Desdemona and their future together. And it is the sudden apprehension of this foreignness within his story that causes Othello to stop and remark on his present prattling and doting – 'O my sweet, / I prattle out of fashion' – which take him away from his old self.

The fact that Shakespeare extends the gap between the event and its conscious registration emphasises the difference between this new place and Othello's previous self. It indicates a kind of trauma. This thing that happened in the past, that is past, is still here with me. I keep re-experiencing it. It is part of me but foreign. It prevents me from returning to myself. And this, perhaps, is another way of thinking about *Othello*'s notorious 'double time'. As Žižek writes, '[t]rauma is "eternal"; it can never be properly temporalized/historicized, it is the point of "eternity" around which time circulates'.[69] The progression of time and narrative is thrown out of kilter. Othello can no longer simply pass through events in chronological order; they keep hitting him after they have gone. Desdemona's foreignness keeps breaking into time and memory, transforming it and turning it to the present. No longer frozen and autonomous, or 'given all at once',[70] his conscious states now melt, 'permeat[ing] one another' like the flow of music.[71] More specifically, the *event* permeates all else. Rather than a 'progression through a homogeneous, empty time', we have, in Benjamin's terms, the sort of revolutionary instant in which a moment of the past is 'blasted out of the continuum of history'.[72] Time is now 'filled by the presence of the now'.[73] And Othello's old music is thrown off key.

The belatedness of Othello's arrival marks a significant departure from *Romeo and Juliet*, in which the gap between the event of love and the action of fidelity, although not nothing – we saw it in the difficult process of creating a new name – was less profound. The event seemed to flow almost inexorably into the lovers' new mode of speaking. The mature tragedies shatter this inevitability. They acknowledge the extreme difficulty of exiling oneself from one's self, from one's identity. The somewhat vacuous Romeo may be able to promise to be 'new baptized', but it's a different matter for those who have already lived and become 'themselves' – for those, who, in Montaigne's words, are 'ready to finish this man, not to make another'.[74] For them, the gap between event and subjective action opens into an abyss. But how is there an abyss? Or, in Othello's words, how is it 'too much of joy'? It is surely frightening for the very reason its joy is overwhelming: because Othello is *subjected* to it. He is taking his cues from a new source and he no longer knows them. As Cassio observes, Desdemona is now 'our great captain's captain' (II.i.75). Or, in Kristeva's words, the fact 'that in love "I" has been an *other*' precipitates a 'state of instability' that leads to both 'the zenith of subjectivity' and 'a degree of psychic as much as physical pain'.[75] Desdemona is taking him away from the only self he knows. Indeed, the old character, the old music with its separateness, is precisely what must be overcome if the vulnerable 'subject' is to emerge.

Othello's movement through the indistinction of the storm brings him to a new realm of possibility, but it is also an unstable ground, trailing towards an undiscerned future. The indistinct event of love thereby opens the fearless Othello to 'fear' (II.i.187): fear of the unknown, of what will come, of the unknown other, and of what that other will make him and make of him. As Badiou writes, if '"some-one" enters into the composition of a subject of truth only by exposing himself "entirely" to a post-evental fidelity, then there remains the problem of knowing what he, this "some-one", will *become* through this testing experience'.[76] The person that was is no more, but the person to come is glimpsed only indistinctly, in shadows. In this obscure space terror resides and with it the possibility of one of Badiou's three forms of Evil: 'to fail to live up to a fidelity is Evil in the sense of *betrayal*, betrayal in oneself of the Immortal that you are'.[77] Badiou may characterise it as an Evil, but its origins lie in the rather more prosaic division between one's old (situational) self and the new (evental) subject: because the 'difficult new demands . . . of fidelity' cause 'a breakdown of the fiction I use to maintain, as an image of myself', one is 'confronted with a pure choice between the "Keep going!" proposed by the ethic of this truth, and the logic of the "perseverance in being" of the mere mortal that I am'.[78] Othello is caught between the terrifying destruction of his old architectural self and the terrifying uncertainty of the new loving subject.

One of the central dilemmas of Shakespeare's tragedies is that his major characters only arrive as subjects through such harrowing division and uncertainty. They must face having their old selves and their old worlds fall apart. In Badiou's terms, this is the very nature of the 'subject': the 'evental rupture always constitutes its subject in the divided form of a '"not … but"'.[79] Indeed, the fact that 'the subjective process occurs from the point of the interruption … as the dialectical division of destruction and recomposition … is what guarantees that the subjective process in part escapes repetition'.[80] It is by pushing him into the unknown that Othello's joyous arrival in Cyprus allows him to escape the repetition of his story, but it also opens a self-division that will force him to choose what he will become. Or as Badiou writes elsewhere, 'for the individual to become a subject it is necessary that he overcome … the fear of losing all identity'.[81] For the moment, in Desdemona's unexpected presence, Othello attains strength in division and weakness. The challenge for Othello, the man of stable substance, is not to admit that he serves, but that he is *in*sufficient, that he needs someone else. As Žižek explains:

> [T]he point of the claim that even if I were to possess all knowledge, without love I would be nothing, is not simply that *with* love, I am 'something' – in love, *I am also nothing* but, as it were, a Nothing humbly aware of itself, a Nothing paradoxically made rich through the very awareness of its lack. Only a lacking, vulnerable being is capable of love: the ultimate mystery of love is therefore that incompleteness is in a way *higher than completion* … only an imperfect, lacking being loves: we love because we do *not* know all.[82]

Such incompleteness connects with a basic aspect of process philosophy: it is by 'affect[ing]' and 'be[ing] affected by another' that an entity obtains 'real existence'.[83] So while Othello feels embarrassed and diminished by his 'prattling' at this newfound interrelation, he thereby obtains a real existence as a subject. In Levinas's terms, exposure to 'the Other Person' reveals 'the ultimate meaning of my "mineness"' by 'tear[ing] me away from my hypostasis, from the *here*, at the heart of being or the center of the world in which, privileged, and in this sense primordial, I place myself'.[84] Othello's prattling marks an arrival because his monumental separateness is punctured. As his exposure to Desdemona breaks down the '*Othello* music', he begins to become a permeable dramatic figure rather than an epic or architectural figure. He emerges from his self-unity – his character-base – to become the conflicted Othello who will heartbreakingly tear himself apart.

'I am not what I am': Iago's Non-Arrival

It is often tempting to think of *Othello* as Iago's play. Its first lines are given to his puppet, Roderigo, who openly admits to giving Iago his 'purse' 'strings' (I.i.2–3), so that Iago seems to be pulling the strings as director, prompter and puppet master. There is, however, a fundamental distinction between Iago's drama and Shakespeare's, for Iago does not believe in the possibility of arrivals. And yet, for all his arresting scepticism and theatrical talent, none of his plotting could have come to anything if Othello were not already shaken by Desdemona. Far from being some bloodless 'utopian possibility',[85] Desdemona's love is the play's central event. The potency of Iago's project rests upon it: on making it seem impossible and grotesque to Othello, on channelling its energies in a poisoned and inverted form. In what follows I do not conduct a full-scale reassessment of Iago but simply explore how he relates to the 'event'.

Iago is a determinist when it comes to the self. It is a product of its history, circumstance and its innate quality rather than of any exceptional moment or defining decision. As such, I take Iago as a force of the 'situation'. Metaphysically, he seeks to re-inscribe its closed structure, which shuts off the void and its excess. Dramatically, he seeks to re-inscribe Othello's self-enclosing language. And culturally, he re-asserts the opposition between Venice and foreign Othello. All of this, of course, involves destroying Desdemona, whose excessive love threatens the situation's foundational structures. The obscure 'Were I the Moor I would not be Iago' (I.i.57) thus suggests a sort of non-arrival. Iago trusts in what is due rather than what comes as grace. Each is what it must be. Yet, there are indications that he too is transformed by the event. Whatever his 'motivations', Iago seems to arrive at his mode of being – his dark workshop of inwardness – through his attempt to destroy Desdemona's love. To understand this we must grasp how Iago's metaphysics relates to those of Desdemona and Othello. At the heart of Iago's metaphysics is his insistence upon a chasm between outward action and inward self:

> For when my outward action doth demonstrate
> The native act and figure of my heart
> In compliment extern, 'tis not long after
> But I will wear my heart upon my sleeve
> For daws to peck at. I am not what I am.   (I.i.61–65).

Iago fundamentally opposes Desdemona's evental stance, which founds the subject on its open and outward action of consecration. His is a tormented position, for if 'outward action' can never demonstrate the 'native act and figure of [the] heart', there is no location for the self in the material world. Iago here resembles Hegel's 'Unhappy Consciousness', which has '*surrendered*' its embodied form ... having *relinquished* it for the enjoyment of consciousness'.[86] Perhaps even more relevant is Kierkegaard's 'demonic', which is a refusal to accept that 'truth is for the particular individual only as he himself produces it in action'.[87] Accordingly, the demonic individual locates its truth or essence *inside* itself. ''Tis in ourselves that we are thus or thus' (I.iii.316), Iago tells Roderigo. And this inner essence is secretive; it will not be brought into the open '[f]or daws to peck at'. Kierkegaard describes this 'hiddenness' as a 'spiritual ... safety-device[] for assuring oneself of having as it were behind reality an enclosure'.[88]

Shakespeare deliberately obscures Iago's motivations regarding Desdemona,[89] but insofar as Iago can be seen as a force of the situation, her love poses an implicit challenge to his existence. In Kierkegaard's terms, 'the demonic ... is in anxiety about the good',[90] for 'the demoniac is consistent in himself and in the consistency of evil', and 'just for this cause he also has a totality to lose'.[91] 'The least inconsistency is a prodigious loss'; 'that same instant the charm is perhaps broken', the 'harmony' is lost.[92] Iago must therefore reduce Desdemona's love to 'a lust of the blood and a permission of the will' (I.iii.329). Why? Because a Venetian, an insider, has broken the rules of the situation. Her consecration takes the form of a 'not ... but': she breaks free from her father and social circumstance ('not') and institutes a new subject ('but'). From inside the situation, there is no discernible reason why her love refuses to follow the traditional path. Excessive and unheralded, it speaks to a different metaphysics in which 'THE IMPOSSIBLE DOES HAPPEN',[93] to an evental superabundance that threatens Iago's disillusioned worldview of false appearances. Because the real is what is inner and secret for Iago, the outer world always gives less than one hopes. 'Your heart is burst, you have lost half your soul' (I.i.87) is almost his summary of the human condition.

Iago's inward reserve also directly opposes Othello's 'Were it my cue to fight'. Whereas Othello harbours an impossible desire for his outward action *to be* his self without any need for interiority – he simply channels the world's cues – Iago harbours an impossible desire for an interiority that does not manifest itself in outward action. Whereas Othello wants unreflective oneness, Iago wants reflective severance. In short, Othello's identity relies on his tale, his actions, his service and his certainty of his cues, while Iago's relies on an inner consciousness or essence that is not revealed. Hence Cefalu's observation that Othello embraces an 'instrumentalized, biographical self, the self defined by service', to which Iago reacts violently when Othello 'projects his own values of service on to Iago'.[94] Tragically, however, these seemingly opposed stances share one important feature: they both require a detachment from the demands of others and, ultimately, from the event. They both exclude Desdemona's consecration. In fact, the way they come together to destroy Desdemona involves something of a marriage between Othello's outwardness and Iago's inwardness.

We get a foretaste of this marriage in the way Iago manipulates his victims through a pincer movement of internal and external identity. He begins with a claim about how the world operates: whatever lies outside the situation – including any subject or transgressive desire – is impossible, unnatural, a deception. There is no event. As he says of Desdemona's unconventional love: 'For, one may smell in such a will most rank, / Foul disproportions, thoughts unnatural!' (III.iii.237–38). While Iago's thought might seem monstrous, it is anything but. It follows Montaigne's insight that when we describe something as 'according to Nature', it simply means that it 'follow[s] according to our understanding', in our custom and time, and that '[w]hatsoever is beyond it, is monstrous and disordered'.[95] In these terms, Iago's thought is typical, even rational. It restricts what is possible to what is seen in the situation. If it is monstrous, it is only in that it creates monsters of what lies beyond it. Once this worldview is established, it is very easy to exploit the gap between Desdemona's actions and her presumed cultural identity. Under his influence, Brabanzio immediately asserts that Othello has used 'foul charms' or 'drugs' (I.iii.74–75) to coerce Desdemona, thereby separating Desdemona's 'love' from her 'self'. Iago is thus intent on Desdemona's destruction long before Othello's threat to 'tear her all to pieces' (III.iii.436). Iago tears her apart from her consecration, from what Kierkegaard calls the 'truth' that the 'self produces in action'.[96] But, in fact, he does more than tear: he also *summons another self* – hidden, secret, twisted by black magic – that exists inside of Desdemona.

Because her love for Othello is unjustified, there must be 'something else' in Desdemona to explain it. Hence Brabanzio's disbelief that 'If she in chains of magic were not bound', she would 'Run from her guardage to the sooty bosom / Of such a thing as thou – to fear, not to delight' (I.ii.66–72). The disconnect between her presumed essence and her inexplicable action becomes 'probable' and 'palpable to thinking' (I.ii.77) both because it confirms Brabanzio's desire that *Desdemona* does not love Othello and because it confirms the ordinary expectations of society. In short, Iago uses the failure of external (cultural) forms of identity to conjure a double spectre of the internal: on the one hand, that there is a self that wants to fulfil these external forms and would do so, if it were not held in magic; on the other, that there is a self that is corrupted by magic and thus monstrously deformed. So whereas Othello's rigid identity begins to crack under the pressure of the event, Iago's more plastic and amorphous inwardness is capable of distorting it, of converting it into inwardness. He operates as a sort of dark form of Hegel's 'tarrying with the negative',[97] which gives consciousness 'the magic power that converts the negative into being'.[98] And he does so by expertly manipulating the external. In Iago's hands, the 'situation' is not just a static and regimented structure (Othello v. Venice, white v. black) but something responsive and *creative*. The inner thus becomes an (imaginary) mask for the outer. It becomes what explains away or forestalls the *truth* of appearances and thereby preserves Desdemona's situational identity.

In these terms, Iago is part of a larger pattern that seeks to exorcise Desdemona's monstrous exception and thereby restore the situation. Iago too is one of the 'credulous fools [who] are caught' by 'medicine' (IV.i.42). Just as Brabanzio half-believes in magic, or Othello half-believes in Desdemona's infidelity ('I think my wife be honest, and think she is not' (III.iii.389)), Iago half-believes in Desdemona's love for Cassio: 'That Cassio loves her, I do well believe it. That she loves him, 'tis apt and of great credit' (II.i.273–74). It is 'apt and of great credit', of course, because it follows the old rules. Iago is not simply an outside-sitting devilish manipulator, playing on players, but a player in this same process. To deny Desdemona's excessive and inexplicable love for a dark and unmerited thing, each clings to the most tenuous 'proof'. Indeed, each mounts a self-annihilating counteroffensive against the event. And yet, in this at least, Iago fails, for Desdemona refuses to return to the fold: 'Unkindness may do much, / And his unkindness may defeat my life, / But never taint my love' (IV.ii.163–65). Ultimately, her love cannot be accounted for by Iago's philosophy.

For all Iago's improvisational genius, then, his drama is a narrow one. As Montaigne writes: 'If that which we have not seene, is not, our knowledge is wonderfull abridged.'[99] Whereas in Shakespeare's drama things arrive from beyond the illimitable horizon, in Iago's world nothing emerges, at least not in an outward 'embodied form'.[100] He is not a creator of new worlds and new subjects but an illusionist. He conjures ghosts in the machine of the situation: spirits held by magic, or simulacrums rather. Nothing genuinely new arrives because there is nothing outside the situation. Here Kierkegaard's description of how one can defraud oneself of love is apposite:

> If it were true, as a conceited cleverness believes, proud of not being imposed upon, that one should believe nothing that one does not see with the sensual

eye, then must one first and foremost cease to believe in love. And if one did this and did it for fear of being deceived, would one then not be deceived? One may be deceived in many ways; one may be deceived by believing the false, but one may also be deceived by not believing the true; one may be deceived by appearances, but one may also be deceived by the appearance of shrewdness, by the flattering conceit which is absolutely certain it cannot be deceived . . . To defraud oneself of love is the most terrible deception of all.[101]

Something similar occurs in postmodern thought, which wants to avoid being 'caught out' by ideology or belief. As Žižek writes, the 'fundamental lesson of postmodernist politics is that there is no Event, that "nothing really happens"'.[102] Rather than following the 'not … but' model of Badiou's fidelity, Iago skewers existing culture – he personifies the 'not' – while utterly rejecting the positive content of the 'but'. This is not the ideologically neutral outlook it might seem: 'Cynical distance is just one way – one of many ways – to blind ourselves to the structuring power of ideological fantasy: even if we do not take things seriously, even if we keep an ironical distance, *we are still doing them.*'[103] It is for this reason that Iago can be both an inveterate sceptic of his fellow Venetians and a force of the old situation. He highlights the rhetorical emptiness of reputation but nonetheless desires it: 'I know my price, I am worth no worse a place' (I.i.11). Iago continues to do what he does not believe. But there is also a deeper layer of repetition. Iago dismantles Badiou's 'dialectical division of destruction and recomposition'[104] and is therefore bound to endlessly repeat the 'destruction' of its first term. Iago must not only repeat the 'not', he must also repeat 'what is not': he must continually repeat what he does not believe – dismissing it over and over – so that he is defined by what he opposes: 'Virtue? A fig!' (I.iii.316).

'My life upon her faith': Othello's Retreat

Iago comes in Desdemona's wake. She makes the impossible happen, but when she turns her back for a moment, Iago steps in and makes the impossible *seem* impossible to Othello. As late as III.iii, Othello is still 'with' Desdemona as they banter and barter over Cassio's reappointment. Kuzner suggests that this 'fraught'[105] exchange reveals both their separation in love and their acceptance of love's imposing demands. In particular, he reads Othello's 'I will deny thee nothing' (III.iii.84) as the performance of one of 'love's most important works: declaring fidelity to the event of love, vowing to deny his beloved nothing without knowing what love is or may ask of him'.[106] Indeed, despite Desdemona's almost unrelenting solicitation of her suit and Othello's clear irritation, their disagreements end happily: 'Farewell, my Desdemona. I'll come to thee straight' (III.iii.88).

Othello, of course, never comes back to her again. It is here, after Othello utters his ominous words – 'Excellent wretch! Perdition catch my soul / But I do love thee, and when I love thee not, / Chaos is come again' (III.iii.91–93) – that Iago steps in front of Desdemona. When she returns soon after, Othello is gone, unreachable. Iago has infected his relation to the event. Part of the problem, of course, is that Othello's relation to the event was already problematic: 'My life upon her faith'. Stanley Cavell has brilliantly unpacked this phrase and the way Desdemona is the 'object' that 'stands for ... the world as such'.[107] For my purposes, what matters is that this is a highly un-eventual wager, given over all at once to the presumed inner quality of Desdemona's 'faith'. By viewing love as an all-in wager rather than as a mutual *'work* of love',[108] Othello is not only reminiscent of Romeo's oaths, he also leaves himself with no way to comprehend his own suspicion except as (her) corruption, as a 'sure thing' gone terribly wrong. Moreover, by treating Desdemona's unverifiable 'faith' as a substance, Othello disconnects it from the action of consecration that constitutes it. As Badiou explains: 'Fidelity must not be understood in any way as a capacity, a subjective quality, or a virtue', rather, it 'is a functional relation to the event'.[109] Othello's thus misses the need for *his* intervention.

Because the event is 'in excess of proof',[110] it necessitates a very different sort of wager. It is not a wager on a sure thing but on the 'undecidable', the sort of wager we saw when Juliet gave herself to the darkness. Here Badiou's thought connects with the Christian idea of strength in weakness:

> Pascal is concerned to save the vulnerability of the event, its quasi-obscurity, since it is precisely on this basis that the Christian subject is the one who decides from the standpoint of undecidability ... rather than the one who is crushed by the power of either a demonstration ... or some prodigious occurrence.[111]

In direct contrast to the popular song 'To Know You (Is To Love You)', Shakespeare shows that loving is antecedent to knowing. For all its iconic status as the classic of fated love, *Romeo and Juliet* in fact shows that 'to love you is to know you'. The leap of faith precedes, indeed founds, the 'you' that is 'known' (and that knows). Othello's tragedy is that he does not have faith in this vulnerable flight into the unknown. The opposite is true of Desdemona, who, even when she is cut off from Othello, unable to know him, maintains her consecration: 'I would you had never seen him', Emilia bemoans; 'So would not I', Desdemona replies (IV.iii.17–18). As Kuzner stresses, 'love in the play' does not have any determinate content but only 'demands a single thing: that lovers cling to love, that they keep going'.[112] Love is a consecration.

Iago's task, in contrast, is to prise open the gap between Desdemona and her action, between her 'faith' and her 'true' self. The lever, here, is the question: 'why did she choose me?' Or, as Othello buries the question: 'Nor from mine own weak merits will I draw / The smallest fear or doubt of her revolt, / For she had eyes and chose me' (III.iii.191–93). Without deserving love on the 'merits', everything rests on a choice that is unfathomable according to the rules of the situation. Othello, who demands to know his cues, is poorly equipped for such uncertainty. Cefalu plausibly speaks of his '[m]indblindness', which 'is of a piece with Othello's romantic notion of himself'.[113] He clings to Iago because Iago *can* read others' minds: 'This fellow's of exceeding honesty, / And knows all qualities with a learned spirit' (III.iii.262–63). To regain certainty, Othello makes Iago his second go-between. Indeed, Cefalu suggests that Iago becomes 'a veritable extension of Othello's mind'.[114] Othello calls him in to translate the undecidable into the situation. The tragedy is not, however, that Othello is 'caught between the need and inability to read other minds',[115] the tragedy is that mind reading was utterly unnecessary. If he'd never looked inward, if he'd accepted the outward, he would have been right. As we've seen, love is a contingent and unjustifiable event. There are no rules or criteria to judge it; we cannot determine 'why' we love someone or someone loves us. There is nothing to read 'inside' the other.

By looking inward, Othello therefore dismisses the woman in front of him – 'she [who] had eyes and chose [him]' (III.iii.193) – and fantasises about the unseen. Othello joins with Iago in turning her into a ghost in the machine. He opens an interiority that *isn't there*. Beyond sight and knowledge, a sort of void within her, Desdemona's 'faith' becomes the terrible unknown of the '*Che vuoi?*': 'What does the Other want?'[116] According to Žižek, 'fantasy' rushes in as the only possible '*answer* to this "*Che vuoi?*"' and it comes in the form of 'an imaginary scenario filling out the void' opened by 'the *desire of the Other*'.[117] For Othello, of course, the fantasy is that Desdemona 'with Cassio has the act of shame / A thousand times committed' (V.ii.217–19). It is in this way that I understand Cavell's point that Othello is 'trying, against his knowledge, to believe [Iago]' because 'it is a thing he would rather believe than something yet more terrible to his mind . . . her faithfulness'.[118] For whereas the fantasy of her faithlessness can be grasped and envisaged, her faithfulness, her unseen fidelity, cannot. Desdemona's unseen love is a hidden terrorism for a man who wants open warfare: 'Had it pleased God / To try me with affliction … I should have found in some place of my soul / A drop of patience' (IV.ii.49–55). The fantasy of her whorish guilt relieves him of his consuming uncertainty.

From the perspective of the event, however, the inner is a lie, a conjuring trick. It is a trick Iago plays compulsively until the end, conjuring spectres within himself, as if there was something in him *more* than his action: 'Demand me nothing. What you know, you know' (V.ii.309). There is less. He never can work out a consistent internal cause for his action. By surrendering his 'embodied form', Iago, like Hegel's Unhappy Consciousness, 'pronounces an absolute vanishing, but the pronouncement *is*, and this consciousness is the vanishing that is pronounced'.[119] Or: 'I am not what I am.' His is the power to convert excess into nothing, like an event in reverse, or a return to the void – a vanishing that converts all into inwardness. And this is precisely what he gives Othello: Desdemona's ghostly, internal identity. Iago creates it by having Othello watch her from the outside, like a voyeur: 'Look to your wife' (III.iii.201); 'Look to't' (III.iii.204). As we've seen with Brabanzio, Iago's genius is to feed the external and the internal off each other, to marry them against the event. He begins by talking of cultural practices: 'I know our country disposition well. / In Venice they do let God see the pranks / They dare not show their husbands' (III.iii.205–7). You might not realise it, Othello, but this is the sort of thing people do. Actually, when you think about it, Desdemona has already *done* this: she already 'deceive[d] her father' (III.iii.210); she already 'seemed to … fear your looks' when she actually 'loved them most' (III.iii.211–12). What is Othello's response? 'I am bound to thee for ever' (III.iii.216). That quickly he is gone. He has not just left Desdemona; he has twinned himself with Iago. They now form the Two. He has 'relinquish[ed] his ability to think on his own':[120]

IAGO	My lord, I see you're moved.
OTHELLO	No, not much moved.
	I do not think but Desdemona's honest.
IAGO	Long live she so, and long live you to think so!
OTHELLO	*And yet how nature, erring from itself –*
IAGO	Ay, there's the point; as, to be bold with you.

(III.iii.229–33, italics mine)

The marriage that Iago effectuates between internal and external identity in some ways reflects a marriage between Badiou's two enemies of the evental subject: the community (external identity) and the individual (internal identity).[121] Once the external – nature, custom, clime, complexion, degree – is acknowledged to *not* be definitive (as Othello's knowledge of his cues would have it), it becomes a powerful force for the internal: 'And yet how nature erring from itself – '. The gap is opened and Othello now 'doubl[es] with Iago' in his 'obsessive mind-reading'[122] of Desdemona. As Iago continues the passage just cited:

> Not to affect many proposèd matches
> Of her own clime, complexion, and degree,
> Whereto we see in all things nature tends.
> Foh, one may smell in such a will most rank,
> Foul disproportions, thoughts unnatural!   (III.iii.234–38).

Carving out one's own little area of self-interest within the situation of 'clime, complexion, and degree' is reasonable and believable, is according to 'nature', consecrating one's self to another is not. Iago's 'Foh' is the rhetorical snap of the fingers that turns Desdemona's exceptional act into disgust, destroying the concept of love as something that comes '*without being due*'[123] by turning its unjustified, excessive quality into something 'unnatural', 'Foul' and 'rank'. The unseen, indistinct quality of the event – the very force behind Othello's arrival in Cyprus – becomes something monstrous: 'By heaven, thou echo'st me / As if there were some monster in thy thought / Too hideous to be shown!' (III.iii.110–12). And the monster becomes Desdemona.

By and large, love is already over when Othello declares, 'She's gone' (III.iii.271), though the torturous process of closing its rupture will take the rest of the play. In fact, when Desdemona returns, less than 200 lines after she left Othello, it is he who is gone: 'Why do you speak so faintly? Are you not well? . . . Faith, that's with watching' (III.iii.287–89). His voice has changed. He speaks 'so faintly'. Desdemona no longer understands where he is coming from. He avoids her words and intent. And he avoids her pity. She ministers to the 'pain upon [his] forehead' (III.iii.288) as he perversely plays on cuckold's horns, but her pity is not enough: 'Your napkin is too little' (III.iii.291). He rejects her napkin, along with her love, and it falls disastrously to the ground. Within another 200 lines Othello kneels with Iago to vow 'wide revenge' (III.iii.462). As Badiou astutely observes, the betrayal of a truth-event 'is something quite different from an abandonment': 'I must always convince myself that the Immortal in question *never existed*, and thus rally to opinion's perception of this point.'[124] It requires a reactionary violence equivalent to the violence of the event. Othello can become himself once more only by blowing away the unknowable desire of the other: 'All my fond love thus do I blow to

heaven – 'tis gone. / Arise, black vengeance, from the hollow hell'
(III.iii.450–51). Certain and stony, it is no surprise that, as Leavis notes,
when Othello 'kneels to take a formal vow of revenge' he returns to 'the
heroic strain of the "*Othello* music"'.[125] 'Never, Iago,' Othello intones, and
then marches through the grand single words of 'the Pontiac', 'the
Propontic' and 'the Hellespont' to the cold certainty of 'revenge', sworn to
'yon marble heaven' (III.iii.456–63). The vulnerable Othello who arrived in
Cyprus is gone forever as 'he sets himself irrevocably in his vindictive
resolution' and thereby 'reassumes formally his heroic self-dramatization'.[126]
It is the marriage of Iago and Othello, each kneeling before the other, that
allows the old '*Othello* music' to return.

The immediate result is Desdemona's utter incomprehension. In the
following scene, Othello presses her relentlessly on the now monumentally
significant handkerchief, culminating in five requests to see it, the last three of
which simply cue Desdemona with 'The handkerchief' (III.iv.89–93).
Excluded from this now all-consuming signifier, Desdemona has no language
with which to reach Othello. In fact, Othello's mind 'now parasitically relies
on Iago's', so that 'Othello even begins to repeat language spoken by and
about Iago'.[127] So whereas Romeo and Juliet together transformed the significance of names, Othello joins Iago in tearing their meanings apart. Most
strikingly, Iago-Othello steals the word 'pity' from Desdemona, so that
Othello's deformed mind jerks uncontrollably between Iago and pity: 'But
yet the pity of it, Iago. O, Iago, / the pity of it, Iago!' (IV.i.186–87). It is a
gruesome deforming of Desdemona's beautiful and foundational pity by a
mind in the tightening noose of a compulsion to kill, yet spasming with regret.
Pity was for love; now it is for death.

'It is the cause': Death March

Desdemona remains fatally cut off from Othello's thought until the very
last moment. Indeed, it is even hard for us to follow Othello's death march.
'It is the cause, it is the cause, my soul' (V.ii.1) marks a shift in Othello from
enraged uncertainty to calm surety. But what is the 'cause'? There is at once
a chilling metaphysical import and an utter emptiness to these words. For
the '"It" has no antecedent'.[128] One wants to leave the words alone, free
from analysis or content. Othello does not do so, however, for he does give
a cause: 'Yet she must die, else she'll betray more men' (V.ii.6). These
words not only fail to match the foreboding of the opening, they seem
facile and evasive. Who is there left to betray? As Leavis writes, 'the accent is
so clearly unrelated to any effectual motive in Othello that the concern for

justice, the self-bracing to noble sacrifice, appears as self-deception'.[129] Tellingly, it is here that Knight locates the apotheosis of the '*Othello* music': 'During the last scene Othello is a nobly tragic figure … [and] he utters the grandest of his poetry.'[130] He gives particular emphasis to Othello's 'cause' speech: 'This is the noble *Othello* music: highly-coloured, rich in sound and phrase, stately. Each word solidifies as it takes its place in the pattern.'[131] What Knight fails to see is that the music's solemn march is precipitated by the violent and deluded return to certainty, rather than any inner 'nobility'. Othello can return to his noble solidity because he is 'certain' that Desdemona is guilty and that she will soon be dead. Violent self-deception is the 'cause' and precondition of Othello's calm, block-like speech. It is, therefore, quite inadequate to declare that the 'exaggerated, false rhetoric'[132] following his discovery of Desdemona's innocence is simply the result of '[t]he Iago-spirit':[133]

> O cursèd, cursèd slave!
> Whip me, ye devils,
> From the possession of this heavenly sight
> Blow me about in winds, roast me in sulphur,
> Wash me in steep-down gulfs of liquid fire!
> O Desdemona! Desdemona! dead!
> Oh! Oh! Oh! (V.ii.283–89).

Although there is undoubtedly intense pain, and self-torture in these lines, it is a pain that allows Othello to expel his uncertainty and return to his old speech, only now – finally – through the certainty of *his* guilt. The painful ugliness of Othello's violent speech is, like his actual violence towards Desdemona, the condition of the 'architectural stateliness'[134] that surrounds it. It actualises his longing that God 'try [him] with affliction' (IV.ii.50) rather than with the unseen corruption of his heart. Alone and afflicted, Othello can return to his old tale. Their identities are now certain. Their characters are readable. There is nothing undecidable and no need for faith.

In this sense, Leavis is quite right that 'he remains the same Othello' even when 'he discovers his mistake'.[135] But this does not mean that he remained the same throughout, for this violence, to both Desdemona and himself, is necessary to *restore* the '*Othello* music'. It needs restoring because the trauma of love wrenched him from himself. Strong walls were always the condition of Othello's music, walls that kept out events and others. But there can be no tragedy unless walls are breached, and we saw them totter upon his arrival in Cyprus, if not quite fall. The breach may only have been partial but it was profound. To return to the '*Othello* music', the price is now tragic. He cannot love and be that Othello. Except, of course, when Desdemona is dead and her purity assured: 'Be thus when thou art dead, and I will kill thee / And love thee after' (V.ii.18–19). The intruder must be torn to pieces, what was living must be turned to stone, and the walls must be re-erected around Desdemona's 'sacrifice' (V.ii.70). Then Desdemona's perfection may be loved again as pure image, 'monumental alabaster' (V.i.5).

Once Desdemona's purity is assured, Othello retreats from Cyprus into the certain tale of his past where he is most at home. The 'quarried speech'[136] returns and with it the effortless mastery of command. 'Behold, I have a weapon':

> I have seen the day
> That, with this little arm and this good sword,
> I have made my way through more impediments
> Than twenty times your stop.   (V.ii.266–71)

He has rediscovered the Othello he knows how to be, the tune he knows how to play. Now he really does know his cue, and it is to death and stillness: 'Be not afraid, though you do see me weaponed. / Here is my journey's end' (V.ii.273–74). He speaks words of retreat and diminishment but in the tone of command. Indeed, the description of another's fear and the power to pacify – ''Tis a lost fear . . . Othello . . . retires' (V.ii.276–78) – denotes his utter mastery of the situation, recalling his night-time confrontation with Brabanzio.

A story-teller first and last, Othello seems to compulsively perpetuate his own myth in his final lines. The almost studied irrelevance of this farewell speaks to a continuing avoidance. Othello's notorious claim that he is 'one that loved not wisely but too well' (V.ii.353), combined with his suggestion that he is 'one whose hand, / Like the base Indian,[137] threw a pearl away / Richer than all his tribe' (V.ii.355–57), grossly misrepresents his tale. Knowing or not knowing Desdemona's worth was never Othello's problem. He was all too aware of the stakes: of Desdemona's monumental value. Martin Meisel quotes Pinter's observation that 'a torrent of language' can be 'employed' as a form of 'silence', designed as a 'stratagem to cover [the] nakedness' of 'true silence'.[138] By cloaking himself in the grand language of his story, Othello follows Iago's demonic trick of 'inclosing reserve', which 'is ingenious enough to transform the disclosure itself into a mystification'.[139] It is, in the end, an avoidance of the naked and vulnerable self that is capable of love. It is an avoidance of the only cue that mattered: that of Desdemona's consecration. That he failed to consecrate himself in return, to give himself in weakness, to endureth all things and believeth all things for her, is smothered, like Desdemona herself, under Othello's all-encompassing music.

The end of *Othello* is thus almost a black parody of Hegel's idea of tragic affirmation, in which 'the heart of the hero recoils into simple unity with itself, when it says: "It is so"'.[140] For Othello, this return to himself is a re-immersion into his self-contained symbolic realm. The motion of life is frozen in his architectural stillness. In Badiou's terms, Othello retreats from '[c]ourage as insubordination to the symbolic order'.[141] What should have been the basis of the subject – his active consecration to the indiscernible event – becomes the abyss in which it drowns. Othello's final speech – the glorious piece of confusion that is his story of the 'turbaned Turk' (V.ii.362) – makes a mockery of Hegel's idea that the tragic hero 'remains true to himself . . . and manifest[s] the cheerfulness and serenity of tranquillity'.[142] Rather, in the cutting words of Eliot, we witness a 'terrible exposure of human weakness': 'What Othello seems to me to be doing in making this speech is *cheering himself up*. He is endeavouring to escape reality, he has ceased to think about Desdemona, and is thinking about himself.'[143] Othello is at once the Turk and the slayer of the Turk. He both revels in and hates himself. He both protects and ravages Venice. There is great scope for cultural analysis in this ending: of Othello seeing himself through Venetian eyes, hating himself for being an outsider, wanting to paint himself as a Venetian even in his alienness. But his confused self-immolating also marks the logical endpoint of the '*Othello* music': he is consumed by himself, becoming everything. Othello is all in this tale: the proud Venetian, the cruel Turk, and the protective warrior. He accuses himself and he punishes himself. He possesses all roles. That they also possess him is no concern for Othello, nor has it ever been. From the start he was possessed by his story. Only Desdemona, the one cue he could neither read nor grasp, broke this totality. But now he knows. He is to play his own executioner and possess himself in full. Action, knowledge and self are united at last.

CHAPTER 4

The Ghostly Event(s) of Hamlet

Hamlet presents something of a problem for the notion of 'arrivals'. When he enters, dressed in black, standing out as an exception to the painted court, it seems that he is already 'Hamlet', possessed of a deep interiority and speaking in an enduring attitude of characterisation: 'O that this too too solid flesh would melt' (I.ii.129). He seems to arrive less through an evental rupture than his declaration of selfhood: 'I have that within which passeth show' (I.ii.84–85). In this sense, Hamlet almost seems something of a Danish Montaigne.[1] Indeed, his rejection of 'show' recalls Montaigne's intention for his *Essays*: 'I desire therein to be delineated in mine own genuine, simple and ordinarie fashion, without contention, art or study; for it is myself I pourtray.'[2] It might seem that Hamlet too arrives by assaying his separateness and inwardness. The similarities to Montaigne are often striking. His famed 'delay' mirrors Montaigne's declaration that his youthful complexion 'had no other fault, but a certaine dull languishing': 'The danger was not, I should doe ill, but that I should doe nothing.'[3] His antic self-diversity reflects Montaigne's many assertions of his wavering, inconstant nature. And his characteristic disgust mirrors Montaigne's own bursts of misanthropy: 'is not a man a miserable creature?'[4] Indeed, Hamlet's disdain for human vanity follows Montaigne all the way down to the diet of worms: 'The heart and life of a mighty and triumphant Emperor, is but the break-fast of a seely little Worme.'[5]

Despite the undoubted similarities, this chapter ultimately serves to more clearly delineate the gulf between Hamlet and Montaigne. Part II explores perhaps the most obvious problem with the idea of a Montaigne-like Hamlet: the play's final act. In scripting Hamlet's (re)arrival from the mysterious voyage to England, which takes place beyond the borders of the play, between Acts IV and V, the play represents something quite foreign to Montaigne: the radically transformative happening. But even before we come to Hamlet's obscure voyage, Part I shows how Shakespeare's dramaturgy and hero are permeated with the evental and the spectral.

Part I: The Ghost

Ghostly Arrivals

We have seen in both *Romeo and Juliet* and *Othello* a certain indistinction in Shakespeare's foundational events. They come from the darkness, from the unseen, from the indistinction of the 'high-wrought flood'. They are not quite locatable or speakable. In *Hamlet*, Shakespeare amplifies this indistinction to the extent that the nature of the play's 'event' is often thrown into confusion. From the very outset, we are thrown into the midst of a 'happening' of porous borders. For even before Hamlet's entrance, the ghost has intruded from the unseen and opened the play-world to excess and uncertainty. The ghost is, as States notes, 'symptomatic of the play's ghostliness', which blurs boundaries and identities.[6] In contrast to the fairly stable dichotomies of Montague and Capulet, Venetian and outsider, *Hamlet* begins with disorientation and confusion on dark midnight ramparts, with coldness and heart sickness at the witching hour. Their identities obscured, the relief mistakenly challenges the watch before Shakespeare further disorientates his speakers as that ultimate figure of the excessive and the unnatural, the ghost, 'comes again' (I.i.38) to interrupt their attempts to 'speak of this' (I.i.32). The opening scene thus ruptures the ordinary world of Denmark, which exists only in report. Shakespeare founds the play-world on the edge of the unseen, from which this ghostly 'thing appear[s]' (I.i.19). We are thrust into a world coming apart at the seams. Unnatural beings creep through the gaps of its stitching. The 'King that's dead' (I.i.39) returns when it shouldn't, marking a world of 'fear and wonder' (I.i.42) quite alien to Venice's or Verona's concrete social orders.

Of course, Denmark's social and dynastic orders are very much part of the play. Margreta de Grazia has rigorously shown how land, conquest and inheritance are far more integral to the play than Romantic notions of inwardness traditionally allowed.[7] In a sense, I highlight the inadequacy of Romantic readings from the opposite angle. If de Grazia rightly brings the ground back into focus, I show how, at key moments, Shakespeare also does quite the contrary: he raises the focus point beyond earthly plots and thereby *blurs* the ground. In such moments, the ground is precisely what is lost; what is pulled from under us; what is crumbling, subsiding or flat out disappearing. Indeed, as de Grazia astutely highlights, land is what is withheld from Hamlet: he is 'dispossessed' and 'disentitled'.[8] None of this is to deny land's importance, but to suggest that something else is also at play: that something also emerges *from* the earth. In fact, I argue that *Hamlet* stages a complex play of ground and groundlessness. Despite the numerous references to land, the ground is not stable in *Hamlet*: Shakespeare points beyond it, as well as to it, in the final act; it slips away on Hamlet's voyage; and it breaks open for the ghost.

From the edge of representation, this 'thing appear[s]', stalking in form familiar but different. Eluding Horatio's philosophical delineations, it is articulable only as 'some strange eruption to our state' (I.i.68). As with Badiou's event, the ghostly happening is both of and from beyond the situation. It is of the state of things, arising on its hard stone battlements and speaking of its political machinations. But it is also alien, irrupting from a darkness beyond the walls, from the 'fires' of an unseen 'prison-house' whose harrowing 'secrets' it is 'forbid [t]o tell' (I.v.11–14). Theatrically, the ghost emerges from the hidden realm under the stage. 'When the ghost first appeared in the original staging he climbed out of the trapdoor in the middle of the Globe's stage', coming from an 'understage area' that, as Gurr and Ichikawa write, 'had a symbolic function as hell'.[9] Whether hell or purgatory, the ghost's entrance from the dark recesses below the stage marks an intrusion from another world, both dramatically and metaphysically.

The intrusive quality of *Hamlet*'s ghost is neither necessary nor typical for early modern stage ghosts. In *The Spanish Tragedy*,[10] for instance, the ghost of Andrea is a mere spectator to events who does not enter the play's life or dialogue. Indeed, Andrea calls attention to his own irrelevance by claiming that Bel-imperia 'loved [him] more than all the world' (II.v.3–6) even as the play shows her falling in love with his former best friend, Horatio, who now 'sit[s] in Bel-imperia's thoughts' as her 'second love' (I.iv.61–64), vibrant and alive. Andrea is a deflated presence into whom Horatio and Bel-imperia blow hollow words; he half-rises for the barest moment before shrinking into nothingness following Horatio's murder in II.iv. As the play's focus shifts to Hieronimo's subject-altering grief, Andrea is less than an afterthought. Unlike the vital passion of Old Hamlet ('O horrible, O horrible, most horrible!' (I.v.80)), Andrea has no presence in the world of the living. The unchanging insignificance of the deflated ghost hangs heavy in the air, not 'promise-crammed' (III.ii.86) but promise-parched. In *Hamlet*, however, we have not a spectral spectator but a radical spectral intrusion. The ghost is harrowingly 'like the King' (I.i.41) but also manifestly, and harrowingly, *not* the King. The 'thing' 'usurp'st' the King (I.i.44). What is the same is also inexplicably different. It is from beyond (the grave, if nothing else).

The ghost's second coming triggers a change in its observers' speech, signalling a break in their ordinary modes of communication. It has Horatio asking it questions, seeking out its nature, but finding no answers, only its disappearance before 'the morn in russet mantle clad walks o'er the dew of yon high eastern hill' (I.i.147–48). The ghost's exceptional appearance unleashes an exceptional burst of lyricism[11] in the sober-minded Horatio and with it the resolution to 'impart what we have seen tonight / Unto young Hamlet' (I.i.150–51). Poetic exuberance breaks into Horatio's level-headed speech, like the ghost intruding into the material world. The opening scene thus triangulates the ghost's appearance, the play's poetry, and the coming of Hamlet. It calls forth the poetic prince from the edge of representation, from beyond the upended situation, and from outside Horatio's philosophical questioning. 'By heaven', Horatio 'charge[s]' it to 'speak' (I.i.47), but it 'stalks away' (I.i.48), awaiting another.

Before Hamlet's famed distinction between 'that within' and 'actions that a man might play' (I.ii.84–85), he has thus already been evoked as the figure who will inhabit both the material dimension of the ramparts and the 'strange' dimension that comes from beyond, inhabit both the ground and the groundless. Everything surrounding the ghost, the 'fear and wonder' of its observers, its movement under their feet, its coming from the unseen, creates the sense of something singular and excessive entering the frame. Something new is coming and its name is Hamlet. In a strange way, the ghost and Hamlet emerge as singularities in the same fashion: in and as an excess of their situations. When he comes, Hamlet, like his ghostly father, does not immediately speak. For his first sixty-four lines onstage, Hamlet simply appears in black silence. He is of the Danish court but he is also manifestly, and disturbingly, outside of it. He too arrives as an intruder, an outsider, a 'strange[r]', dark like the ghost, and secretive too. For both, it is their undefined *difference* from their surrounds that makes them compelling singularities. While I advance this further in Part II, it is worth noting that this marks a confluence of divergent philosophies: 'Badiou and Levinas share with Paul (as do Derrida and Marion) the conviction that subjectivity is not, as it is for cultural historicism, socially determined: it is exactly what exceeds social determination.'[12]

The ghost's intrusion is, to adapt Lowell Gallagher's words, the play's dark and conflicted form of the 'sheer excessiveness of grace [that] disrupts and alters the entire field of the given'.[13] It thereby permits the emergence of something beyond the 'given' situation and perhaps even its given forms of remembrance (mourning and revenge). That said, while the force infiltrating Denmark may be an event, it is a 'strange' event of uncertain origins and ends, and this uncertainty filters into the opaqueness of a character that constantly eludes our grasp. When Hamlet enters silent and unheralded, we have a hero who, like the event itself, refuses to be defined by his surrounds. Hamlet is not fully present or stably located but as with his first line – 'A little more than kin and less than kind' (I.ii.65) – awaits some future moment for his full significance. For one thing, he awaits the ghostly encounter.

Before that encounter, Hamlet's rejection of 'seem[s]' (I.ii.76) opens a chasm between inner being and outward action that is reminiscent of Iago's attempt to sever his 'heart' from any 'outward action' (*Othello*, I.i.61–62). A Pauline disgust permeates Hamlet's pre-ghost soliloquy, in which Elsinore is overrun by the 'unweeded' postlapsarian 'garden', full of 'things rank and gross in nature' (I.ii.135–36). Here Hamlet echoes Paul's palpable disgust at the 'sinful flesh' (Romans 8:3) that defines human life under the 'the curse of the law' (Galatians 3:13). Something is indeed 'rotten in the state of Denmark' (I.v.67). We have a sense of what John Gillies describes as 'the intellectual intuitiveness of original sin in late Elizabethan England': 'That the timber of humanity is crooked – the heart desperately wicked – is never in need of demonstration.'[14] It is a sentiment that clearly flows into the systematic corruptions of revenge tragedy. And it is also evident in Montaigne's *Essays*, which, like *Hamlet*, touch both upon sexual disgust (nature 'hath pell-mell lodged our joyes and filthes together'[15]) and a spiritual disgust at man's lofty pretensions: that lying in the 'filth and mire of the world', man 'yet dareth imaginarily place himselfe above the circle of the Moone, and reduce heaven under his feet'.[16] In the opening scenes, this disgust is potent and debilitating. Hamlet is paralysed by an enervating abyss between internal truth and the falseness of outward manifestations in this corrupt, filth-ridden kingdom. Hamlet's anguished remembrance of his father is therefore cut off from any outward action: 'Heaven and earth, / Must I remember?' (I.ii.142–43), 'But break, my heart, for I must hold my tongue' (I.ii.159). Not unlike Montaigne, he holds his tongue (and hand) in public only to let loose in private soliloquies (or essays).

There is, however, more to Hamlet than disgust, for his 'melt[ing]' flesh also calls us back to the ghost, melting between worlds, fleshless, waiting. Here we begin to sense something far removed from either Montaigne's withdrawal from the 'common presse'[17] or the systematic corruptions of revenge tragedy. In Shakespeare's radical rewriting of the genre, Hamlet's despair sits alongside a world-altering wonder that is evidenced in the ghost's invigorating appearance. After Hamlet's moralising speech about the 'custom / More honoured in the breach' (I.iv.18), Horatio's 'it comes' (I.iv.19) cues him to enter into a different, evental, register:

> Be thou a spirit of health or goblin damned,
> Bring with thee airs from heaven or blasts from hell,
> Be thy intents wicked or charitable,
> Thou com'st in such a questionable shape
> That I will speak to thee. I'll call thee Hamlet,
> King, father, royal Dane. O answer me! (I.iv.21–26)

To some extent, Hamlet's reckless disregard for spiritual consequences mirrors Laertes' 'Conscience and grace to the profoundest pit! / I dare damnation' (IV.v.128–29). And yet, its direction is altogether different, for it focuses not on revenge but on the desire to question and communicate with his father again in his inimitability.[18] It is for this reason that Hamlet views his mother as bestial, because, by marrying her husband's brother, she has effaced this singularity: 'O God, a beast that wants discourse of reason / Would have mourned longer!' (I.ii.150–51). In fact, she becomes less than a beast for Hamlet: an automated role; a name, 'Queen'; an act 'that a [wo]man might play'.

Perhaps most importantly, the ghost's shifting appearance opens Hamlet to something beyond the disillusioned and debilitating severance of inward truth and outward show. Hamlet's energy becomes future orientated: 'I will speak to thee.' The ghost comes in 'questionable shape' that draws forth speech and draws forth Hamlet: 'I'll call thee Hamlet.' The ghostly visitation fills the watchers '[w]ith thoughts beyond the reaches of [their] souls' (I.iv.37). It transports Hamlet beyond what is speakable in the stale, flat and unprofitable situation: 'There are more things in heaven and earth, Horatio, than are dreamt of in your philosophy' (I.v.174–75). It exposes Hamlet to an urgent and energising mode of existence (and representation) that is outside the realm of Denmark's knowledge. The spectre, itself ungrounded, serves to unground Hamlet. And this ungrounding is swiftly marked in Hamlet's language. In I.ii he is melting, thawing, becoming dew; the world is weary, stale, flat, rank and gross. Following his encounter, however, Hamlet is no longer the same disgusted, withdrawn figure. His language in I.iv expresses not a melting Hamlet but an energised, almost bursting, Hamlet:

> Let me not burst in ignorance, but tell
> Why thy canonized bones, hearsèd in death,
> Have burst their cerements, why the sephulchre

> Wherein we saw thee quietly enurned
> Hath oped his ponderous and marble jaws
> To cast thee up again. What may this mean[?]   (I.iv.27–32)

For a moment, Hamlet seems on the verge of 'burst[ing] [his] cerements'. For a moment, he seems to leave behind the customary ceremonial containments of grief to something pressing, fearful and absolutely present. The passive anguish of remembrance now competes with an energising encounter in which things are opened up and cast into the dramatic moment, forcing Hamlet to grasp blindly for some handhold: 'What may this mean?' The explosive face-to-(non)face sends him spinning beyond the simple material situation: 'beyond the reaches of [his] soul[]'. His debilitating melancholy is not gone, but it is now mixed with urgency and action: 'Say, why is this? Wherefore? What should we *do*?' (I.iv.38, emphasis mine). Above all, then, the ghost opens Hamlet to the notorious question of *action*. In this invigorating evental world, Hamlet must now think action – what is he to do? – even if action itself is obscured and deferred. Dramatically speaking, Hamlet's distinctive interiority – both pressed into and oppressed by action – is not pre-existing or innate but is produced by outwardness. It is produced by what *happens* to Hamlet: by the tearing apart of the old world, the disorientation on the ramparts, the undead figure coming from the void. Indeed, Hamlet's newly energised and antic mode of being – with its 'Hillo, ho, ho, boy[s]' (I.v.119) and 'wild and whirling words' (I.v.137) – springs to life immediately upon his ghostly encounter (and thus before he 'think[s] meet / To put an antic disposition on' (I.v.172–73)).

And yet, what 'happens' to Hamlet is far from straightforward. Indeed, Hamlet's exchange with the ghost in I.v shows us that the excessive, urgent Hamlet that emerges on the ramparts is fundamentally divided. The ghost ceases to be a pure happening (this 'thing appeared') and is named as his father, thereby entering the discourse of Denmark's rotten state. If the ghost's appearance was a sudden spectral emergence of the singular, its command is of an altogether different nature. The ghost is no clean break. The unprecedented, questionable intrusion speaks generic and restrictive words. The ghost is almost immediately re-grounded in the dynastical (and revenging) concerns traced by de Grazia. In Badiou's terms, we might say that when it speaks, the ghost ceases to reveal the situation's void and instead declares the situation itself. It does so in the most statist terms possible: Father, King, Command, Duty, Obey, Revenge. Hamlet is thus hailed by '"an eminent, idealized, exalted" Other – his father'.[19] The ghost is, of course, a return of the past, demanding remembrance and duty. It demands the structures of honour and revenge tragedy be fulfilled. And it returns to the debilitating language of disgust at fallen humanity's sexual corruption, at lust-ridden 'radiant angel[s]' come to 'prey on garbage' (I.v.55–57). In short, the ghost is constitutionally divided. On the one hand, its spectral appearance operates in an evental manner to open the situation to its void. On the other hand, its command reasserts the situation and seeks to reclose the ground.

The closing, situational aspect of the ghost is evident in the way that its call for vengeful remembrance follows the same automated logic as Claudius's forgetful mourning: 'your father lost a father; / That father lost, lost his; and the survivor bound / In filial obligation for some term / To do obsequious sorrow' (I.ii.89–92). Both attempt to shut down the situation's excess. Both dutiful vengeance and obsequious sorrow bear no relation to the singularity of Hamlet's loss, or encounter, but impose an automatic equivalence that must be enacted on the basis of 'filial obliga-tion'. The wretched uncle has stolen the beloved father's life and wife, and now the father asks Hamlet to act as if they were the same after all by slaying Claudius to 'set things right' (I.v.190). The ghost's command both binds Hamlet's memory of his father to Claudius and binds him to the 'revenger' role:

HAMLET:	Speak, I am bound to hear.
GHOST:	So art thou to revenge when thou shalt hear.
HAMLET:	What?
GHOST:	I am thy father's spirit,
	. . .
	If thou didst ever thy dear father love –
HAMLET:	O God!
GHOST:	Revenge his foul and most unnatural murder. (I.v.6–25)

It is worth taking this language seriously. Both the ghost and the genre do bind Hamlet to revenge. As de Grazia notes, '[o]nce the command (or vow) has been uttered, the deed is as good as done: the dictates of convention demand it'.[20] But if Hamlet is 'bound', what makes him 'Hamlet'? What distinguishes him from his ghostly forefathers, from revenging heroes such as Hieronimo? What makes the deed not quite as 'good as done'? While there are doubtless many answers, what I intend to explore is how Hamlet emerges from this very *division* between the binding to revenge and the unlocatable but foundational energy of the ghost's appearance, in short, from the complex play of ground and groundlessness.

In fact, this division is immediately registered by Hamlet. His responses to the ghost's command – 'What?' and 'O God!' – speak to a sudden unravelling of the ghost's bindings. Not that the injunction to revenge disintegrates; rather, Hamlet is taken aback. He is separated from it. 'What?' is both a questioning of what crime he is bound to revenge and a sort of double take; a surprised reaction to a non sequitur. It jars open a gap between the automated task of revenge and Shakespeare's representation of Hamlet's interiority. For Cavell, this gap indicates how revenge is what 'debars Hamlet from existence': the ghost 'asks the son to take the father's place, to make his life come out even for him', which ultimately 'deprives the son of his identity'.[21] There is certainly a sense that Hamlet is being effaced when he cries, 'Haste, haste me to know it, that with wings as swift / As meditation or the thoughts of love / May sweep to my revenge' (I.v.29–31). But something subtler is also at play, for the ghost (dis)embodies not only the duty to revenge that threatens to subsume subjectivity but also an intrusive excess that cannot be subsumed and which jolts subjectivity into life.

Cavell misses this uneasy duality: the way that the ghost combines a spectral appearance that stresses singularity, excess and memory, with a restrictive command that stresses equivalence, repetition and confining duty. And it is this duality that produces a divided Hamlet that is self-questioning, turbulent and multiply located. As Greenblatt writes:

> the metaphors Hamlet uses have the strange effect of inadvertently introducing some subjective resistance into the desired immediacy, since meditation and love are experiences that are inward, extended, and prolonged, experiences at a far remove from the sudden, decisive, murderous action that he wishes to invoke … This corrosive inwardness – the hallmark of the entire play and the principal cause of its astonishing, worldwide renown – is glimpsed even in his first frantic response to the Ghost.[22]

If we accept that Hamlet arrives through division, the ghost's push toward revenge does not threaten to erase the subject, it gives rise to this divided subject. Not only is Hamlet's 'corrosive inwardness … glimpsed *even* in his first frantic response to the ghost', it is *born here*. To put it more clearly, although some sense of Hamlet's inwardness certainly pre-exists the ghost's command, the command brings to a head the most recursive and corrosive aspect: the question of action and 'delay'. Before the ghost's intrusion, no action is possible. Hamlet must simply 'hold [his] tongue' (I.ii.159). He must withdraw in black. It is the ghost's command that gives rise to

Hamlet's obsession with a bloody action that is incommensurate to the wonder of the ghost's appearance.

Philosophically, the importance of this division to Hamlet's arrival can be seen from two angles. First, according to Badiou's theory of the event, 'an evental rupture always constitutes its subject in the divided form of a "not . . . but"',[23] the 'not' being the evental rupture of the existing situation and the 'but' being the subject's new action of fidelity. In these terms, it is the ghost's situational command that sets up the 'not' for Hamlet. Hamlet will *not* be fully interpellated by the customary role of the revenger, which follows the violent rules of the situation (emblematised by the 'coagulate gore' (II.ii.441–42) of Pyrrhus's vengeance). It is the very failure of full identification with the imposed, generic duty that opens the division that defines Hamlet's antic, agitated role-play.[24] What is so difficult about the ghost is that as well as commanding the role that Hamlet will 'not' fulfil, it also seems to produce the evental rupture that separates Hamlet from that role. Dramatically speaking, the ghost's intrusion also introduces the spectral excess, the state of exception, the poetic break that separates Hamlet from the command. What is so confounding, then, if one looks to articulate Hamlet in terms of 'arrivals', is that the ghost seems to be both situation and event. That which gives rise to the 'not' also separates Hamlet from the 'not'. And there is a further complication too, for the ghost's excess also raises the spectre of the 'but': of a different mode of being that is not captured by the situation or its revenger models. That said, while the ghost raises this spectre, it gives it no clear outlet, no sense of what the 'but' demands. The excessive, spectral aspect of the ghost may create a rift between Hamlet and the commanded action but the excess has no content. It hardly flows into a 'fidelity' in the sense of Badiou's truth-events or the love-event of *Romeo and Juliet*. Rather, the spectral seems to evoke the situation's void without drawing anything from it. Indeed, it often seems that Hamlet would prefer to follow the 'not' (the revenging Pyrrhus or unthinking Fortinbras) than the ghostly excess of the 'but'.

The preceding may seem to be yet another tortured attempt to fit Hamlet into a pre-existing critical category. Speaking of the ghostly excess of the 'but' certainly risks a descent into farcically vague theoretical depths (if not cruder places). Yet I think it is worth the risk, because it expresses something of what is tortured and difficult in *Hamlet*. It gets at the conflict between an obviously nameable thing that Hamlet is and yet is not (the dutiful revenge hero) and something else that he is but which cannot be named. It gets at the ghostly excess, the 'something more', that has long surrounded Hamlet and haunted critics. Despite the fact that the 'but' that arises from the ghost's appearance is obscure, Badiou's model is relevant because Hamlet does emerge as something exceptional rather than something structural. He arises from the rift between the situation and its unspeakable void. He arrives as 'Hamlet' by becoming other than his old self. The Hamlet that we encounter is irrevocably divided from '[t]he glass of fashion and the mould of form' that Ophelia describes as 'o'erthrown' (III.i.149–52). Claudius expresses the point in his typically functional address: 'Something have you heard / Of Hamlet's transformation – so I call it, / Since not th'exterior nor the inward man / Resembles that it was' (II.ii.4–7). All this should tell us not that Hamlet possesses innate depths of inwardness but that he has been transformed by what has happened: that inwardness is new and it comes from without. Indeed, Claudius searches for an external event that, 'More than his father's death [has] put him / So much from th'understanding of himself' (II.ii.8–9). As if he feared a ghost.

The importance of the ghost's divided nature can be further clarified through the lens of process philosophy. The ghost's command to revenge plays a strangely similar role to animal instinct for Bergson: 'Where consciousness appears, it does not so much light up the instinct itself as the thwartings to which instinct is subject; it is the *deficit* of instinct, the distance between the act and the idea, that becomes consciousness.'[25] Rather than 'debar[ring] Hamlet from existence',[26] the duty of revenge induces consciousness by revealing the '*deficit*' of this automated response, its distance from the singularity of his encounter with the ghost. In other words, Hamlet emerges as a ghostly excess of location and genre through the opposition between Shakespeare's dramaturgy of unseen excess and the restrictive command to revenge. Hamlet cannot follow the enclosing customary response and this gives rise to something *other*, to choice and thought:

> [C]onsciousness is the light that plays around the zone of possible actions or potential activity which surrounds the action really performed by the living being. It signifies hesitation or choice. Where many equally possible actions are indicated without there being any real action (as in a deliberation that has not come to an end), consciousness is intense. Where the action performed is the only action possible (as in activity of the somnambulistic or more generally automatic kind), consciousness is reduced to nothing.[27]

The ghost's division strands Hamlet between thought and action, self and instinct, which is the very (non)place of consciousness: the degree of consciousness expands with 'the zone of indetermination which surrounds its activity'.[28] Hamlet's division thus creates 'room' for the 'light' of consciousness.[29] It is the rupture by which Hamlet emerges *as an exception* to 'somnambulistic' instinct, as embodied by Laertes and Pyrrhus. It thereby suggests a synergy between Bergson's thought (which Badiou generally rebuts) and Badiou's idea that the subject is not a 'point of origin ... [but] essentially touches upon scission':[30] 'the subjective effect takes hold' through 'occurrences of "or else", "unless" ... "except that"', which are signifiers of 'a caesura between two orders'.[31] Ultimately, then, Hamlet's desire to fully coincide with his dutiful role – to 'wipe away all' else 'from the table of [his] memory' (I.v.98–99) – does not debar subjectivity but makes the necessarily divided consciousness so intense for Hamlet. It throws the spectral, shifting nature of the ghost, and, indeed, of Hamlet's subjectivity, into stark relief.

Delayed Consciousness

Such an understanding of Hamlet's division also gives new meaning to his so-called delay. Speaking of Hamlet's delay obviously has its risks: 'When organized around' Hamlet's delay, 'the play lends itself to infinite repro-gramming: any theory of what makes a subject, however construed, tick (or stop ticking) can be fed into the machinery of the play.'[32] The Romantics, for instance, tend to explain the tragedy through Hamlet's (Romantic) inner nature: Hamlet fails to act 'merely from that aversion to action which prevails among such as have a world within themselves'.[33] There are two points to be made here, however. First, 're-programmings' are the lifeblood of literary criticism. Second, and more specifically, the re-programming I attempt is quite different from that which de Grazia critiques. Indeed, I fully agree that we should 'do without' the Hamlet that is 'distinguished by an inner being so transcendent that it barely comes into contact with the play from which it emerges'.[34] Such a Hamlet goes against the very idea of 'arrivals'. Rather than offer a new diagnosis of Hamlet's inwardness, then, I seek to re-examine how 'the machinery of the play' creates 'Hamlet'.

Most basically, of course, I posit that the subject is not already there: that it must arrive. That is not the view of Coleridge, who writes that Shakespeare 'portray[s] a person in whose view the external world and all its incidents and objects were comparatively dim, and of no interest in themselves'.[35] Apart from the obvious objection that the 'external world' and its ghost are of intense interest to Hamlet, the very concept of 'interest' indicates how such readings locate the play's driving force in Hamlet's presupposed (and imaginatively surmised) inner nature. They follow the basic Hegelian idea that everything new 'is immanent to the "already"'.[36]

Hamlet has always already arrived. The tragedy 'turns ... on Hamlet's personal character. His noble soul is not made for this kind of energetic activity.'[37] What is startling, when one considers the diffused energy of the play's opening scenes, is that such readings ignore what *happens* to Hamlet. The ghost's disorientating intrusion is normalised as an effect of Hamlet's inner being – a being that the intrusion helps to create. The causation is backwards. Bloom is a good example: because he begins from the assumption that Hamlet's inner richness already 'contains every quality',[38] he must 'discount' the idea that the ghost 'brought about a radical change in him'.[39] The play and the 'plot cannot change Hamlet',[40] even if they *made* him. Consciousness becomes the source of all mysterious happenings rather than their product.

The theoretical reaction against 'character' did not stop critics searching for something 'already' in Hamlet to explain his delay. De Grazia notes that there is 'now a long tradition in which critics identify Hamlet's delay as the play's problem and propose a new disorder to account for it, often drawing upon the latest theories in philosophy, psychology, and psychoanalysis'.[41] Perhaps the most typical postmodern re-programming has been to point to the absence of Hamlet's inner essence, to show how Hamlet slides between roles without ever residing in one:

> 'That within' ... this essence, the heart of Hamlet's mystery, has been the quarry not only of Rosencrantz and Guildenstern, agents of the king's surveillance, but of liberal-humanist criticism ... The quest is, of course, endless, because the object of it is not there. As [Francis] Barker goes on to argue, 'this interiority remains, in Hamlet, gestural ... At the centre of Hamlet, in the interior of his mystery, there is, in short, nothing.'[42]

While it is clearly not 'possible to locate the true, the essential Hamlet',[43] Belsey and Barker's approach does not account for how something *does* arrive. By focusing on the absent centre, they are still defined by the concept of 'centre'. They are still looking for something already in Hamlet, only now it is a typically postmodern absence: Hamlet revolves around the 'nothing' of postmodern subjectivity, sliding endlessly between roles and signifiers. What arrives in *Hamlet* is not a centre, I argue, but something more dispersed and creative. Hamlet's interiority is not a mass Romantic hysteria, but neither is it straightforwardly within Hamlet. An analogy might here be drawn to Whitehead's processual understanding of 'physical things': although there 'is a focal region, which in common speech is where the thing is ... its influence streams away from it with finite velocity throughout the utmost recesses of space and time'.[44] The entity under observation, be it a star or a molecule, is not simply 'here' and 'now', it is 'a state of agitation'[45] that spills beyond itself. However, the modern physicist does not conclude that the star is an illusion because it is not self-sufficient, self-centred or simply located. The fact that it is dispersed in a 'stream of influence' does not negate its reality; it merely means that it exists differently, more interconnectedly, than had been thought.

Rather than being already there in either an essential self or the linguistic system, Hamlet's interiority arrives through the 'state of agitation' created by Shakespeare's dramaturgy. The ghost is the originating 'generator' of Hamlet's divided consciousness, but its shifting, excessive intrusion streams into the play-world at large. Bergson is again helpful in showing how the outward is productive of interiority:

> When we mechanically perform an habitual action . . . unconsciousness may be absolute; but this is merely due to the fact that the representation of the act is held in check by the performance of the act itself, which resembles the ideas so perfectly, and fits it so exactly, that consciousness is unable to find room between them. *Representation is stopped up by action.* The proof of this is, that if the accomplishment of the act is arrested or thwarted by an obstacle, consciousness may reappear . . . This inadequacy of act to representation is precisely what we here call consciousness.[46]

Both Hamlet's impossible desire to 'wipe away' all but the ghost from his 'memory' (I.v.98–99) and Laertes' fusion of action and nature when he cries that the 'drop of blood that's calm proclaims me bastard' (IV.v.114) suggest mechanical responses by which '[r]epresentation is stopped up by action'. There is no 'room' for consciousness to operate. Everything else is 'wipe[d] away' by the act. Consciousness only emerges 'if the accomplishment of the act is arrested or thwarted by an obstacle'. Whereas, for the Romantics, this obstacle – the delay – was within Hamlet's (surmised) consciousness, I follow Bergson in concentrating on the outward. Consciousness emerges because revenge is blocked – blocked by the ghost's irruptive spectrality, and the new mode of representation it unleashes. That the 'obstacle creates nothing positive . . . [but] simply makes a void, removes a stopper'[47] may seem to support the idea of an empty gestural Hamlet. But, as Bergson stresses, the void is where consciousness emerges as a creative force.

We see this gap in operation in the 'rogue and peasant slave' soliloquy. Hamlet's self-accusations express his continuing inability to overcome the obstacle and link representation to action. In part at least, Hamlet wants to be like Pyrrhus and let fall the 'bleeding sword' (II.ii.471). He longs to escape the 'monstrous' (II.ii.528) excess that prevents him from 'forc[ing] his soul' (II.ii.529–30) within its role. He longs to smooth over the void of consciousness. But while Pyrrhus may resemble Hamlet in inexplicably stopping before the act – 'his sword ... seemed i'th' air to stick' and he, 'like a neutral to his will and matter, [d]id nothing' (II.ii.457–62) – this 'delay' never reorients Pyrrhus's consciousness or divides him from himself. Rather, it immediately dissipates as he strikes Priam with '[a] rousèd vengeance' (II.ii.468). But Hamlet cannot close the gap. Unlike Othello's claim to know his cues, Hamlet never achieves even a temporary oneness with his task. Nor would we want him to, for the gap marks the rupture by which Hamlet emerges as an exception to his surrounds. However much Hamlet may struggle to close it over, the void is not a problem to be solved, for 'without this infimous and total gap, without this grammar of exception, there would only be the monotonous and infinite efficacy of the grinding of being under the law of an absence',[48] only the grinding repetition of the situation's cyclical violence. There would be no subject without the void, no arrival. We would be left with bloody Pyrrhus.

Although it is not fully taken up by Hamlet until the final act, the spectral, evental aspect of the ghost is nonetheless maintained in the dramaturgy. We see it in the strangely superfluous nature of II.ii, in which this ghostly excess of representation fragments into the antic faces, conflicting voices, assumed roles, and dramatic constructs of Hamlet's collaborations and confrontations with the players. Here, Hamlet's conflicted voicing of ghostly duty not only reflects a mind at work; it becomes dramatic, spilling out into the opposing voices of his soliloquy. Hamlet is both enticed by the bloody serenity of full interpolation by the command and tortured by its impossibility: 'Who calls me villain, breaks my pate across ... Who does me this?' (II.ii.549–52). The speech puts on trial the chasm between the ghost's Pyrrhic command and the excessive Hamlet that arrives from the spectral encounter:

> Remorseless, treacherous, lecherous, kindless villain!
> O, vengeance! –
> Why, what an ass am I? Ay, sure, this is most brave.　　(II.ii.558–60)

Hamlet attempts to don the Pyrrhic role of unreflective revenger but he runs aground on a short line ('O, vengeance!') and this leads to yet more reflection and self-condemnation. The speech reveals what Robert Weimann calls the play's 'disturbing gulf between what is represented and what is representing'.[49] For Weimann, Hamlet's 'antic disposition' involves a 'release from representivity' (as neoclassical verisimilitude), which is 'at the centre of a nonrepresentational dramaturgy as manifested in the achieved strategy of dissociating Hamlet from the courtly world of dramatic illusion and aristocratic decorum'.[50] It is 'representation' but representation that points beyond the situation, to the 'inadequacy of [the] act'[51] of revenge. The result is that the overcharged workings of Hamlet's mind, firing like double-cracked canons, explode with a non-representative excess of association: 'Words, words, words' (II.ii.192). Hamlet's speech thereby *does justice* to the diffused dramatic event of the ghost's appearance – to 'what is representing (i.e. the Shakespearean activity in the text . . .)'[52] – in a way that Pyrrhus's 'somnambulist'[53] action cannot. Indeed, Hamlet's awareness of the gap, or surplus, drives him not to action in the traditional sense but to the action of theatre, to representativity. The obstacle – 'the inadequacy of [the] act [of revenge] to [Shakespeare's] representation' – unleashes a prolonged burst of 'representation' *per se*, which centres on the players and culminates in the play-within-the-play.[54] It is as if the void between act and representation becomes the whole show.

We see this void clearly in Hamlet's most famous soliloquy. For Bergson, although consciousness originates in the ghost-like '*interval between representation and action*',[55] it always remains 'relative to the needs of action'.[56] But Hamlet's speculative 'To be, or not to be' (III.i.58) removes this relation and stares into the 'undiscovered country' (III.i.81) of the gap itself. Hamlet begins by contemplating an act – 'tak[ing] arms' (III.i.61) against Claudius or himself or both – that will be followed by a death, a 'sleep' (III.i.62). But then there is 'perchance' (III.i.67). '[P]erchance' is the dissociative (or associative) break from sleep, from the act, 'to dream' (III.i.67) and 'what dreams may come' (III.i.68). The metaphor of sleep awakens the spectre of what happens to consciousness afterward: of a further, perhaps more terrible, zone of consciousness or choice *after* the act. The act disappears and the 'void', which gave rise to consciousness, becomes consciousness's central concern. The event does not solidify into an actable fidelity but trails into the groundless unknown of 'something after' (III.i.80): the 'know not of' (III.i.84) that 'lose[s] the name of action' (III.i.90). Hence Davis's point that 'that within' never solidifies in *Hamlet*, that Hamlet's 'consciousness' is 'just "something", almost unnamed'.[57] The ungrounding 'perchance' overruns and disappears all else.

The disconnect between possibility and actuality is in evidence when Hamlet tells Ophelia that he is 'indifferent honest' but nevertheless could accuse himself 'of such things that it were better my mother had not borne me' (III.i.124–26). There is again something Montaigne-like about Hamlet's self-condemnations: 'I accompt my selfe of the common sort except in that I deeme my selfe guiltie of the basest, and culpable [of the] most popular defects: but not disavowed nor excused.'[58] And he also follows Montaigne's sense of the 'infinite' variety of 'strange lustfull longings' that have 'possest us'.[59] But whereas Montaigne writes of defects he actually possesses, Hamlet looks into himself and views the array of offences he *might* commit. These are not enacted offences, or even future offences, but 'perchance' offences. His unknown future-self mutates with its (potential) offensive action: '[He has] more / offences at [his] beck than [he has] thoughts to put them in, imagination to / give them shape, or time to act them in' (III.i.127–29).

There is an extraordinary sense of *excess* at play here. Somehow, these galaxies of offence swirl around him, ready to be incarnated at any moment. However we might imagine offences that are not done, thought or imagined, Hamlet here speaks of streaming beyond himself, his situation and any action that he actually performs, indeed, beyond material life, with its limited opportunities to act. One can understand why Bloom speaks of 'Hamlet's unlimitedness',[60] of how Hamlet 'contains every quality',[61] although I clearly disagree that it is 'contain[ed]' *within* him. Rather, Hamlet's mind seems to trail off into a multiverse of corruption, in which all possible offences are somewhere committed – though not here. By infecting the future in this manner, Hamlet's disgust penetrates the 'beyond' in a highly un-Pauline manner. The future-to-come becomes an infinite repetition of the fallen material world, with its debased dreams, crimes and foul imaginings.

Here we may return, at last, to the problem of the obscure, spectral nature of the excess – the 'but' – introduced by the ghost. What we find is not an answer, however, but a bleeding. Hamlet is 'not' the revenger, but he is not any thing else either. He bleeds, rather, into the void, into what is not, into groundlessness. Indeed, in Badiou's terms, Hamlet's thought dives beyond the void, which is a particular situation's suture to being, and into infinite multiplicity itself. Whether it is the possibility of dreams after death, or of his possible offences, the Hamlet that arrives through 'delay' is unbound, not tied to any one spot. He seems to drift, ghost-like, toward the undiscovered countries of pure multiplicity and infinite possibility. Here Kierkegaard's writing on possibility and necessity is instructive:

> Now if possibility outruns necessity, the self runs away from itself, so that it has no necessity whereto it is bound to return – then this is the despair of possibility. The self becomes an abstract possibility ... floundering in the possible, but does not budge from the spot, nor get to any spot, for precisely the necessary is the spot; to become oneself is precisely a movement at the

> spot . . . At last it is as if everything were possible – but this is precisely when the abyss has swallowed up the self.[62]

Hamlet is 'swallowed' by the void between the ghost's irruptive spirit and its 'commandment'. So while the gap between action and subject creates the space for thought, thought itself becomes 'a prison' (II.ii.239). For Kierkegaard, however, there is a 'spot' for the subject and 'the necessary is the spot'. Whereas 'anxiety is the dizziness of freedom' in which '[f]reedom succumbs',[63] freedom is restored by 'submit[ting] to the necessary'.[64] In Part II, I show how Hamlet's (re)arrival in Act V marks the coming of necessity, through which Hamlet gains a 'spot', however unstable or dispersed. In Lafeu's words, Hamlet comes to 'submit [himself] to an unknown fear' (*All's Well That Ends Well*, II.iii.5). Hamlet's mysterious voyage abruptly halts his fearful circling around the 'undiscovered country' and leads to a radical submission to the 'unknown'. Worldly corruption no longer infects the beyond; rather, Hamlet's obscure voyage brings the beyond into the material present and energises a new mode of being in the situation: 'readiness'.

Part II: The Voyage

According to Aristotle, every good tragedy has a recognition scene that enacts 'a change from ignorance to knowledge', and '[t]he best sort of recognition is that accompanied by *peripeteia*'.[65] But what if the moment of recognition is itself obscure? It is clear that Hamlet recognises something in his sudden regard for divine 'providence' (V.ii.157–58), that there has been a 'reversal', but *what* exactly this entails and *how* Hamlet reaches this point is uncertain: 'when he returns from his sea voyage . . . he is a changed man – although what precisely constitutes the change may not be agreed.'[66] Most obviously, Hamlet's (re)arrival is prompted by a second obscure event: the never-present voyage to England. Whereas Hamlet's delay teased us inward, Shakespeare now foregrounds the outward. Although 'many have felt' that the 'key' to his transformation 'lies somewhere in Hamlet's inner life', Ronald Levao notes that 'Shakespeare seems wilfully to have blocked that mastery; once Hamlet returns to Denmark, there is an abrupt cessation of soliloquy'.[67] In the non-represented voyage between acts, the sudden assertion of providence, the confrontation with life's material end, and the extravagant foregrounding of chance in Hamlet's encounter with pirates – which in turn highlights the overseeing influence of Shakespeare's hand – we have a series of pointers to what lies outside 'Hamlet's inner life'.

Hamlet's transformation, his *peripeteia*, thus stems from a cross-pollinating combination of his journey across the seas, the materiality of the graveyard, his movement towards final action and, above all, his recounting of the rashness that overcame him and secured his return.

The Graveyard

When Hamlet enters the graveyard, it is he and not the ghost that arrives from the unseen and his relation to the event has been transformed. After his inflamed experience of 'rashness' (V.ii.7) on the voyage, Hamlet no longer circles compulsively around the 'undiscovered country' of the void; rather, the void is externalised as 'providence'. Ewan Fernie, who tackles the fifth act in light of Badiou's and Žižek's thought, captures this change when he writes that Hamlet's 'mystical experience' of rashness reveals a '"divinity" [that] irradiates and operates through the very imperfections of existence'.[68] Hamlet is finally able to act because he embraces the grave's materiality through 'the novel spirituality of immanence that *Hamlet* develops in its last act': 'a spirituality *of* the graveyard – of time, mortality and the event'.[69] For Fernie, the graveyard thereby 'snuffs out the ghost, but ... at the same time spirituality is transfused into material life'.[70] Whereas Hamlet confronted the unknown, spiritual ends of death in his 'To be, or not to be' soliloquy, pushing him into the abyss, he now confronts the material ends of death, pushing him into the earth. And whereas speculative thought on the 'undiscovered country ... puzzles the will' (III.i.81–82), Hamlet's contemplation of the grave – 'To what base uses we may return, Horatio!' (V.i.187) – is somehow liberating. It recalls Montaigne's thinking on death: 'It is uncertaine where death looks for us; let us expect her everie where: the premeditation of death, is a forethinking of libertie.'[71] It is liberating, perhaps, because it is not puzzling. All life's possibilities come to one final destination. We return to dust.

At one level, then, the graveyard's materiality puts time back into joint. Whereas time seemed 'abstract' or infinite in Hamlet's 'perchance to dream', 'I knew him, Horatio' (V.i.171) marks a more immediate and human register of time – akin to Bergson's 'duration' – that is tied to mortal remains.[72] Rather than drifting into infinite multiplicity, the graveyard to some extent re-grounds him.[73] Hence Fernie's emphasis on immanence:

> in the startling fifth act of *Hamlet* what is spiritually other and ultimate is not beyond but *immanent* in events ... Shakespeare's most famous play ultimately dramatises a kind of eschatological presentism that suggests that our

present is the place – the only and, therefore, the absolute place – of agency
and decision where all time may and perhaps must be consummated.[74]

The problem, however, is that this 'immanence' is *too* grounded. Fernie's
touchstones of 'agency' and 'presentism' do not quite do justice to the
difficulty of Shakespeare's dramatic structure, which, rather than resting in
the present as the 'absolute place', tosses us back and forth between
the material present of the graveyard, the mysterious past of the offstage
voyage, and the unknown future evoked by Hamlet's 'readiness'.
Moreover, the event that transforms Hamlet is no one of these but flows
throughout them all. The diffusion between temporalities (and speakers)
suggests a sense of give and take between Hamlet and his world that is in
stark contrast to his earlier imprisoning thought. Hamlet's second coming
thus stages a confluence of the present, the past, and the future, the
material and the 'beyond', that is not simply 'immanent'.

Such a confluence also breaks down Montaigne's strict division between
our miserable earthly existence and the absolutely other and unthinkable
realm of the divine. Whereas Fernie brings the divine beyond into the
material present (perhaps to the extent that there is no longer any 'beyond'
to speak of), Montaigne keeps the divine beyond our earthly reach: 'No
eye can behold, (saith Saint *Paul*) *The hap that God prepareth for his elect,
nor can it possibly enter the heart of man* (1 Corinthians ii. 9).[75] To make
us 'capable' of such beholding, our 'being' and 'essence' would have to
undergo 'so extreme and universall a change, that . . . we shall be no more
ourselves'.[76] However, Montaigne misses Paul's next verse: 'But God hath
revealed them unto us by his Spirit: for the Spirit searcheth all things, yea,
the deep things of God' (1 Corinthians 2:10). He therefore misses the
mysterious sense of advent, or 'Spirit', in which the divine and human
worlds meet. For Paul, of course, this meeting is radically transformative.
We are, indeed, 'no more ourselves'. The same can be said of Act V Hamlet:
his 'being is reformed and essence changed'. He has, in Bloom's words,
'experienced resurrection'.[77] Hamlet is not reborn of inwardness, however.
As Romeo from love, or Othello from the 'high-wrought flood', Hamlet is
reborn from the unseen voyage. Hamlet's second happening may be an
event, but the nebulous mode of its (non)representation – the way it is
constructed through an unstable temporal movement between the material
presence of the graveyard and the offstage voyage – complicates both
Badiou's event and the concept of 'immanence'.

We know that something has happened to Hamlet, but where and when
it happens are difficult to discern. To some extent the graveyard is the

aftermath, or embodiment, of what has taken place between Acts IV and V. But Hamlet does not here arrive all at once, or as a finished product. In fact, the fifth act establishes an increasingly porous Hamlet. Before his entrance, we have learned of his return to Denmark and his encounter with the pirates, but only through 'Horatio reading a letter', with the result that Hamlet's 'offstage heroics' are 'elaborately distanced from us'.[78] In what is in some ways a repetition of the first scene, we are made to wait for Hamlet himself. Instead of his anticipated return, however, we are first given clowns in a graveyard. As they equivocate about Ophelia's death, the gravediggers remind us not only of the harm that Hamlet's actions have caused but also of the underlying relationship between action and subject: 'if I drown myself wittingly, it argues an act; / and an act hath three branches: it is to act, to do, and to per- / form' (V.i.10–12). The Gravedigger does not offer a serious definition of action but exposes what has been missing: the one act, deed, and performance we have waited for all along. The Gravedigger's talk of action points to a non-doing: to the non-killing of Claudius, to action that is yet-to-come. The scene thus refuses to rest in the present as the 'absolute place'. The dramatic meanings created by these clowns may arise in the present of the graveyard, but they also flow into what is absent (Hamlet), what is past (Old Hamlet and Ophelia), what has been deferred (the witting act), and what will soon be done (killing Claudius).

Even when Hamlet does finally re-enter, he is made to share the stage and we must continue to wait. In the Folio-text, Hamlet re-enters via what Gurr and Ichikawa call a 'broken entrance': 'the stage direction reading *"Enter Hamlet and Horatio a farre off"* is marked nine lines earlier [than in the Q2-text], i.e. five lines before the First Clown begins to sing', and thus nine lines 'before Hamlet's first speech'.[79] While even in Q2, 'Hamlet's first remark' – 'Has this fellow no feeling of his business? A sings in grave-making' (V.i.61–62) – 'implies that he and Horatio have been watching and listening to the First Gravedigger'.[80] The gravediggers are thus an intimate part of Hamlet's (re)arrival. They both tee it up and are part of it. They share the stage as Hamlet returns and speak as he enters, in a sense delaying his speech. His broken, shared, and elongated entrance, while only a small dramaturgical point, shows how Hamlet is not simply immanent in *his* action and speech. Rather, dramatic immanence is heterogeneous, layered, broken up. Hamlet is never fully his own. Rather, there is a strange 'reciprocal sympathy between the satellite characters and the hero of *Hamlet*'.[81] We have something analogous to Tribble's idea that 'cognition is distributed' across a system rather than a property of 'each individual'.[82] The result is not that 'individual agency has no place', rather, the 'cognitively rich [environment] . . . is precisely calculated to maximize individual contributions'.[83] Hamlet becomes *more* through the richness of his sharing with the gravediggers and the 'distanced' event.

We might link this ghostly diffusion to Keir Elam's observation that 'it is not possible to talk of a single theatrical message: the performance is, rather, made . . . of "multiple messages in which several channels [of communication] . . . are used simultaneously"'.[84] Although the dramatic world arises immanently – through here-and-now events, actions, dialogue – this immanence is fragmented into multiple messages rather than existing as a smooth, single present. In this sense, the gravediggers almost become the play's form of 'readiness': readiness for Hamlet, readiness for change and readiness for the end. A readiness that, like Hamlet's, is never fully present. Much of what we think of as 'Hamlet' is thus projected from outside of him. But what is projected from the play-world also returns to Hamlet: the Gravedigger speaks of action only as doing, divorced from intention, and suddenly Hamlet re-emerges, having just acted as if without intention in the swapping of the commissions. We have an interweaving of dramatic codes that Elam calls '*transcodification*'.[85]

Until this point Hamlet has played both Clown and Hero, but in the graveyard Hamlet is 'on the receiving end of the "antic disposition"'.[86] De Grazia therefore argues that the much noted 'change . . . in Hamlet's mood' is really 'a shift in social position after his stint in the *dis*-position of the antic'.[87] It is not Hamlet 'himself' who turns serious in any internal sense (he has yet to recognise providence) but the Clown who vicariously, punningly turns him serious by taking over his role of equivocator-in-chief. Hamlet is, in this sense, atoned by the Gravedigger, who now bears the puns of equivocation, and who almost literally tees up the skull of 'poor Yorick' (V.i.171) for Hamlet's swing into tragic contemplation. He thus frees Hamlet from the curse of the law of association and allows him to reveal himself unequivocally: 'This is I, / Hamlet the Dane' (V.i.241–42).[88]

It is the dramaturgy, then, that communicates the meaning of Hamlet's (re)arrival. To a great extent, the offloads and uploads between Hamlet and the gravediggers, the shared codes, broken entrances, substitutions, other voices and mingled temporalities *are* Hamlet's transformation. This over-determined 'Hamlet' now shares porously with his environs rather than divorcing himself from them in speculative soliloquy. Far from 'the grave-yard scene . . . snuff[ing] out the ghost',[89] I suggest that Hamlet here finally lives up to, and perhaps accepts, its spectral dimension. He becomes a shifting, ghost-like being, moving through others' voices and other places.

He begins to achieve a ghostly openness to what is outside of him. From his staggered not-yet-here entrance to the neither present nor past voyage, the event's 'stream of influence'[90] builds a dispersed Hamlet who is not simply present.

Recounting the Voyage

Thus far I have focused on the immediate aftermath of the voyage. The multiple codes and temporalities of the graveyard are, in a sense, ripples from this nebulous occurrence. I will now try to get closer to its *origins*. The task is a difficult one, however, because although Hamlet-the-character may experience rashness as a 'fighting' 'in [his] heart' (V.ii.4) that is immanent in the voyage, this is not true for either Hamlet-the-actor or the audience. Despite being primed by Hamlet's sustained absence to give his account a privileged importance, we are not given the voyage directly. His rashness may acquire a sort of presence in Hamlet's retrospective narration, but his account also shuttles us back into a moment of rupture we never see and forward into an end we don't see yet. The time is still not in joint. And this, of course, affects the Hamlet we are given in the scene, which is shifting, unstable and distended in place and time.

The fact that the critical moment is not directly represented as action on stage suggests that what happened was beyond ordinary, expressible experience. Again, it is not just what Hamlet says — a divinity shaping our ends perhaps does not tell us much — but how it is orchestrated. Shakespeare uses a midline shift to highlight how the voyage's strangeness breaks into his speech and re-orients his regard:

> Sir, in my heart there was a kind of fighting
> That would not let me sleep. Methought I lay
> Worse than the mutines in the bilboes. *Rashly —*
> *And praised be rashness for it*: <u>let us know</u>
> Our indiscretion sometime serves us well
> When our dear plots do pall, and that should teach us
> There's a divinity that shapes our ends,
> Rough-hew them how we will — (V.ii.4–11, emphasis added)

A number of potential shifts cascade towards the break in narration. The cascade begins with the adjective 'Rashly', which describes the action of coming 'Up from [his] cabin' (V.ii.13) that Hamlet narrates seven lines later. It builds with 'And praised be rashness for it', which glosses his adjective and highlights the remarkable, positive ends of his rashness. And it breaks midline with the rather clunky 'let us know'. Here we witness an obvious break from the narration, which is more than an adjective or a gloss: it is a thought, and a mind, that is separated in time and space from the narrated action.

Palfrey and Stern describe 'the midline shift' as a 'location for *thinking*: for an effectively invisible process of coming to terms with the world'.[91] By interrupting the narration of the voyage with Hamlet's reflection on its significance, Shakespeare produces the impression of consciousness pushing up against its world, struggling to understand it. The shift from specific events to the general conclusion, 'let us know', indicates that a critical realisation has occurred. Hamlet's language first expresses an awe at his own experience – 'in my heart', 'a kind of fighting', 'Rashly', 'praised', 'rashness' – that suggests that something wondrous and foreign has taken place. It then takes on a distinctly 'preachy' feel: 'let us know', 'serves us well', 'should teach us', 'divinity that shapes our ends'. It is an almost quintessential religious movement: a personal experience of the unknown brings Hamlet into a state of confusion and awe, but through this disorientation he discerns the divine and attempts to draw general principles. But this is not simply Coleridgean generalising,[92] for it is through Hamlet's midline shift that the unthinking voyage enters and transforms the present and thereby re- orients the subject. After returning to his feeling in the past ('rashness'), he rejoins the present and searches for some meaning or structure to carry it forward ('let us know'). As Witmore puts it, Hamlet's 'digression ... serves as audible evidence that he has paused to recognize something, that he has responded to some sign of God's presence in the world'.[93] It is a 'spontaneous recognition ... [of] divine power'[94] intruding. Otherness and the beyond are thus not banished by immanence but are the very gateway to immanence.

Glimpsed only through a retelling, the absent voyage gestures towards what is 'cut off' from the drama, to pirate Nancy's words about the 'sacred'.[95] For all its bloody and messy immanence, there is something mysterious, something of the 'sacred', in Hamlet's (re)arrival. The religious intimations, the sense of awe, the apprehension of deep consciousness, do not belong to Hamlet-the-character, however, but are drawn from what he is cut off from. For Nancy, the 'sublime' is a matter of a 'movement' – as seen in Hamlet's narration – along *the border of the limit, and thus on the border of presentation*.[96] The 'limit' is where the new crosses the horizon, where '*everything* comes to pass'.[97] Shakespeare's lines draw our eyes to the play's outer limits along which the transformed Hamlet passes into existence as an alien singularity. The new Hamlet may become 'here' in the graveyard but the process of his arrival involves an at times confounding crossing over from formlessness to form. Both dramatically and metaphysically, then, the 'spiritually other and ultimate' only becomes '*immanent in events*' by touching upon the 'beyond'[98] – or void – of the voyage.

To help express this difficult oscillation between here and beyond, it is worth returning briefly to Badiou's understanding of how the event and the void interrelate. Although the 'evental site' is 'presented in the situation' (here through Hamlet's account of the vanished voyage), '"beneath" it nothing from which it is composed is presented'.[99] What 'compose[s]' the evental site is the void: the situation's invisible, and thus unknown, suture to the infinite multiplicity of being. Providence, for Hamlet, is the situation's void: the invisible truth that structures the situation (albeit a notoriously obscure truth). In Badiou's terms, then, Hamlet's pivotal moment of recognition – in which he embraces the material present – draws its energy and impetus from outside the dramatic frame. As we saw with Othello's voyage through the 'high-wrought flood', the movement to and from the void both un-grounds the subject – taking it from its old situation and mode of being – and re-grounds it in relation to the event. The idea of the void is critical because it complicates the standard historicist creed 'that nothing comes of nothing, even in Shakespeare'.[100] A similar attitude, albeit in a very different form, underpins Eliot's 'objective correlative', which requires 'a set of objects, a situation, a chain of events' to serve as 'the formula of [a] *particular* emotion'.[101] Hamlet is defective for Eliot because he is 'dominated by an emotion which is inexpressible, because it is in excess of the facts as they appear'.[102] For Badiou, however, the event is always in excess of the facts, for it enters from the void, which is 'outside situations, unpresentable' and 'in excess of being as a thinkable disposition'.[103] The new thus always comes from 'nothing'; it is unsourced and without correlative. And its coming is explosive: 'the void, once named "in situation" . . . proceeds "explosively", or "everywhere", within [it].'[104]

The void's explosiveness helps articulate how Hamlet's voyage not only goes beyond the 'situation' but returns to transform it. Hamlet moves outside presentation into what 'is not' and yet what 'is not' returns to the situation, after the fact, as Hamlet re-enters 'a farre off'.[105] Moreover, he returns with a changed relation to the void. Hamlet no longer seeks unity with the ghost's restrictive command but assumes its spectral excess by embracing the ungraspable 'divinity that shapes our ends' (V.ii.10). Hamlet, the symbol of independent self-consciousness, like Othello, the figure of self-contained heroism, arrives belatedly as an active subject by being opened to what happens. He now shares with others, with the dramaturgy, and with unseen providence. The way the void explodes everywhere like shrapnel – through clowns and skulls and pirates and dust and limits and providence – suggests that the ghost's spectral excess is not 'snuff[ed] out'[106] in the graveyard but streams into a new spectral Hamlet.

'The Readiness Is All'

The voyage, like the ghost, emerges from the unseen, upsets time, exposes the gap between act and representation, and strikes Hamlet with a transformative wonder. Both events are – dramatically – creative of Hamlet's 'consciousness'. There is, however, a critical difference in the play's second coming of the void. Whereas the ghost's creative force flowed into Hamlet's debilitating preoccupation with the void itself, with the unknown consequences of action, Hamlet's 'readiness' connects the void's explosive excess to the material – to the ground – and unleashes the bloody action of the play's finale. To grasp this movement, it is vital to distinguish this readiness from the rashness that precedes it. Despite its prominence, rashness is not Hamlet's ultimate mode of being in the final scene. They are two distinct stages of Hamlet's (re)arrival: its origin in the rashness that lies beyond and its inscription in the world through readiness. Readiness both distances the void, placing it outside the subject and within the province of providence, and accepts that it is integral to the subject's action.

Put otherwise, the event and its attendant action were not fully realised at the time. Hamlet's rashness was not 'divinity' or 'providence' when it happened; it was just rashness. It is only in retrospect, on second glance, that there is a 'divinity that shapes our ends'. The initial event of coming up from his cabin and swapping the commissions is only 'retroactively ground[ed]'[107] as genuine action in Hamlet's subsequent reflection. What was not strictly subjective action, but came from the outside as divine rashness, is *recuperated* as action after the fact – as readiness. As Benjamin puts it, '[t]o articulate the past … does not mean to recognize it "the way it really was"' but to 'seize hold of a memory as it flashes up at a moment of danger'.[108] Like Othello's disorientating arrival in Cyprus, Hamlet's midline shift to recognise providence thus bends dramatic time. It suggests Agamben's understanding of Paul's 'messianic time' as 'introduc[ing] a remnant, a zone of undecidability, in which the past is dislocated into the present and the present is extended into the past'.[109] Hamlet's regard wavers in a 'zone of undecidability', fluctuating between the pre-voyage Hamlet, the Hamlet experiencing rashness, the present Hamlet reconstituting rashness as providence, and the unseen Hamlet who will fulfil providence through readiness. We again see that dramatic immanence is not reducible to presence. Indeed, much of our attention is future orientated.[110]

Not that Hamlet's movement to readiness is easy or unqualified. The rapid and gratuitous death sentence meted out to Rosencrantz and Guildenstern lies at the birth of this new Hamlet, where his evasive justifications make conscience begin to look a little like bad conscience: 'Why, man, they did make love to this employment. / They are not near my conscience' (V.ii.58–59). We are left to wonder how this first, dubious, invocation of conscience or, indeed, the absence of conscience, infects his second conscience nine lines later:

> Does it not, think'st thee, stand me now upon –
> He that hath killed my king and whored my mother,
> Popped in between th'election and my hopes,
> Thrown out his angle for my proper life,
> And with such coz'nage – is't not perfect conscience
> To quit him with this arm? And is't not to be damned
> To let this canker of our nature come
> In further evil? (V.ii.64–71)

Despite the troubling connection, it is possible to differentiate Hamlet's second conscience. The first conscience retrospectively (and perhaps a little guiltily) excuses the deadly act of rashness. The second conscience establishes an ongoing readiness that invokes conscience positively rather than evades it. Rashness, then, is the unthinking, unknowable 'beyond conscience'. Readiness is the mediated and attached 'active conscience'. Readiness does not condemn Laertes as rashness did Rosencrantz and Guildenstern. Moreover, Hamlet does not, in fact, pursue any definite plan to 'quit [Claudius] with this arm'. Hamlet does not dole out further death sentences but *waits in readiness*, suggesting that Hamlet paradoxically achieves agency – an active conscience – by submitting to providence. Most famously, he determines to enter the duel not with passionate rashness, or a plan to kill Claudius, but with a detached, philosophic objectivity:

> Not a whit. We defy augury. There's a special providence in the fall of a sparrow. If it be now, 'tis not to come. If it be not to come, it will be now. If it be not now, yet it will come. The readiness is all. (V.ii.157–60).

No longer demanding to know final consequences of action (in Act V there 'are no fantasies of poetic omnipotence'[111] such as demanding to damn Claudius), Hamlet is now committed to accepting each fight as it comes.

Critics have not necessarily agreed. Belsey, for instance, contends that Act V 'presents a second Hamlet who no longer struggles towards identity and agency'.[112] Belsey may be right that 'Hamlet utters no soliloquies'[113] in Act V, but he nonetheless continues to speak to himself within speeches that are ostensibly addressed to Horatio. Belsey thus oversimplifies when she writes, '[t]his Hamlet is an inhabitant of a much older cosmos, no more than the consenting instrument of God'.[114] Hamlet's newfound providentialism does not merely evoke some simplistic 'older cosmos' of divine law; it involves an understanding of the interconnectedness and diffusion of existence. In a sense, Hamlet now follows Shakespeare's dramaturgy rather than rebelling against it. Whereas Hamlet was trapped in a proto-existentialist 'prison' of the mind, in which the outside world reflected his own melancholy thoughts, 'readiness' implies Hamlet's subjectedness to both the divine rashness that precipitated it and the material circumstances he must act within. Hamlet's providence clears space for action by creating a space that is outside Hamlet.

Such subjectedness to providence recalls Kierkegaard's 'necessity'. Hamlet was floating adrift in the possible, but he has now found his 'spot' by 'submit [ting] to the necessary'.[115] It is the event, intruding from outside this groundless world, that *enables possibility* as a material fact. It grounds the previously groundless 'perchance'. Hamlet's providence mirrors, albeit more dramatically than religiously, Kierkegaard's central paradox: it is only through submission to the necessity of God that 'all things are possible'.[116] Far from being a retreat into dogmatic certainty, this strange sense of agency 'is fraught and provisional'.[117] As Eagleton elaborates, Kierkegaard's 'process of endless becoming' is more than 'aesthetic self-fashioning', not only because of its 'radical one-sidedness' but also because of 'its openness' to what is 'sheerly given'.[118] The subject's 'origin lies beyond its own mastery' and its 'end is nowhere in view'.[119] Abandonment to what is 'sheerly given' is not an abandonment of the 'struggles towards identity and agency' but their paradoxical, yet provisional, culmination.

Indeed, Fernie has shown that 'Hamlet's crucial transition from "To be, or not to be" (3.1.58) to "Let be"' ties into a 'rich history of indifference and letting-be . . . in the Western tradition'.[120] We saw in Chapter 3 how Paul posits a strength in weakness, whereby the subject reaches its apotheosis by submitting to grace. While for Luther, '*man must utterly despair of his own ability before he is prepared to receive the grace of Christ*'.[121] For the more sceptically minded Montaigne, the idea was translated not only into one's subjectedness to chance, custom and circumstance but also into the consequent recognition that wisdom necessitates acknowledging reason's weakness (and therefore submitting to ancient faith). Even Nietzsche reaches an analogous conclusion:

> [A] living thing can be healthy, strong and fruitful only when bounded by a horizon; if it is incapable of drawing a horizon around itself, and at the same time too self-centred to enclose its own view within that of another, it will pine away slowly or hasten to its timely end.[122]

In these terms, then, Hamlet's recognition of the bounding 'horizon' of providence (or necessity, or the event) is far from an unthinking embrace of fate. Hamlet's rashness may not be 'agency', but his move to readiness draws a new form of agency from that rashness: 'The interim's mine' (V.ii.74).[123] Indeed, readiness is a highly political mode of being despite its references to supra-historical notions of providence. It re-grounds the sublime voyage as action and flows into Hamlet's re-engagement with the public sphere in the duel.

The Future-to-Come

Waiting allows Hamlet to act and seize the 'interim', and yet, as much as it leads to agency, it still *waits*. Having voyaged into the unseen, Hamlet now trusts the unseen future. The result is that Hamlet's readiness not only stems from the beyond, it *flows into* the beyond. The ground again gives way. Marion's description of the painter's task illuminates what it means to arrive through the 'unseen':[124]

> He is trying to let burst onto the scene much more than what is pre-delineated [*prévu*], more than what is seen, more than what he desires or wills ... The authentic painting fulfils the expectation of the painter and the visitor, strictly speaking, by surprising it, disorientating it, and flooding it.[125]

The act of painting here is bizarrely non-situated. The painter must have glimpses of the painting to begin to paint, but what, precisely, will come remains to be seen. It requires a faith that something will come and that it will exceed expectation, that it will be more than just paint on a canvas. There is a similar faith in Hamlet, and in us for Hamlet: something will come and it will involve killing Claudius but it will also exceed expectation; it will be more than just blood on a floor. There is an artistic method, therefore, in Hamlet's readiness: he looks for the 'unseen' that will, 'up to the point of its final appearance', remain 'unforeseen'.[126]

Such waiting marks a fundamental break from previous revenge tragedy. After corrupted authority and extravagant violence dismantle the hero's place within the seemingly 'natural' order, revenge offers a means of wresting back some measure of control over this Machiavellian but also postlapsarian rottenness, of 'set[ting] it right'. Hieronimo, almost driven mad by the debased power structures that have rendered his old role unplayable, is able to script his revenge. Death may be the cost, but the revenge hero is the author of his own (and his enemies') end. Not so with Hamlet. He does not script his own end but 'let[s] it be' (V.ii.280).[127] He does not plot but blunders into his enemies' plots, foiling them through blind fate or luck. Hamlet kills Claudius but he hardly does so in revenge of his father, let alone in control. He is not the author of his own end but passes his voice over to others. Why? In part, at least, because of how Shakespeare orchestrates the 'invisible event' (Q2.IV.iv.49). The transformative voyage is beyond Hamlet's control. It does not bring order to the old situation but comes from beyond its borders. Almost a second coming of the ghost, transported to the seas, turning pirate against the revenge tradition, it opens Hamlet to something other than the old corrupted order.

What is this something other? We are never quite sure. It is both here and it isn't. One might call it a leap of faith: both Hamlet's faith in providence and ours in Hamlet. In his writing about poetry, Badiou addresses the difficulty of having faith in what is not quite present:

> If poetry is an essential use of language, it is not because it is able to devote the latter to Presence; on the contrary, it is because it trains language to the paradoxical function of maintaining that which – radically singular, pure action – would otherwise fall back into the nullity of place. Poetry is the stellar assumption of that pure undecidable, against a background of nothingness, that is an action of which one can only *know* whether it has taken place inasmuch as one *bets* upon its truth.[128]

Even if immanent, poetry does not bring about 'Presence'. The reason may be traced to the fundamentals of Badiou's event: as 'an un-founded multiple . . . the event can only be indicated beyond the situation, despite it being necessary to wager that it has manifested itself therein.'[129] The 'wager' is necessary because the poetic event is not simply 'here' or stably grounded. It can never be encapsulated or grasped, else it would not be poetry. Like Hamlet's transformational voyage, it is 'indicated beyond the situation'. It is simultaneously here, in the play's words, and beyond them, like an apparition, in meanings that are not simply accessible, in evocations and feelings that may or may not come. The aesthetic is ever ghostly.

For Badiou, it is this non-presence that enables poetry to escape the 'nullity of place' and become something 'radically singular'. The singularity here is multiple: it is Hamlet's dramatic (re)arrival, the event of the voyage, and our own experience of the two in the theatrical event. Similarly, the 'nullity of place' is both the automated customary role of revenger and the critical tendency to explain character by something that is 'already' there, whether it be material ground or groundless interiority. The 'stellar assumption of the pure undecidable' is thus opposed to the scholarly desire to '*know*': to draw character from its known 'place' in language or history or presupposed essence. Hamlet, certainly, does not come to clear-sighted knowledge in Act V. He does not see his end. Hamlet and we remain unsure of what has happened to him and where it will take him. Rather, his readiness is closer to Badiou idea of 'courage' as what 'effectuates the interruption of the dead law in favour of the excess'.[130] There is no knowledge or rule that determines the event, rather, 'one *bets* upon its truth'. Hamlet puts his faith in an unseen path. And just as Hamlet must 'bet' on readiness or providence, *we* must bet on Hamlet's obscure arrival. The play's last act thus triangulates the 'pure undecidable', which is at once Hamlet himself, forever eluding us, the unseen voyage in the past, and the event's unseen future.

We are now far from the events of *Romeo and Juliet* and *Othello*, whose trajectories materialise into fidelities and betrayals that are identifiable, and nameable, as 'love'. In *Hamlet* we are always in the event's undecidable midst. Shakespeare's drama therefore complicates Badiou's suggestion that '[d]espite being unknown', the 'generic parts' that arise from an event must be 'named'.[131] Hamlet attempts to name what has happened but always stops short: 'Had I but time ... O, I could tell you – / But let it be' (V.ii.278–80). Even as Hamlet is transformed by the event, this diffusion debars him from a nameable fidelity. The impossibility of pinning down what happens to Hamlet perhaps suggests that, within Shakespeare's drama at least, the event need not be pinpointed in such categorical terms but may spread out, incorporating multiple strands, temporalities, characters and modes of speech. In other words, the event in *Hamlet* is aesthetic. It is a skilful construction of poetry and scenic form that does not designate a 'truth' beyond itself. And yet, in another sense, it *is* a truth for us, the audience. In these terms, then, Hamlet's (re)arrival both is and is not a Badiouan event. It is, once more, undecidable. Here it is worth turning to Andrew Gibson's *Beckett and Badiou*,[132] which argues that unlike philosophy, poetry has a capacity to represent the event-as-such, a sort of meta-event without a specific 'truth' or content. Accordingly, 'art's relationship to the event is actually different from that of the other truth-domains. Art can always concern itself with … the event in its absolute form, the event of the event.'[133] Or, better yet, the event in free play. Such an artistic event remains obscure and ungrounded. For instance, Gibson writes that Mallarmé 'is concerned with the possibility or the conditions of the arrival of the event and, above all, with its undecidability'.[134] Perhaps, in these terms, we can see the voyage–graveyard nexus not as a distinct, nameable event but as a dramatisation of the *eventual*, of '*événmentialitié*'.[135]

The way *Hamlet*'s event refuses to pass into a nameable fidelity – the way its 'poetry' is 'poised on the edge of a truth-procedure, rather than engaged in one'[136] – opens the door to what Fernie calls the 'ecstatic, aspirational energy' of Derrida's messianic 'to come'.[137] For Fernie, however, 'justice' in *Hamlet* 'is *not* achieved by exposure to difference as in Derrida's prescription for it' but by 'Hamlet's engagement with the absolute'.[138] But we may wonder what is meant by the terms 'difference' and 'absolute'. For Fernie, 'difference' entails 'the system of differences (of individuality, of gender, of class) that constitutes social life' and which Hamlet was 'stuck in' before Act V.[139] Such difference is, in effect, Montaigne's infinite confusion of opinion. But Derrida offers a more nuanced concept of difference and its relationship to the absolute of justice. Derrida begins *Spectres of Marx* with the question of how '[t]o live otherwise' or 'more justly'.[140] The question of justice 'arrives' not through cultural differences but through a 'regard [of] what will come in the future-to-come'.[141]

If we co-opt Derrida's messianic 'to come' for a moment and place it within the process of 'arrivals', we can see that it is not entirely incongruent with Badiou's thought. For Derrida, the 'regard' for the future-to-come ruptures 'the self' and 'exceed[s] any presence'.[142] And this disjuncture fits easily enough with Badiou's eventual rupture. For there to be an active commitment (a 'there must be'), Derrida claims that one must first experience 'disjunction, interruption, the heterogeneous'.[143] The 'absolute' is not something simply here or present but opens from what is other, beyond, obscure or not-yet. As Levao writes of Nicholas of Cusa: '[the] transition from relative to absolute vision requires a vertiginous moment, a disorientating of the individual from the point of view he was initially asked to assume.'[144] Where Derrida differs sharply from Badiou is on the nature of this break. For Derrida, disjuncture occurs not through an event that has already happened but through openness to, and the thinking of, the 'future-to-come'. In this way, Derrida helps to articulate the invigorating way in which *Hamlet*'s second event remains unknowable and unclassifiable, a point that escapes Badiou's concept of 'nomination'. The subject's confrontation with the (unnamed) alien other is what energises its commitment (readiness). The exorbitant future-to-come therefore 'does not mean only (as some people have too often believed and so naively) deferral, lateness, delay, postponement', rather, in this 'irreducible differance the here-now unfurls'.[145] Openness to the future's otherness, or difference, may allow us to act now, in the interim. Or again: 'If it be not now, yet it will come. The readiness is all' (V.ii.159–60).

We might link this openness to Gibson's major problem with Badiou's event: that it is too clear. Badiou's event may be 'difficult insofar as it is rare and has a complex structure', but it is 'almost luminously clear, because it and its consequences alone matter or have weight'.[146] The '[e]vent and subject' can thus be 'isolated' from the 'world around them'.[147] Derrida helps point to what is less clear in Hamlet's (re)arrival: how although 'divinity' enters the material, the fifth act is also filled with the feeling of imminence. Arising in response to the voyage's mysterious 'otherness', Hamlet's readiness is also directed to an obscure what-is-to-come: providence. If this is an apprehension of truth, it is an almost intuitive apprehension without clear content, a faith without nameable fidelity, a trust in what it cannot yet see. It is an unknown trajectory. We might link Derrida's openness to Gibson's idea, referencing Heidegger, that 'the modern poet is "the guardian of the Open"; that is, he or she is a custodian, not of a truth or truths, but of the conditions which make it possible for a truth to appear'.[148] In this sense, the modern poet is (*pace* Badiou) the poet of an event that does not quite come: the 'poet ... watches out for and awaits the event when it seems recalcitrant or unforthcoming'.[149] Art can thus get itself into a position of the pre-event and thereby create a fragile sense of evental imminence as well as immanence: of immanence-to-come.

The need for a pre-evental 'openness' is one of Gibson's key ideas. He argues that a Kantian or Proustian 'concept of sensibility' – 'an openness to affect, a power of being affected' – is needed 'to fill out Badiou's theory of the event and subjectification'.[150] For Gibson, the '"suddenness" of the encounter' simply cannot 'be imagined other than as involving some kind of openness to an exteriority, and therefore receptivity'.[151] Whatever the case with Beckett, this does not seem true for Shakespeare. We've seen with Othello and Romeo how a violent rupture or break may open what was not already open or receptive. Of course, once the event has occurred, one can retrospectively posit *some* sort of openness, but this hardly seems to be a 'sensibility'. If anything, Othello's sensibility is to closure not openness. Shakespeare's arrivals are more sudden, unconditioned and unjustified than Gibson envisages, for Shakespeare's lightning does not always take the path of (receptive) least resistance. In short, Gibson's receptivity is too *structural* for Shakespeare. What Gibson does help with, however, is the peculiar case of *Hamlet*'s last act, in which the event remains obscure and incomplete. Here we must indeed 'wait'. And here, in Hamlet's readiness, there is indeed a sense of 'openness to supplementation'.[152]

As a theatrical event that stages an unprecedented coming together of evental immanence and messianic promise, *Hamlet* therefore suggests a rare point of mutual augmentation between the widely different philosophies of Badiou and Derrida. *Hamlet* can bring them together because it blurs the gap between before and after. This is important because what Derrida writes of the *before* of an event – of waiting for justice that is to come – reflects what Badiou writes of the *aftermath* of the event and the subject's never-complete construction of its truth. For Badiou, the subject only '*approximat[es] truth*', which is to say 'locally discerns the connections and disconnections between . . . the situation and the name of the event'.[153] Because the subject is 'local', whereas the truth – the void – is 'global' and 'un-presented', the truth-event's full realisation is always to come, or indeed transcendent: 'Here, belief is what-is-to-come, or the future, under the *name* of truth.'[154] But in *Hamlet* the event is both past and to come. The event has both happened on the voyage and we wait for it in 'readiness'. The play's last act creates a messianic 'zone of undecidability'[155] that dislocates the before and after, and thereby blurs the distinction between Derrida's pre-evental and Badiou's post-evental 'to come'. Indeed, the play's finale seems to be at once an advent and a pointer to messianic justice.

The Messianic and Justice

Although Hamlet is caught, ensnared, killed, forced into an action that takes everyone else down with him, and thus completes a cycle of vengeance, many have also felt a contradictory and unlocatable rush of hope and justice.[156] The play's finale hints at a justice to come. Where can this be found amidst the slaughter? It must be on the edges and in the cracks. There is a strange moment before their duel in which Laertes accepts Hamlet's apology and peace offering in 'nature' but 'stands aloof' in 'honour', which offers no precedent that allows him to save face: he will allow 'no reconcilement / Till some elder masters of known honour / [he has] a voice and precedent of peace / To keep [his] name ungored' (V.ii.181–89). Here we see what Hamlet has in part escaped and what Laertes remains caught within: the 'law' of the father, the 'commandment', the 'elder masters', the automated desire of the other that directs one's action. What perhaps offers some hope, some sense of another kind of justice, is the way their later exchange of forgiveness provides a new 'precedent' that points beyond the overarching cycle of violence: 'All courage amounts to passing through there where previously it was not visible that anyone could find a passage.'[157] The new path is opened too late to save Hamlet but, like Badiou's truth or Derrida's justice, awaits the future.

The sense of justice somehow survives the bloody mess of the finale and even the somewhat farcical nature of Hamlet's apology to Laertes, in which he absolves himself by 'proclaim[ing] [it] was madness' and '[n]ever Hamlet' that 'wronged Laertes' (V.ii.169–70). It is as if, within the existing frameworks of familial violence and revenge tragedy, there is no room to think justice. It perhaps connects to Heffernan's broader point about 'the unredeemable closure of the Elizabethan political world', which 'lacked historical precedents that could count as true political events'.[158] In *Hamlet*, justice is not within, but outside, the situation. Hence why it only slips through the cracks, why we see only glimpses of another order. Justice is sustained not by the plot but by traces of the void, which trail from the voyage and filter through the last act. Rather than simple 'causal connection' and narrative progression, we have a present that 'is shot through with chips of Messianic time'.[159]

Following Whitehead's idea of a 'stream of influence',[160] we need not dismiss these chips of justice as mere fantasies, hovering in the ether, but can see them as part of Hamlet's diffused existence. Just as Hamlet's (re)arrival was staged through a layering of dramatic codes, his death incorporates a layering of divergent images and strands that produces an excess over what he says or does:

> Hamlet dies, as Benjamin notes, contingently – 'as the fateful stage-properties gather around him, as around their lord and master'. He is referring to those images of poisoned honor, sexuality, and stagecraft – the poisoned sword and chalice, this last enhanced with a 'union' or pearl that . . . seems to symbolize both death and sex. But he is also pictured by Horatio, after all this darkness, as a soul ascending to heaven with an angelic squadron leading him on. In short, in the event-packed concluding moments of Hamlet, there is a careful balance between a motif of continuing emptiness and another, contradictory one of redemption and even triumph.[161]

It is the excess produced by this clustering of the here-now and future-to-come that is able to sustain the contradictory ideas of revenge and forgiveness, hope and waste, accident and redemption that filter through Hamlet's farewell. Even here, at the end, the to come is envisaged by Horatio's winged flight. Rather than being absolute or essential, we have flecks of justice and Hamlet. Arrivals are not final but are dramatic moments of confluence that easily dissipate. Before they do, however, the diffused images create an excess that, in Benjamin's words, 'points, before its extinction, to the Christian providence in whose bosom his mournful images are transformed into a blessed existence'.[162] There is, then, something unique in *Hamlet*: 'Only Shakespeare was capable of striking Christian sparks from the baroque rigidity of the melancholic, un-stoic as it is un-Christian, pseudo-antique as it is pseudo-pietistic.'[163]

We are able, then, to give Derrida's messianic future some ballast in the present. Justice in *Hamlet* is not purely to come. It is never fully here, never present, and yet it exists. Latour's 'positive [understanding] of relativism', which 'define[s] existence not as an all-or-nothing concept but as a gradient',[164] helps us understand how the fifth act forces us into both the present moment of action and a feeling of the beyond. The idea of 'relative existence'[165] frees up justice, allowing it to exist like a ghost, both here and not here, its presence spectral but real. As Derrida writes, 'the logic of the ghost . . . points towards a thinking of the event that necessarily exceeds a binary . . . logic that distinguishes or opposes *effectivity or actuality* (either present, empirical, living – or not) and *ideality* (regulating or absolute nonpresence).'[166] The ghost is not 'snuff[ed] out' but comes to exist as a spectral Hamlet and a spectral justice. Here Badiou's own writing on justice connects with Derrida's: '*Justice* . . . amounts to relativizing the law', a '*blurring of the places*, the opposite, therefore, of the right place'.[167] The 'blurring' suggests the importance of registering the diffusion and obscurity of Hamlet's (re)arrival, of not treating Hamlet as purely present or grounded in the graveyard.

Ultimately, of course, the messianic hints of justice occur amidst the ruin of Hamlet and the Danish state: 'In the ruins of great buildings the idea of the plan speaks more impressively than in lesser buildings, however well preserved they are.'[168] *Hamlet*'s finale is almost a becoming-ruin of its hero. He becomes our object, handed over to our possession. He becomes *our* subject. From the point that Laertes tells him, 'Hamlet, thou art slain' (V.ii.256), he, like Romeo and Juliet, becomes dead whilst alive, the walking dead, no longer an agent but a (ruined) monument for us. Hamlet himself declares this transition as he passes his agency to Horatio:

> I am dead, Horatio. Wretched Queen, adieu!
> You that look pale and tremble at this chance,
> That are but mutes or audience to this act,
> Had I but time – as this fell sergeant Death

Is strict in his arrest – O, I could tell you –
But let it be. Horatio, I am dead,
Thou liv'st. Report me and my cause aright
To the unsatisfied.   (V.ii.275–82)

Hamlet here passes over to the survivors. He passes over to Horatio, who has always been Hamlet's audience, been our onstage representative, but he most of all passes over to us, who 'liv'st'. In an almost direct address to the audience – 'You that look pale and tremble at this chance' – Hamlet makes us part of the play. He hands over his energies and voice so that *we* must speak of what he 'could tell' us. Action thus becomes ours in the present. Through this shift of agency, Hamlet stops being *the* subject, or actor, and lies silent: 'The rest is silence' (V.ii.300). All we are left with are the voices of survivors and the dying 'Os' of a voice that will speak no more words. As Frank Kermode notes of *King Lear*'s catastrophe: although 'tragedy assumes the figurations of apocalypse, of death and judgment, heaven and hell . . . the world goes forward in the hands of exhausted survivors'.[169] And so, 'when the end comes it is not an end'.[170]

It is here, as agency passes over, that ruin and bloodshed begin to give way to something else. As Benjamin stresses, it is precisely at the point of death and destruction that the 'allegory of . . . baroque' drama 'returns', in 'the second part of its wide arc . . . to redeem'.[171] The vision of death 'does not faithfully rest in the contemplation of bones, but faithlessly leaps forward to the idea of resurrection'.[172] It leaps, in *Hamlet*, through the voices of those to whom Hamlet passes his voice. Laertes asks 'noble Hamlet' to '[e]xchange forgiveness' (V.ii.271). Horatio, the play's spectator, declares that here 'cracks a noble heart' and wishes that 'flights of angels sing [him] to [his] rest' (V.ii.302–3). And Fortinbras, who has Hamlet's 'dying voice' (V.ii.298), orders 'four captains' to 'Bear Hamlet like a soldier to the stage, / For he was likely, had he been put on, / To have proved most royal' (V.ii.339–42). These voices begin our speculation about what was 'likely' for, and of, Hamlet. In doing so, they build a monument of hope and expectation for Hamlet, setting him up for his afterlife, which continues in these words. Beginning with Fortinbras's speculative 'had he . . . ', they build an alternative vision of Hamlet and an alternative end that exists in parallel to, and is intermingled with, the bloody end we see. The speculations and hopes of the survivors thereby reflect Žižek's point:

> the past itself is not simply 'what there was,' it contains hidden, non-realized potentials, and the authentic future is the repetition/retrieval of *this* past, not of the past as it was, but of those elements in the past which the past itself, in its reality, betrayed, stifled, failed to realize.[173]

Hamlet is again more than his own words and deeds. The subject that arrives is broader than any individual but flows into the theatrical event and its spectators. Death is, therefore, not the end of Shakespeare's tragedy. Action and the subject pass over. Some of the play's action is not recuperated as action but remains to be grasped by us, to be collected in the future. There is a sense in which we are always left waiting for the 'event' in *Hamlet*: 'The spirit of man has broken with the old order of things' but, as Hegel writes of the moment before the dawn, the new arrival is but yet an 'undefined foreboding of something unknown'.[174] That which will break apart the old corrupt order and found the new never quite arrives. At the same time, however, it is disseminated throughout the play. Our faith in Hamlet is disappointed and yet somehow bolstered in the failure, transferred to the future. This latency suggests that while something is deferred, it is also present as a potential that lies in wait – if we are ready.

CHAPTER 5

Macbeth: *The Arrival of Evil*

We saw with *Othello* how the event's indistinct, unseen quality places it in the borderlands between wonder and terror. The same is true of *Macbeth*, only now the obscurity of the event tips far more quickly, and completely, into the realm of horror. For much of the play we are dealing with the event's ghastly afterlife. What arrives is dead, stillborn. Nevertheless, unlike almost every other character, Macbeth *does* arrive and he does so through his rapturous, even wondrous, embrace of the dark and mysterious realm opened by the weird sisters. Something more than historical narrative is going on, something that makes normative readings about ambition or usurpation inadequate to our imaginative responses. They are true as far as they go, but they do not go as far as the weird sisters who, from the very start, puncture the circularity of Holinshed's Scotland.

'Thunder and lightning' – The Weird Sisters

The play opens with the strange and unnatural. '*Thunder and lightning*' cues the entrance of three mysterious figures who chant and rhyme, their purposes unknown, except that they go to 'meet with Macbeth' (I.ii.7). We are not within 'history', or at least not merely within history. In Holinshed's *Chronicles*, Makbeth's tale begins not with supernatural happenings but political intrigue. Under threat from Makdowald, Duncane calls on his nobles for advice due to his 'small skill in warlike affaires'.[1] Makbeth, after 'speaking much against the kings softnes', declares that 'if the charge were committed vnto him and vnto Banquho' then 'the rebels should be shortly vanquished'.[2] The weird sisters are only a secondary and subsidiary concern, an interlude in the serious business. Although 'thrée women in strange and wild apparel' do meet Makbeth and Banquho as they 'iournied towards Fores', and 'haile Makbeth' as 'Glammis', 'Cawder', then 'king of Scotland',[3] that is the end of their influence. They make no further incursions into the tale, they do not infect its language or alter its structure, and they do not infect Makbeth's mind. In fact, Makbeth appears to take them lightly:

> This was reputed at the first but some vaine fantasticall illusion by Mackbeth and Banquho, insomuch that Banquho would call Mackbeth in iest, king of Scotland; and Mackbeth againe would call him in sport likewise, the father of manie kings. But afterwards the common opinion was, that these women were either the weird sisters, that is (as ye would say) the goddesses of destinie, or else some nymphs or feiries, indued with knowledge of prophesie.[4]

Although Shakespeare's representation of Scotland's upheavals recalls Holinshed's form of narrative, his representation of the weird sisters – now irruptive and darkly influential – is altogether different. By recalibrating the relation between the weird sisters, Macbeth, and the historical narrative, Shakespeare establishes two distinct worlds in the play: the historical world of Holinshed and the mysterious, excessive world of dark conjurings. The worlds overlap, but they do so marginally and weirdly. In terms of character, they overlap almost solely in Macbeth.

The atmospherics of *Macbeth*'s supernatural opening are therefore very different from *Hamlet*'s founding spectral intrusion. In *Hamlet*, the characters onstage register the ghost's intrusion. It is upsetting things, putting them out of joint. Dread and confusion grip the watchers on the walls. In *Macbeth*, there is nobody there to upset. Whereas *Hamlet* and *Othello* 'open with conversations which lead into the action', in *Macbeth* 'the action bursts into wild life amidst the sounds of a thunderstorm and the echoes of a distant battle'.[5] Unlike *Hamlet*'s ghost, which disturbs a world that is in some sense already there, the weird sisters *precede* and almost direct our experience of this historical world. They set the time and place for our meeting of Macbeth:

FIRST WITCH	When shall we three meet again?
	In thunder, lightning, or in rain?
SECOND WITCH	When the hurly-burly's done,
	When the battle's lost and won.
THIRD WITCH	That will be ere the set of sun.
FIRST WITCH	Where the place?
SECOND WITCH	Upon the heath.
THIRD WITCH	There to meet with Macbeth.

(I.i.1–7)

Macbeth is the object, the target, of their weirdness and conjuring. They *name* him, which has its own peculiar power. They are without identifiable history, but they are somehow entering the historical realm, altering it, and calling Macbeth out of this world in almost comic language. The 'comic', here, is language's excessive and shifting quality. It does not stay where it should but breaks the rules and inverts things. Their almost childlike rhyme, playful word choice ('hurly-burly'), reference to legendary tales ('Grimalkin' the Scottish faery cat) and characteristic inversions ('[f]air is foul, and foul is fair') speak to a sort of superabundant playfulness (I.i.8–11). Describing the weird sisters as 'the heroines of the piece', Eagleton writes that '[t]heir riddling, ambiguous speech . . . promises to subvert' the existing hierarchal 'structure' and reveal 'the pious self-deception of a society based on routine oppression and incessant warfare'.[6] Their origin-less, over-spilling quality not only defies teleology; it relates to the historical world of Duncan's Scotland in a manner that recalls Badiou's *'eventalsite'*: while the 'site, itself, is presented', '"beneath" it nothing from which it is composed is presented' in the situation.[7] The event is, as ever, *'on the edge of the void'*.[8] Although the weird sisters are presented to the audience, with the exception of Macbeth (I distinguish Banquo later), they are not presented to those *within* the old situation. They, like Hamlet's voyage, exist on the borders of the play-world; they come from an unknown dimension. We cannot see 'beneath' them. We cannot discern their origins or desires.

'What bloody man is that?' – The Situation

The historical world, from which the weird sisters conjure, is established in the second scene. Whereas in *Hamlet* the pre-evental, unconscious unity of the situation is immediately thrown 'out of joint' by the ghost and is thus only retrospectively glimpsed in Hamlet's shattered 'glass of fashion and . . . mould of form' (III.i.152), in *Macbeth* this unconscious unity is pressed alongside the evental as a sort of competing reality. Indeed, their weirdness dissolves with the martial 'Alarum' (I.ii) that cues our entrance into Duncan's starkly different realm. The spectral vanishes and Duncan's feudal Scotland is established as the world from which Macbeth will be conjured by the weird sisters, as well as the historical world from which Shakespeare conjures *Macbeth*. Duncan's world is thus a sort of pre-history or canvas for conjured arrivals. In Badiou's terms, the implacable surface of Duncan's world is the 'situation' that will be ruptured when Macbeth is seized by the 'void' and thereby 'produces' an explosive 'irruption of inconsistency'.[9]

The King and his followers have not seen the weird sisters but are embroiled in a bloody upheaval. The first line of this world's more utilitarian dialogue has the King asking, 'What bloody man is that?' (I.ii.1). Soon we hear of the battle in which Macbeth turns the tide by 'unseam[ing]' the rebel Macdonald 'from the nave to th' chops' (I.ii.22). There is a gleeful barbarism to the Captain's account and to the reaction of the King, who praises Macbeth as his 'valiant cousin' and 'worthy gentleman' (I.ii.24) for this unseaming. It is all far more grotesque and explicit than the weird sisters' opening. And it has its own gory economy: through his bloody deeds 'noble Macbeth hath won' what Cawdor 'hath lost' (I.ii.66). The end result of this economy is, of course, the unseaming of Macbeth's head from his shoulders. Roles and fortunes will be reversed in this realm of cyclical violence and undifferentiated subjects. Duncan's 'What bloody man is that?' thus takes on a deeper meaning, suggesting that singularity is precluded by the general slaughter. Duncan's world here resembles the cyclical instability of Holinshed's *Chronicles*, in which Scotland veers between destruction and renewal. The cycle also defines Holinshed's rulers themselves, making individuals indistinct. Like Cawdor, who, without explanation, moves from commanding the King's 'absolute trust' (I.iv.14) to being 'that most disloyal traitor' (I.ii.52),[10] Holinshed's cast of rulers undergoes sudden and inexplicable changes between seemingly absolute states. The individual subject seems inseparable from the broader oscillation between crisis and restoration. So, for instance, King 'Culenes reigne, begun with righteous execution of iustice' but then, 'shortlie after', he ends up 'loosing the rains of lasciuious wantonnesse' and governing with 'negligence'.[11] While King 'Grime', 'at length of a chast & liberall prince, long slouth and increase of riches, became a most couetous ty[. . .]ant'.[12]

Amidst the perpetual upheaval, nothing new emerges in Holinshed. There is only a tidal movement of blood, now more and now less. Such a perpetual crisis recalls Benjamin's idea that in the 'tradition of the oppressed … the "state of emergency" in which we live is not the exception but the rule'.[13] In other words, the military tumult that begins *Macbeth* and mirrors Holinshed is not a genuine 'emergency' but expresses this world's underlying structure. We get a hint of this structure when the Captain describes the '[d]oubtful' outcome of the battle through the metaphor of 'two spent swimmers that do cling together / And choke their art' (I.ii.7–9). As Harry Berger Jr shows, the metaphoric 'clinging together' of authority and rebellion 'produces a dysfunctional solidarity'.[14] It is the weird sisters, then, that follow Benjamin's 'task' of 'bring[ing] about a real state of emergency',[15] as opposed to this entrenched quasi-emergency. They interrupt the cyclical model of history, which is soon overrun by Macbeth's presence and vitality. We almost have a dramatisation of Nietzsche's belief that we do not 'need history' for 'knowledge' but 'for the sake of life and action'.[16] The weird sisters turn dead history into something living: into dramatic history. It is only the weirdness of the disembodied or not fully embodied – 'The earth hath bubbles', Banquo tells us, 'And these are of them' (I.iii.77–78) – that can get under the skin of this corpse-ridden feudal merry-go-round and engender the divisions and imaginings of a subject.

The serene surface of Duncan's subject-less world is established by the unproblematic unity of words and events. There is no gap between act and representation, which, as we saw in *Hamlet,* is the space for consciousness. The seemingly straightforward ability to name events is evident as the Captain reports his 'knowledge of the broil' (I.ii.6): for a moment, 'fortune' smiles on its 'damnèd quarry' (I.ii.14) Macdonald, but 'justice' (I.ii.29) promptly destroys him. Justice comes in the form of Macbeth who is justly rewarded. Not only are events capable of simple narration, they are also susceptible to clear judgement. 'Justice' is here a motionless absolute that sublates everything local, vaporising all difference and singularity. Soon 'noble Macbeth' (I.ii.66) will be unseaming enemies not for justice but for evil, and so 'justice' and 'rebel' become hollowed-out, static concepts. Within the language of the situation – that of Duncan, Malcolm and Macduff – these terms are overlaid on all circumstances, so that Macbeth can replace Macdonald, and Macduff Macbeth, without any change in language or structure. But this language of measurement and nominality is, like Romeo's oaths, utterly inadequate to our experience of the poetic event. Macbeth's arrival is simply not expressible in Duncan's proper names or instrumental political language, which remain untouched by the play's convulsions.

Indeed, Duncan's language cocoons him from the scandalous intrusion of evil. He seems hermetically sealed, without the physicality or puns that are the usual lifeblood of Shakespearean speech. Everything exists in report for Duncan. He alternates between questioning others about events, 'Dismayed not this our captains, Macbeth and Banquo?' (I.ii.34), and dealing out praise and courtesies, 'O valiant cousin, worthy gentleman!' (I.ii.24). Duncan's almost content-less language does not touch the physical world or connect images to the material, or does so only ironically and unintentionally: 'I have begun to plant thee, and will labour / To make thee full of growing' (I.iv.28–29). Sealed from the vital and irruptive, the only value expressed by Duncan's language is formal courtesy: 'O worthiest cousin, / The sin of my ingratitude even now / Was heavy on me!' (I.iv.14–16).

Whereas the 'situation' attempts to make everything nameable and presentable, the weird sisters' riddling play suggests Badiou's 'theorem of the point of excess': 'it is formally impossible, whatever the situation be, for *everything* which is included (every subset) to belong to the situation.'[17] Such belonging is, of course, precisely what Duncan's sealed language seeks to establish: an eternal state – this 'justice' – with nothing outside it. It recalls Badiou's idea that 'the State pursues ... the one-effect beyond the terms which belong to the situation'.[18] In other words, 'the State' attempts to expand its 'mastery' to *all* multiples and thereby to shut down all 'inconsistency' and excess: 'It is not for nothing that governments, when an emblem of their void wanders about – generally, an inconsistent or rioting crowd – prohibit "gatherings of more than three people", which is to say they explicitly declare their non-tolerance of the one of such "parts."'[19]

Duncan's closed language seeks to shut out the void. Any 'one' existing outside its official count is labelled a rebel, traitor or villain. With the only possibilities being complete belonging to the established order or complete chaos, Duncan's Scotland recalls Holinshed's oscillation between destructive vice and restorative virtue. There is no movement between the situation and its void, no subjectivity or politics. There is no revolutionary moment in the endless crisis but only evil rebellion, which is fated to annihilation. The speeches condemning the 'damnèd' 'rebel' (I.ii.9–14) Macdonald thus foreshadow how Macbeth will be viewed within this situation: 'this dread butcher and his fiend-like queen' (V.xi.35). The result is the odd situation in which the 'good' characters are detached from our dramatic experience. 'Clearly', as Berger puts it, 'the Macbeth *we* see from 1.3 on is very different from the Macbeth *they* see.'[20] With the exception of Lady Macbeth, who is twinned with Macbeth, most of the play's other characters are half-asleep, awash in the flow of narrated action but fundamentally removed from the dramatic present. Shut away in their linguistic completeness, they lie outside the metaphoric excess of the play's imaginative conjurings. They form only the base register of the play, from which Macbeth soon bursts into life. In this sense, it is Macduff and the forces of Duncan's cyclical Scotland, rather than the weird sisters, that play the role of 'fate'. Theirs is the situation that will be reinstituted at the play's end.

'I have almost slipped the hour' – Macduff's Non-Arrival

The strangely undramatic nature of the 'good' characters is exemplified by Macbeth's nemesis, Macduff. The play, like the Porter, defers opening the door to Macduff and instead allows its own hellish imaginings to run wild. Palfrey and Stern explain how the Macduff role is structured upon a 'curious belatedness':

[T]he play is almost half over by the time Macduff speaks his first words; he arrives after the most dilated 'entrance cue' in all of Shakespeare, with his 'knocking' first interrupting the Macbeths' guilty terror, and then sustained throughout the Porter's long soliloquy; Macduff's purpose upon arriving is to waken Duncan, but of course Duncan is already dead.[21]

Macduff may be the figure of historical and narrative progression that ends Macbeth's imaginings and restores the episodic world of I.ii, but, working almost as Macbeth's surrogate, the Porter's dark imaginings keep this progress at bay. Macduff's ironic reference to his already failed task of waking Duncan – 'He did command me to call timely on him. / I have almost slipped the hour' (II.iii.45–46) – becomes 'the calling card of the part'.[22] Macduff is pushed off time and out of key. He is never *with* the play's dramatic moment. He is always too late for something, trying to catch up with what has already happened.

Even when he acts with forthright passion after discovering Duncan's murder, crying 'O horror, horror, horror!' (II.iii.62), it only seems to confirm Macduff's non-presence. He is again too late. His 'horror' is too late for us, who have already sat through an entire scene (II.ii) dedicated to the murder's horror. For us, it has been registered by Macbeth's ghastly visions and voices. The declarative style of Macduff's wordy '[c]onfusion now hath made his masterpiece' (II.iii.65) does not stand up to the spooky invasiveness that precedes it but is more comparable to Macbeth's feigned grief: 'There's nothing serious in mortality' (II.iii.92). After Macbeth's trance-like account of his inability to 'say Amen' (II.ii.26), it seems withdrawn or journalistic. It never quite hits Macduff as a subject. Macduff, in other words, never quite arrives. He is shocked by events, but there is no psychic tumult or transformation. That is not to say we condemn him, or even dislike him; rather, he and his sufferings happen in the half-light that characterised Duncan's world. They are not gripping in the manner of Macbeth's haunted interiority. They are not, in the end, what the play is about.

Macduff's chief involvement comes directly after Macbeth settles upon 'giv[ing] to th'edge o'th' sword / His wife, his babes' (IV.i.167–68). As sympathy for Macbeth is drowned by the rising tide of cruelty, it seems fitting that our attachments should shift to the good and patriotic Macduff. But Shakespeare does not allow it. He forestalls our investment in Macduff, treating him somewhat brutally. Macduff's call to 'Hold fast the mortal sword' (IV.iii.4) may be defiant and notionally inspiring, but it is undercut by the bitter irony of his talk about 'widows' and 'orphans' (IV.iii.5). Macduff was not there with 'mortal sword' to defend his wife and child. While their murders also occur in Holinshed, Shakespeare makes a critical change in not giving Macduff *knowledge* of them when he speaks to Malcolm. It allows Shakespeare to exploit his actor, who shares the character's helplessness: '"Macduff" knows nothing, his actor knows it all: but neither of them can *do* anything.'[23] An undermining of Macduff's heroism is thus inscribed in the part.

Macbeth may be cut off from every other character, but Macduff is cut off from us. He never knows what we know or feels what we feel. The embarrassment of both actor and audience builds as Malcolm torturously asks, 'Why in that rawness left you wife and child[?]' (IV.iii.27), a question to which Macduff is permitted no response. For more than 200 lines the news of his family's slaughter is withheld, and cannot be acted. Even when Ross enters, bearing the news, Macduff is not given a straight answer for forty-five lines. First Ross tells him that his family are 'well at peace' (IV.iii.180), true only in the most evasive religious sense. And then, even when Macduff commands Ross 'If it be mine, / Keep it not from me; quickly let me have it' (IV.iii.200–201), Ross delays further. Shakespeare never lets him fully 'have it' and never lets us, or his actor, fully have him. Nothing is given to Macduff straight, so, in his longest scene, he ends up despairing over the wrong things (Malcolm's 'voluptuousness' (IV.iii.62) and 'avarice' (IV.iii.79)) and not despairing over the right things (his murdered family). Macduff may belatedly catch up with the dramatic moment as he settles on revenge, but we then leave him immediately. His role is all but over at the moment he catches up with the play.

'Speak, if you can' – Dark Openings

From the stillness of I.ii to the belatedness of Macduff, Shakespeare establishes a base world of history and narrative that does not contain the play's hero. It seems designed to prepare for, and emphasise, the arrival of something utterly different. I must therefore reject Hegel's characteristic argument that, despite 'appear[ing] as external powers determining Macbeth's fate', the weird sisters really declare 'his most secret and private wish'.[24] Rather, the weird sisters are given the dramatic and imaginative force to convulse the dead world and conjure Macbeth. There is no 'wish', no Macbeth, before their appearance. One might here turn Hegel's master–slave dialectic against his Shakespeare criticism: it is only by encountering the weird sisters that Macbeth's 'consciousness has been fearful', that his 'whole being has been seized with dread, and everything solid and stable has been shaken to its foundations'.[25] For Hegel, this fearful shaking, this 'absolute melting-away of everything stable, is the simple, essential nature of self-consciousness'.[26] It is through such a seizure or 'melting-away' that Macbeth becomes an 'other' for himself. It is pure fantasy, then, to imagine (with Bradley) that 'when Macbeth heard them he was not an innocent man'.[27] For it is only through the weird sister's invocation of the imagination that Macbeth comes to be. Indeed, 'innocence' and 'guilt' do not seem to pre-exist their intrusion. Bradley's focus on individual agency means he must treat them as 'dangerous circumstances with which Macbeth has to deal',[28] rather than as a foundational force through which the play's 'action bursts into wild life'.[29]

The weird sisters' second entrance is again marked by '*Thunder*', which concludes the one-dimensional battle talk and prompts the arrival of another dimension. They mirror their martial counterparts by recounting their recent endeavours. But while the military talk was functional and enclosing, the weird sisters' account of 'tempest-toss[ing]' a hapless sailor (I.iii.3–24) is non-functional and excessive. There is again something almost comic about their speech and its irrelevance to the main plot, something absurd in the pre-occupation of these profound forces with a sailor's wife who refused to hand over the 'chestnuts in her lap', which she 'munched, and munched, and munched' (I.iii.3–4). The comic specificity of the 'chestnuts' speaks to a very different sort of history than Duncan's, in which an overlying concept of 'justice' determines all action and overrides all particularity. Rather than such indistinct mass movements and faceless cycles – 'What bloody man is that?' – we have significance and action at the lowest level of detail. The weird sisters are a bubbling broth of repetition, rhyme, reversal and, above all, relentless doing: 'I'll do, I'll do, and I'll do' (I.iii.9). Spirits can come anywhere, anytime, to transform lives. Even for chestnuts. Creativeness creeps in through the gaps and cracks of the situation. It speaks to the almost unavoidable potentiality of arrivals, which may attach themselves to the smallest details, so that nothing is inconsequential. The world 'bubbles' (I.iii.77) with dark life.

Macbeth enters on the back of the weird sisters' account, and his speech is immediately distinct from Duncan's battle talk, in which he made simple, unambiguous pronouncements – 'Great happiness' (I.ii.58) – about events at which he was not present. While Duncan speaks belatedly, Macbeth is part of the day: 'So foul and fair a day I have not seen' (I.iii.36). His words not only establish a clear link between Macbeth and the weird sisters' originating 'foul is fair' inversions; they establish that Macbeth is *present* in the day. He has 'seen' it. He is disorientated by its weirdness and is conscious of his own disorientation. We are no longer in a historical narrative; rather, strange things are happening right now before us. In a sense, Macbeth exits the historical tale – in which his deeds are recounted in I.ii – and begins to become something else in his very first line. He emerges as the only character who perceives the full register of the play, apprehending the worlds of both Duncan and the weird sisters. He alone experiences the play as we experience it: not merely as a normative account of revolt and restoration but also as the spectral emergence of a mind.

The weird sisters of *Macbeth* are, in large part, the weird sisters of Macbeth. From the outset, it is he whom they conjure: they go to 'meet with Macbeth'. What happens – the spectral that invades the structural violence – happens to him. Indeed, the fact that Macbeth's difference, his consciousness and his consciousness of difference are revealed in the weird sisters' 'fair is foul' language suggests that something has already happened before his entrance, that he has already been conjured. As Palfrey and Stern note, Macbeth's first line is cued by the weird sisters' charm:

> ———— [Charme's] [wound] up. *Enter . . .*
> So foule and faire a day I have not seene.[30]

Shakespeare's cue raises questions about the relation 'between the wound-up "charm" and [the actor's] own entrance': 'Has his character been conjured up by black magic?'[31] It highlights the character's indebtedness to a weirdness that lies outside of it: to an 'alien [un]righteousness'[32] that has already begun to transform and perhaps even possess the character.

Banquo's mundane and functional first words, 'How far is't to Forres' (I.iii.37), immediately tell us that he is not a twin to Macbeth. Despite his evocative description of the earth's 'bubbles' (I.iii.77), his communication with the weird sisters is quite different from Macbeth's. He is not operating in the same dual sense:

> How far is't called to Forres? – What are these,
> So withered, and so wild in their attire,
> That look not like th'inhabitants o'th'earth
> And yet are on't? – Live you, or are you aught
> That man may question? You seem to understand me
> By each at once her choppy finger laying
> Upon her skinny lips. You should be women
> And yet your beards forbid me to interpret
> That you are so.   (I.iii.37–45)

Banquo's long-winded questioning is plainly inadequate to this strange happening. The gap, or hyphen, between his mundane opening and his 'What are these' marks the convergence of two worlds hereto separated.

The explosiveness of the moment is lost on Banquo, however, who tries to place the weird sisters in a nameable and material context through a series of dichotomies: on the earth or not, alive or not, questionable or not, women or not. In this sense he is Duncan's heir, demanding that existence fits within simple categories (justice or rebellion). Although his speech does attempt to get at the strangeness of the happening, the 'not' in the second half of each equation suggests a bewildering beyondness with which his language cannot deal. In Latour's terms, Banquo 'define[s] existence ... as an all-or-nothing concept' rather than 'as a gradient'.[33] The event is not nameable in the situation's language of rigid binaries, however, so Banquo's questions run away from him. (Hence why the weird sisters raise their fingers to their lips, signalling him to silence and permitting Macbeth to speak.)

Macbeth is similarly eager to know what these alien figures are, but he is not blocked by the need to name events as 'here' or 'not'. Whereas Banquo creates a wall of sound that insulates him, Macbeth exposes himself to their speech: 'Speak, if you can. What are you?' (I.iii.45). After Banquo's flailing attempts to answer his own questions, Macbeth's short question and command to speak (the qualifying 'if' recognising their inhuman quality) indicate a radical openness to their bubbling excess. It is this sense of risk and exposure that blunts Bradley's claim, in comparing Macbeth to Banquo, that 'no innocent man would have started, as he did, with a start of *fear* at the mere prophecy of a crown'.[34] Rather, their differing responses stress Macbeth's opening to a dimension beyond Duncan's realm, the sort of opening that the situation's language sought to repress. The failure of this enclosing language (seen in Banquo's questioning) when faced with the excessiveness of the weird sisters, is, in Badiou's terms, a marker of the 'event': of the 'dysfunction of the count' that permits 'the void to become localizable at the level of presentation'.[35] It marks, in other words, the inability of the situation's 'count' to account for the event's 'excess-of-one'.[36] Unlike Banquo, however, Macbeth turns to face the void from whence the excess comes. We might draw a dark parallel between the road to Forres and the road to Damascus. In both, something intrudes into existing chronicles and language, and in both the intrusion is only really heard by one man: 'And [Saul] said, Who art thou, Lord?' In contrast, 'the men which journeyed with him stood speechless, hearing a voice, but seeing no man' (Acts 9:5–7). The voice speaks before others but calls forth only one new man, one 'chosen vessel' (Acts 9:15). 'We go to meet Macbeth'. Macbeth may share elements with vice-characters but he is not 'closed' to the event's excess as is Iago. Rather, it is the old world that is closed. Macbeth's opening to the unaccountable entrance of another dimension – the only event that happens in this self-contained world – is what founds the play. It *is* the play. And it brings Macbeth to life.

Evil

That Macbeth comes alive through an opening that ultimately closes him from life poses a potential problem for 'arrivals', for it appears that the event is in league with 'evil'. We might wonder, then, whether any intense experience, however destructive or politically regressive, might count as an event. How to distinguish between a 'truth-event' and an 'evil' is also a central difficulty for Badiou. As Žižek writes of Foucault's political writings on Iran: 'Foucault ends up at a point at which one should effectively raise the question usually addressed to Badiou: why, then, is Hitler's Nazi "revolution" not also an Event?'[37] If 'a subject retroactively assigns sense to the event' and 'there are no objective criteria' to determine whether it is a genuine event, one may wonder, with Oliver Feltham, the translator of Badiou's *Being and Event*, if it is possible to distinguish between 'subjectivization in a truth procedure and ideological interpellation'.[38] 'In fact', Feltham continues, 'Badiou has built in one safeguard to prevent the confusion of truth procedures and ideologies, and that is that the former is initiated by the occurrence of an event *at an evental site*'.[39]

So what, precisely, does Badiou's 'safeguard' entail? And why is the Nazi 'revolution' not founded on an 'evental site'? Badiou answers these questions in *Ethics*, in which he establishes a definition of Evil that is the flipside of his idea that the subject arises from 'the singular truths of which he is capable'.[40] If the subject arises in fidelity to an event (the Good), Evil is what destroys this event or fidelity. Badiou identifies three types of Evil: betrayal, disaster, and the simulacrum. The one that Feltham is pointing to is the 'simulacrum' of a truth-event.[41] The Nazi movement is Badiou's prime example: it is 'formally indistinguishable from an event'[42] because it uses 'borrowed names – "revolution", "socialism" – justified by the great modern political events (the Revolution of 1792, or the Bolshevik Revolution of 1917)' to legitimise 'the break with the older order'.[43] It is fundamentally different, however: 'When a radical break in a situation . . . convokes not the void but the "full" particularity or presumed substance of that situation, we are dealing with a *simulacrum of truth*.'[44] It is not 'initiated by the occurrence of an event *at an evental site*' because, rather than naming 'the void of the earlier situation', the Nazi movement sought to carry 'the absolute particularity' of 'a particular community, the German people, toward its true destiny, which is a destiny of universal domination'.[45] The result of '[f]idelity to a simulacrum ... is the unending construction' of 'the closed particularity of an abstract set ... and it has no other means of doing this than that of "voiding" what surrounds it'.[46] Death is directed to all that lies outside this pre-established 'set'.

There is certainly something of Badiou's 'simulacrum' in Macbeth's murderous course, which involves '"voiding" what surrounds it'. Here the 'closed particularity' is Macbeth-as-King, based on a prophecy addressed only to him, with death addressed to all. Whereas Saint Paul's conversion led to a message intended to save all, the weird sisters' message is intended to damn one (and kill many). And yet, while the particularity of Macbeth dominates all politics, there is also a dramatic creativity and vitality that does not conform to Badiou's philosophical categories. Macbeth's event may be closed to others in Duncan's situation, but it is genuinely new and irruptive, giving rise to an imaginative subjectivity and language that was impossible in that situation. It is open to *us*. That said, the fact that this newness is ultimately closed over in Macbeth's isolating violence suggests that the event's excess is paralysed within the existing political structures. It has nowhere to go, no way out in language or thought. It may not summon the '"full" particularity' of the old situation in the manner of the simulacrum, but neither does it fully summon that situation's void. Indeed, in many ways Macbeth *repeats* the structural violence of Duncan's world in his unending murders and closure from others.

The difficulty of this bind – of Macbeth's arrival to darkness – again suggests that dramatic arrivals need not fit neatly within Badiou's categories. Marion writes that painting is not 'a matter of inscribing upon a neutral surface ... a complex of foreseen objects', but 'of representing the dark opening from which the unseen nevertheless expels the unforeseen, to the great horror of the gaze'.[47] It 'surprises, overwhelms, and subverts the painting'.[48] Here we get at why the weird sisters' conjuring of Macbeth is not simply a simulacrum, even if it challenges the positive understanding of arrivals. The weird sisters do not close the situation but *open* it to the unforeseen and creative. Žižek stresses that an event is an 'opening' in his discussion of how the Iranian Revolution, however briefly, produced 'something new ... beyond the existing options of Western liberal democracy or a return to pre-modern tradition':

> Foucault's blunder in no way implies that the Iranian revolution was a pseudo-Event (in a Badiouian sense) comparable to the Nazi 'revolution': it was an authentic Event, a momentary *opening* that unleashed unprecedented forces of social transformation, a moment in which 'everything seemed possible'.[49]

Given the darkness and, ultimately, the deadness of what arrives in *Macbeth*, perhaps what we are left with is a bleeding between the openness of the void, the stolidness of the situation and the irruption of the event, so that we cannot distinguish adequately between them. It is very difficult to draw a line between the undeniable openness of Macbeth's conjuring from the void and the undeniable closure of his return to the cyclical situation, in which all conjurings fade as he assumes Cawdor's role of the heroically resigned rebel. *Macbeth* slides between the instrumental and the super-natural, the situation and the void. We are at once left with a world that has been transformed completely by Macbeth, and a world that returns to the old situation as Malcolm restores 'measure, time, and place' (V.xi.39). The world is the same, but different; different, but the same – another of the play's chiasmuses. And yet, while in narrative terms the old order is resumed, in dramatic terms it is not resumed for us. Macbeth dominates our imaginative experience of the play and we depart the play-world with his demise. Moreover, on closer examination, our view of Duncan's Scotland *is* changed, for it is only through riddling prophecy that the old regime is restored. Its supposed 'naturalness' and 'self-unity' are now infiltrated by the unnatural. It, like Macbeth, ends up in league with the weird sisters – who are given the prophetic and dramatic agency to bring the wood to Dunsinane – so that the once separate worlds end up blurring. The weird sisters both provide the means to return to the old world of linear history and instrumental language and produce an excess that waits in the wings. Their prophecies are not yet fulfilled but wait with Banquo's heirs. Malcolm is not the end of the story and the weird sisters' world is not finished. And yet, of course, Malcolm is the end of the story.

'What is not' – Horrible Imaginings

Despite the obvious difficulties, Badiou's concept of the event is none-theless important for showing how Macbeth arrives as a haunted subject. The road to Forres event may be tied to evil, but it still lies at the origin of Macbeth as a singular subject: of how he becomes something more than another link in the subject-less chain of rebellion and restoration. Insofar as Macbeth's opening to darkness ruptures the old order, it is not reducible to a simulacrum but resembles Badiou's void, which is 'outside situations, unpresentable' and therefore 'in excess of being as a thinkable disposition, and especially as natural disposition'.[50] Breaking into the seemingly 'natural' order, Macbeth unleashes the imagination's explosive force as a transformed and inescapably metaphoric language. The centrality of

Macbeth's imagination has long been recognised. Bradley articulates its divided nature in his essay on Hegel: 'Macbeth's imagination deters him from murder, but it also makes the vision of a crown irresistibly bright.'[51] He pursues this thought in *Shakespearean Tragedy*:

> This bold ambitious man of action has, within certain limits, the imagination of a poet ... Macbeth's better nature – to put the matter for clearness' sake too broadly – instead of speaking to him in the overt language of moral ideas, commands, and prohibitions, incorporates itself in images which alarm and horrify. His imagination is thus the best of him, something usually deeper and higher than his conscious thoughts; and if he obeyed it he would have been safe.[52]

Macbeth's conscience is here a sort of linguistic surplus or remainder that works through poetic images rather than functional speech. It infiltrates Macbeth as 'images which alarm and horrify', making Duncan's simple self-presence and hollowed-out language impossible. Macbeth's speech and mind teem with metaphors and imaginings. Bradley may attempt to distinguish between the 'good' and 'bad' aspects of this imagining, indeed, to limit Macbeth's imagination to 'moral' conscience, but the play does no such thing. As we'll see, Macbeth's imagination is not the best of him in a moral sense, even if it is in a dramatic sense. Morally, it is equally the worst of him. His entire consciousness and not just his 'better nature' work through imaginings.

After asking them to speak, Macbeth says nothing when the weird sisters hail him as Cawdor and King. His silence is far from dumb, however, as Banquo's question indicates: 'why do you start and seem to fear / Things that do sound so fair?' (I.iii.49–50). While Banquo is outwardly eager to know his prophecy, he is not transported elsewhere like Macbeth, who is envisioning something different to his ordained future within the situation, something different to life as Glamis. The weird sisters thus open the possibility of an imaginative and poetic Macbeth. That he is possessed by his vision of the future-to-come is confirmed twice more. First, Banquo again takes up the questioning because Macbeth 'seems rapt withal' (I.iii.55), indicating that Macbeth's mind remains elsewhere. Second, after Ross and Angus confirm that he is Cawdor, Macbeth barely speaks to these emissaries from the King's world but is again rapt: 'Look how our partner's rapt' (I.iii.141). We might link this rapture to theatre itself. States quotes Heidegger's observation that in 'the vicinity' of the work of art 'we are suddenly somewhere else than we usually tend to be'.[53] The 'somewhere else' is not a 'spatial elsewhere' so much as 'the sense that what is before us, the painting itself, offers a different kind of *here*'.[54] In this, the audience and Macbeth coincide: as Macbeth is lifted out of Holinshed's time (Duncan's time), our usual sense of time is suspended. His conversion, his 'truth', is thus open to us: we are both transported into a new 'here'.

Macbeth's rapture also recalls the ambivalence of Montaigne's writing about imagination. On the one hand, Montaigne seems almost proud to 'feele a very great conflict and power of imagination'.[55] It lies at the heart of his empathetic and wide-ranging thought, allowing him to 'insinuate [his] selfe into [the] place' of others.[56] Indeed, a sense of imagination is essential to a full life: 'If that which we have not seene, is not, our knowledge is wonderfull abridged.'[57] One might say that Duncan's closed language entails a narrow and sterile view of life. On the other hand, however, Montaigne's very sensitivity to imagination's power, his 'want of strength to resist her', causes him to 'avoid it'.[58] He withholds himself from the passionate raptures of the 'vulgar sort':

> [T]he principall credit of visions, of enchantments, and such extraordinary effects, proceedeth from the power of imaginations, working especially in the mindes of the vulgar sort, as the weakest and seeliest, whose conceit and beleefe is so seized upon, that they imagine to see what they see not.[59]

Such moderate and reasonable judgements are present in Shakespeare too. Banquo warns Macbeth that the 'instruments of darkness [may] tell us truths' to 'win us to our harm' (I.iii.121–22), and we are well aware that Macbeth will be tricked, condemned and destroyed. The play again and again registers the terrifying and dominating power of the imagination. And yet, although being the 'seeliest' may open Macbeth to destruction and duplicity (to being 'seized upon'), it is what brings him to life. Imaginings are not *just* imaginings in Shakespeare. Montaigne sees no path between such fantastical imaginings and the everyday world – there is, again, no 'advent' – but in *Macbeth* such imaginings transform the world, albeit in nightmarish fashion. As Ewan Fernie puts it in his recent book on the demonic: 'Duncan's murder acts as a ritualistic induction into a new existential or spiritual state, which is at once a state of death but equally and troublingly of more vivid life.'[60] Imagination and material existence blur, as exemplified by the famous moment when the 'dagger of the mind' becomes 'palpable' (II.i.38–40) to the hand. 'Things are *hatching*'[61] and new forms of life are being born. Indeed, there is an almost insane escalation from words and visions into horrific reality. In an extraordinary passage, we first hear that Duncan's horses ran 'wild' after his murder; then that the horses 'ate each other'; and finally that Ross, who had first told us of the horses running, actually saw this cannibalistic scene with his own 'eyes' (II.iv.14–20).

Macbeth is certainly not content to rest in the imaginary world. Even amidst his initial scepticism there is a smothered but urgent desire for his imagining to come true: 'The Thane of Cawdor lives, / A prosperous gentleman, and to be king / Stands not within the prospect of belief, / No more than to be Cawdor' (I.iii.24–27). From their arrival as fantastical figures, suddenly present on the road, the weird sisters bring the imagination to life, but what radically shifts Macbeth's 'prospect of belief' is the revelation that he has been made Thane of Cawdor. As such, the prophecy does not just entice Macbeth's imaginings; it establishes their *reality*. That Macbeth is subjected to a trick here – of the sort usually foisted upon Macduff – is suggested by the fact that, following the King's announcement in I.ii, we know that Macbeth is Cawdor *already*. That is not so in Holinshed, where it is 'shortlie after' the prophecy that Cawdor was 'condemned at Fores' and 'his lands, liuings, and offices were giuen of the kings liberalitie to Mackbeth'.[62] The fact that, in Shakespeare, this is not really a prophecy at all sheds some light on what the weird sisters are doing: by linking an occurrence to an alluring narrative they entice Macbeth to imaginatively invest in it so that it seems miraculous once confirmed.

There is here, perhaps, a bitter echo of Hamlet's 'providence'. 'God's providential presence is uncovered', Witmore writes, 'in encounters with accidents'.[63] Understood 'as occasions for storytelling and the expression of immanent forms of value',[64] however, the providence revealed by such accidents need not be godly. For instance, for '[a] man who is plowing a field [and] stumbles upon buried treasure ... it was "as if" he were doing the ploughing to find the treasure'.[65] The accident fuses with, or activates, a narrative that inspires the imagination: buried treasure. More profoundly, Hamlet's voyage showed how accidents may strike the individual with 'wonder', which 'marks the moment when an individual's attention or "regard" is suddenly detached from the concerns of the world and turned elsewhere'.[66] Macbeth is not only 'hailed' by the weird sisters; he is hailed by the accident of becoming Cawdor and transported 'elsewhere'. Or, as Lady Macbeth puts it: 'Thy letters have transported me beyond / The ignorant present, and I feel now / The future in the instant' (I.v.54–56).

Once Macbeth's imagination is gripped by the narrative of his path to kingship, in which becoming Cawdor is the critical first step, the confirmation of its happening is incredible and energising – hence Macbeth's declaration that '[t]he greatest is behind' (I.iii.114). While this is often glossed straightforwardly as the greatest is 'to come',[67] the line has another important resonance. The greatest has already happened – 'is behind' – because the accident of becoming Cawdor shows that the world of imagining can enter the material. Dreams can come true. Life can be transformed. 'Because they represent[] a lapse of intelligible order in the world',[68] accidents challenge the seemingly unalterable facts of the world in which Glamis is Glamis, Cawdor is Cawdor, and Duncan is King. The feudal scales fall from his eyes. Material facts certainly lose their inevitability for Macbeth: 'what seemed corporal / Melted as breath into the wind' (I.iii.79–80). Imaginings become his reality:

> Present fears
> Are less than horrible imaginings.
> My thought, whose murder yet is but fantastical,
> Shakes so my single state of man that function
> Is smothered in surmise, and nothing is
> But what is not. (I.iii.136–41)

Contrary to the old idea that 'Macbeth's character is determined by his passion of ambition',[69] ambition is not a stable, pre-existing trait but only becomes meaningful and powerful insofar as it is a fantastical vision whose realisation is suddenly believable. Macbeth arrives not through already being an 'ambitious man',[70] but because he becomes conscious of the fact that something has happened to him. He is strikingly aware that the exhilarating vision enticed by the weird sisters has *changed* him: that he is 'unfix[ed]', 'knock[ed]', 'shake[n]' and 'smothered' by this 'horrid image'. It is by this convulsion that he gains 'the imagination of a poet'.[71] Unlike in Holinshed, where Makbeth is established as a 'valiant gentleman' but 'somewhat cruell of nature' at the outset (Duncane is 'soft and gentle of nature'[72]), there is no Macbeth before the weird sisters. And, even if we were to infer a pre-existing Macbeth, it must be in terms of the Holinshedian world of I.ii, which is to say a flat and immediate Macbeth whose unified 'single state' and 'seated heart' allowed no 'surmise', contradiction or difference.

Macbeth's imagination – the imaginings that constitute his so-called ambition – spills from the void opened by this surmise. He is invigorated by the realisation that visions can be made real. As such, he repeatedly describes ambition in the language of the imagination: 'suggestion', 'horrid image', 'horrible imaginings', 'thought', 'fantastical', 'surmise', 'what is not'. There are, of course, clear signs of conscience in imagination's 'horribleness', but the overwhelming feeling is of an irresistible, albeit awful, allure that 'make[s] [his] seated heart knock at [his] ribs'. It usurps the material so that 'nothing is / But what is not'. It is worth recalling, at this point, Badiou's conclusion 'that the void *is not*; if by "being" we understand the limited order of presentation, and in particular what is natural of such order'.[73] The weird sisters open another 'order' – 'beyond / The ignorant present' – into which Macbeth, dreamlike, plunges. Fittingly, it is here, sharing a line with Macbeth's 'what is not', that Banquo observes, 'Look how our partner's rapt' (I.iii.141). Macbeth is possessed by an imagining that is far more electric than guilty conscience: it is the opening of a new horizon of possibility. He arrives as a mind committed to the obscure power of 'what is not'. Badiou's idea of courage as 'insubordination to the symbolic order' is here apposite: 'Courage positively carries out the disorder of the symbolic, the breakdown of communication, whereas anxiety calls for its death.'[74] Whereas Banquo was caught in an anxious series of dichotomies between what is and what is not, Macbeth ventures into 'the disorder of the symbolic', into 'what is not'. Although we may glimpse 'anxiety' in Macbeth's subsequent paranoia – ultimately suggesting how *Macbeth* blurs philosophical categories – in comparison to Banquo's and Duncan's rigid 'subordination' to their closed language, Macbeth is surely courageous here: 'Courage effectuates the interruption of the dead law in favour of the excess.'[75] He re-animates Scotland's dead world.

It is here worth returning to Montaigne, who describes how the 'Poeticall furies, which ravish and transport their Author beyond himselfe' must be put down to 'good fortune', since the author 'acknowledgeth to proceed from elsewhere, than from himselfe, and that they are not in his power'.[76] Perhaps because it is contained within the safe confines of poetic endeavour, Montaigne here casts the enrapturing power of imagination in a far more positive light. It is, in fact, an almost evental view of poetry: poetry comes from outside, from 'elsewhere', as a sort of unexplained and fortuitous happening that transports the author away from 'himselfe' and thereby creates something new. Here we perhaps see why Macbeth can be said to have 'the imagination of a poet'. It is not only because his imaginings are poetic but also because the manner in which he arrives as an imaginative consciousness resembles the poetic process itself – or at least the violent ravishment of the sublime. And the sublime lies at the heart of Shakespeare's tragic arrivals: the crossing over (and back) from formlessness to form, from night to day, from the immensity of the void to the material world. The confronting implication of *Macbeth* seems to be that this crossing over is uncontrollable. That it is beyond, or at least before, good and evil.

Indeed, Macbeth's energising excess recalls Nietzsche's view that 'we are most ourselves when we are in this destructive, dangerous and suffering state of freedom, violating the restraints of the very history which has produced us'.[77] As Dollimore continues, '*Macbeth* does not warn against hubris and ambition; on the contrary it affirms their attraction'.[78] *Macbeth* also rebuffs the historicist impulse, deadening the world of historical progression whilst animating the passionate, brutal action of one man. As Nietzsche poses: 'imagine a man seized by a vehement passion, for a woman or for a great idea: how different the world has become to him!'[79] Such a seizure transforms the world so that 'all is so palpable, close, highly coloured, resounding, as though he apprehended it with all his senses at once'.[80] Far from being unproblematically liberating, however, Nietzsche's description of this experience could easily apply to Macbeth:

> It is the condition in which one is least capable of being just; narrow-minded, ungrateful to the past, blind to dangers, deaf of warnings, one is a little vortex of life in a dead sea of darkness and oblivion: and yet this condition – unhistorical, anti-historical through and through – is the womb not only of the unjust but of every just deed too.[81]

In a manner that ironically links with Saint Paul's conversion and Badiou's event, Nietzsche affirms that transfiguring action requires a dangerous break with history in which the present bursts with irreducible life and urgency. We are far from Locke's empiricist common sense, which urges us to be satisfied with understanding in 'proportion' to 'our faculties' and not to 'demand certainty, where probability only is to be had'.[82] As Nietzsche suggests, the drive for 'more' is enlivening and creative; it is the womb of action. Macbeth becomes 'a little vortex of life' within the 'dead seas' and 'oblivion' of the Holinshedian realm. Although I.ii sets up the pattern that Macbeth will repeat by taking up Duncan's enticing words – 'More is thy due than more than all can pay' (I.iv.21) – and adopting Cawdor's role of traitor, the historical narrative is quite simply 'less than [Macbeth's] horrible imaginings'.

Nietzsche's 'vortex' is, in many ways, the antithesis of Montaigne's quest for moderation, in which he declares that 'Wee never governe that thing well, wherewith we are possessed and directed'.[83] As much as Montaigne might be 'right', his praise of the moderate man who 'marcheth alwaies with the reines in his hand' (Ibid., p.260) sounds more like Malcolm than Macbeth. Shakespeare's major tragic figures seldom march 'with the reines in ... hand'. Indeed, they regularly arrive by letting the reins fall. They arrive, to adapt Montaigne's words against immediate passion, through 'torment' and 'affliction', through the 'violent' and at times 'tyrannical' intrusion of events, and through the 'rash motions' that 'transport' them to radically new modes of being.[84] Montaigne values control. Duncan and Malcolm value control. By and large, criticism values control, and doubtless I have tried to exert some measure of control through the conceptual framework developed in this book. Even Badiou, with his open-ended and excessive concept of the event, values control when it comes to the nameable categories of 'truth-events' and 'evils'. In plays such as *Macbeth*, however, Shakespeare escapes our control. Dark things flame forth only to return to darkness: things that elude our names and categories. We do our best, of course, and the attempt to name is neither unprofitable nor avoidable, but there is a gap between his worlds and our words. And perhaps, in the end, what we say of it need not be complex: something dark flames forth and it lives. Or as Hazlitt writes:

> Poetry puts a spirit of life and motion into the universe . . . It does not define the limits of sense, or analyze the distinctions of the understanding, but signifies the excess of the imagination beyond the actual or ordinary impression of any object or feeling.[85]

Badiou remains important, in all this, because he can get us a step closer to the dark void of this 'excess of imagination'. He shows us that this flaming to life stems not simply from the way of things, or a pre-determined character, but from the excessive event. Badiou may not be able to adequately name the events of Shakespeare's drama, but he gives us a starting point for thinking about how their excess comes from 'what is not', how it crosses over, like a 'dagger of the mind', and pierces the material situation.

'The eye wink at the hand' – The Act

Darkness may come to life in *Macbeth* but the flaming is short lived. And the end of life, the cessation of the flame is where words begin again. We attempt to analyse and categorise, to exert control over the ashes, to ask how the flame dies. We might say that while Macbeth's opening to 'what is not' brings him to life, it comes to close him off from 'what is'. Not only are his imaginings black, Macbeth envisages shrouding the act of realising them in darkness:

> Stars, hide your fires,
> Let not light see my black and deep desires;
> The eye wink at the hand; yet let that be
> Which the eye fears, when it is done, to see.   (I.iv.50–53)

Macbeth attempts to separate what is imagined from the action that will realise it, to insulate the mind from the act. It is an ambivalence towards action that Lady Macbeth seems to expect: 'Thou'dst have, great Glamis, / That which cries "Thus thou must do" if thou have it' (I.v.21–22). In contrast, Lady Macbeth's 'unsex me here' (I.v.39) speech is a brutal commitment to enacting desire at any price. In a sense, the couple forms one agent, he supplying the imagination and she the willpower to enact its visions. Her critical contribution comes shortly after Macbeth's sustained speech on the relationship between imagination and act:

> If it were done when 'tis done, then 'twere well
> It were done quickly. If th'assassination
> Could trammel up the consequence, and catch
> With his surcease success: that but this blow
> Might be the be-all and the end-all, here,
> But here upon this bank and shoal of time,
> We'd jump the life to come. (I.vii.1–7)

The 'If' of this speech is deeply problematic. Macbeth immediately negates it by pre-visioning how Duncan's murder will play in the minds of others. He in fact concludes that the act is not 'done', first, because it will 'teach / Bloody instructions' that 'return / To plague th'inventor' (I.vii.8–10), and second, because 'pity' will 'blow the horrid deed in every eye' (I.vii.17–24). The explicit focus on the outward consequences of the act (particularly evident in Macbeth's tremulous question: 'If we should fail?' (I.vii.59)) gives some credence to Bradley's conclusion that Macbeth's 'conscious or reflective mind . . . moves chiefly among considerations of outward success and failure, while his inner being is convulsed by conscience'.[86] And yet, surely Macbeth *does* consciously address the moral horror of the act when he describes 'pity . . . blow[ing] the horrid deed in every eye'. He is picturing the murder as others will, which is a form of shamed conscience. The trouble is – and this is the critical point Bradley misses – that Macbeth separates the 'horrid deed' from the allure of 'what is not'. There is thus a deeper conflict at play than Bradley's opposition between 'good' imagination and 'bad' conscious thought: there is a split between the subject and the act. As we saw with his '[s]tars, hide your fires', Macbeth divorces his vision of the future from the act that will consummate it. Hence how Macbeth can somewhat contradictorily foresee that others will be both inspired to *repeat* the action (it will 'teach / Bloody instructions') and be *repulsed* by the 'horrid deed'. What is 'horrible' about his imaginings is attributed to the act, while what is 'enticing' about them is attributed to the vision that the act will bring about. The separation between the two implies – or hopes – that the act will be over and 'done' *for Macbeth*, even as it continues to horrify (or inspire) others. It brings about a settled state by way of a 'be-all' and 'end-all' blow: 'The future in the instant' (I.v.56).

The separation also reveals a fault line between Macbeth and his wife. Although Macbeth understands that the murder will lead to more bloodshed by instructing others, he fails to imagine what the act will make *him* become – that it will keep acting on him. In contrast, Lady Macbeth clearly apprehends that the act will change her. Indeed, the brutal imagery of her 'unsex me now' speech seeks to pre-empt its transformative psychic violence. As Bradley notes, however, Lady Macbeth 'hardly imagines the act'.[87] She lacks Macbeth's imagination of the act's *horror*. In fact, she almost deliberately smothers it: 'Come, thick night . . . That my keen knife see not the wound it makes' (I.v.48–50). What they might know, if they were not divided, is that they will be changed into horror. As Davis shows, 'character', in *Macbeth*, derives from the 'fact that a man becomes what he has done'.[88] It is no more possible to bypass the horrific act by having the 'eye wink at the hand' than it is to pre-empt the act by calling on spirits to 'fill [one] from the crown to the toe top-full / Of direst cruelty' (I.v.39–41).

In Badiou's terms, one might say that Macbeth's done-ness seeks a transcendent and subject-less 'truth' that is outside any particular situation. Macbeth does not envisage a relation between the situation and its void but a future that is wholly consumed within the void of 'what is not'. Unlike Hamlet's readiness, which brought the 'beyond' into the situation's contingency and action, in *Macbeth* the beyond annihilates the material world. In this sense, it bears some relation to Badiou's 'evil' of 'disaster', which involves the 'absolutization of [the event's] power'.[89] Although an event '*changes the names* of elements in the situation',[90] it 'does not have the power to name all the elements of a situation'.[91] That would imply 'the *total* power of a truth'.[92] Of course, Badiou's category of 'disaster' is far from capturing the full allure or complexity of Macbeth's wavering guilt. The conflicted movements of his consciousness – the eye winking at the hand – show that, to some extent, Macbeth does not want to make the event, or his own murderous act, 'total' in Badiou's sense. Nevertheless, Badiou's 'disaster' does help articulate one important aspect of Macbeth: the way his insistence on finality seeks to wipe out the very situation that gave rise to the event.

To return to Badiou's fundamentals, while an evental truth is '*supplementary*', it always remains 'the truth *of* the situation, and not the absolute commencement of another'.[93] It is, in other words, not 'the be-all and the end-all'. The 'subject', which strives towards 'the incorporation of the event into the situation',[94] 'cannot ruin the situation'.[95] The ruining of the situation is precisely what Macbeth desires. As Cavell writes, 'I hear

Macbeth's speculation of deeds done in the doing, without consequence, when surcease is success, to be a wish for there to be no human action', a 'wish for an end to time'.[96] Indeed, his murderous course is a bloody Sisyphean effort to strike the end-all blow. His idea that he is 'in blood / Stepped in so far that, should [he] wade no more, / Returning ere was as tedious as go o'er' (III.iv.135–37), implies that there *is* a place 'o'er' it; a foothold on the other side of this river of blood; a final resting place, free from others and action, 'renown and grace' (II.iii.90). (Though the dark aural joke that turns 'go o'er' to gore suggests that there is only more blood, that blood is the same as gore.) Far from the 'flowing time' of Shakespeare's drama or Bergson's 'duration',[97] Macbeth seeks to ground time's flow 'here, / But here upon this bank and shoal of time'. The double 'heres' form an impossibly absolute present that recalls Duncan's closed language. They shut down the relation between situation and its void and with it Macbeth's foundational 'scission'[98] from the dead unity of Duncan's world.

And this, perhaps, is why there is a subjective abyss to Macbeth as king. If we consider what he wants to do as king, we can find no answer.[99] He has no plans or politics, only more imaginings and murders. It reveals the ultimate voiding that takes place when the void is detached from the situation and turned into an absolute. Macbeth's story thus slides into Holinshed's ongoing cycle of murderous usurpation and restoration. For Badiou, however, '[a] subject is equally the process of recomposing, from the point of interruption, another place and other rules', and this is what allows the subject to escape 'repetition'.[100] Although Macbeth may envisage 'another place', by absolutising that 'place' he guts it of reality. He severs it from his violent actions, which repeat the 'rules' of cyclical violence, and which come to consume him. So although Macbeth's openness to darkness begins as a form of 'courage', it ends in a form of 'anxiety' that calls for the 'death' of the 'symbolic' order rather than its 'splitting'.[101] The world is 'full of sound and fury, / Signifying nothing' (V.v.26–27). In the end, Macbeth stops short of Badiou's 'courage . . . [of] passing through there where previously it was not visible that anyone could find a passage'[102] and returns to old, well-worn paths. Ultimately, in fact, he seeks the transcendent finality of prophecy. But now the weird sisters are no longer vital forces of the void. The apparitions that arise from their cauldron are no longer irruptions but pure images, incapable of communication: 'Listen, but speak not to't' (IV.i.105). We come close to Deleuze and Guattari's 'death instinct', which is 'pure silence, pure transcendence'.[103] 'Death is not desired, but what is desired is dead, already dead: images.'[104] He is left stranded in a life beyond life: 'Tomorrow and tomorrow and tomorrow' (V.v.18).

'Renown and grace is dead' – Living Deadness

But that is not the whole story, for Macbeth's desire to reach a final resting place fails both metaphysically and dramatically. The result is that he is perpetually embroiled in the present that he wants to leap over. His mind is never still but moves with the phantoms that possess it. And this tortured movement *births* the play's peculiar form of life. As Davis notes, in becoming 'what he has done', there is, 'almost incredibly, a sort of horrified innocence of realization. Look at me! at what I have come to!'[105] Like us,[106] Macbeth cannot follow his wife's prosaic advice – 'These deeds must not be thought / After these ways. So, it will make us mad' (II.ii.31–32) – but stares in appalled fascination at his own nightmare: 'Methought I heard a voice cry "Sleep no more, / Macbeth does murder sleep"' (II.ii.33–34). As Bradley writes, 'the image of his own guilty heart or bloody deed . . . hold[s] him spell-bound and possess[es] him wholly, like a hypnotic trance which is at the same time the ecstasy of a poet'.[107] The 'horrible imaginings' that overtook 'present fears' now overrun the solid world.

In fact, Macbeth comes to apprehend everything as an imagining. 'Conscience' comes to consciousness as the uninvited trespass of a foreign voice: 'Sleep no more'. At one level, this is a brilliant way of dramatising how conscience encroaches as an external force: 'Of such marvailous-working power is the sting of conscience: which often induceth us to bewray, to accuse, and to combat our selves.'[108] But it is also fundamental to Macbeth's mode of life: not only is conscience apprehended in this manner, Macbeth apprehends all ideas and actions through traumatic visions. Fittingly, Duncan's murder, the play's central action, is not staged. It is not that sort of play. We do not see it, as we see Desdemona's murder, but apprehend it as Macbeth does: as a haunting. It disappears, along with the rest of the material world. Whereas Othello's fearful repudiation of the unseen swells into furious action, Macbeth's mind shrinks from the material act and *into* 'what is not', which is both the promise of the imagination (new life) and Macbeth's desultory isolation (death). Macbeth hears a voice crying that he 'does murder sleep'. *That* is the act for Macbeth. It is an intrusion he cannot stop. He is 'afraid to think what [he] has done' (II.ii.49). The act therefore becomes something else, is translated into voices and apparitions. But, in a sense, it is not translated at all. It always was that. That was its appeal: that horrible imaginings would be all.

The Porter, who appears from nowhere before disappearing again, is characteristic of the play's gripping intrusions. He embodies the uncontrollable, overriding power of sublime imagining that overruns the play-world. Like Macbeth, the Porter suspends historical narrative, refusing to let it in. He translates the situation's knocking into an unrelenting flow of hellish associations, as he admits farmers and equivocators and tailors into hell but does not open the door to Macduff. Ultimately, however, Macbeth's 'place is too cold for hell' (II.iii.16). The play-world's life is now an afterlife or rigor mortis. There is 'nothing serious in mortality' (II.iii.89) because life has been usurped by the dead. Banquo's ghost is, of course, the most striking representation of the act's afterlife. As with the weird sisters' riddling, things are, in a darkly comic fashion, not in their right place:

> The time has been
> That, when the brains were out, the man would die,
> And there an end. But now they rise again
> With twenty mortal murders on their crowns,
> And push us from our stools. This is more strange
> Than such a murder is. (III.iv.77–82)

The strange experience of deadness is so vivid and vital that it becomes the life of the play. It possesses 'a horribly animating power'.[109] So, just as Macbeth first arrived through his awareness of being '[s]hake[n]' by his imagining, he now arrives as a subject of hell through his awareness that he cannot escape the act's haunting: 'Can such things be / And overcome us like a summer's cloud, / Without our special wonder?' (III.iv.109–11). It is tempting, then, to conclude that Macbeth enacts a sort of demonic fidelity. There is, as Fernie notes, 'something desperately grand and exhilarating about adventuring beyond all determinism'.[110] The matter is not straightforward, however, for as strikingly conscious as he is of his changed self, Macbeth's torturous guilt also operates, paradoxically, to *maintain* his old self. Guilt insulates him from the full terror of the act, which becomes a floating, foreign vision, a haunting ghost, never fully belonging to 'Macbeth'. It is for this reason that Kierkegaard uses Macbeth to illustrate '[d]espair over sin', which is 'an attempt to maintain oneself by sinking still deeper' into sin, reaching the point where 'it is eternally decided that one will hear nothing about repentance, nothing about grace'.[111] Kierkegaard points to Macbeth's lines after the murder:

> from this instant
> There's nothing serious in mortality.
> All is but toys. Renown and grace is dead. (II.iii.88–90)

'The masterly double stroke is in the last words, "*renown* and *grace*."'[112] In Badiou's terms, Macbeth is closed to both the situation ('renown') and the irruptive event ('grace'). Shut off within himself, no longer really speaking to anyone living, he now dismisses the possibility of transformation. But this despair also serves a 'positive' function: it serves to maintain his self-consistency. In a sense, he avoids the full terror that would come if grace and goodness were admitted – if he could go back. We see this in Macbeth's ultimate response to his ongoing hell: 'Strange things I have in head that will to hand, / Which must be acted ere they may be scanned' (III.iv.138–39). The most straightforward reading is that he must enact his murderous thoughts before others suspect them. He must kill Macduff. But it also implies that he refuses to scan them before they are put to hand. To some extent, acting before scanning is a continuation of the eye winking at the hand, of his attempts to escape horror by avoiding thought and to act with closed eyes.

And yet, perhaps there is something of dark fidelity here too, for Macbeth now knows that the horror *will* follow the act: that these '[s]trange things' will be 'scanned'. Just as Banquo is only really there for Macbeth after his murder, these dark thoughts will only be truly felt (always through a visual scanning) once they are done. Knowing this, Macbeth's decision to put all his horror to hand is almost a moment of consecration: he pushes 'what is not' to its consummation so it can be scanned. For Kierkegaard, a thinker acutely aware of the closeness of good and evil, most people are 'only momentarily conscious, conscious in the great decisions', and therefore only 'spirit (if this word may be applied to them) once a week for one hour', which 'is a pretty bestial way of being spirit'.[113] In contrast, Macbeth's nightmare visions speak to a mind inescapably aware of its being in sin. Macbeth thereby achieves a demonic consistency – a 'continuity of sin'[114] or 'consistency in something higher'[115] – which, however dark, makes him a man of 'spirit'. He does, in some sense at least, arrive as a subject. The demonic rejection of the good can thus be seen as simultaneously an evasive attempt to 'maintain' his old 'self' by 'sinking still deeper' into 'sin'[116] and as a courageous pursuit of 'what is not'.

More positively put, greatness for Kierkegaard is not essential but is a matter of what one is attached to: 'everyone became great in proportion to his *expectancy*'.[117] Insofar as Macbeth expects a new horizon of life and thought, the weird sisters are an event. Insofar as he expects to usurp the role of King, to merely reshuffle the deck of the old order, the weird sisters are a simulacrum. Rather than reaching a final name for Macbeth's tragedy, rather than settling on one of Badiou's categories, or dismissing them altogether, we can turn again to Latour's notion of 'relative existence'.[118] Shakespeare creates a hero who embodies both event and simulacrum, truth and evil, fidelity and disaster – a hero whose horizons of expectation are both the greatest and the lowest. We have another indication of drama's ability to rest in uncertainty, in a way that philosophy cannot. As Empson famously writes of Shakespeare's 'dramatic ambiguity': we should avoid 'taking sides between two viewpoints instead of letting both be real'.[119] Or, to return to Bradley: 'the elements in' Macbeth's 'nature are so inextricably blended that the good in him, that which we admire, instead of simply opposing the evil, reinforces it'.[120] The event still operates; it still prompts Macbeth's arrival as he moves beyond the blankness of Duncan's feudal world, but he also returns to that world, to the old situation, and fulfils its cycle of rebellion and restoration.

Embarrassments and Conclusions

The belatedness and embarrassments that Macduff is forced to experience suggest *Macbeth*'s potential to embarrass various critical approaches. The play embarrasses a certain historicist impulse by placing a non-historicisable intrusion at the heart of a play that is about historical figures and drawn from historical chronicles. What is potentially embarrassing to the idea that context offers the best means of understanding a work is the brutal dominance of this excess. The unnatural weird sisters conjure the imaginative world of *Macbeth*, gripping the vision of its hero and its audience. Meanwhile, Macduff, the figure of historical progression, is thrust to the sideline and deferred. The play's life seems to bubble from the 'irreducible point of originality' of 'writing', around which 'an immense series of structures, of historical totalities of all orders, are organized, enveloped, blended'.[121] Its irreducible and otherworldly excess cannot be satisfactorily accounted for by historical sources.

The play also embarrasses the humanist impulse by placing the powers of imagination and poetry in the service of an attractive evil. Shakespeare's technology of character creation does not produce Promethean heroism but utter alienation in a living hell. The play also embarrasses my impulse to draw positive subjective possibilities from Shakespeare's arrivals. What arrives in *Macbeth* is magnetic and alive – it conjures consciousness – but it is hardly the joyous creation of *Romeo and Juliet*. Shakespeare's arrivals simply need not be affirmative. The play also poses a problem for Badiou by showing how the subject's founding event can be as much an 'evil' as a 'truth'. While Badiou attempts to distinguish evils from events, Macbeth's experience, and our experience of Shakespeare's theatrical event, does not fall easily within his categories. Rather, Macbeth seems to slide indistinctly between the old situation, its void, and the irruptive event. Things never remain where they should but keep bursting from, and disappearing into, 'what is not'. The weird sisters and their chestnuts, the ghost of Banquo, the Porter, the visions of Macbeth keep rising to the top of the cauldron and sinking down again. There seems to be no way out, no settled fidelity, no release point like Hamlet's readiness, by which Macbeth can channel the void into even an obscure 'truth'. He remains forever stranded between the old situation and the new excess.

Relevant, here, is Fernie's recent work on the demonic, which convincingly argues that while the 'demonic *is* evil ... in its violent hostility to being', it also 'involves a potential for creativity over against what merely is, which is something other than evil'.[122] The 'demonic' is not just 'evil'; 'it is evil as a form of *life*.'[123] This stresses just how conflicted Macbeth is as an 'evental' subject: how he both bursts into 'wild life' from a dead situation and also comes to destroy all that lives. Macbeth may (to put it mildly) tip too far into the negative, but that tipping, with all its violence, with all its terror and peril, is absolutely essential to *all* arrivals. Of course, Juliet shows that such arrivals may be loving and creative, but there is nonetheless something violent, destructive and absolutist to her break from 'what is'. For a moment at least, each of Shakespeare's arrivals resembles Macbeth: Juliet's violence towards her name, family and past joys; Desdemona's violence towards her father and place; Othello's violence towards his old story-of-himself; Hamlet's murderous rashness. Badiou gets at this too with his radical understanding of the subject as something exceptional, destructive, and inimical to established 'identity'. And yet, Badiou's arrival does not seem terrifying enough. *Macbeth* reveals that the tearing birth of Shakespeare's character is far closer to evil, to demonic birth, than Badiou's categories allow. In *Macbeth*, Shakespeare seems to extract and distil the violent, destructive aspect of arrivals – the 'not', the break, the negative – and make *it* the fidelity. And he thereby has us asking whether this is, at base, what arrivals means: is becoming 'what is not', and thereby destroying the world that is, what it means to arrive as a dramatic subject? Is this what it means to create? Is this the heart of Shakespeare's extraordinary power to conjure character? For in Shakespeare's tragedies, the void engenders both good and evil, and though Juliet offers a more hopeful path, Macbeth comes to cast a shadow there too.

Macbeth, in death, thus brings us face to face with something at the heart of life. And it is hard not to acquiesce. Besmeared in blood, gore and baby's brains, the devil yet has an attractive face – for the devil is in us, if we truly live. Of course, we may not. According to Kierkegaard, we are often lifeless Malcolms, dispensing our judgements, complacent in our conventional 'virtue', happy to pronounce 'justice' and 'fiend'. These days, we are moralisers of tolerance. We respect 'others' above all. Unless they are truly others, creatures of the night, then things become tricky, and bloody; or we turn away. But *Macbeth* makes us look. It may even make us face a creature within: the other that lurks somewhere behind our words. The demon that by day pulls strings from the shadows here bursts into glorious flame. I will be different. I will create. I will set fire to the world. I *will*! And is that not, in the end, the beginning of all creation, as well as all destruction? Is that not how the new arrives: in flames?

The issue is an ancient one, with us since eyes 'beheld Satan as lightning fall from heaven' (Luke 10:18): how to distinguish evil from the sublime? Such arresting and domineering experiences are, as Montaigne writes, 'beyond rules, and above reason': 'the splendor of a lightning flash ... hath no communitie with our judgement; but ransacketh and ravisheth the same'.[124] The overt difficulties with *Macbeth* thus reveal difficulties implicit in other plays. In particular, if Shakespeare's events are dependent on sublime poetic language and structure, what is the nature of this lightning? It suggests that they fork from somewhere beyond Badiou's categories of 'truth'. The irreducible point of originality in Shakespeare's events may turn out to be poetry: art. That might make them 'artistic events', in Badiou's terminology, but, as in *Hamlet*, this designation doesn't tell us much. Or, perhaps we do not like what it tells us: that poetic events need have no grounding in anything moral, political or emancipatory; that new horizons of possibility may turn out to be nightmares; that new subjects may turn out to be murderous paranoiacs. Shakespeare's 'impartiality makes us uncomfortable', Bradley writes: 'we cannot bear to see him, like the sun, lighting up everything and judging nothing.'[125] Shakespeare's evental process of character creation remains in force in *Macbeth*, but it gives birth to a living deadness.

Philosophical and ethical categories, along with historical context, struggle in the face of Shakespeare's evental drama because its creation of presence – that Macbeth *does* arrive – almost becomes a cardinal virtue that overruns regular virtues.[126] Drama is animating: it brings 'what is not' to life. But the lightning, *Macbeth* tells us, is not without cost. And I think Shakespeare saw this too; or, at least I imagine he did. And I think he was not unmoved. For, after the flame dies for Coriolanus, we have Paulina and Prospero. There is an effort to recover something from the ashes, to bring life from the scorched ground. And there is something of both in *Lear*: something of the lightning strike of arrivals and the romances' resurrections, though both abortive. *Macbeth* thus prompts us to consider Shakespeare's relation to his art. Macbeth's substitution of the world for the linguistic excess of the weird sisters' supplementary realm is a deal with the devil that both brings spirits to life and makes the world barren. The black arts, but also 'art', are supplements that are gained at the expense of living. It is reminiscent of Faust's fatal refusal to burn his books, but it also foreshadows how Prospero's drowning of his book leads to a recuperated (if diminished) life.

Books, reading, writing, creativity, magic, illusion and imagining are both gateways and threats to living in these tales. 'What is not' threatens to usurp 'what is'. It recalls the double-edged writing of Derrida's 'Dangerous Supplement'.[127] First, '[t]he supplement adds itself, it is a surplus, a plenitude enriching another plenitude, the *fullest measure* of presence'.[128] It is, for Macbeth, energising and animating; it brings 'something more' into the self-presence of Duncan's realm. But, secondly, the 'supplement supplements'; it 'adds only to replace'.[129] The supplement 'intervenes or insinuates itself *in-the-place of* . . . the thing itself'.[130] The weird sisters' realm supplants the world it supplements. Macbeth destroys his situation so that 'nothing is but what is not'. Macbeth's 'horrible imaginings' give birth to an impossible desire for a world beyond action or representation, for a world that is fully present, for an end of the story and its subject. '[F]rom the abyss of representation, from the representation of representation, etc' is 'born' a 'desire of presence'.[131] This fraught aspect of imagination connects with a concern about tale-telling that is evident from Othello's tale of himself to winter's tales. There is, in the stories Shakespeare's subjects tell themselves, or behind them, an impulse towards the final, the settled state.

And yet, even in *Macbeth*, life is given to us. Whitehead writes that '[t]he meaning of "givenness" is, that what *is* "given" might not have been "given"; and that what *is not* "given" *might have been* "given"'.[132] By 'giving' life to Macbeth and refusing it to others, Shakespeare leaves us with the question of 'what if'. The play calls us to think how this life is given and whether it might have been given otherwise: to consider a 'potentiality . . . for creativeness' that might be divorced from its particular 'given'.[133] We are left with the feeling that there is a potentiality in Macbeth's arrival, all but smothered, that means more than judgements of 'justice and 'traitor'. If any hope resides in *Macbeth* it resides in this thinking of what might have been: in a 'potentiality' that was present but is lost, and in thereby following Macbeth into 'what is not'. Such thinking is far from Hegel's idea of tragic affirmation, which sees the hero's death as the 'resurrection of the spirit out of . . . the finitude which is inadequate to it'.[134] One can hardly sense a 'resurrection of the spirit' in Macbeth's nihilistically resigned death, 'signifying nothing'. Hope resides only in the unrealised idea of surpassing the simple dichotomy between the sterile world of Duncan and the living death of Macbeth. As Žižek writes of lost causes, from Maoism to the Islamic Revolution, 'while these phenomena were, each in its own way, a historical failure and monstrosity . . . *this is not the whole truth*: there was in each of them a redemptive moment which gets lost in the liberal-democratic rejection – and it is crucial to isolate this moment'.[135] There is a history that is not written by the Malcolms. *Macbeth*'s redemptive potential, which is a barest hint, lies in the unrealised possibility of breaking the deadlock between the irruptive Macbeth and the closed Macbeth that repeats the situation. Not an answer, then, but a push to think: how can one live with the negative power – the 'what is not' – without it becoming all? Is there a balance between being and event, between what is and what is not?

These are questions with which Shakespeare's 'late plays' grapple. While it would be conjecture to claim that Shakespeare himself was 'embarrassed' by the way his technology of character creation could create a subject of alluring evil, in the late plays there is a movement away from such single dominating consciousnesses, as character becomes more diffused and tentative. Perhaps in response to the electric evil of *Macbeth*, we are not given a single subject but, as in *The Tempest*'s isle, a world of subjective orbits and interrelations. Perhaps there is, in the fading light of Prospero's abjuration, a search for a supplement that does not supplant but reconciles, albeit at a loss. If the arrivals of Shakespeare's tragic subjects are in some way 'right' – that it is only fitting that Romeo and Juliet should be transformed by love, that Othello should be shaken in Cyprus, that Hamlet should return in readiness, and even that Macbeth should scan the horrors of imagination – this dynamic is fundamentally altered in the late plays. In a sense they are about characters who refuse or defer arrivals. And, even when they do arrive, there is a sense that it is too late, that something has been irrevocably lost. The trend starts with *King Lear*, the story of a man who avoids exposure to the event of love and whose transformation is not an originary lightning strike but a painful recovery.

CHAPTER 6

The Cordelia Event: Seizing the Vanished in King Lear

Lear is different. It has Lear but it also has Cordelia, France, the Fool, Edgar, Edmond, Kent and Gloucester. In what follows, I suggest that the diffused subjectivity of *Lear* trails into the very different 'arrivals' of Shakespeare's late plays. To do so, I analyse the play through what I label the 'Cordelia event'. Whereas 'what is not' was an alluring vision of finality towards which Macbeth quested, Cordelia's silent love, expressed as 'Nothing' (F.I.i.85), is *King Lear*'s point of emergence. It dismantles the static, mechanistic worldview that underpins Lear's love-test and unleashes the creative energy of the void. This energy no longer settles on one subject, however, but haunts the play as its foundational 'vanishing term'. It arrives only to vanish but then vanishes only to reappear fleetingly in disparate and unpredictable subject points.

The Love-Test

The play begins with a kingdom that is to be divided according to a test but, as Coleridge observes, Lear's 'triple division' of the kingdom is 'already determined ... previously to the trial of professions':[1]

> Know that we have divided
> In three our kingdom, and 'tis our fast intent
> To shake all cares and business from our age,
> Conferring them on younger strengths *while we*
> *Unburdened crawl toward death.*
>
> (F.I.i.35–39, Folio-only text is italicised)

Because it is predetermined, Coleridge views the 'trial of professions' as 'but a trick'.[2] It is a ceremonial show, performed after the fact of division, in which nothing is at stake (until Cordelia's 'Nothing' puts everything on the table). The Folio text, which is the primary text for this chapter due to its emphasis on the centrality of 'Nothing', highlights this point by adding Lear's pronouncement that he has 'this hour a constant will to publish' (F.I.i.41). The will is already written; it just needs to be 'publish[ed]' through the formal exchange with his daughters. The Folio also adds the important phrase 'while we / Unburdened crawl toward death', which fairly well sums up Lear's project. As Cavell observes, Lear's plan is to 'exchang[e] his fortune for his love at one swap'.[3] He attempts to reach a settled state in which all debts have been paid, he securely possesses his daughters' love, and he can therefore rest 'unburdened' by future obligations and actions, including the burden of loving. As another Folio addition makes clear, he tries to bank these absolute expressions of love, along with his 100 knights, '[s]ince' he will no longer have the power to command them: 'Tell me, my daughters – / *Since now we will divest us both of rule, / Interest of territory, cares of state* – / Which of you shall we say doth love us most' (F.I.i.46–49, Folio-only text italicised). By treating love as a property to be possessed, Lear reveals his inability to 'tolerate' the 'incalculable emotional possibilities and costs' of 'immanence'.[4] Rather, 'in the manufactured "occasion" of the love contest' Lear 'attempts to cancel any further dependence on occasion for the remainder of his life (crawling "unburdened" to "death")'.[5] But if the subject is 'the *bearer* of a fidelity',[6] it *must* be burdened. The subject is its process. Lear thus exiles love by replacing its irruptive 'occasion' with his mechanistic quasi-event. He 'unburden[s]' himself of the process that *constitutes* subjectivity.

Bergson's processual worldview rebuts the 'mechanical explanation', which 'regard[s] the future and the past as calculable functions of the present, and thus . . . claim[s] that *all is given*'.[7] Considered in these terms, Lear's love-test operates as a mechanism that specifies a calculable input and a calculable output: an absolute expression of love brings a third of a kingdom. Moreover, the result is already '*given*': the will is written, the kingdom divided, and his daughters' loves already counted upon before their final exchange. Lear's calculations thus resemble 'radical finalism' and 'radical mechanism', which are both 'reluctant to see . . . an unforeseeable creation of form'.[8] 'Nothing will come of nothing' (F.I.i.88). In fact, according to Bergson, asking 'why bodies or minds exist rather than nothing' necessarily leads to a search for 'a logical principle, such as A = A', that has 'the power of creating itself'.[9] By passing 'through the idea of the nought in order to reach that of being, the being to which we come is a logical or mathematical essence'.[10] And so 'a static conception of the real is forced on us: everything appears given once and for all, in eternity'.[11] Ultimately, Lear's strict opposition between something and nothing (rather than processes and gradations) absolutises something – substance – and exiles nothing from the kingdom as a 'stranger' (F.I.i.113).

The conflict between Lear and Cordelia also ties into an Early Modern tension between the mechanical and 'Nothing'. For Francis Bacon, it was the newly discovered scientific methods and mechanical instruments that revealed the mechanical nature of nature itself[12] and thereby gave rise to the belief 'that the world' was 'on the brink of being rendered calculable and hence predictable'.[13] While the 'idea of analysing human and animal bodies in terms of mechanisms' is typically 'associated with Cartesian [thought]', Jonathan Sawday has shown that this 'system of metaphors and similes' was 'in play' in Shakespeare's time.[14] For example, in 'Thomas Dekker's *The Seuen Deadly Sinnes of London* (1606), we read how humans are restless mechanisms, anatomical machines in perpetual motion'.[15] But while '[w]heels and mechanical motion seem to haunt *King Lear*'[16] – including the repeatedly evoked wheel of Fortune and Lear's 'wheel of fire' (IV.vi.40) – the play is very far from mechanistic. Indeed, a wheel of Fortune seems paradoxical given Fortune's capriciousness, while a wheel of fire has no immediately obvious function. Machines and mechanistic thinking may be integral to Lear's kingdom, but they are ultimately unable to control its excess. Fortune and fire soon send their respective wheels spinning out of control.[17] Moreover, while Lear's love-test may operate in a mechanical fashion, the fact that the kingdom is already divided also makes it quite superfluous. It is a showman's 'trick' devised to facilitate Lear's desire for extravagant expressions of love. It facilitates a surplus or 'superflux' (F.III.iv.35) that is at odds with its mechanical operation.

What, then, distinguishes the surplus Lear seeks from the surplus Juliet describes in her depthless bounty? The answer is surely exposure. Whereas Juliet exposes herself to the obscure event of love and the unseen other, Lear insulates himself. Whereas love 'exposes the subject to everything that is not its dialectic and its mastery',[18] the love-test is an elaborate apparatus for containing the excess of love within the logic of measurement and thereby avoiding exposure to others and events. The love-test treats 'love' as a 'substance' to be possessed rather than the utterance 'I love you', which, as Nancy stresses, is an ongoing 'promise [that] does not anticipate or assure the future'.[19] By staging a once-and-for-all trade, Lear seeks to avoid the helplessness of relying on a promise. And he thereby avoids becoming the 'autonomous' individual who, in Nietzsche's words, 'has developed his own, independent, long-range will, which dares to make promises'.[20] Lear, like Macbeth, longs to reach the future in an instant.

Considered in Badiou's terms, one might say that Lear is the 'one' that 'results' from the unifying structure, or 'count', of his love-test: 100 knights and three professions of 'love' are given over to the one King of a kingdom he has already divided in three. But as Badiou stresses, '[t]*he one as such* ... *is not*', which is to say that '[i]t is always the result of a count, the effect of a structure',[21] which excludes all inconsistent multiples. The 'one' is not the origin or centre Lear wants it to be. The 'manufactured "occasion"'[22] of the love-test is thus not an event but a 'simulacrum'. Although the simulacrum uses 'names borrowed from real truth-processes', such as 'love', it 'convokes not the void but the "full" particularity or presumed substance of that situation'.[23] Lear attempts to extract the 'presumed substance' of Cordelia's love, and of his own kingly self, from its process. The result is closure: 'Fidelity to a simulacrum' leads to the 'unending construction' of the 'closed particularity of an abstract set'.[24] Love is closed off from its constitutive promise and possessed by Lear as this 'abstract set' of one. Cordelia's 'Nothing', then, is the 'dysfunction of [Lear's structuring] count'.[25] It punctures Lear's 'one' and reveals the situation's void. Her soft words burst into Lear's situation with extraordinary violence, revealing the artificial nature of Lear's mechanistic structure along with the inconsistent excess, or 'superflux', that makes love possible.

'Nothing'

Even amidst the clanging of Lear's machine-like ritual, another force is operating. Before her 'Nothing' brings the gears to a shuddering halt, Cordelia's love works between them silently. Her asides form little pockets of genuine feeling amidst her sisters' gross flattery:

GONERIL   A love that makes breath poor and speech unable.
             Beyond all manner of so much I love you.
CORDELIA   What shall Cordelia speak? Love and be silent.
LEAR   Of all these bounds even from this line to this.   (F.I.i.58–61)

Cordelia is faced with a problem: how does one participate in a simulacrum of love when one really does love?[26] 'She hits on the first solution to her dilemma: Love, and be silent. That is, love *by being* silent.'[27] It is, of course, a decisive moment. Cordelia maintains her silent love despite being hemmed in by the long, formal and very public speeches of her family, with her dissembling sisters on the one side and the implacable droning of Lear's pre-determined division on the other: 'Of all these bounds even from this line to this'. The same pattern occurs in her second speech, which follows Regan's extravagances:

CORDELIA   Then poor Cordelia –
            And yet not so, since I am sure my love's
            More ponderous than my tongue.
LEAR   To thee and thine hereditary ever
            Remain this ample third of our fair kingdom.   (F.I.i.73–78)

While Cordelia's forthright words arise in the situation, they are also cut off from it, contained in their own little bubble. They elicit no response from Lear, who goes on measuring and dividing. It is, of course, being cut off from, and set off by, the heartless economy of exchange that (as with Hamlet's rejection of 'seems') makes Cordelia's words so powerful. Compressed between her sisters' theatricality, her asides evoke an alternative vision of love as something bare and honest: a divested, stripped-down love, free from the lendings of property and titles. It supports Yachnin and Selkirk's argument that '[m]etatheater deepens character': 'It seems to cast off theatricality as an inferior or questionable representational mode so that what is being acted is given the status of non-theatrical representation.'[28] We believe in Cordelia's silent love.

As affecting as they may be, Cordelia's trapped asides also seem powerless, unable to avert the march of Lear's mechanical logic. Indeed, the ineffectuality of Cordelia's love in a harsh, bleak world is a fairly dominant reading of the play, and one that led to Tate's much maligned happy-ending rewrite. Tate's Cordelia is neither silent nor sublime but explains her refusal to participate in the love-test in calculated terms, determining to 'tempt the choleric king / Rather to leave me dowerless, than condemn me / To loathed embraces!' (Tate, I.i.92–95).[29] In this conventional battle between obedience to her father or her heart, Cordelia's beautiful refusal becomes cynical and disingenuous. While the contemporary appreciation of *Lear* rejects Tate's response, it similarly accepts *Lear*'s bleakness. It accepts the powerless nature of Cordelia's silent love: 'Pity, like kindness, seems in *Lear* to be precious yet ineffectual.'[30] I reject both positions. Cordelia's silent love is not merely a sublime failure; it is the play's central event, the force behind its arrivals. Indeed, in theatrical terms, it is immediately effectual: 'Even though Cordelia's passages are spoken as "asides"', it is they (rather than Regan's and Goneril's speeches) that 'directly cue Lear'.[31] Her silence thus has an obscured dramatic power. It *does* something, both to us and to Lear. And it soon does much more: prompting France's arrival and Lear's explosive rejection.

The violent breakdown of Lear's mechanistic love-test stems from his exchange of 'Nothing' with Cordelia, the play's pivotal moment. The exchange directly follows Lear's question, 'what can you say to draw / A third more opulent than your sisters? Speak' (F.I.i.83–84). The term 'to draw' suggests a mechanical purpose for the expression of love, tainting any participation with the idea that love is exchanged for kingdoms. As such, Cordelia does not necessarily refuse to love, or even to express her love, but refuses to participate in a competition that *is not love*. To match her sisters would pander to the absolutism that severs Lear from the process of love. 'Cordelia's real transgression is not unkindness as such, but', as Dollimore writes, 'speaking in a way which threatens to show too clearly how the laws of human kindness operate in the service of property, contractual, and power relations'.[32] By separating her 'heart' from her 'mouth' she breaks up the unity of love and show, love and kingdoms, and thereby unbalances all Lear's equations:

CORDELIA	Nothing, my lord.
LEAR	Nothing?
CORDELIA	Nothing.
LEAR	Nothing will come of nothing. Speak again.
CORDELIA	Unhappy that I am, I cannot heave
	My heart into my mouth. I love your majesty
	According to my bond, no more nor less.

(F.I.i.85–91)

As an 'inconsistency' within Lear's mechanistic 'count', Cordelia's love – like her asides – is 'not actually presented'[33] in the situation. It is a 'phantom remainder',[34] excluded from the count, expressible only obliquely, as 'Nothing'. As Badiou writes, because within 'set theory what is presented is multiple of multiples ... the unpresentable can only figure within language as what is "multiple" of *nothing*'.[35] The eventual subject, however, must 'try to *name* the very thing which is impossible to *discern*': 'to name [it] without naming it'.[36] Hence Juliet's struggle to alter the language of love following the unjustified event, to speak it as a process rather than as a final name. Cordelia arrives within a similar dilemma. Meisel notes that 'Cordelia is the first instance I at least have met in drama where the gap between feeling and capacity for its expression in words is taken seriously'.[37] Because love emerges from the void, reasons, justifications and explanations cannot account for it. Love is again that which cannot be discerned and Cordelia names it 'without naming it': 'Nothing'.

Cordelia's speech also works to reveal what Lear's legalistic love-test is really asking for: a 'bond', a binding of love to him in exchange for kingdoms. Lear, of course, doubles down on his equation by threatening material deprivation – 'Mend your speech a little / Lest you may mar your fortunes' (F.i.92–93) – and thereby prompts Cordelia's harsh elaboration of her 'bond'. Her speech, which precipitates Lear's breakdown, is expressed in short, sharp words, many monosyllabic:

> Good my lord,
> You have begot me, bred me, loved me.
> I return those duties back as are right fit –
> Obey you, love you, and most honour you.
> Why have my sisters husbands if they say
> They love you all? Haply when I shall wed
> That lord whose hand must take my plight shall carry
> Half my love with him, half my care and duty.   (F.I.i.93–101)

There may be love in here, but it is a difficult speech. Its starkness brutally rejects not only Lear's grandiose ceremony but also the very human feelings underpinning it. Lear is almost left behind, weak and bereft, for this future 'lord'. What's more, Cordelia herself uses the language of measurement and exchange. She refuses to love Lear 'all' because her future lord will 'carry half' her 'love'. For this reason, Bradley writes that '[t]here surely never was a more unhappy speech' and concludes that Cordelia 'perverts the truth when it implies that to give love to a husband is to take it from a father'.[38] At best this is only half the truth, however. Enmeshed in a situation in which love is infected by property and measurement, we have a twinned Cordelia. On the one side, she speaks as a resolute daughter and combative sister, who, in the violence of the situation, offers an almost cruel assertion of her integrity. (And, one might add, refuses what is surely an inappropriate fatherly demand for absolute love.) Not that *Cordelia* is cruel, but the starkness of her speech, the aloofness of her truth from Lear's emotional needs, allows her to be interpreted as such: as an heir to *Measure for Measure*'s Isabella. Hence Bradley's reference to her 'failure' to make the 'unreasonable old King feel that he was fondly loved'[39] and Coleridge's reference to her 'some little faulty admixture of pride and sullenness'.[40] Shakespeare does not foreclose such judgements. On the other hand, however, Cordelia is almost a fairy-tale figure: she is the 'good' sister who opposes the 'evil' sisters; she loves honestly from the start; she speaks to us directly; and she speaks truth that we do not question. It is thus hard to do her justice. There is a tendency to either psychologise – to blame or excuse – or treat her as an emblematic figure of love.

I want to suggest another approach, for, despite being implicated in the language of measurement, Cordelia also *releases something new* into the situation. Cordelia's language may express the mechanistic, legal nature of the love-test, which treats love as a 'return' on investment, but her asides and silence also introduce a love *beyond* these bounds. Cordelia's refusal to give 'all' does not reject love but rejects Lear's love-test, while affirming an alternate vision of love that is left undetermined, anticipated, and almost transcendent.[41] Of course, the whole thrust of *Being and Event* is 'that for the void to become localizable at the level of presentation . . . a dysfunction of the count is required, which results from an excess-of-one'.[42] Seen as a dysfunction of Lear's attempted restructuring, Cordelia's 'nothing' infinitely exceeds his 'count'. It reveals that his structure is not natural or complete, that it has omitted key data, that it does not cover the field. It forces Lear to glimpse a blind spot, an abyss, in his count.

We see this in the fact that Cordelia's speech not only flows from 'Nothing'; it is directed towards a shadowy future husband who is as yet nothing. This 'lord' enrages Lear, raising the spectre of multiple loves and multiple others that would fracture his unified structure. In the context of 'Nothing', however, Cordelia's reference to 'half' her love is immeasurable. The logic of calculation breaks down – as it does so consistently in this play. If love is an uncounted excess, there is no 'thing' to be halved. What is half of nothing or half of infinity? Rather than simple divisibility, Cordelia's 'lord' implies multiplicity. There are multiple loves to be given, not one. As Witmore puts it, if we treat love not as a 'quantity', but 'as a quality, love would no longer have degrees, only varieties'.[43] Of course, by treating it as a quantifiable property, Lear sees Cordelia's future 'lord' not as a different variety of love but a corruption of her love for him, indeed, the voiding of love.

Ultimately, what Cordelia's 'Nothing' reveals is not some inward, privileged world that Lear misses, but the fact that Lear's situation is not 'natural': that it derives from an artificial 'count', from property, power and show. To maintain his stable structure, then, Lear must reject what is inconsistent with it. Having glimpsed the abyss, Lear can no longer turn a blind eye – he must blind it. As Othello sacrifices Desdemona to maintain his romantic self-image, Lear sacrifices Cordelia to maintain his kingly image of himself:

> Here I disclaim all my paternal care,
> Propinquity, and property of blood,
> And as a stranger to my heart and me
> Hold thee from this for ever.   (F.I.i.111–14)

Lear's attempt to efface Cordelia's existence is almost the definition of 'all or nothing'. '[He] loved her most' (F.I.i.121), but as her love is not given absolutely, it is absolutely rejected: 'Better thou / Hadst not been born than not t'have pleased me better' (F.I.i.231–32). Lear's extravagant profession of severance is the dark mirror of Goneril's and Regan's extravagant professions of love. Its absoluteness and highly wrought imagery reflects the sort of once-and-for-all declaration he expected. Perhaps most striking is that it happens so fast: from '[m]end your speech a little' (F.I.i.92) to 'Let it be so. Thy truth be your dower' (F.I.i.106) in fourteen lines. We are barely 100 lines into the play and something terrible has come from 'Nothing': Lear's absolute disclaiming of 'paternal care'. As if one could remove one's humanity by a kingly performative.[44] We have the monstrous seed of the play's extravagant curses of creation: 'If she must teem, / Create her child of spleen' (F.I.iv.243–44).

We can tie the monstrousness of 'Nothing' back to ideas of process. Lear's demand to possess love absolutely suggests a problem inherent in Cartesian dualism: 'Descartes' notion of [independent] "substance"' treats the object of perception 'in complete disconnection from any other such existent'.[45] The result is the 'burden[ing of] th[e] solitary mind with the impossible task of finding absolute certainty instead of plugging it into the connections that would provide it with all the relative certainties it needed to know and to act'.[46] We saw a similar movement in *Othello*: by treating Desdemona's 'faith' as a substance to be perceived 'out there', Othello turns the interrelation between subject and event into an unfathomable gap. The 'collapse' of his supposed knowledge, or 'best case', leads to a radical unmooring from existence – 'a self-consuming disappointment that seeks world-consuming revenge'[47] – that is manifested in excessive, violent oaths of severance. Cavell describes this as 'the human wish to escape the bounds or bonds of the human': 'the human craving for, and horror of, the inhuman, of limitlessness, of monstrousness'.[48] And so Lear's monstrous curses turn nature against nature once the 'naturalness' of his structure breaks down. The 'sacred radiance of the sun', 'The mysteries of Hecate and the night' and the 'operation of the orbs' (F.I.i.107–9) are all aligned against 'paternal care, / Propinquity, and property of blood'. A 'world-consuming revenge' indeed.

Here, the play's tragic trajectory leaps out before us, as a torch into darkness. We know that in Shakespeare such oaths have consequences. All Lear's careful measurements, his threes and ones, are annihilated in an instant. And that is the play, in a way: the razing of measurements and calculations, both for richer and for poorer, for better and for worse. The play famously takes a sledgehammer to poetic justice and its source material. Indeed, Bradley contends that 'the "moral" of *King Lear* is presented in the irony of this collocation:

> *Albany.* The gods defend her!
> *Enter Lear with Cordelia dead in his arms.*[49]

In one sense, then, Lear's kingly performative is successful: it strips 'paternal care' from the world and makes the 'barbarous Scythian' his 'neighbour[]' (F.I.i.114–17). There is no going back, except through pain, blood and barbarity. And, of course, the going back cannot undo what is done. As in *Macbeth*, words have a terrible power. Nothing indeed comes of Cordelia's 'Nothing', but nothing is not an emptiness or non-being; nothing, in this play, has presence. It enters the world, or the world enters it, in all its monstrous and lawless excess.

We see this very quickly. Lear makes a void in nature by turning it against itself and, in the very next scene, Edmond, the lively agent of darkness, kneels before it as his 'goddess' (F.I.ii.1). What is Edmond's catechism? 'Nothing'. Gloucester is in a state of shock as the known world dissolves and suddenly he finds the dark materials in his own home: 'What paper were you reading?' / 'Nothing, my Lord' (F.I.ii.30–31). Edmond here uses 'Nothing' in expert, Iago-like fashion to conjure the monstrous, and it again leads to the violent expulsion of a loved one. Edmond, of course, repeats Cordelia's line exactly: 'Nothing, my Lord.' He re-activates its explosive charge. Gloucester is thus quite wrong to claim that 'The quality of nothing hath not such need / to hide itself' (F.I.ii.33–34). As the situation's inconsistency, or void, 'nothing' must be repressed, exiled, destroyed: 'Abhorred villain, unnatural, detested, brutish villain' (F.I.ii.73): 'Into her womb convey sterility' (F.I.iv.240). 'Nothing' threatens the whole edifice of 'something' if one presumes that 'Nothing will come of nothing'.

Cordelia's 'Nothing' prompts not just an intrusion from the void, in the mode of *Hamlet*'s ghost, but a full-scale collapse into it, like a world swallowed by a black hole. The terrain is vague and indistinct,[50] and its characters are pulled like magnets to the places (the heath, Gloucester's castle) where lightning crashes. Individuals too are not distinct in this inverted underworld where nothing circulates like spirits through the air, waiting to strike at the opportune (or inopportune) moment. 'Nothing' comes (in one of its guises) as inverted repetition. We've already seen Edmond repeat Cordelia's 'Nothing', and we soon see Cornwall repeat France's 'seiz[ure]' (F.I.i.250) of Cordelia when he embraces Edmond:

'You we first seize on' (F.II.i.115). Edmond raises the prospect of 'Tom o' Bedlam' (F.I.ii.123) and his brother then embraces nothing and becomes Poor Tom. Lear curses Goneril: 'You nimble lightnings, dart your blinding flames / Into her scornful eyes' (F.II.ii.330–31), but the flames fork uncontrollably, and Gloucester is blinded. The normal, calculable mode of existence is ripped apart and these lightnings arc and curl through the void-world, striking and re-striking – lightning always strikes twice in *Lear*.

What 'Nothing' unleashes is the opposite of mechanistic or 'constructivist thought', which is built 'around the exclusion of the indiscernible, the indeterminate, the un-predicable'.[51] Because mechanical thought 'does not tolerate interruption', there 'is no event, since everything which happens is locally calculable'.[52] Montaigne mocks such reasoning (that '[b]ecause nothing is made of nothing: God was not able to frame the world without matter'[53]) as the height of human vanity: 'This law thou aleagest is but a municipall law, and thou knowest not what the universall is.'[54] What is at stake here is the possibility of creation. In claiming that the future can be explained by what 'immediately preceded it', mechanistic thought rejects 'pure chance' and 'miracles',[55] which are critical to Badiou's irruptive events and to Shakespeare's irruptive drama. But even if we accept that, physically, 'something cannot come from nothing', 'experience alone will tell us which aspects or functions of reality must count for something, and which for nothing'.[56] Although the void 'counts ... for nothing' in the situation, it *becomes something* through the chance of the event. For Lear, it is only as his machine collapses that the reductive consequences of this mechanistic logic are revealed:

GONERIL   What need you five and twenty, ten, or five,

          . . .

REGAN   What need one?
LEAR   O, reason not the need! Our basest beggars
         Are in the poorest thing superfluous.   (F.II.ii.427–31)

It is in response to this countdown, plummeting to zero, that Lear recognises that calculability is not enough, that something 'superfluous' is what makes us human. 'O, reason not the need!' is, as Grady writes, 'a shift away from the implications of the instrumental, reductive logic employed earlier by Lear in his quantification of love and reductive banishment of Cordelia'.[57] It is the beginning of his movement, through the 'Nothing' of madness, to Cordelia's alternative vision of love.

What Comes of Nothing

What comes from this void? Hatred and disclaiming, certainly, and the horrors to come, but also love: the love of Kent, who throws himself before the dragon, and the love of France, which emerges from nowhere. Uncalculating love irrupts into the situation almost the moment it is ruptured by 'Nothing'. The 'Cordelia event' is immediately and explosively effectual. But what of Cordelia herself? We might say that she arrives as a subject in the second clause of her first line. Cordelia's initiating aside not only establishes an inward-looking consciousness but also addresses a crossroads, a very specific problem in the here-and-now: 'What shall Cordelia speak?' She does not know what to do. She is faced with circumstances that force her to decide what to become. There is a gap, albeit minimal, between the question and her answer: 'Love and be silent.' And that is, perhaps, space enough for a condensed arrival. Of course, the fact that these words are 'unprepared for' means that traditional character criticism posits a pre-existing reticence, truthfulness or pride, to explain them. But, in processual terms, Cordelia is founded here and only here, in loving and being silent. It is only *through* this action that she becomes Cordelia. Her statement is situational rather than essential; it is not a mantra for life. There is nothing to indicate she previously loved silently; in fact, Lear's reaction suggests quite the opposite. Ultimately, however, this line of enquiry does not get us very far. To say that Cordelia arrives in her first line begs the question: how do we know? It is not really an arrival in the sense I've discussed. We do not, for instance, see her shaken or re-oriented (even if an actor might play her that way). Given Cordelia 'herself' remains unyielding, I think it is more profitable to examine what arrives *from* the 'Cordelia event'.

The Unexpected Arrival of France

Although Cordelia is something of an emblematic character and disappears for much of the play, the 'Cordelia event' is different. As the void of Lear's mechanistic situation, it has an efficacy that goes beyond 'Cordelia'. The creativity of her 'Nothing' streams into a dispersed constellation of subject points. The first of these is France. Initially an empty and conventional suitor, France arrives by taking up and reactivating Cordelia's loving 'Nothing', before he disappears back into nothing. We here witness a mode of emergence radically different from Lear's mechanism. According to Lear's logic of calculation and exchange, the consequences of Cordelia's

'Nothing' are inevitable: she loses her third of the kingdom and Burgundy discards her. But then something far from inevitable happens. As Fernie remarks in the context of Badiou's insistence that 'the impossible happens': 'The impossible happens, too, when France throws his lot in with the discarded and disgraced Cordelia.'[58] Not only does France's sudden intervention shatter the equation of love with rewards, it is also in no way prepared for by his 'character'. It is not just that no pre-existing relationship with Cordelia explains this decision – there is no France whatsoever.

France does not arrive all at once, however. His initial speeches do not convey love but bewilderment at Lear's sudden turn against his 'best object' (F.I.i.211). France is not automatically 'here' in his mode but awakens slowly, as if from a deep sleep. His initial defence of Cordelia is not impassioned and personal, but detached and stilted: 'Love's not love / When it is mingled with regards that stands / Aloof from th'entire point' (F.I.i.236–38). France soon becomes something more than a stereotypical suitor, however, not least because he channels the audience's energies. Cavell speaks of one's 'rush of gratitude toward France, one's almost wild relief as he speaks his beautiful trust'.[59] Even if he is not yet speaking *to* Cordelia, he embodies and expresses our desire to defend Cordelia and embrace her alternate vision of love: 'Will you have her? / She is herself a dowry' (F.I.i.238–39). He is thus something of an audience surrogate, which, as Meisel writes, is often 'a learner, open and vulnerable to experience, and typically suffering change'.[60] Most fundamentally, France shows how openness to an unjustified and uncalled-for happening can transfigure one's being.

France emerges not merely in opposition to the feeble 'love' propounded by Lear and the 'dukes in wat'rish Burgundy' (F.I.i.256), but also in confluence with Cordelia. The little pockets of silence formed by Cordelia's asides are what animate France. France recuperates Cordelia's silent love – crushed into 'Nothing' by the patri-mechanical situation – and makes it something. He activates its latent power. Indeed, almost all of France's speeches work by taking up the stifled potential in Cordelia's speech. If the 'Cordelia event' is the 'not' that ruptures Lear's situation, one might think of France as the 'but' of Badiou's fidelity. He operates almost as a *refrain* that picks up Cordelia's words and actualises them. He takes up Cordelia's rejection of the 'oily art' of flattery (F.I.i.222) when he speaks of the 'tardiness in nature' that 'leaves the history unspoken / That it intends to do' (F.I.i.233–35). He takes up her implied affirmation of love when he challenges Burgundy to love Cordelia without 'mingl[ing]' her with her portion of the kingdom (F.I.i.236–37) (which in turn prompts Cordelia's rejection of Burgundy). And he immediately takes up her rejection of love as 'respect and fortunes' (F.I.i.246) when he embraces her as 'most rich, being poor' (F.I.i.248). France here 'seize[s] upon' her words not in generalisations, or merely as our surrogate, but as his own most cherished possession:

> Fairest Cordelia, that art most rich, being poor;
> Most choice, forsaken; and most loved, despised:
> Thee and thy virtues here I seize upon.
> Be it lawful, I take up what's cast away.
> Gods, gods! 'Tis strange that from their cold'st neglect
> My love should kindle to inflamed respect. –
> Thy dowerless daughter, King, thrown to my chance,
> Is queen of us, of ours, and our fair France.   (F.I.i.248–55)

The speech builds and swells with its powerful oppositions – 'most choice, forsaken; and most loved despised' – that culminate in the action of 'seiz[ing]' and 'tak[ing] up'. Here, France is doing. The first four lines mark the arrival of an *active* subject that seizes love. The next two lines, beginning with 'Gods, gods!', are an aside that speaks to a suddenly emerging inward regard that is reminiscent of Othello's wonder in Cyprus. Taken aback, France's speech turns to the fact that something 'strange' has happened to him and stopped him in his tracks. The legal language of goods and seizure gives way to something more introspective, as France, seeing himself as if from the outside, confronts his own transformation.

As against Lear's attempt to treat love as a given, France's refrain gives rise to something that was not there before. From Cordelia's 'Nothing' and France's initial emptiness we have the dramatic emergence of something from nothing: the emergence of a subject. 'Nothing' is thus given a dramatic creativeness. We are dealing not with an 'astronomical, physical and chemical fact' whose future 'is foreseen', but with the creativity of 'an original situation' that 'imparts something of its own originality to its elements'.[61] Far from his initially stilted verse, we have the triumphant rhyme of 'chance' meeting 'France'. The triumph is of course short lived. France's archaic, almost chivalric poetry cannot survive in Shakespeare's tragedy. His form of restitution is not possible and he soon disappears. Where France differs from typical romance heroes, however, is in his very discontinuity. He does not possess a stable mode of chivalric being but emerges from an initial emptiness by seizing upon 'Nothing' – upon the void.

We can break this down further. 'Gods, gods!' speaks to the way his sudden apprehension of Cordelia's silent love intrudes as an almost divine force. Like Luther's 'alien righteousness', it comes 'from without' the individual.[62] ''Tis strange' speaks to its newness and unaccountability. While the dubious legality of the happening – 'Be it lawful' – shows how it is, in Badiou's terms, '*supplementary*; thus absolutely detached from, or unrelated to, all the rules of the situation'.[63] Even France's old-fashioned rhyme expresses how the givenness of the event comes unlooked for, 'thrown' to him by 'chance'. It suggests Badiou's idea that '[t]o be faithful is to gather together and distinguish the becoming legal of a chance'.[64] The chance thrown from the event must *become* 'lawful' because, like Pascal's miracle, it is an 'interruption of the law'.[65] France thereby foreshadows the wondrous response to the 'miracles' at the end of the romances, such as Leontes's 'O, she's warm! / If this be magic, let it be an art / Lawful as eating' (*TWT*, V.iii.109–11). He is not quite able to comprehend what has transformed him but, unlike Othello, he takes it up.

Importantly, Cordelia is not most rich *despite* being poor but is most loved *because* she is despised. It is because she is nothing within the existing structure that Cordelia becomes everything to France. As Fernie puts it, 'Cordelia's disgrace is a revelation to France. His plunge into love for his abject bride discovers different values.'[66] In other words, Cordelia's failed love is 'a dysfunction of [the situation's] count'.[67] Cordelia's abjectness names the situation's void – a love that is not exchanged for dowries but arrives like grace from 'Nothing' – and so her valueless, abject quality is what is most valued and extraordinary. There is therefore something sublime in France's seizure, as the infinite value of Cordelia's love is revealed through its abject failure. I here use 'sublime' in Žižek's sense of the 'magic ruptures which momentarily break the inexorable chain of tragic necessity'.[68] Žižek's formulation is poignant for arrivals:

> In schematized time, nothing really *new* can emerge – everything is always-already there, and merely deploys its inherent potential. The Sublime, on the contrary, marks the moment at which something emerges out of Nothing – something new that cannot be accounted for by reference to the pre-existing network of circumstances. We are dealing here with another temporality, the temporality of freedom, of a radical rupture in the chain of (natural and/or social) causality.[69]

Žižek moves beyond the usual idea of the sublime as occurring when an 'object or event is such that words fail and points of comparison disappear',[70] to the way that the void's excess enters the material world as an active force. Not that France 'himself' is sublime in his old-fashioned speech, but there is something sublime in Shakespeare's orchestration of France's union with Cordelia, whereby Cordelia's rejected love, like Badiou's event, 'proceeds "explosively", or "everywhere"',[71] creating new formations and new subjects – creating France – so that 'something emerges out of Nothing'.

We have, then, moved definitively away from Cartesian 'substance' and its 'chain of . . . causality'. We've seen, for Whitehead, that 'relatively to any actual entity, there is a "given" world of settled actual entities and a "real" potentiality, which is the datum for creativeness beyond that standpoint'.[72] *King Lear*'s tragic end undoubtedly shows that much of the world is 'given', is unresponsive to our hopes and dreams, and that breath doesn't stir from nothing. But the play also dramatises this world's 'creativeness': that the new also rises. Whereas the twentieth-century descendants of the Cartesian subject – be it the Bradleian subject trapped by 'character' or the postmodern subject trapped by language – focus on what is 'given' and thus miss this 'potentiality', Shakespeare's tragic vision powerfully reveals *both*: the inescapable tragic 'given' and the incredible creative 'potentiality'. Because France is initially subject-less, the process of this potentiality is made apparent. Grace is only materialised if it is 'seize[d] upon' and forced into the situation:

> Everything hinges on knowing whether an ordinary existence, breaking with time's cruel routine, encounters the material chance of serving a truth, thereby becoming, through subjective division and beyond the human animal's survival imperatives, an immortal . . . [I]t is incumbent upon us to found a materialism of grace through the strong, simple idea that every existence can one day be seized by what happens to it.[73]

The subject is not inoculated from existence, crawling unburdened to death, but is 'seized by what happens to it'. France's 'Gods, gods!' here points to a 'materialism of grace'. France, who far more obviously than Cordelia emerges from 'ordinary existence', becomes a subject, becomes 'an immortal', because he 'encounters the material chance of serving [the] truth' that Cordelia's silent love reveals. Because he 'seize[s] upon' it.

And then he is gone. Although I have resuscitated France from his disappearance in the play and its critical history, the play does not rest with France. France arrives from nothing only to disappear again. With Cordelia, he is exiled from the kingdom. The foundational moment is over and its agents are gone, the baton of arrivals passed to others. And while Cordelia will return, she returns not as the irruptive force of 'Nothing' but as a force of restoration and redemption. Rather than breaking up Lear's situation, the later Cordelia reconciles him to her love. The vanishing event does not flow into one subject as the weird sisters flow into Macbeth. *Lear* is thus less a story of one subject than a dramatisation of an event as such: how it flashes up before vanishing into the situation as a haunting excess that may (or may not) be reactivated by various subject points.

Vanishing Terms

Useful, here, is Badiou's 'vanishing term',[74] which is a forerunner to his 'truth-event'. The concept stems from his examination of the 'Greek atomists', who posited a 'strong (qualitative) difference … between atoms and the void'.[75] In this initial situation, the void is on one side and all the atoms on the other, which means that all atoms are qualitatively the same: they are 'identical with regard to the void' and so 'movement is perfectly null, for lack of a reference point with which to mark it'.[76] Everything is identical and hence indistinguishable. For the atoms to form *something*, something distinct or singular, deviation is required, or, in other words, an evental site: 'An atom is deviated, the world can come into being. The sudden obliqueness of a trajectory interrupts the identical movement of the atoms and produces a collision of particles from which is finally born a combined multiplicity, a thing, sufficient to make up a world.'[77] To 'deviate from its course', the atom 'except[s] itself from the law' that 'arranges for the identical rain of particles under the unanimous effect of the void'.[78] The vanishing term's deviation thus '*marks the void*, since it is affected by it in a singular way'.[79] Its errant 'movement … interrupts the isotropism of the domain',[80] founding the new through its difference to what was previously identical (or isotropic). In these terms, not only does Cordelia arrive from the situation's void, her 'Nothing' creates a new 'world', with a new relation to the void. It is the world of the play, with its arrivals and creations that do not obey Lear's demand that something emerge calculably from something.

It is, of course, a divided world, with two distinct texts, two distinct plots, and two distinct families, with Gloucester's family having its own originating act in his dark deed. And yet, this divided world is given its creative impetus by Cordelia's deviating 'Nothing', which dismantles the kingdom by marking the void. But although the 'vanishing term' founds a new 'Whole', it 'is none of the elements of the Whole' and 'is thus nothing' within it.[81] The new world of *King Lear* emerges 'under the effect of the deviation of one One' – of Cordelia, who is 'marked by the void' – but this deviating 'One' soon 'vanishe[s] in the whole'.[82] It is diffused throughout the play whose obsessive preoccupation with nothing constantly recalls its founding moment. Cordelia and France not only quietly haunt the play;

their shadows return to reactivate the void in strange ways. Take, for instance, the *Cat in the Hat* style exchange between Lear-Shadow and Kent-Caius about who put Kent in the stocks: 'No.' / 'Yes.' / 'No, I say.' / 'I say yea.' / 'By Jupiter, I swear no.' / 'By Juno, I swear ay.' / 'They durst not do't, They could not, would not do't. 'Tis worse than murder' (II.ii.189–93). In a sense this is 'worse than murder'. Worse than any murder in Shakespeare at least, far more demeaning and diminishing, albeit amusing too in a guilty way. But it is also, not coincidentally, a volleyed rally of something and nothing, yea and nay. And, again, something comes from nothing. Kent's 'ay[s]' have it. 'They could not', Lear declares, but they have. And so 'respect' (II.ii.194) is dead. Respect, of course, signifies the standard, calculable, modes of honour and exchange. And its collapse leads to an almost deranged, more than Fool-like, mode of speech. We know where this will lead: 'O, let me not be mad' (F.I.v.41), to resurrection or annihilation.

The Vanished and the Foolish: Dark Angels

The foundational deviating term may vanish into the new 'whole', but we experience its echoes and after-effects everywhere. The 'Cordelia event' unleashes a discontinuous 'stream of influence'[83] – of the evental, creative and even redemptive – that cuts through the 'given' mechanical world, albeit without offering any final salvation. By following this 'stream', I offer an alternative to bleak postmodern readings that see suffering and loss as the play's givens.

It is the Fool who most immediately takes up Cordelia's mantle of 'Nothing'. He is the bitter twin to the lady he 'pine[s] away' (F.I.iv.63) for, constantly reminding Lear that he is nothing within his mechanical kingdom: 'I am a fool; thou art nothing' (F.I.iv.159). The Fool relentlessly harps on the fact that, in calculable terms, Lear has given away everything for nothing; that he is no longer owed anything; that he is without the land and power that made him something. He thereby pushes Lear to the logical endpoint of his mechanistic worldview: 'This is not Lear' (F.I.iv.191). It is, ultimately, only from this 'not', from nothing, that the unjustified can emerge *'without being due'*.[84] In other words, the Fool's inversions call for a collapse of the old order that will clear a space for the creation of something other than Lear's debtor-creditor existence. We see this in the way the Fool articulates transactional logic – 'Let go thy hold when a great / wheel runs down a hill' (F.II.ii.238–39) – but then declares that he 'would have none but knaves follow' such 'counsel' (F.II.ii.241–42). Unlike the one who 'serves and seeks for gain', and therefore leaves 'when it begin[s] to rain', he 'will tarry, the fool will stay, / And let the wise man fly' away (F.II.ii.244–49). Although he will be dragged down with Lear's malfunctioning wheel, the Fool remains. He articulates the wise course but follows the foolish. He articulates the calculable end but follows the incalculable. In this, admittedly limited fashion, the Fool reflects an element of Kierkegaard: 'but he who expected the impossible became greater than all'.[85] And in this sense we might agree with Enid Welsford's conclusion 'that in this play [Shakespeare's] mightiest poetry is dedicated to the reiteration of the wilder paradoxes of the Gospels and of St Paul'.[86] Of course, the Fool too is soon replaced, first by Edgar's Poor Tom and then by Cordelia's return.

Edgar's multiple, incomplete selves are the most comprehensive, and difficult, example of the play's discontinuous arrivals from nothing – these flecks of the 'Cordelia event' that do not settle on one subject. Without consistent subjecthood, he performs his own series of vanishing (and reappearing) acts: from his initial emptiness, through Poor Tom and his demons, to the hint of an 'Edgar' voice in his compassionate asides, followed by his deeply ambivalent 'miracle working' on Dover's cliffs, and finally the return of something that was never there (Edgar). Despite being part of a different family, Edgar's vanishings and re-appearings also receive their impetus from the 'Cordelia event'. At his first appearance, he is a cipher deployed by his brother. Shakespeare withholds the usual 'subjectivity effects' given to a major character. He has no long speeches, asides, soliloquies, midline shifts, witticisms, or personal reflections. He is, in short, the empty fop that Edmond thinks he is. But all this changes after his re-entry is cued by Kent's ambiguous use of 'Nothing' ('from Cordelia'):

> Nothing almost sees miracles
> But misery. I know 'tis from Cordelia,
> Who hath now fortunately been informed
> Of my obscurèd course, and shall find time
> For this enormous state, seeking to give
> Losses their remedies.
> . . .
> Fortune, good night;
> Smile once more; turn thy wheel.   (F.II.ii.150–59)

The miracle Kent seeks is Cordelia. It is she who must 'give / Losses their remedies' and turn the wheel of Fortune. She knows; she sees; she will act. But there is also a hint that Cordelia is irrecoverable in Kent's 'Nothing almost sees miracles / But misery'. The darker implication is, of course, that misery *almost* sees miracles: miracles that do not come. In an essay devoted to Kent's phrase, Thomas Roche writes that this open-ended 'sentence becomes almost a paradigm of the various ways of interpreting the play, from a Lear transcending his misery into a miracle beyond our ken to a Lear descending into a further misery that deludes him as a miracle'.[87] But Kent's speech also does something more immediate: it cues Edgar's re-emergence as he determines 'To take the basest and most poorest shape' (F.II.ii.164). '[T]urn thy wheel', Kent implores, and it is Edgar who (in the same line) turns: 'I heard myself proclaimed' (F.II.ii.158). Cordelia may not answer Kent's prayer but the wheel does turn: it turns Edgar into something new through 'filth' and 'nakedness' (F.II.ii.166–68). He is not yet Poor Tom, but he has begun to strip off his foppish lendings, begun to become another.

Although Cordelia's incalculable 'Nothing' establishes 'an absolutely qualitative difference'[88] from the mechanical situation, the new world it produces is far from one of pure event or miracle. Between miracle and misery is Edgar's dirtier creativity. Whereas Cordelia is the miracle that haunts the 'misery' of *Lear*'s play-world – is the miracle that is 'almost' seen, that 'almost' breathes, and 'almost' gives losses their remedies – Edgar is the miracle it has to make do with.[89] He is the child who outlives its parents. Kent wants Cordelia's plenitude but he gets Edgar's emptiness as he plans to take shapes, cover himself in filth, roar, wander and disappear. Before Lear, Edgar becomes something new by first becoming nothing: '"Poor Tuelygod, Poor Tom." / That's something yet. Edgar I nothing am' (F.II.ii.177–78). Given the distinct lack of life or personality in Edgar's early scenes, it seems hard to disagree with Fernie's point that 'Edgar really speaks for the first time when he speaks of this transition into Poor Tom'.[90] The 'miracle' is that here, on the edge of 'Nothing', something alive begins to emerge through Kent's invocation of 'Nothing', 'miracles' and 'misery'. Edgar here mirrors France, who was summoned by Cordelia's 'Nothing' from the 'misery' of her rejection and thereby emerged almost as a 'miracle': 'Gods, gods'. And so, Edgar, in the 'happy hollow of a tree' (F.II.ii.159), begins his metamorphosis.[91] The chrysalis is offstage,[92] an absence, a happy hollow of darkness. And offstage, outside the frame, is where he returns to morph and to wait.

For what? Another prayer, soon to be uttered. Upon a storm and a prayer, Edgar is resurrected as Poor Tom: 'Come not in here, nuncle. Here's a spirit. Help me, help / me!' (III.iv.38–39). Such miracles as misery sees are seen now. But what is this miracle? Edgar has ever been hard to fathom – at once dispossessed and possessed by Poor Tom – and the answers are as multiple as his guises. Perhaps most obviously we can approach Edgar-Tom through Lear. From the hollow of the hovel, Poor Tom emerges in answer to Lear's prayer: 'the figure of Tom is almost literally cued by Lear's famous prayer for the "poore naked wretches"'.[93] More specifically, Edgar's transformation is again prompted by another character's invocation of misery and miracle, of nothingness ('Poor naked wretches') and divine justice ('show the heavens more just') (F.III.iv.28, 36). In response, Edgar-Tom rises from the depths of divested humanity: 'Fathom and half! Fathom and half! Poor Tom!' (F.III.iv.37). Edgar's arrival as Poor Tom is, of course, entwined with the breakdown of Lear's calculable worldview. As the old structures are ripped away, a wild poetry emerges from Edgar, who re-emerges from the depths as a conglomerate of persecuted suffering – pursued by the 'foul fiend' (F.III.iv.44) – and strange blessing – 'Bless thy five wits, Tom's a-cold! O, do, de, do, de, do de. Bless thee from whirlwinds, star-blasting, and taking' (F.III.iv.55–56). The effect upon Lear is well known. Love, for Lear, begins when exchange ends, when there is nothing left. Such non-calculability resembles Levinas's 'interhuman', which is 'a responsibility of one for another, but before the reciprocity of this responsibility, which will be inscribed in impersonal laws, comes to be superimposed'.[94] 'Unaccommodated man' (F.III.iv.95–96), 'tears [Lear] away' from his old self: 'I expose myself to the other person.'[95] Here, finally, is the exposure that Lear avoided in the love-test: 'Expose thyself to what wretches feel' (F.III.iv.34). Hence why, in the previous scene, 'wits begin[ning] to turn' (F.III.ii.66) entailed a movement from the 'saneness' of calculable debt and obligation – 'I am a man / More sinned against than sinning' (III.ii.58–59) – towards the 'madness' of naked and incalculable fellow feeling: 'How dost, my boy? Art cold? / I am cold myself' (F.III.ii.67–68).

The risk with these sorts of observations, however, is not only that they are so well known but also that they are too 'humane' to do justice to Edgar. It risks translating wild poetry into a prosaic common humanity. The humanity may be there, but there is a darker, fathomless side of this transition that is difficult to capture. For long periods, Edgar's 'self' is gone, there are no asides, and we cannot pinpoint the 'I' that speaks: Edgar, Tom or fiend. He seems to exist in a sort of indistinct interim, before or between subjecthood, that he can never call 'mine'. Of some help, perhaps, is Hegel's idea that mind 'only wins to its truth when it finds itself utterly torn asunder'.[96] It is only by 'looking the negative in the face and dwelling with it' that consciousness gains 'the magic power that converts the negative into being'.[97] Edgar seems to have something of that 'magic power' of tarrying with the negative.

Nonetheless, it is hard to appreciate this sort of thing as one sits and reads in comfort: 'Poor Tom, whom the foul fiend / hath led through fire and through flame' (F.III.iv.49–50). Roasted by devils and somehow sanctified, Poor Tom is a burnt offering to Lear's prayer, or an angel sent through fire, seen by an 'astonied' king (Daniel 3:24), who can only now understand. But this angel flames only to sink into the dark of 'whirlpool[s] … bog[s] and quagmire[s]' (F.III.iv.51) … and then coldness … and then blessing … a strange blessing from a poor prayer … or a demonic miracle from nothing. Prose struggles to paraphrase this, but, from Lear's perspective, perhaps the best I can say is that Poor Tom is the second coming of the 'Cordelia event'. Cordelia's 'Nothing, my lord' may trigger the play's fall into nothing, but then nothing rises: 'Here's a spirit … Poor Tom' (F.III.iv.38–41). The fall from Cordelia's sublime is followed by the ascent through Edgar's filth – through a self that is dismembered or 'torn asunder': 'Off, off, you lendings!' (F.III.iv.97). A counter-equation begins to emerge incalculably: one play, two angels, one of light and one of dark; the light falling, the dark rising – to tearing life. In fact, at the play's end, Edgar's is the only life. The kingdom is abdicated to dark angels. Better than devils, one supposes.

But I am being unfair on the prosaic, for Lear's divestment undoubtedly connects to various philosophical and religious divestments, even if it is not quite captured by any of them. In some ways, the emphasis on dispossession makes *Lear* Shakespeare's most Montaigne-like tragedy. In his great statement of learned ignorance, 'An Apologie of Raymond Sebond', Montaigne writes that *'Man is a thing of nothing'* who, in the words of Augustine, best knows God *'by our not knowing him'*.[98] In more philosophical terms, Montaigne concludes that after humanity's 'long search' for knowledge and meaning, 'all the benefit [we] hath gotten by so tedious a pursuit, hath been, that [we] hath learned to know [our] owne weaknesse' and to acknowledge the 'ignorance which in us was naturall'.[99] Divestment is also the starting point of the evental tradition – its point of emergence 'from zero point'.[100] Or, in the more doctrinal words of Luther, 'it is impossible for someone who does not first hear the law and let himself be killed by the letter, to hear the gospel and let the grace of the Spirit bring him to life'.[101] New life only comes about by first dying, by first becoming nothing. So, for Kierkegaard, 'if repentance were to emerge, one would first have to despair completely, to despair out and out, and then the spirit-life might break through from the very bottom'.[102] Lear must reach deep into despair so that his 'externals' ('immediate man … recognizes that he has a self only by externals'[103]) are pulled from him: 'Come, unbutton here' (F.III.iv.97–98). Nor is this a purely religious or Stoic sentiment. Put in

Deleuze and Guattari's terms: whereas Lear previously 'invent[ed] heavy apparatuses for the regimentation and the repression of the desiring-machines',[104] the wildness of the storm moves him from the 'paranoiac' to the 'schizoid', which is defined 'by lines of escape that follow the decoded and deterritorialized flows, inventing their own nonfingurative breaks or schizzes that produce new flows'.[105] Out of his 'deterritorialized' madness comes a new, less rigid or axiomatic Lear: 'When thou dost ask me blessing, / I'll kneel down / And ask of thee forgiveness' (F.V.iii.10–11).[106]

But what of Edgar-Tom qua Edgar? Is there an Edgar subject? It is hard, for he is multiple. It seems as if he has been, or could be, a million men or devils. In Badiouan terms, he seems to arrive from, and signal towards, the excess of the void: to the suture where the known world is stitched to infinite multiplicity: 'Nero is an angler in the lake of darkness' (F.III.vi.6–7) and the 'foul fiend haunts Poor Tom in the voice of a nightingale' (Q.13.24–25). But how is this depth, this multiplicity, possible in one subject? It is not. Fernie is surely right that Edgar arrives as a figure of 'possession': 'passive possession is the risk always involved in … real susceptibility and openness.'[107] Edgar is possessed by Poor Tom – 'Poor Tom is in fact much more alive than Edgar is and easily overwhelms his personality'[108] – and Poor Tom is forcibly possessed by a never-ending series of spectral intrusions. Indeed, Fernie memorably suggests that the description of the '[f]ive fiends' in the Quarto-text 'intimates a sodomitical rape' by a gang of devils 'who have been in Tom at once and have since possessed chambermaids and waiting-women'.[109] 'Who gives anything to Poor Tom' (F.III.iv.49), he asks. No-one. No-one but the foul fiend who gives him everything: the spirits, depths and storms; the poison and the knife; the fire and bog; the whirl-winds and star-blasting; the servingman; the frogs and cowdung; and the Modos and Mahus and assorted devils. Let us look at one possession:

LEAR What hast thou been?

EDGAR A servingman, proud in heart and mind, that curled my hair, wore gloves in my cap, served the lust of my mistress' heart, and did the act of darkness with her. (F.III.iv.77–79)

Has he 'been', perhaps, the servingman he comes to kill? Oswald? The proleptic quality of the play is well known,[110] with its double-strike lightnings, and so who knows, perhaps Edgar-Tom has pre-possessed, or been pre-possessed by, Oswald too. He seems open to everything. Or, as Fernie puts it: 'By its very essence radical susceptibility must be subject to demons as well as more beneficent influences.'[111] Does Edgar's openness come down, ultimately, to the sort of receptivity to events that I raised in the *Hamlet* chapter? Fernie and Palfrey seem to suggest as much in their separate, though in many ways compatible, recent readings. For instance, Palfrey argues that Edgar's initial 'absent-minded gullibility' indicates 'an emptiness which is somehow open to experiment, and therein abuse'.[112] I largely follow these powerful readings of Edgar's openness but, perhaps unsurprisingly, take issue with one point: from where this openness arrives. In particular, can we meaningfully say that Edgar is 'open' (Palfrey) or 'susceptible' (Fernie) *before* he begins to transform in his happy hollow? Is susceptibility a pre-existing quality, or is it something that happens? For emptiness can exist without openness, and there seems little in Edgar's opening scene to suggests that openness is already in him. It seems more accurate to say that he needs 'Nothing' to *happen* to him – to prise him open – before he can open himself to anything. I have already traced 'Nothing's' broken lightning chain of custody. From Cordelia to Edmond to Gloucester to Kent's speech in the stocks, 'Nothing' is passed along to strike Edgar. Only then does he become something, after its rupture. Fernie at times seems to make Edgar-Tom a demon-saint of openness,[113] but this perhaps places too much emphasis on the individual (vessel). It is Shakespeare's lightning – the 'Nothing … from Cordelia' (F.II.ii.150–51) – that sets off this chain reaction.

If Cordelia opens the world to the void, the void seems to open within Edgar. Its electric excess runs through his veins, jolts his corpse into new life, and then does it all over again. For Juliet, the lightning struck once, for Macbeth also. But Edgar seems to live in a constant evental stream, as a mast in the storm, aglow in the dim. And then he refracts the lightning that has struck him: it breaks into the proud servingman, the fiend, Childe Rowland in the darke tower, and into Lear too. What is he? No one thing, but more a stream of dark lightning that gives as it receives; a bounty as deep as the sky; a lightning rod for his own back, and his father's, and perhaps for ours too; a perpetual event without clear outlet – or with too many outlets, never becoming one path, one self. So perhaps never a 'subject', as I have discussed it. Perhaps we have, rather, a sort of pre-subject or blank canvas. In the storm, the play strips away the symbolic justifications of the self. It asks us to feel ourselves, for a moment, as the naked Lear. Perhaps, if we allow it, even as Edgar in the hollow. What do we become if we are stripped of name, status, identity and cliché? What do we seize upon? What seizes upon us? There is no answer, of course, but there is Edgar and there is France. And, in both, there is a sense that it is in such moments of forsakenness that something can arrive: from the void, from absence. In this sense, then, his openness makes Edgar the bare bones of arrivals: from nothing something comes. He is ruptured, shaken, and transformed into life. Despite all the transformations, he arrives to haunt the 'thing itself'.

And yet, the thing that comes then dissolves again. Edgar is born, like Macbeth he is *animated*, but then he is re-animated as something else. He does not become himself but has to suffer the arrival of multiple demonic children. If this is a 'fidelity', it is a fidelity to openness itself:[114] to what Fernie describes as a sort of 'wild receptivity' that opposes 'Cordelia's righteous reserve'.[115] It is, in an even more extreme sense than *Hamlet*, a fidelity without fidelity: without constancy or consecration or name. But then isn't this *too* open? Isn't it too detached from the dramatic occasion, event or situation: an openness to anything and everything? In fact, Fernie himself recognises this point, writing that Edgar's receptivity

> begs the question of the limits of ethical and erotic openness, which has arguably been sentimentalised in recent, Levinasian ethical theory of the primacy of 'the Other.' Just how open to the Other should I be? And to how many others should I open myself?[116]

It is a question, too, for this book's notion of arrival: why does *this* event transform the self? Why not another? And then another? But few of us can handle more than one road to Damascus happening. Perhaps even Shakespeare could not handle another Edgar – radical receptivity is certainly not Prospero's problem. And, of course, even in *Lear*, Poor Tom disappears. Radical receptivity is not Edgar's final destination, though it is hard to tell what is. He can never arrive as Poor Tom, for we know that Edgar waits in the wings. He can never arrive as Edgar, because we have now seen the intensity of Poor Tom. In short, he is never himself but veers and pops and haunts without inhabiting. In another sense, then, Edgar points to a different model of the subject that lies beyond the arrivals of Shakespeare's tragic figures. His multiplicity points to the diffusions and subjective orbits of the late plays. Both Edgar and the play are born – and give birth – in the dark space between romance and tragedy.

Vanishing Breath

Cordelia does not simply vanish but, like Christ, vanishes and then returns, only to vanish once more. She returns after Lear's territorial divisions are erased. The nature of her return varies, however, in the Quarto and Folio texts. I have largely followed the Folio because of its greater emphasis on the power of 'Nothing'. Whereas Scene 17 of the Quarto foreshadows Cordelia's return through the First Gentleman's description of her piteous tears – 'There she shook / The holy water from her heavenly eyes' (Q.17.30–31) – in the Folio, which omits this scene, 'Cordelia appear[s] abruptly, with no preparation'.[117] She again arrives from nothing, without being due. The Folio also stresses that Cordelia returns as an *active* force. Whereas, in the Quarto, the French army is led by the 'Maréchal of France' (Q.17.9), by removing such references the Folio transforms Cordelia 'late in the play from an emblem of pity into a fighting Queen of France',[118] who 'appears abruptly with no preparation at the head of an army'.[119] That said, Cordelia's redemptive force is soon defeated, as she herself seems to foresee:

> O thou good Kent, how shall I live and work
> To match thy goodness? My life will be too short,
> And every measure fail me.   (F.IV.vi.1–3)

Kent ironically calls attention to the same fact. He asks Cordelia that she not reveal his identity to Lear until 'time and I think meet' (F.IV.vi.10), but time never does 'think meet' for Kent. There is no time for Kent and precious little for Cordelia. The readiness is not quite all. In fact, Edgar's reformulation, 'Ripeness is all' (F.V.ii.11), is revealing, for while one may be ready, not all fruit ripens. We may be ready for a divinity that does not come, for a providence that does not fall: 'My life will be too short, / And every measure fail.'

And yet, perhaps, not 'every measure'. Perhaps one scene is enough for a 'li[f]e and work' of 'goodness'. Perhaps one line is enough, or half a line even, reason not the need: 'No cause, no cause' (F.IV.vi.69). For although Cordelia's redemptive force is defeated, it is not only defeated. There is a moment in which it ceases to hover tantalisingly and lands tenderly. In overseeing Lear's awakening, she is indeed the restorative romance heroine that the Quarto describes, but she is so in her own action rather than the Gentleman's description:

> O my dear father, restoration hang
> Thy medicine on my lips, and let this kiss
> Repair those violent harms that my two sisters
> Have in thy reverence made!   (F.IV.vi.23–26)

For the first and only time, she is given circumstances in which she can act productively, as her kiss precipitates Lear's gradual, touching awakening. We thus have a palpable and physical restoration – almost a resurrection. As Žižek affirms, 'THE IMPOSSIBLE DOES HAPPEN' and '"miracles" like

Love ... DO occur'.[120] Rather than the sham of Edgar's 'divine' miracle, however, we have an honest human miracle. Cordelia is, as Cavell points out, 'the only good character whose attention is wholly on earth, on the person nearest her'.[121] Here the contrast with Edgar is particularly striking. Whereas Cordelia opens Lear's eyes, Edgar's staged 'miracle' (F.IV.v.55) is – to return to Kent's 'Nothing almost sees miracles / But misery' – only possible because Gloucester 'almost sees': because he is blind and miserable and cannot see the cliff's (and the miracle's) absence. And yet, the play's ambivalence somewhat blunts Cavell's assessment that Edgar thereby 'deprives Gloucester of his eyes again'.[122] He does, but Gloucester sees better afterwards. Edgar is again the angel of darkness to Cordelia's angel of light. They are the two 'spirits' of the play. 'Here's a spirit' (F.III.iv.38), Edgar, who pushes Lear into 'madness'. And here is Cordelia when he awakes: 'You are a spirit, I know. Where did you die?' (F.IV.vi.42). Soon.[123]

The change in Cordelia's re-arrival also entails a change in France's vanishing. Foakes points to 'the consistent excision in F of all references to the King of France from Act 3' onwards.[124] He therefore speculates that 'Shakespeare may have had an early conception of his play that was closer to the old [play of *King*] *Leir*', in which 'the King of Gallia invades England ... and restore[s] Leir'.[125] The removal of France's potential intervention not only gives Cordelia a more active role, it also makes France less active in his absence. Whereas France hovers on the Quarto's borders as the warlike figure envisaged by Goneril – 'France spreads his banners in our noiseless land, / With plumèd helm' (Q.16.55–56) – the Folio's France hovers in a different way. He is recalled only once explicitly as an individual (rather than a kingdom), by Cordelia as she re-enters the play: 'Therefore great France / My mourning and importuned tears hath pitied' (F.IV.iii.25–6; Q.18.26–27). Once again, France is the facilitator of Cordelia's latent power. He endows her with a force to set about her father's work: 'O dear father, / It is thy business that I go about' (F.IV.iii.23–24). He is, again, what releases the power of forsaken love. And this is particularly true of the Folio, where this is *all* France is.

The absent France, or the absence of France, thus helps facilitate the great moment of reconciliation. Madness melts from Lear along with his rage and his heart's hardness. He slowly accepts that Cordelia's 'tears [are] wet' (F.IV.vi.64), that she is really here, that he is alive, that she has 'some cause' against him (F.IV.vi.68). And then she utters those beautiful words of forgiveness: 'No cause, no cause' (F.IV.vi.69). What is Lear's response? He asks, 'Am I in France?' (F.IV.vi.69). 'France' thus shares a line with Cordelia's most cherished words of love. 'In your own kingdom, sir'

(F.IV.vi.70), Kent corrects Lear. At this, the moment of his awakening, it is inconceivable to Lear that he is in his 'own kingdom'. In Lear's kingdom there is only the 'poison' (F.IV.vi.65) he imagines Cordelia has for him. He 'will drink it' (F.IV.vi.65), because he has 'cause' to, because he deserves it, because he owes her: the last dregs of his mechanistic world.[126] 'No cause' is Cordelia's soft but emphatic rejection of that logic. She effaces the debt.

Unlike the harshness of the opening scene, Cordelia's speech is now magically in tune with Lear's emotional needs. As Blanchot admonishes: 'Do not forgive. Forgiveness accuses before it forgives. By accusing, by stating the injury, it makes the wrong irredeemable.'[127] Cordelia instead 'wipes the slate clean as in the sacrament of penance'.[128] For Lear, it seems impossible that such unjustified words, that such gifts, undeserved, could arise in his calculable kingdom. They could only arise 'in France'. Already redeemed by Cordelia, and no longer warlike, the Folio's France moves to the fringes as an alternative model of kingdoms. He is transformed into a land of healing and redemption, a land that works otherwise, outside mechanistic laws. It is a land only glimpsed at, between sleep and awakening, madness and reality – a land where breath stirs. France thereby connects with, and helps carry *in absentia*, a seemingly contradictory feeling of affirmation amidst the suffering of *Lear*'s finale:

> The feeling I mean is the impression that the heroic being, though in one sense and outwardly he has failed, is yet in another sense superior to the world in which he appears; is, in some way which we do not seek to define, untouched by the doom that overtakes him; and is rather set free from life than deprived of it.[129]

Although Bradley captures the indefinableness of this affirmation, the trouble is that he follows Hegel's privileging of 'spirit' over 'the finitude which is inadequate to it'.[130] The inadequacy of the world is not Shakespeare's dramaturgy, however. If we take France as our guide, affirmation pertains not to the subject's undefined 'superior[ity] to the world', but to its seizure of, and arrival in, *this* world. Both France and Cordelia show that the subject must be outward, that it must be 'touched', if it is to be anything. They neither transcend the world nor renounce it – and Cordelia is crushed rather than 'set free' – but they nonetheless 'seize upon' (F.I.i.250) failed and finite love. As I've noted, Cordelia is the most earthed character in the play. Her clear-sighted final speech makes no reference to fate, providence, gods or even justice. She recognises, without resignation or despair, that things often go horribly and undeservedly wrong. Unlike Bradley, however, and unlike almost all the other characters, she does not draw lessons from terrible circumstances, for such lessons are irrelevant to her fidelity:

> We are not the first
> Who with best meaning have incurred the worst.
> For thee, oppressèd King, am I cast down,
> Myself could else outfrown false fortune's frown.
> Shall we not see these daughters and these sisters? (F.V.iii.3–7)

For Cordelia, unjust death does not destroy love. It leads not to bleak resignation but defiance. She goes hence in fidelity and 'best meaning' to her love. She does not turn away from evil but rejects it sternly, even to death: 'Shall we not see these daughters and these sisters?'

Such an attitude contrasts with the bleak postmodern view of the play. As Jeffrey Kahan observed in 2008: 'As of this writing, it is safe to say that in the public's mind the story of Lear's physical and spiritual suffering, and, above all, his heartbreaking end, aptly sum up the human condition: "When we are born, we cry that we are come / To this great stage of fools."'[131] The conflict between this resigned suffering and Bradley's affirmation suggests yet another opposition between something and nothing. For Bradley, there is an undefined greatness of spirit behind the tragedy, which becomes everything; for postmodern critics there is nothing. In both cases we reach a settled view of the world's supposed essence. As Foakes outlines, from 'about 1960' the play was transformed 'into a bleak vision of negation' as it was 'considered in direct relation to a new political consciousness engendered by the Cold War, the rediscovery of the Holocaust … and the development of the hydrogen bomb'.[132] *King Lear* implicitly becomes a timeless representation of a world in which virtue is not rewarded, innocents suffer, the gods are silent, meaning is elusive, and frail human life 'progresses towards despair rather than towards redemption'.[133] But Shakespearean worlds are never so settled. They are always arriving from, and perishing into, their voids. Helpful here is Nietzsche's idea that '[a]rt is not an imitation of nature but its metaphysical supplement'.[134] The play is a creative event, not a representation of a stable world. We can thereby rethink Nietzsche's idea that tragedy's supplement is able to 'justify the existence of even the "worst possible world"'.[135] There is a feeling of awe in this worst of possible endings: that even amidst crushed possibility, such loves and forgiveness, such seizures and subjects, could arrive. They were not simply extinguished by the terrors of this storm-tossed world, they arose in and through these terrors; they were born and delivered amongst them. We have, perhaps, a different sense of the *birth* of tragedy.[136]

If we return to France as an instance of Badiou's 'materialism of grace', by which 'ordinary existence' is seized by a truth,[137] we can forgo the old oppositions that focus on the play's outcome: 'Interpreters have generally sought to show either that the tragic close evinces a redemptive possibility, notwithstanding its horror, or that Tate was right, that *King Lear* in fact subverts a Christian or even Enlightenment world view and anticipates the absurd universe of existentialism or postmodern materialism.'[138] Rather, France's seizure of Cordelia's crushed potential provides a model for our response to the sublime failure of the tragic end. As an 'audience surrogate', France 'offers the playwright an engaging means for leading an actual audience in the paths, emotional and intellectual, wherein it should go'.[139] He calls us to embrace love that has been cast aside, to affirm what has been rejected and to thereby become something different. He calls us to recognise another kingdom, but one that *is* of this world.

Appreciating *King Lear* as 'a profound, if bleak, meditation on the human experience'[140] does lead to something sublime: the sublime of love's fragile light extinguished in the black storm of indifferent suffering. It is, however, a passive and reductionist sublime. Shaw writes that the postmodern understanding of the sublime 'lays stress on the inability of art or reason to bring the vast and the unlimited into account', but 'affirms nothing beyond its own failure, and it does so without regret and without longing'.[141] The sublime is here deadened, if not accounted for via the back door, because its unaccountability and terrible vastness are seen as the unavoidable 'way of things'. In a reversal of Tate's version, suffering and not redemption becomes the inescapable rule of existence, its uncompromising law of gravity. It thereby renders it familiar and comfortable. The sublime is stripped of its active force, so that *Lear* comes to embody a structural suffering and not an evental drama in which something can come of nothing. It misses the sublime potential of arrivals: that the subject and even redemption can emerge from the void, even amidst suffering. Arrivals shows that love, like grace, comes without being due, works silently and acts creatively, that even vanished events may transform worlds. In the too-late arrivals of Edgar and Lear, of course, this potential is only ever recuperated in incomplete, provisional fashion. Nonetheless, France shows how it is also a potential for us. It is we, at the play's end, who witness love's abject failure; it is now in our hands to 'take up what's cast away'.

Treating *King Lear* as a representation of structural suffering ultimately creates a second 'Restoration' version of the play that, like Tate's, misses the sublime's creative potential. Badiou describes the period from around 1980 onwards as the twentieth century's Restoration, which retreats from revolutionary movements and, above all, from the attempt to create a 'new man':

> [T]he interval between an event of emancipation and another leaves us fallaciously in the thrall to the idea that nothing begins or will ever begin, even if we find ourselves caught in the midst of an infernal and immobile agitation. We have thus returned to classicism, though we are deprived of its instruments: everything has always already begun, and it is vain to imagine that foundations are built on nothing, that one will create a new art, or a new man.[142]

There is a retreat, in other words, from the power of 'Nothing'. Rather than an active force that founds France, summons Edgar from emptiness, restores Lear after the nothing of madness, and inspires our investments, Cordelia's love becomes an ineffectual light in the darkness. Such a pallid *Lear* misses the connection between the sublime and action: how failure can inspire the creation of a new subject and thus a new world. The failure of love may be bleak, but France shows us that *we* must respond to it: that we must seize the potential that ends in 'Nothing'. Affirmation lies not in the character's 'spirit' but, ultimately, in our 'taking up' of their actions, and thus in our actions. So while Bradley contends that 'the world' of *Lear* 'is convulsed by evil, and rejects it',[143] it is in fact we who must reject it. And while postmodern criticism contends that the play reveals that nature is indifferent to suffering, the play also reveals that we are not indifferent. It is not that the plot is 'affirming', but that the play prompts us to rebel against its suffering. Badiou quotes André Breton on the strange moment in which suffering is translated into rebellion:

> It's there, at the poignant moment when the weight of endured suffering seems about to engulf everything, that the very excessiveness of the test causes *a change of sign* … One must go to the depths of human suffering, discover its strange capacities, in order to salute the similarly limitless gift that makes life worth living. The one definitive disgrace one can bring upon oneself in the face of such suffering, because it would make that conversion of sign impossible, would be to confront it with resignation … Rebellion is its own justification, completely independent of the chance it has to modify the state of affairs that gives rise to it. It's a spark in the wind, but a spark in search of a powder keg.[144]

Like Cordelia and France, our guides to active rebellion, we must respond to failure and injustice; we must refuse it. Only then can there be '*a change of sign*' from suffering to creativeness. Such a rebellious affirmation celebrates how the seizure of 'Nothing' creates *new* subjects and *new* loves even amidst suffering, how 'Nothing' is not a bleak 'state of affairs' but a point of emergence. Not that the rebellious course is assured. It is uncertain and tragic, flowing into both Cordelia's revival of Lear and his cruel inability to revive her. And yet, as Cordelia's 'We are not the first' speech affirms, her rebellious 'Nothing' is 'its own justification'. It opens the *possibility* of creativeness beyond the given world, with its structures of language, calculation and suffering. As Badiou puts it, '[a] creative disposition, be it vital or artistic, must be the conversion of a negative excess into an affirmative excess; of an unfathomable pain into an infinite rebellion'.[145] We might call it a dramatic feeling of grace. Love is not simply to be preserved; it is an active force to be unleashed, the artistic force that may change the sign and resuscitate vanishing breath. A criticism of arrivals thus helps us evade the trap of thinking that 'Nothing comes of nothing' and that 'everything has always already begun'.[146]

Afterword

When I first began, long ago, I had hoped to locate a transformative potential in Shakespeare's plays: to move from the tragedies to action in our world. I cannot say I have achieved this, at least not in any immediate sense. What I have achieved, I hope, is to get closer to the techniques and moments through which Shakespeare's tragic figures spring into new life. I'm afraid I cannot, in the end, offer more. In Shakespeare's tragedies, the sublime emergence from the void is simply not stable, controllable or aphoristic. It leads to Cordelia's loving 'Nothing' but also to Macbeth's terrible arrival into 'what is not'. There is no idealising in Shakespeare's arrivals. They are not in the service of any overarching concept, spirit, nature or even Badiouian 'truth'. Rather, the void in Shakespeare's plays is as terrifying as it is creative. The trajectory of its sublime arrivals is not linear but errant: it may explode into life, close over or slide into horror.

Indeed, the inability to name the event has haunted the second half of this book. There was love, then there was betrayal, and then there was *Hamlet*. And, as ever in *Hamlet*, action lost its name. If Shakespeare does not cue us to any particular fight or particular politics, the reason, I think, is that the 'fermenting', the 'continual composition and decomposition of [the drama's] elements',[1] is irrevocably local. Life rises and perishes from each play's singular situation–event nexus. As with the weird sisters' intense particularity when they fret over the sailor's wife's 'chestnuts', Shakespeare's plays turn – unjustifiably – on contingent details: a look or a word, a sudden recognition or misrecognition, an obscure accident or change in regard. In one sense, then, the events I trace are not as satisfying as I once hoped. They need not unfold in a heroic path of fidelity. They do not offer a political path or theology.

And yet, if my first hopes and raptures end disappointed, others have followed, with abundant recompense. For against my first intent and inclination, I have learned to look on Shakespeare with something closer to an aesthetic eye. I have, I suppose, been subjected to events that I do not fully own or understand. And if I have lost the direct name of action – the immediate link to politics – I have sensed the beauty of the path taken, even when it ends in ruin. It seems to me that an outcomes-based assessment is doomed to failure when it comes to literature, and to tragic literature in particular. Instead I see a constellation of 'exquisite pauses' that arrests us – without amounting to any one thing – in a momentary awe of 'the fullness of existence', before our inevitable return to dust.[2] It is hard to say if I'm better for it, though at times I see a cherub that says so. Whatever the case, it is by escaping our control that Shakespeare's arrivals become powerful aesthetic events that can be taken up in new worlds through the ages. They do not stay dead but return, with four centuries of critical wounds on their crowns, to push us from our stools and inhabit our various presents. They cannot be satisfyingly mapped onto a historical source or philosophical concept. They escape us and thus reanimate. They (re)arrive as an undue beauty to which criticism may yet be faithful. Not because they offer a 'programme' or because they makes us 'citizens' but because in ever unforeseen ways, they chip away at the limits of what is said, and what is sayable, about our experience and world. And thereby, slowly, like a river, or quickly, like a lightning strike, but always unpredictably, Shakespeare's arrivals *form new worlds*.

If we need Shakespeare, we need him not because of what we know but because of what we do not know, because of what it might open us to: the bolt that might cast the world in a different light, the caesura that turns Romeo and Juliet into 'Romeo and Juliet'. In an era that highly values identity, and in which it seems increasingly impossible to 'put on the new man' (Ephesians 4:24), Shakespeare's tragedies provide a confrontingly different model: the existential peril of becoming a subject. It is a model quite foreign to the insistent Polonius-like imperative to 'be one's self' and 'tell it like it is'. Perhaps, in such an era, Shakespeare gains a new countercultural relevance by forcing us to ask: what 'self'? What is the 'it' to be told? Arrivals, creations, eruptions from the void, these do not rest within self-contained interpretive communities but shatter communities and identities. They clear a space; they open a door, for … something. Shakespeare, of course, cannot tell us what may come. But he speaks to a mode of existence in which things *do* come. The fact that something emerges that is not there 'already'[3] – whether in the manner of Hegel's spirit, postmodernism's linguistic superstructures or historicism's explanatory contexts – is an invigorating aspect of Shakespeare's dramaturgy. '*That which founds a subject cannot be what is due to it.*'[4] If we at times feel imprisoned, Shakespeare's drama suggests that there remain spaces in our nutshells that may birth new worlds, structures, languages, selves. Space is relative, after all, and filled with dark matter.

Not that Shakespeare's arrivals are a faithful representation of our world; they are, rather, a 'metaphysical supplement'.[5] Shakespeare's creation of the new at the situation's limit provides energy for our own transformations. The 'limit' is where '*everything* comes to pass'.[6] It offers the freedom of creation, even if what is created remains undetermined, which is to say left open, or 'free'. But Shakespeare's plays are also events that continue to act on us, both in the straightforward sense of being the most performed plays in this, the twenty-first century, and in the present action, energy and thought of those who perform and reinterpret them. They continue to irrupt into our inner worlds. Shakespeare's tragedy is thus an event we remain exposed to, which offers itself to us, which continues to arrive. And it is an event that requires us to act upon it and for it, to which we must offer ourselves. Shakespeare's plays remain 'promise-crammed' (*Hamlet*, III.ii.86). They arrive through a continuing poetic 'action' – 'the stellar assumption of that pure undecidable, against a background of nothingness' – 'of which one can only *know* whether it has taken place inasmuch as one *bets* upon its truth'.[7] They arrive because we continue to seize upon them in the present. This book, then, is one small act of seizing onto the new in Shakespeare, of betting upon its truth and not letting it sink into a background of nothingness.

Notes

Introduction

1. Paul Yachnin and Jessica Slights, eds., *Shakespeare and Character: Theory, History, Performance, and Theatrical Persons.* Basingstoke: Palgrave Macmillan, 2009, p. 1. Edward Pechter references this comment when he points to 'six Shakespeareans during the . . . last ten years' who have signalled a return to character: 'Character is certainly back'; "character criticism seems to be coming back"; "Character has made a comeback"; there is a "powerful resurgence of academic interest in character-based approaches to Shakespeare"': Pechter, 'Character Criticism, the Cognitive Turn, and the Problem of Shakespeare Studies', *Shakespeare Studies* 42 (2014), 196–228, p. 197.
2. All references are to *The Norton Shakespeare*. Stephen Greenblatt et al. Eds. New York: Norton, 1997.
3. Michel de Montaigne, *Montaigne's Essays*. John Florio. Trans. Vol. 3. London: Dent, 1980, Ch. 13, p. 322.
4. Ibid., p. 323.
5. Ibid., Vol. 2, Ch. 1, p. 12.
6. Ibid., Ch. 12, p. 248.
7. This is far from a new observation. Even in his postmodern-inflected reading, Jean Starobinski writes that 'Montaigne is undoubtedly one of those writers most responsible for fleshing out our Western notion of individual existence': *Montaigne in Motion*. Arthur Goldhammer. Trans. Chicago: University of Chicago Press, 1985, p. 307.
8. Montaigne, Vol. 2, Ch. 18, p. 392.
9. Ibid., Vol. 1, Ch. 22, pp. 117–118.
10. Ibid., Ch. 38, pp. 254–255.
11. In Chapter 1 we will see Philip Davis make a similar point: *Sudden Shakespeare: The Shaping of Shakespeare's Creative Thought*. Athlone: London, 1996.
12. Bert O. States, *Hamlet and the Concept of Character*. Baltimore: Johns Hopkins University Press, 1992, p. xiv.
13. Ibid., p. xv.
14. Ibid., p. 19.
15. Yachnin and Slights, p. 6.

16. Chapter 1 outlines how critics ranging from William Hazlitt to Philip Davis and Simon Palfrey contend that character is not always 'all there'.

17. Montaigne, Vol. 3, Ch. 13, p. 323.

18. Alain Badiou, *Being and Event*. Oliver Feltham. Trans. London: Continuum, 2005, p. 145.

19. All references to the King James Bible.

20. Friedrich Nietzsche, *Untimely Meditations*. R. J. Hollingdale. Trans. Cambridge: Cambridge University Press, 1983, p. 60.

21. Walter Benjamin, *Illuminations*. Harry Zohn. Trans. London: Fontana, 1992, p. 255. Julia Lupton similarly seeks to plot 'constellations that persist, that appear in, before, and after Shakespeare': *Thinking with Shakespeare*. Chicago: University of Chicago Press, 2011, p. 18.

22. William Hazlitt, *Lectures on the English Poets*. London: Macmillan, 1903, p. 281.

23. Nietzsche, *Untimely*, p. 59.

24. T. S. Eliot, *On Poetry and Poets*. London: Faber, 1957, p. 112.

25. Simon Palfrey writes that 'Shakespeare doesn't simply download his principal characters, fully formed'; rather, '[t]hey may endure multiple births': *Shakespeare's Possible Worlds*. Cambridge: Cambridge University Press, 2014, p. 258.

1 Thinking Arrivals

1. Jacques Derrida, 'Structure, Sign and Play in the Discourse of the Human Sciences', in P. Rice and P. Waugh, eds., *Modern Literary Theory: A Reader*. London: Edward Arnold, 1989, 149–165, p. 165.

2. A. C. Bradley, *Shakespearean Tragedy: Lectures on Hamlet, Othello, King Lear, Macbeth*. Second Edition. Macmillan: London. 1932.

3. L. C. Knight's 1933 essay 'How Many Children Had Lady Macbeth?' is usually noted as the beginning of this, but as James Wells notes, Bradley's 'long-deceased corpse' was 'exhumed', and then retried and re-executed, by cultural materialist and New Historicist critics in the late twentieth century: Yu Jin Ko and Michael W. Shurgot, eds., *Shakespeare's Sense of Character: On the Page and From the Stage*. Farnham: Ashgate, 2012, p. 225. For a good summary of this re-execution of Bradley see: Alan Sinfield, 'From Bradley to Cultural Materialism', *Shakespeare Studies* 34 (2006), 25–34. For Sinfield, Bradley's '"character" [is] a typical mystification of bourgeois ideology, tending to efface the realities of class, race, gender and sexuality, oppression, cooperation, history, and ideology': p. 33.

4. Bradley, *Shakespearean*, pp. 1–2.

5. Ibid., p. 26.

6. Ibid., p. 23.

7. G. W. F. Hegel, *Aesthetics: Lectures on Fine Art.* T. M. Knox. Trans. Oxford: Clarendon, 1988, p. x.

8. See Jim Vernon and Antonio Calcagno, eds., *Badiou and Hegel: Infinity, Dialectics, Subjectivity.* Lanham: Lexington, 2015. According to Badiou himself, Hegel begins his 'dialectical odyssey by positing that "There is nothing but the Whole"', whereas Badiou begins from the maxim that 'There is no Whole': *Logic of Worlds.* Alberto Toscano. Trans. London: Continuum, 2009, p. 141. Badiou nonetheless 'admire[s] in Hegel the power of local dialectics': *Logic*, p. 146.

9. Alberto Toscano, 'Taming the Furies: Badiou and Hegel on *The Eumenides*', in Vernon and Calcagno, 193–205, p. 194.

10. G. W. F. Hegel, *The Phenomenology of Mind.* J. B. Baillie. Trans. Second Edition. London: George Allen & Unwin, 1961, p. 511.

11. Ibid., p. 96.

12. Ibid., p. 93.

13. Ibid., p. 96.

14. Ibid., pp. 92–93.

15. Ibid., p. 92.

16. Bradley, *Shakespearean*, p. 28.

17. Hegel, *Phenomenology*, p. 75.

18. States, *Hamlet*, p. 41.

19. Ibid., p. 13.

20. Ibid., p. 41.

21. Ibid., p. 47.

22. Ibid., pp. 47–48.

23. Bradley, *Shakespearean*, p. 7.

24. Hegel, *Phenomenology*, p. 96.

25. Bradley, *Shakespearean*, pp. 37–39.

26. A. C. Bradley, *Oxford Lectures on Poetry.* London: Macmillan, 1926, p. 91.

27. Bradley, *Shakespearean*, p. 34.

28. Ibid.

29. Hegel, *Aesthetics*, p. 179.

30. Alain Badiou, *Theory of the Subject.* Bruno Bosteels. Trans. London: Continuum, 2009, p. 49.

31. Frank Ruda, 'Badiou with Hegel: Preliminary Remarks on A(ny) Contemporary Reading of Hegel,' in Vernon and Calcagno, 105–121, p. 113.

32. Hegel, *Aesthetics*, p. 218.

33. Ibid., p. 578.

34. Bradley, *Shakespearean*, p. 13.

35. Ibid., p. 12.

36. Peter Holbrook, *Shakespeare's Individualism*. Cambridge: Cambridge University Press, 2010.
37. Ibid., p. 189, p. 187.
38. Lorna Hutson, *The Invention of Suspicion: Law and Mimesis in Shakespeare and Renaissance Drama*. Oxford: Oxford University Press, 2007, p. 116.
39. Ibid., p. 224.
40. Hutson writes of Shakespeare's 'character realism': pp. 10–11.
41. Bradley, *Shakespearean*, p. 14.
42. Ibid., p. 15.
43. Aristotle, *Poetics*, in D. A. Russell and M. Winterbottom, eds., *Ancient Literary Criticism*. Oxford: Clarendon, 1972, p. 98.
44. See, for instance: Philip Davis, *Shakespeare Thinking*. London: Continuum, 2007; Michael Witmore, *Shakespearean Metaphysics*. London: Continuum, 2008; Richard Allen Shoaf, *Lucretius and Shakespeare on the Nature of Things*. Newcastle: Cambridge Scholars, 2014.
45. Bruno Latour, *Pandora's Hope: Essays on the Reality of Science Studies*. Cambridge Mass.: Harvard University Press, 1999, p. 4. David Hillman evocatively describes Descartes' meditative closure as 'annihilating the material world': *Shakespeare's Entrails: Belief, Scepticism and the Interior of the Body*. New York: Palgrave Macmillan, 2007.
46. Hegel, *Aesthetics*, p. 98.
47. G. W. F. Hegel, *Introductory Lectures on Aesthetics*. Bernard Bosanquet. Trans. London: Penguin, 1993, p. 121, footnote 8.
48. Latour, p. 21.
49. Ibid., p. 24.
50. Ibid., pp. 49, 51.
51. Ibid., p. 310.
52. Various critics have suggested that fictional characters have a certain 'reality'. For instance, Amie L Thomasson argues that characters have metaphysical reality as 'abstract artifacts': *Fiction and Metaphysics*. Cambridge: Cambridge University Press, 1999, p. 37. Stanton B. Garner Jr writes more generally that human experience is always displaced 'by the imaginary in the guise of memories, anticipations, daydreams, fantasies' but that '[o]ur vocabulary fails to capture … this mutuality of the real and the unreal at the heart of what we call "actuality"': *Bodied Spaces: Phenomenology and Performance in Contemporary Drama*. Ithaca: Cornell University Press, 1994, p. 42. I broadly agree but seek to address why Shakespeare's characters seem *more* real.
53. Alfred North Whitehead, *Process and Reality: An Essay in Cosmology*. Cambridge: Cambridge University Press, 1929, p. 82.
54. Ibid.

55. Alfred North Whitehead, *Adventures of Ideas*. Cambridge: Cambridge University Press, 1933, p. 354.
56. Ibid., p. 153.
57. Witmore, *Metaphysics*, p. 16.
58. Ibid.
59. Ibid., p. 39.
60. Ibid., p. 19.
61. Henri Bergson, *Creative Evolution*. Arthur Mitchell. Trans. London: Macmillan, 1911, pp. 39–40.
62. Ibid., p. 47.
63. Ibid., p. 7.
64. Latour, pp. 125–126.
65. Hazlitt, *Poets*, p. 276.
66. Ibid., p. 277.
67. Ibid.
68. Ibid., p. 281.
69. Davis, *Thinking*, p. 16.
70. Ibid., p. 23.
71. Holbrook, p. 188.
72. Ibid., p. 189.
73. Ibid., p. 187. My emphasis.
74. Ibid, pp. 117–118, p. 187.
75. Davis, *Thinking*, p. 39.
76. Davis, *Sudden*, p. 236.
77. Ibid., p. 26.
78. Ibid., p. 236.
79. Palfrey, *Possible*, p. 30.
80. Ibid., p. 121.
81. Ibid., p. 316.
82. Ibid., p. 124.
83. Davis, *Sudden*, p. 14.
84. Part of character's resurgence is also due to 'cognitivism', which Paul Cefalu claims has 'reopened the possibility of character criticism for both cognitive and psychoanalytic literary criticism': *Tragic Cognition in Shakespeare's Othello: Beyond the Neural Sublime*. London: Bloomsbury, 2015, p. 47. Such approaches are generally too broad to help explore *specific* Shakespearean events. They are said to apply to '[a]ny performance and *any* literary work': Pechter, p. 215. However, ideas of 'distributed cognition' are at times relevant: for instance, Evelyn Tribble's idea of 'extended cognitive architectures' in *Cognition in the Globe: Attention and Memory in Shakespeare's Theatre*. New York: Palgrave Macmillan, 2011, p. 8. In one sense, I map an extended

architecture of character that includes the dramatic 'events' that interrupt, surround and envelop it.

85. Paul Yachnin and Myrna Wyatt Selkirk, 'Metatheater and the Performance of Character in *The Winter's Tale*', in Yachnin and Slights, 139–157, p. 152.
86. Thomasson, p. 47.
87. Ibid., p. 37.
88. Harold Bloom gets at this with his idea that Shakespeare's characters 'develop because they reconceive themselves' and that '[s]ometimes this comes about because they overhear themselves talking': *Shakespeare: The Invention of the Human*. London: Fourth Estate, 1999, p. xvii. However, Bloom's intense focus on inwardness does not get us very far in analysing Shakespeare's *technique*: what happens outwardly and dramatically to give rise to these transformative overhearings.
89. A Deleuzean study relevant to 'arrivals' is Bryan Reynolds' *Transversal Enterprises in the Drama of Shakespeare and his Contemporaries*. Basingstoke: Palgrave Macmillan, 2006. 'For transversal theory, subjectivity is processual and develops positively through becomings and comings-to-be': p. 10.
90. Shakespeare's 'language lock[s] into the very structures of creation': Davis, *Thinking*, p. 18.
91. Shoaf, p. 112.
92. Witmore, *Metaphysics*, p. 37.
93. Palfrey, *Possible*, p. 3.
94. Ibid., p. 119.
95. Alain Badiou, *Deleuze: The Clamor of Being*. Louise Burchill. Trans. Minneapolis: University of Minnesota Press, 2000, p. 97.
96. Ibid.
97. Ibid.
98. Shoaf, p. 111.
99. Davis, *Thinking*, p. 25.
100. Davis, *Sudden*, p. 70.
101. Ibid., p. 237.
102. Davis, *Thinking*, p. 29.
103. Simon Palfrey and Tiffany Stern, *Shakespeare in Parts*. Oxford: Oxford University Press, 2007, p. 93.
104. Ibid.
105. Ibid., p. 490.
106. Ibid., p. 119.
107. Montaigne, Vol. 2, Ch. 17, p. 385.
108. Hazlitt, *Poets*, pp. 277–278.

109. John Lee, *Shakespeare's Hamlet and the Controversies of Self.* Oxford: Clarendon, 2000, p. 223.
110. Starobinski suggests that Montaigne follows the old religion to maintain 'public tranquillity' but strips it of '"mystical" authority': pp. 253–254.
111. Montaigne, Vol. 1, Ch. 56, p. 365.
112. Ibid.
113. Starobinsi, p. 79.
114. As Montaigne describes the promise of the afterlife: Montaigne, Vol. 2, Ch. 12, p. 223.
115. In my final revisions, I was encouraged to read James Kuzner's *Shakespeare as a Way of Life: Skeptical Practice and the Politics of Weakness.* New York: Fordham University Press, 2016. Although Badiou is not a major focus, Kuzner's chapter on *The Winter's Tale* discusses the connection between Badiou and Saint Paul in light of what he sees as a 'non-confessional' type of 'faith' that transcends the old law: p. 81. Lupton also discusses Badiou, Agamben and Saint Paul 'beyond any confessional framework': p. 240.
116. Ken Jackson and Arthur F. Marotti, 'The Turn to Religion in Early Modern English Studies', *Criticism* 46 (2004), 167–190, p. 179.
117. Martin Luther, *Martin Luther's Basic Theological Writings.* Second Edition. Timothy F. Lull. Ed. Minneapolis: Fortress, 2005, p. 81.
118. Ibid., p. 101.
119. Ibid., pp. 135–136.
120. Giorgio Agamben, *The Time That Remains: A Commentary on the Letter to the Romans.* Patricia Dailey. Trans. Stanford: Stanford University Press, 2005, p. 61.
121. Montaigne, Vol. 3, Ch. 10, pp. 261–262.
122. Ibid., Ch. 9, p. 198.
123. Ibid.
124. Slavoj Žižek, *On Belief.* London: Routledge, 2001, pp. 148–149.
125. Slavoj Žižek, *The Ticklish Subject: The Absent Centre of Political Ontology.* London: Verso, 1999, p. 143.
126. Soren Kierkegaard, *The Concept of Anxiety.* Reidar Thomte and Albert B. Anderson. Trans. Princeton: Princeton University Press, 1980, p. 85.
127. Soren Kierkegaard, *The Sickness Unto Death.* Walter Lowrie. Trans. Princeton: Princeton University Press, 1970, p. 238.
128. Soren Kierkegaard, *Fear and Trembling.* Alastair Hannay. Trans. London: Penguin, 1985. p. 50.
129. Trevor Ponech, 'The Reality of Fictive Cinematic Characters', in Yachnin and Slights, 41–61, p. 42.
130. Alain Badiou, *Ethics: An Essay on the Understanding of Evil.* Peter Hallward. Trans. London: Verso, 2001, p. 41.

131. Ibid.
132. Ibid., p. 43.
133. Kuzner, p. 82.
134. Badiou, *Ethics*, pp. 42–43.
135. Ibid., p. 42.
136. Ibid., p. 68.
137. Ibid., p. 43.
138. Ibid., p. 69.
139. Ibid., p. 68.
140. Ibid., pp. 25–26.
141. Jackson and Marotti, pp. 175–176.
142. Julián Jiménez Heffernan, *Shakespeare's Extremes: Wild Man, Monster, Beast*. Hampshire: Palgrave Macmillan, 2015, p. 62. Heffernan argues that '*[i]n Marlovian drama there is a radical absence of genuine events*': p. 75. Although Shakespeare's heroes are '[m]ore alive' to 'traces of the future, the beacons of jural or moral possibility', for Heffernan they are still 'unable to take the road of a faithfully human subjectivation' and so 'Shakespeare's world is still that of Marlowe': p. 43. This would seem to directly oppose my argument; however, in the end, I think we are talking about very different things. I speak of events in terms of Shakespeare's creation of character (dramatic and aesthetic), whereas Heffernan speaks of events in terms of politics ('jural or moral possibility'). Put otherwise, even if there is no politically actable fidelity *for* a character, this does not mean in terms of our response *to* a character that Shakespeare does not work in an evental manner. In short, dramatic events need not follow a happy road of fidelity, a point I address in Chapter 3 onwards and particularly in Chapter 5.
143. Badiou, *Ethics*, p. 27.
144. Montaigne, Vol. 2, Ch. 12, p. 248.
145. Ibid., pp. 248–249.
146. Ibid., p. 276.
147. Ibid., Vol. 2, p. 523.
148. Ibid., Ch. 12, p. 186.
149. Ibid., p. 277.
150. Alain Badiou, *Saint Paul: The Foundation for Universalism*. Ray Brassie. Trans. Stanford: Stanford University Press, 2003, p. 58.
151. Ibid., p. 64.
152. Žižek, *Ticklish*, p. 135.
153. Ibid.
154. Badiou, *Paul*, pp. 76–77.
155. Badiou, *Being*, p. 44.
156. Ibid., p. 28.

157. Ibid., p. 45.
158. Ibid., p. 28.
159. Ibid., p. 24.
160. Ibid.
161. Ibid.
162. Ibid., p. 52.
163. Ibid., p. 53.
164. Ibid.
165. Ibid.
166. Ibid.
167. Ibid., p. 86.
168. Ibid., p. 74.
169. Bradley, *Shakespearean*, p. 25.
170. Badiou, *Being*, p. 84.
171. Ibid.
172. Ibid., p. 75.
173. Ibid., p. 56.
174. Hegel, *Aesthetics*, p. 585.
175. Badiou, *Being*, p. 162.
176. Badiou, *Subject*, p. 49.
177. Badiou, *Being*, p. 74.
178. Ibid., p. 209.
179. Ibid., p. 239.
180. Ibid., p. 391.
181. Ibid., p. 393.
182. Ibid., p. 221.
183. Ibid., p. 197.
184. Ibid., pp. 215–216.
185. Ibid., p. 216.
186. Ibid., p. 432.
187. Ibid. For Badiou, this 'linguistic idealism' mirrors the 'great classical tradition of idealism' but makes language and not self-consciousness the point of being 'through which all access to existence as such must pass': Ibid., p. 278.
188. Ibid., p. 430.
189. Badiou, *Subject*, p. 279.
190. Badiou, *Being*, p. 3.
191. Ibid.
192. Badiou, *Subject*, p. 259.
193. Ibid.
194. Ibid., p. 279.

195. Ibid., p. 28.

196. Benjamin, *Illuminations*, p. 253.

197. Alain Badiou, *The Century*. Alberto Toscano. Trans. Cambridge: Polity, 2007, p. 140.

2 The Subject of Love in *Romeo and Juliet*

1. Montaigne, Vol. 2, Ch. 1, p. 13.

2. Badiou, *Being*, p. 24.

3. Susan Snyder observes that these contentless names operate ideologically to define the situation: 'Capulets define who they are against Montagues, Montagues against Capulets': 'Ideology and the Feud in *Romeo and Juliet*', *Shakespeare Survey* 49 (1996), 87–96, pp. 90–91.

4. Palfrey, *Possible*, p. 73.

5. Holbrook, p. 214.

6. Holbrook, p. 217.

7. Hegel, *Aesthetics*, p. 219, italics mine.

8. States contends that our 'further exposure' to a character merely 'confirms what we see at the outset respecting the character's way of being before us': p. 12.

9. Paul A. Kottman, 'Defying the Stars: Tragic Love as the Struggle for Freedom in *Romeo and Juliet*', *Shakespeare Quarterly* 63.1 (2012), 1–38.

10. Garner Jr. quoting Maurice Merleau-Ponty, p. 4.

11. Samuel Taylor Coleridge, *Coleridge's Criticism of Shakespeare*. R. A. Foakes. Ed. London: Athlone, 1989, p. 151.

12. Petrarch, *Petrarch's Lyric Poems: The Rime Sparse and Other Lyrics*. Robert M. Durling. Ed. Cambridge Mass.: Harvard University Press, 1976, p. 98, Poem 37.

13. Montaigne, Vol. 2, Ch. 10, p. 97.

14. 'Shakespeare generally makes fun of the traditional signs of love melancholy, especially in male lovers. He is sympathetic, but also amused': Maurice Charney, *Shakespeare on Love and Lust*. New York: Columbia University Press, 2000, p. 22.

15. Roland Knowles, 'Carnival and Death in *Romeo and Juliet*: A Bakhtinian Reading', *Shakespeare Survey* 49 (1996), 69–85, p. 74.

16. Jonathan Goldberg, 'Romeo and Juliet's Open Rs', in R. S. White, ed., *Romeo and Juliet, William Shakespeare*. Basingstoke: Palgrave, 2001, 194–212, p. 197.

17. William Empson, *Some Versions of Pastoral*. Third Impression. London: Chatto, 1968, p. 30.

18. Ibid.

19. Slavoj Žižek, *The Fragile Absolute or, Why Is the Christian Legacy Worth Fighting For?* London: Verso, 2000, p. 128.
20. Kottman, 'Defying', p. 10.
21. Emmanuel Levinas, *Entre Nous: Thinking-of-the-Other*. Michael B. Smith and Barbara Harshav. Trans. London: Continuum, 2006, pp. 74–75.
22. Alain Badiou, *In Praise of Love*. Peter Bush. Trans. London: Serpent's Tail, 2012, p. 43.
23. Ibid., p. 28.
24. Jean-Luc Marion, *The Crossing of the Visible*. James K.A. Smith. Trans. Stanford: Stanford University Press, 2004, p. 87.
25. Ibid., pp. 56–57.
26. Badiou, *Paul*, p. 54.
27. Arthur Broke, *Romeus and Iuliet*. Amsterdam: Da Capo, 1969, Fo. 6.
28. Ibid., Fo. 7.
29. Ibid., Fo. 9.
30. Lloyd Davis, '"Death-Marked Love": Desire and Presence in *Romeo and Juliet*', *Shakespeare Survey* 49 (1996), 57–67, p. 65.
31. Badiou, *Love*, p. 22.
32. Ibid., p. 27.
33. Ibid., p. 28.
34. Kottman, 'Defying', p. 5.
35. Ibid.
36. Badiou, *Subject*, p. 6.
37. Starobinski, p. 26.
38. Kottman, 'Defying', p. 6.
39. Ibid., p. 12.
40. Ibid.
41. Ibid., pp. 12–13.
42. Kottman uses this term constantly without giving it a clear content: pp. 3, 5, 6, 8, 9, 15, 17, 18, 21, 26, 29, 31, 34, 37.
43. Ibid., p. 22.
44. Ibid., pp. 24, 26, 27, 30.
45. Badiou, *Being*, p. 3.
46. Kottman, 'Defying', p. 5.
47. Palfrey, *Possible*, p. 73.
48. States writes that the 'character-base . . . involves the behavioral equivalent of musical key': *Hamlet*, p. 32.
49. Hegel, *Phenomenology*, p. 93.
50. Ibid.
51. Kuzner, p. 75.
52. Badiou, *Love*, p. 29.

53. Ibid.
54. Kiernan Ryan, 'The Murdering Word' in White, 116–128, p. 121.
55. Goldberg, p. 197.
56. Badiou, *Love*, pp. 80–81.
57. Ibid., p. 80.
58. Ibid., p. 82.
59. Catherine Belsey, 'The Name of the Rose in Romeo and Juliet' in White, 47–67, pp. 55–56.
60. Badiou, *Being*, p. 209.
61. Badiou, *Love*, p. 42.
62. Vernon, 'Love', p. 158.
63. Eliot, *Poetry*, p. 87.
64. Ibid.
65. Ibid., p. 88.
66. Belsey, 'Name', p. 54.
67. Ibid., p. 65.
68. Jacques Derrida, *Acts of Literature*. Derek Attridge. Ed. New York: Routledge, 1992, p. 423.
69. Ibid.
70. Ibid., pp. 426–427.
71. Ibid., p. 419.
72. Broke, Fo. 16.
73. Marcel Mauss, *The Gift: The Form and Reason for Exchange in Archaic Societies*. W. D. Halls. Trans. London: Routledge, 1990, p. 3.
74. Paul A Kottman, *A Politics of Scene*. Stanford: Stanford University Press, 2008, p. 175.
75. Badiou, *Love*, p. 28.
76. Palfrey and Stern, p. 148.
77. Ibid.
78. Ibid., p. 149.
79. Žižek, *Ticklish*, p. 138.
80. Badiou, *Love*, pp. 28–29.
81. Philip Sidney, *Astrophil and Stella*. M. H. Abrams et al., eds., *The Norton Anthology of English Literature*. 7th ed., Vol. 1. New York: Norton, 2000, pp. 917–931.
82. Tybalt, that force of the situation, is '"the . . . captain of compliments", or conventions,' whereas Juliet fights against such 'lifeless social forms and courtesies': Holbrook, p. 220.
83. Badiou, *Paul*, p. 17.
84. Montaigne, Vol. 2, Ch. 29, p. 431.
85. Badiou, *Paul*, p. 14.

86. Jacques Derrida, *Politics of Friendship*. George Collins. Trans. London: Verso, 1997, p. 220.
87. Ibid.
88. Kottman, *Scene*, p. 175.
89. Ibid., pp. 176–177.
90. Ibid., 'Defying', p. 13.
91. Badiou, *Ethics*, p. 26.
92. Kottman, 'Defying', p. 33.
93. Though, as I noted, the 'other' is very quickly transcended in favour of individual self-realisation.
94. Badiou, *Love*, p. 46.
95. Ibid., p. 25.
96. Ibid., p. 98.
97. Jim Vernon, 'Badiou and Hegel on Love and the Family', in Vernon and Calcagno, 155–176, p. 156.
98. Ibid., p. 158.
99. Žižek, *Belief*, pp. 148–149.
100. States, *Hamlet*, p. 32.
101. Julia Kristeva, *Tales of Love*. Leon S. Roudiez. Trans. New York: Columbia University Press, 1987, pp. 221–222.
102. Ibid., p. 217. According to Kristeva, '[e]ither time's alchemy transforms the criminal, secret passion of the outlaw lovers into … a tired and cynical collusion' or 'the married couple continues to be a passionate couple, but covering the entire gamut of sadomasochism': p. 217.
103. Ibid., p. 3.
104. Ibid.
105. Hugh Grady, *Shakespeare and Impure Aesthetics*. Cambridge: Cambridge University Press, 2009, p. 203.
106. Badiou, *Love*, p. 27.
107. I here draw on Žižek's essay, 'Courtly Love, or Woman as Thing' in S. Žižek, *The Metastases of Enjoyment: Six Essays on Woman and Causality*. London: Verso, 1994.
108. Kuzner, p. 14.
109. Kottman, *Politics*, p. 177.
110. Žižek, *Belief*, p. 90.
111. Badiou, *Subject*, p. 159.
112. Vernon, 'Love', p. 150.
113. Montaigne, Vol. 2, Ch. 29, p. 431.
114. Badiou, *Love*, p. 40.
115. Badiou, *Ethics*, pp. 41–42.
116. Badiou, *Being*, p. 393.

117. Kottman, 'Defying', p. 23.
118. Badiou, *Love*, p. 26.
119. Hélène Cixous, 'The Laugh of the Medusa', in Vincent B. Leitch Ed. *The Norton Anthology of Theory and Criticism*. New York: Norton, 2010, 1942–1959, p. 1959.
120. Ibid.
121. Jean-Luc Nancy, *A Finite Thinking*. Simon Sparks. Ed. Stanford: Stanford University Press, 2003, p. 253.
122. Kristeva, p. 3.
123. Nancy, *Finite*, p. 262.
124. Ibid., p. 265.
125. Soren Kierkegaard, *Repetition: An Essay in Experimental Psychology*. Walter Lowrie. Trans. London: Oxford University Press, 1942, p. 6.
126. Žižek, *Fragile*, pp. 128–130.
127. Kottman, 'Defying', p. 36.
128. Kottman emphasises Hegel's claim that 'freedom is won' by 'risking one's life' (Ibid., p. 8) but ignores the fact that while the master achieves glorious separation, the slave ultimately achieves a higher form of consciousness because he *works* in the world.
129. Badiou, *Paul*, p. 88.
130. Brian Gibbons, ed., *Romeo and Juliet*. Arden Shakespeare. London: Methuen, 1980. p. 44.
131. Badiou, *Being*, p. 216.
132. Kristeva, p. 214.
133. Žižek, *Fragile*, pp. 125–126.
134. Ibid., p. 127.
135. Ibid., p. 126.
136. Vernon, 'Love', p. 159, p. 161 (quoting Badiou's *The Meaning of Sarkozy*).
137. Badiou, *Being*, p. 197.
138. Broke, Fo. 29.
139. Joan Ozark Holmer, 'The Poetics of Paradox: Shakespeare's Versus Zeffirelli's Cultures of Violence', *Shakespeare Survey* 49 (1996), 163–179, p. 163.
140. I am reminded of René Girard's joke 'that back in the twentieth century no more was needed than the request of some ghost, and the average professor of literature would massacre his entire household without batting an eyelash': *A Theater of Envy*. New York: Oxford University Press, 1991, p. 287.
141. Kottman, 'Defying', p. 26.
142. Holmer, p. 175.
143. For Snyder, Romeo's sudden return to 'conventional reactions and conventional language' shows how 'the grip of ideology is tenacious,

and apt to tighten in moments of emotional crisis': Romeo is 'total[ly]' absorbed 'into the avenger-role prescribed for him in the code of honour': p. 94.
144. The demands of 'fidelity' are nothing if not harsh.
145. Badiou, *Subject*, p. 168.
146. Paul A. Kottman, *Tragic Conditions in Shakespeare: Disinheriting the Globe*. Baltimore: Johns Hopkins University Press, 2009, p. 17.
147. Badiou, *Love*, p. 60.
148. Lloyd Davis, p. 65.
149. 'When Juliet lapses into her feud-assigned form of subjectivity as outraged Capulet, her speech changes. All at once, she is speaking in hackneyed images and formally balanced end-stopped lines': Snyder, p. 94.
150. Broke, Fo. 30.
151. Badiou, *Paul*, p. 77.
152. Belsey, 'Name', p. 55.
153. Whitehead, *Adventures*, pp. 200–202.
154. Emrys Jones, *Scenic Form in Shakespeare*. Oxford: Clarendon, 1971, p. 35.
155. Ibid., pp. 35–36.
156. Kottman, 'Defying', p. 25.
157. Even their deaths become a triumph of 'active individuation' in which they 'embrace their final separation as their own': Ibid., p. 37.
158. Ibid., p. 25.
159. Kottman, *Politics*, p. 167.
160. Lupton, p. 89.
161. Kristeva, p. 217.
162. Žižek, *Belief*, p. 41.
163. Žižek, *Fragile*, p. 127–128.
164. Derrida, *Literature*, p. 419.
165. Bergson, *Creative*, p. 172.
166. Petrarch, p. 44, Poem 10.
167. Holbrook remarks: 'Genuine lovers remake the world around them … [t]hey can redescribe a nightingale as a lark and daylight as the light from a meteor': p. 218.
168. Belsey, 'Name', p. 55.
169. Geoffrey Hill, *Collected Critical Writings*. Kenneth Haynes. Ed. Oxford: Oxford University Press, 2008, p. 349.
170. Badiou, *Ethics*, p. 43.
171. Vernon, 'Love', p. 158.
172. Bert O. States, *Great Reckonings in Little Rooms: On the Phenomenology of Theater*. Berkeley: University of California Press, 1985, p. 27.

173. Bryan Reynolds and Janna Segal speak of a 'some-other-where-but-here-space' in *Romeo and Juliet*: 'a non-represented yet aesthetically-invoked dimension': Reynolds, p. 156.

174. I here adapt Tony Tanner: 'As Professor Mahood very accurately puts it, Romeo and Juliet "stellify each other"': *Prefaces to Shakespeare*. Cambridge Mass.: Belknap, 2010, p. 105.

175. Ibid.

176. Badiou, *Logic*, p.432.

177. Whitehead, *Adventures*, p. 305.

178. Ibid., p. 227.

179. States, *Reckonings*, p. 198.

180. Ibid., p. 199.

3 Love's Late Arrival: Wonder and Terror in *Othello*'s 'High-Wrought Flood'

1. T. S. Eliot, *Selected Essays*. London: Faber, 1932, p. 130.

2. F. R. Leavis's account of Othello is particularly damning: 'Diabolic Intellect and the Noble Hero', in J Wain, ed., *Shakespeare: Othello: A Casebook*. Second Edition. Houndmills: Macmillan, 1994, pp. 120–124.

3. Cefalu, p. 6.

4. Ibid., p. 95.

5. Cefalu describes his story as an 'unpeopled narrative': p. 94.

6. G. Wilson Knight, 'The Othello Music', in Wain, 72–95, p. 94.

7. Bradley, *Shakespearean*, p. 23.

8. Knight, p. 73.

9. States, *Hamlet*, p. 205, n.12.

10. Ibid., p. 32.

11. Knight, p. 75. For example: 'Anthropophagi, Ottomites, Arabian trees, "the base Indian", the Egyptian, Palestine, Mauretania, the Sagittary, Olympus, Mandragora, Othello, Desdemona'.

12. Ibid., p. 79.

13. Bradley, *Shakespearean*, p. 176.

14. That said, I'll show that Kuzner's focus on weakness as a means of achieving subjecthood in many ways chimes with my own focus on the vulnerability of relying on the event.

15. Kuzner, p. 55.

16. Cefalu, pp. 41–42.

17. Knight, p. 78.

18. Hegel, *Aesthetics*, p. 200.

19. Ibid.

20. Bradley, p. 190.
21. Knight, p. 78.
22. Palfrey and Stern, p. 118.
23. Ibid., p. 93.
24. Ibid., p. 94.
25. Ibid.
26. He will, of course, also demand to know Desdemona's thoughts.
27. Hegel, *Introductory*, p. 121, n.8.
28. Badiou, *Love*, p. 98.
29. Christopher Pye, '"To throw out our eyes for brave Othello": Shakespeare and Aesthetic Ideology', *Shakespeare Quarterly* 60.4 (2009), 425–447, p. 435.
30. Kuzner, pp. 56–57.
31. Ibid., p. 190, n.9.
32. Laurie Maguire, '*Othello*, Theatre Boundaries, and Audience Cognition', in L. C. Orlin, ed., *Othello: The State of Play*. London: Bloomsbury, 2014, 17–43, p. 18.
33. Ibid.
34. Nicholas Potter, *Othello*. London: Continuum, 2008, p. 101.
35. Shawn Smith, 'Love, Pity, and Deception in *Othello*', *Papers on Language and Literature* 44.1 (2008), 3–51, pp. 20–21.
36. The Geneva Bible (1560) uses 'pity' twice here but 'compassion' in the following passage. It similarly uses 'pitiful' in the 1 Peter 3 verse.
37. Cefalu, p. 42.
38. Lupton, p. 243.
39. Pye, p. 428.
40. Ibid.
41. Ibid., p. 425.
42. Ibid., p. 428.
43. Ibid., p. 430.
44. Badiou, *Being*, p. 175.
45. Ibid.
46. Ibid.
47. Ibid., p. 391.
48. Knight, p. 86.
49. Kuzner, p. 68.
50. Ibid., p. 67.
51. Badiou, *Love*, p. 39.
52. Kuzner, p. 190, n.9.
53. Badiou, *Love*, p. 98.
54. Hegel, *Phenomenology*, p. 96.
55. Ibid., p. 237.

56. Levinas, *Entre*, p. 13.
57. Luther, p. 135.
58. Kuzner, p. 6.
59. Ibid.
60. Ibid.
61. Ibid.
62. Ibid, p. 14.
63. Cefalu, p. 95.
64. Žižek, *Ticklish*, p. 57.
65. Kuzner, p. 67.
66. Knight, p. 93.
67. Badiou, *Love*, p. 39.
68. Kuzner, p. 59.
69. Žižek, *Fragile*, p. 96.
70. Henri Bergson, *Time and Free Will: An Essay on the Immediate Data of Consciousness*. F. L. Pogson. Trans. London: George Allen, 1912, p. 98.
71. Ibid., p. 100.
72. Benjamin, *Illuminations*, pp. 252–53.
73. Ibid.
74. Montaigne, Vol. 3, Ch. 10, pp. 261–62.
75. Kristeva, pp. 4–5.
76. Badiou, *Ethics*, p. 46.
77. Ibid., p. 71.
78. Ibid., p. 78.
79. Badiou, *Paul*, p. 64.
80. Badiou, *Subject*, p. 259.
81. Badiou, *Century*, p. 124.
82. Žižek, *Fragile*, pp. 146–47.
83. Whitehead, *Adventures*, pp. 152–53.
84. Levinas, *Entre*, p. 74.
85. Which is what Hugh Grady argues is 'missing' from Pye's reading: 'Theory "After Theory": Christopher Pye's Reading of Othello', *Shakespeare Quarterly* 60.4 (2009), 453–459, p. 457.
86. G. W. F. Hegel, *The Hegel Reader*. Stephen Houlgate. Ed. Oxford: Blackwell, 1988, p. 108. I here use A. V. Miller's translation of *Phenomenology* as it better captures the idea of embodiment.
87. Kierkegaard, *Anxiety*, p. 138.
88. Kierkegaard, *Sickness*, pp. 206–207.
89. Shakespeare pointedly departs from Cinthio's tale, in which the Ensign's motivations are clear: he loves Disdemona and unsuccessfully attempts to seduce her (before murdering her in revenge). As Bradley shows, the

'difficulty' with Shakespeare's Iago is not that he doesn't provide motives but 'that he assigns so many' and that these 'appear and disappear in the most extraordinary manner': Bradley, p. 225.

90. Kierkegaard, *Anxiety*, p. 119.

91. Kierkegaard, *Sickness*, p. 239.

92. Ibid., p. 238.

93. Žižek, *Belief*, p. 84.

94. Cefalu, p. 42.

95. Montaigne, Vol. 2, Ch. 12, p. 232.

96. Kierkegaard, *Anxiety*, p. 138.

97. Miller's translation: Hegel, *Reader*, p. 56.

98. Hegel, *Phenomenology*, p. 93.

99. Montaigne, Vol. 2, Ch. 12, p. 141.

100. Hegel, *Reader*, p. 108.

101. Soren Kierkegaard, *Works of Love*. David F. Swenson. Trans. Princeton: Princeton University Press, 1946, p. 5.

102. Žižek, *Ticklish*, p. 135.

103. Slavoj Žižek, *The Sublime Object of Ideology*. London: Verso, 1989, p. 33.

104. Badiou, *Subject*, p. 259.

105. Kuzner, p. 70.

106. Ibid., p. 73.

107. Stanley Cavell, *Disowning Knowledge in Seven Plays of Shakespeare*. Updated Edition. Cambridge: Cambridge University Press, 2003, p. 19.

108. Žižek, *Fragile*, p. 128.

109. Badiou, *Being*, p. 233.

110. Ibid., p. 216.

111. Ibid., p. 218.

112. Kuzner, p. 75.

113. Cefalu, p. 87.

114. Ibid., p. 92.

115. Ibid., p. 94.

116. Žižek, *Sublime*, p. 114.

117. Ibid.

118. Cavell, p. 133.

119. Miller's translation: Hegel, *Reader*, p. 103.

120. Cefalu, p. 92.

121. Heffernan observes that 'Badiou's meta-ontology is premised upon two exclusions: the individual and the community': p. 62.

122. Cefalu, p. 85.

123. Badiou, *Paul*, p. 77.

124. Badiou, *Ethics*, p. 79.

125. Leavis, p. 131.
126. Ibid.
127. Cefalu, pp. 92–93.
128. Potter, p. 72.
129. Leavis, p. 134.
130. Knight, p. 94.
131. Ibid., p. 79.
132. Ibid., p. 77.
133. Ibid., p. 94.
134. Ibid., p. 78.
135. Leavis, p. 135.
136. Knight, p. 78.
137. Or 'Judean' in the Folio.
138. Martin Meisel, *How Plays Work: Reading and Performance*. Oxford: Oxford University Press, 2007, p. 169.
139. Kierkegaard, *Anxiety*, p. 128.
140. Hegel, *Aesthetics*, p. 158.
141. Badiou, *Subject*, p. 160.
142. Hegel, *Aesthetics*, p. 158.
143. Eliot, *Selected Essays*, p. 130.

4 The Ghostly Event(s) of *Hamlet*

1. Unless that would be a Kierkegaard.
2. Montaigne, Vol. 1, p. 15.
3. Ibid., Ch. 25, p. 188.
4. Ibid., Ch. 29, p. 213.
5. Ibid., Vol. 2, Ch. 12, p. 155.
6. States, *Hamlet*, p. 96.
7. Margreta De Grazia, *Hamlet Without Hamlet*. Cambridge: Cambridge University Press, 2007.
8. Ibid., pp. 1–2.
9. Andrew Gurr and Mariko Ichikawa, *Staging in Shakespeare's Theatres*. Oxford: Oxford University Press, 2000, p. 49.
10. Thomas Kyd, *The Spanish Tragedy*, in K. E. Maus, ed., *Four Revenge Tragedies*. Oxford: Oxford University Press, 2008.
11. T. S. Eliot describes Horatio's exchange with Marcellus as 'great poetry' that culminates in Horatio's words on the morn – words by which 'we are lifted for a moment beyond character': *Poetry*, pp. 76–77.
12. Lowell Gallagher, 'Waiting for Gobbo', in E. Fernie, ed., *Spiritual Shakespeares*. London: Routledge, 2005, 73–93, p. 81.

228 *Notes to Pages 106–115*

13. Ibid.
14. John Gillies, 'The Question of Original Sin in *Hamlet*', *Shakespeare Quarterly* 64.4 (2013), 396–424, p. 399.
15. Montaigne, Vol. 3, Ch. 5, p. 105.
16. Ibid., Vol. 2, Ch. 12, p. 142.
17. Ibid., Vol. 1, Ch. 12, p. 118.
18. Whether Hamlet Snr *is* inimitable is clearly open to doubt but Hamlet certainly *wants* him to be. Moreover, the encounter on the ramparts is itself singular.
19. Holbrook, p. 89, quoting Lacan's 1959 seminar.
20. De Grazia, p. 196.
21. Cavell, p. 188.
22. Stephen Greenblatt, *Hamlet in Purgatory*. Princeton: Princeton University Press, 2001, p. 208.
23. Badiou, *Paul*, p. 64.
24. Holbrook writes that 'Hamlet's alienation from the world', like Kierkegaard's despair, 'recommends him to us' because it distinguishes him from the spiritless repetition of the everyday world: '[w]e like Hamlet *because* he is a failure': p. 49.
25. Bergson, *Creative*, pp. 152–153.
26. Cavell, p. 188.
27. Bergson, *Creative*, p. 152.
28. Bergson, *Matter and Memory*. Nancy Margaret Paul. Trans. New York: Zone, 1988, p. 32.
29. Bergson, *Creative*, pp. 151–152.
30. Badiou, *Subject*, p. 180.
31. Ibid., p. 88.
32. De Grazia, p. 170.
33. Coleridge (1989), p. 68.
34. De Grazia, p. 1.
35. Coleridge (1989), p. 67.
36. Badiou, *Being*, p. 162.
37. Hegel, *Aesthetics*, pp. 1225–1226.
38. Harold Bloom, *Hamlet: Poem Unlimited*. New York: Riverhead, 2003, p. 15.
39. Ibid., p. 9.
40. Ibid., p. 132.
41. De Grazia, p. 170.
42. Catherine Belsey, *The Subject of Tragedy: Identity and Difference in Renaissance Drama*. London: Routledge, 1985, pp. 41–42.
43. Ibid., p. 42.
44. Whitehead, *Adventures*, pp. 201–2.

45. Ibid., p. 202.
46. Bergson, *Creative*, pp. 151–152.
47. Ibid.
48. Badiou, *Subject*, p. 89.
49. Robert Weimann, 'Mimesis in *Hamlet*' in P. Parker and G. Hartman, eds., *Shakespeare and the Question of Theory*. New York: Routledge, 1990, 275–91, p. 277.
50. Ibid., p. 284.
51. Bergson, *Creative*, p. 152.
52. Weimann, p. 277.
53. Bergson, *Creative*, p. 151.
54. 'For almost a thousand lines' (from II.ii to III.ii) 'Shakespeare cuts a gap into his representation of reality': Bloom, *Unlimited*, p. 19.
55. Bergson, *Creative*, p. 152.
56. Ibid., p. 161.
57. Davis, *Sudden*, pp. 105–106.
58. Montaigne, Vol. 2, Ch. 17, p. 359.
59. Ibid., Ch. 12, p. 166.
60. Bloom, *Unlimited*, p. 71.
61. Ibid., p. 15.
62. Kierkegaard, *Sickness*, p. 169.
63. Kierkegaard, *Anxiety*, p. 61.
64. Kierkegaard, *Sickness*, p. 169.
65. Aristotle, p. 104.
66. Jones, p. 80.
67. Ronald Levao, *Renaissance Minds and Their Fictions*. Berkeley: University of California Press, 1985, p. 356.
68. Ewan Fernie, 'The Last Act: Presentism, Spirituality and the Politics of Hamlet', in Fernie, *Spiritual*, 186–211, pp. 202–203.
69. Ibid., p. 201.
70. Ibid.
71. Montaigne, Vol. 1, Ch. 19, p. 80.
72. Bergson, *Creative*, pp. 22–23.
73. De Grazia shows 'the extent to which Hamlet's renunciation of earthly things' in the graveyard 'concentrates on earth itself': p. 145.
74. Fernie, 'Last', p. 188.
75. Montaigne, Vol. 2, Ch. 12, p. 223.
76. Ibid.
77. Bloom, *Unlimited*, p. 94.
78. Levao, p. 355.
79. Gurr and Ichikawa, pp. 76–77.

80. Ibid., p. 77.
81. States, *Hamlet*, p. 89.
82. Evelyn Tribble, 'Distributing Cognition in the Globe', *Shakespeare Quarterly* 56.2 (2005), 135–155, p. 135.
83. Ibid.
84. Keir Elam, *The Semiotics of Theatre and Drama*. Second Edition. London: Routledge, 2002, p. 33.
85. Ibid., p. 76.
86. De Grazia, p. 138.
87. Ibid., p. 139.
88. De Grazia argues that Hamlet's supposed 'tranquil[ity]' (p. 130) cannot be reconciled with the 'outrageous lack of control' (p. 152) of his histrionic leap into the grave. However, at this point Hamlet has *yet* to recognise providence. The 'tranquility' is yet-to-come. Even so, Hamlet's non-evasive declaration helps prepare for the final scene's calmer readiness.
89. Fernie, 'Last', p. 201.
90. Whitehead, *Adventures*, p. 202.
91. Palfrey and Stern, p. 389.
92. For Coleridge, 'let us know' reflects the 'characteristic of Hamlet's mind, ever disposed to generalize, and meditative to excess': *Coleridge on Shakespeare*. T. Hawkes. Ed. Harmondsworth: Penguin, 1959, p. 89.
93. Michael Witmore, *Culture of Accidents: Unexpected Knowledges in Early Modern England*. Stanford: Stanford University Press, 2001, p. 96.
94. Ibid., p. 97.
95. Jean-Luc Nancy, *The Ground of the Image*. Jeff Fort. Trans. New York: Fordham University Press, 2005, p. 1.
96. Nancy, *Finite*, pp. 222–223.
97. Ibid., p. 229.
98. Fernie, 'Last', p. 188.
99. Badiou, *Being*, p. 175.
100. Greenblatt, *Purgatory*, p. 4.
101. Eliot, *Selected Essays*, p. 145.
102. Ibid.
103. Badiou, *Being*, p. 74.
104. Ibid., pp. 74–75.
105. Gurr and Ichikawa, p. 77.
106. Fernie, 'Last', p. 201.
107. Badiou, *Subject*, p. 125. In 'certain ruptures' the event 'comes to inscribe itself two times': 'The political time of the universal Church, of which Saint Paul is

the brilliant and ill-humoured Lenin, retroactively grounds the Incarnation as fact': Ibid., pp. 125–126.

108. Benjamin, *Illuminations*, p. 247.
109. Agamben, *Time*, pp. 74–75.
110. 'During a performance of a play ... what most concerns us is the immediate future, what is going to develop out of the present moment': Jones, p. 52.
111. Levao, p. 356.
112. Belsey, *Subject*, p. 42.
113. Ibid.
114. Ibid.
115. Kierkegaard, *Sickness*, p. 169.
116. Ibid., p. 172.
117. Terry Eagleton, *The Ideology of the Aesthetic*. Oxford: Blackwell, 1990, p. 180.
118. Ibid.
119. Ibid.
120. Fernie, 'Last', p. 204.
121. Luther, p. 57.
122. Nietzsche, *Untimely*, p. 63.
123. For Lupton, this is Hamlet 'laying claim to that Messianic *kairos*, that precious time that remains for action': p. 238.
124. Marion, *Visible*, p. 28.
125. Ibid., p. 32.
126. Ibid., p. 28.
127. 'Hamlet's deed suggests the possibility of an authentic act *not* determined by prevailing conventions, in this case revenge': Fernie, 'Last', p. 206.
128. Badiou, *Being*, p. 192.
129. Ibid., p. 197.
130. Badiou, *Subject*, p. 294.
131. Ibid., p. 427.
132. Andrew Gibson, *Beckett and Badiou: The Pathos of Intermittency*. Oxford: Oxford University Press, 2006.
133. Ibid., p. 173.
134. Ibid., p. 140.
135. Ibid.
136. To adopt Gibson's words about Rimbaud: ibid., p. 110.
137. Fernie, 'Last', p. 194.
138. Ibid., p. 204.
139. Ibid.

140. Jacques Derrida, *Spectres of Marx: The State of the Debt, the Work of Mourning, and the New International.* Peggy Kamuf. Trans. New York: Routledge, 1994, p. xvii.
141. Ibid., p. xix.
142. Ibid.
143. Ibid., p. 35.
144. Levao, pp. 77–78.
145. Derrida, *Spectres*, p. 31. Derrida refuses to read Marx as a 'great philosopher', but stresses 'Marx's injunction . . . to act': p. 32.
146. Gibson, p. 190.
147. Ibid.
148. Ibid., p. 106.
149. Ibid., p. 105.
150. Ibid., pp. 167–168.
151. Ibid., p. 168.
152. Ibid., p. 169.
153. Badiou, *Being*, p. 397.
154. Ibid., pp. 396–397.
155. Agamben, *Time*, pp. 74–75.
156. Bradley speaks of 'apprehend[ing] some vaster power' that we cannot 'name' (*Shakespearean*, pp. 171–172), while Fernie speaks of an 'undecidable' sense of 'justice' in the last act: 'Last', p. 206.
157. Badiou, *Subject*, p. 294.
158. Heffernan, pp. 77–78.
159. Benjamin, *Illuminations*, p. 255.
160. Whitehead, *Adventures*, pp. 201–202.
161. Grady, *Aesthetics*, p. 185.
162. Walter Benjamin, *The Origin of German Tragic Drama.* John Osborne. Trans. London: NLB, 1977, p. 158.
163. Ibid.
164. Latour, p. 310.
165. Ibid., p. 156.
166. Derrida, *Spectres*, p. 63.
167. Badiou, *Subject*, p. 296.
168. Benjamin, *German*, p. 235.
169. Frank Kermode, *The Sense of an Ending: Studies in the Theory of Fiction.* New York: Oxford University Press, 1967, p. 82.
170. Ibid.
171. Benjamin, *German*, p. 232.
172. Ibid., p. 233.
173. Slavoj Žižek, *In Defense of Lost Causes.* London: Verso, 2008, p. 141.
174. Hegel, *Phenomenology*, p. 75.

5 *Macbeth*: The Arrival of Evil

1. Ralph Holinshed, *Chronicles of England, Scotland and Ireland*. Text of 1587. www.cems.ox.ac.uk/holinshed/. The Holinshed Project, 2008–2010, p. 169.
2. Ibid.
3. Ibid., p. 170.
4. Ibid., p. 171.
5. Bradley, *Shakespearean*, p. 332.
6. Terry Eagleton, *William Shakespeare*. Oxford: Basil Blackwell, 1986, p. 2.
7. Badiou, *Being*, p. 175.
8. Ibid.
9. Ibid., p. 75.
10. And who is almost indistinguishable from 'merciless Macdonald – / Worthy to be a rebel, for that / The multiplying villainies of nature / Do swarm upon him' (I.ii.9–12).
11. Holinshed, p. 152.
12. Ibid., p. 161.
13. Benjamin, *Illuminations*, p. 248.
14. Harry Berger Jr, *Making Trifles of Terrors: Redistributing Complicities in Shakespeare*. Stanford: Stanford University Press, 1997, p. 75.
15. Benjamin, *Illuminations*, p. 248.
16. Nietzsche, *Untimely*, p. 59.
17. Badiou, *Being*, p. 97.
18. Ibid., p. 109.
19. Ibid.
20. Berger, p. 84.
21. Palfrey and Stern, pp. 125–126.
22. Ibid., p. 126.
23. Ibid., p. 129.
24. Hegel, *Aesthetics*, p. 231.
25. Hegel, *Reader*, p. 97.
26. Ibid.
27. Bradley, *Shakespearean*, p. 344.
28. Ibid., p. 343.
29. Ibid., p. 332.
30. Palfrey and Stern, p. 98.
31. Ibid.
32. Luther, p. 135.
33. Latour, p. 310.
34. Bradley, *Shakespearean*, p. 344.
35. Badiou, *Being*, p. 56.
36. Ibid.

37. Žižek, *Lost*, p. 113.
38. Badiou, *Being*, p. xxix.
39. Ibid.
40. Badiou, *Ethics*, p. 16.
41. Ibid., p. 71.
42. Ibid., p. 73.
43. Ibid., p. 72.
44. Ibid., p. 73.
45. Ibid., pp. 72–73.
46. Ibid., p. 74.
47. Marion, *Crossing*, p. 40.
48. Ibid.
49. Žižek, *Lost*, p. 114.
50. Badiou, *Being*, p. 74.
51. Bradley, *Oxford*, p. 89.
52. Bradley, *Shakespearean*, p. 352.
53. States, *Reckonings*, p. 4.
54. Ibid.
55. Montaigne, Vol. 1, Ch. 10, p. 92.
56. Ibid., Vol. 1, Ch. 36, p. 243.
57. Ibid., Vol. 2, Ch. 12, p. 141.
58. Ibid., Vol. 1, Ch. 10, p. 92.
59. Ibid., p. 94.
60. Ewan Fernie, *The Demonic: Literature and Experience*. London: Routledge, 2013, p. 61.
61. Ibid., p. 63.
62. Holinshed, p. 171.
63. Witmore, *Accidents*, p. 10.
64. Ibid.
65. Ibid., p. 36.
66. Ibid., p. 148.
67. Shakespeare, p. 2569; i.e. the 'greatest', being the kingship, lies *behind* Cawdor, lies next in line.
68. Witmore, *Accidents*, p. 43
69. Hegel, *Aesthetics*, p. 578.
70. Bradley, *Shakespearean*, p. 352.
71. Ibid.
72. Holinshed, p. 168.
73. Badiou, *Being*, p. 75.
74. Badiou, *Subject*, p. 160.
75. Ibid.

76. Montaigne, Vol. 1, Ch. 23, p. 128.

77. Jonathan Dollimore, *Radical Tragedy: Religion, Ideology and Power in the Drama of Shakespeare and his Contemporaries*. Third Edition. Basingstoke: Palgrave Macmillan, 2004, p. xxxi.

78. Ibid., p. xxxii.

79. Nietzsche, *Untimely*, p. 64.

80. Ibid.

81. Ibid.

82. John Locke, *An Essay Concerning Human Understanding*. London: J. M. Dent, 1961 p. 7.

83. Montaigne, Vol. 3, Ch. 10, p. 258.

84. Ibid., pp. 258–260.

85. Hazlitt, *English Poets*, p. 220.

86. Bradley, *Shakespearean*, p. 353.

87. Ibid.

88. Davis, *Sudden*, p. 25.

89. Badiou, *Ethics*, p. 85.

90. Ibid., p. 82.

91. Ibid., p. 85.

92. Ibid., p. 83.

93. Badiou, *Being*, p. 417.

94. Ibid., p. 393.

95. Ibid., p. 417.

96. Cavell, pp. 233–234.

97. Bergson, *Creative*, pp. 22–24.

98. Badiou, *Subject*, p. 180.

99. Fernie similarly asks: 'what does this murderer truly want from the kingship? We do not know; *he doesn't*': *Demonic*, p. 55.

100. Badiou, *Subject*, p. 259.

101. Ibid., p. 291.

102. Ibid., p. 294.

103. Gilles Deleuze and Félix Guattari, *Anti-Oedipus: Capitalism and Schizophrenia*. Robert Hurley, M. Seem, and H. R. Lane. Trans. London: Athlone, 1984, p. 332.

104. Ibid., p. 378.

105. Davis, *Sudden*, p. 25.

106. And ultimately like Lady Macbeth herself.

107. Bradley, *Shakespearean*, p. 354.

108. Montaigne, Vol. 2, Ch. 5, p. 45.

109. Fernie, *Demonic*, p. 63.

110. Ibid., p. 64.

111. Kierkegaard, *Sickness*, p. 241.
112. Ibid.
113. Ibid., p. 236.
114. Ibid.
115. Ibid., p. 238.
116. Ibid., p. 241.
117. Kierkegaard, *Fear*, p. 50.
118. Latour, p. 310.
119. William Empson, *Essays on Shakespeare*. Cambridge: Cambridge University Press, 1986, p. 37.
120. Bradley, *Oxford*, pp. 88–89.
121. Derrida, *Literature*, p. 105.
122. Fernie, *Demonic*, p. 10.
123. Ibid.
124. Montainge, Vol. 1, Ch. 36, p. 246.
125. Bradley, *Oxford*, p. 255.
126. 'We find ourselves relishing villains . . . simply because of their "intensity"': Holbrook, p. 173.
127. Derrida, *Literature*, p. 78.
128. Ibid, p. 83.
129. Ibid.
130. Ibid.
131. Ibid., p. 108.
132. Whitehead, *Process*, p. 160.
133. Ibid., p. 90.
134. Hegel, *Aesthetics*, p. 523.
135. Žižek, *Lost*, p. 7.

6 The Cordelia Event: Seizing the Vanished in *King Lear*

1. Coleridge (1989), p. 95.
2. Ibid.
3. Cavell, p. 61.
4. Witmore, *Metaphysics*, p. 61.
5. Ibid.
6. Badiou, *Ethics*, p. 43. Italics mine.
7. Bergson, *Creative*, pp. 39–40.
8. Ibid., p. 47.
9. Ibid., p. 292.
10. Ibid., p. 315.
11. Ibid.

12. Francis Bacon, *The Major Works*. Oxford: Oxford University Press, 2002, p. 178: 'the passages and variations of nature cannot appear so fully in the liberty of nature, as in the trials and vexations of art.'

13. Jonathan Sawday, *Engines of the Imagination: Renaissance Culture and the Rise of the Machine*. London: Routledge, 2007, pp. 3–4.

14. Ibid., p. 234.

15. Ibid., pp. 234–235.

16. Ibid., p. 153.

17. *Pace* Tate, in which the world operates according to an overarching mechanism of redemption, which rewards and punishes pre-determined virtue and vice.

18. Nancy, *Finite*, p. 254.

19. Ibid., p. 265.

20. Friedrich Nietzsche, *The Genealogy of Morals*. Francis Golffing. Trans. New York: Doubleday, 1956, p. 191.

21. Badiou, *Being*, p. 90.

22. Witmore, *Metaphysics*, p. 61.

23. Badiou, *Ethics*, p. 73.

24. Ibid., p. 74.

25. Badiou, *Being*, p. 56.

26. Adapted from Cavell's observation that while one may 'pretend publicly to love, where you do not love . . . to pretend to love, where you really do love, is not obviously possible': p. 62.

27. Ibid.

28. Yachnin and Selkirk, p. 151.

29. Nahum Tate, *The History of King Lear*. James Black. Ed. London: Edward Arnold, 1976.

30. Dollimore, p. 193.

31. Palfrey and Stern, p. 109.

32. Dollimore, p. 198.

33. Badiou, *Being*, p. 52.

34. Ibid., p. 53.

35. Ibid., p. 67.

36. Ibid., p. 376.

37. Meisel, p. 164.

38. Bradley, *Shakespearean*, p. 321.

39. Ibid., p. 318.

40. Coleridge (1989), p. 98.

41. Bergson explains that '[i]f I pronounce the negative proposition, "This table is not white," I mean that you ought to substitute for your judgment, "The table is white," another judgment . . . the nature of which, however, is not specified': *Creative*, p. 305.

42. Badiou, *Being*, p. 56.

43. Witmore, *Metaphysics*, p. 21.

44. Albeit for the most human reasons of shame and wounded pride.

45. Whitehead, *Adventures*, pp. 144–145.

46. Latour, p. 12.

47. Cavell, pp. 5–6.

48. Ibid., p. 229.

49. Bradley, *Shakespearean*, p. 326. Similarly, see Kent's 'the gods reward your kindness!' (F.III.vi.5), which cues Gloucester's exit from the hovel. Gloucester is blinded in the following scene.

50. Bradley writes of 'the vagueness of the scene where the action takes place' in *Lear* 'and of the movements of the figures which cross this scene; the strange atmosphere, cold and dark, . . . enfolding these figures and magnifying their dim outlines like a winter mist': *Shakespearean*, p. 247.

51. Badiou, *Being*, p. 319.

52. Ibid.

53. Montaigne, Vol. 2, Ch. 12, p. 229.

54. Ibid.

55. Badiou, *Being*, p. 319.

56. Bergson, *Time*, p. 151.

57. Hugh Grady, *Shakespeare's Universal Wolf: Studies in Early Modern Reification*. Oxford: Clarendon, 1996, p. 147.

58. Fernie, *Spiritual*, p. 16.

59. Cavell, p. 65.

60. Meisel, p. 110.

61. Bergson, *Creative*, pp . 29–30.

62. Luther, p. 135.

63. Badiou, *Ethics*, p. 68.

64. Badiou, *Being*, p. 232.

65. Ibid., p. 216.

66. Fernie, *Spiritual*, p. 17.

67. Badiou, *Being*, p. 56.

68. Žižek, *Belief*, p. 17.

69. Žižek, *Ticklish*, p. 43.

70. Phillip Shaw, *The Sublime*. London: Routledge, 2006, p. 2.

71. Badiou, *Being*, p. 74.

72. Whitehead, *Process*, p. 90.

73. Badiou, *Paul*, p. 66.

74. Badiou, *Subject*, p. 69.

75. Ibid., pp. 55–56. Shoaf also analyses *King Lear* in terms of atoms and the void, but his Lucretian worldview makes the *clinamen* or 'swerve' a rule of being:

'*All* things *always* change' (p. 112). But Shakespeare's swerves seem more exceptional than structural. In short, the explosive 'Nothing' of the 'Cordelia event' is what sends the atoms swerving, not some pre-existing 'vitality'.

76. Badiou, *Subject*, p. 57.
77. Ibid., p. 58.
78. Ibid.
79. Ibid.
80. Ibid., p. 69.
81. Ibid.
82. Ibid.
83. Whitehead, *Adventures*, p. 202.
84. Badiou, *Ethics*, p. 77.
85. Kierkegaard, *Fear*, p. 50.
86. Enid Welsford, 'The Fool in *King Lear*', in F. Kermode, ed., *King Lear: A Casebook*. London: Macmillan, 1969, 137–149, p. 149.
87. Thomas P. Roche Jr., '"Nothing Almost Sees Miracles": Tragic Knowledge in *King Lear*', in J. L. Halio, ed., *Critical Essays on Shakespeare's King Lear*. New York: G. K. Hall, 1996, 149–169, p. 151.
88. Badiou, *Subject*, p. 68.
89. In this, and in his unsatisfying redemptions and dubious miracle workings, he may foreshadow Prospero.
90. Fernie, *Demonic*, p. 224.
91. Grady similarly writes: 'Edgar begins his strange series of metamorphoses after, in his turn, being disowned and losing the name of his father, by hiding in "the happy hollow of a tree" (II. iii. 2) and proclaiming, "Edgar I nothing am" (II.iii.21)': *Wolf*, p. 145.
92. In this, Edgar's transformations resemble Hamlet's transformative off-stage voyage, but Edgar is transformed off-stage *multiple* times.
93. Palfrey and Stern, p. 248.
94. Levinas, *Entre*, p. 86.
95. Ibid., p. 74.
96. Hegel, *Phenomenology*, p. 93.
97. Ibid.
98. Montaigne, Vol. 2, Ch. 12, pp. 199–200.
99. Ibid., p. 201.
100. Žižek, *Belief*, p. 148.
101. Luther, p. 83.
102. Kierkegaard, *Sickness*, p. 193.
103. Ibid., p. 187.
104. Deleuze and Guattari, p. 364.

105. Ibid., p. 367.
106. Michael Ryan makes a similar connection but concludes that 'the play represents the multiple as dangerous', 'side[s] with the unitary' and is 'about the need to restore a territorialization organized around a single paternal centre': *Literary Theory: A Practical Introduction*. Malden, MA: Blackwell, 1999, p. 76. I argue that 'Nothing' deterritorializes: that it *breaks down* the calculable and thereby creates something dangerously new.
107. Fernie, *Demonic*, p. 224.
108. Ibid.
109. Ibid., p. 234.
110. As is the connection between the 'servingman' and Oswald: Simon Palfrey, *Poor Tom: Living King Lear*. Chicago: University of Chicago Press, 2014, pp. 210–211.
111. Fernie, *Demonic*, p. 236.
112. Palfrey, *Tom*, pp. 26–27.
113. He refers to a 'potentially sacred abjection' (p. 229), links Edgar to Christ's 'passion' (p. 232) and concludes that he 'retains a flavour of the sacred' (p. 236): *Demonic*.
114. While I dispute the source of Edgar's openness, I largely concur with Fernie's account of it.
115. Fernie, *Demonic*, p. 234. However, his description of Cordelia's 'reserve' does not account for how her irruptive 'Nothing' helps create this new world in which a non-calculable receptivity is possible.
116. Ibid., p. 236.
117. R. A. Foakes, 'French Leave, or Lear and the King of France', *Shakespeare Survey 49* (1996), 217–223, p. 222.
118. R. A. Foakes, 'The Reshaping of *King Lear*', in Kahan, 104–123, p. 121.
119. Ibid., p. 119.
120. Žižek, *Belief*, p. 84.
121. Cavell, p. 74.
122. Ibid., p. 55.
123. Lear's line is often emended to 'When did you die?' in accordance with the Second Quarto (though my formulation does not rely on this emendation).
124. Foakes, 'Reshaping', p. 119.
125. Foakes, 'French', pp. 221–222.
126. Lear has already rejected mechanistic logic in his 'madness' and, indeed, foreshadowed Cordelia's 'No cause': 'I pardon that man's life. What was thy cause? / Adultery? Thou shalt not die. Die for adultery!' (F.IV.v.106–107).
127. Maurice Blanchot, *The Writing of Disaster*. Ann Smock. Trans. Lincoln: University of Nebraska Press, 1986, p. 53.

128. R. V. Young, 'Hope and Despair in King Lear: The Gospel and The Crisis of Natural Law', in Kahan, 253–277, p. 272.

129. Bradley, *Shakespearean*, p. 324.

130. Hegel, *Aesthetics*, p. 523.

131. Jeffrey Kahan, *King Lear: New Critical Essays*. New York: Routledge, 2008, p. 1.

132. R. A. Foakes, '*Hamlet* versus *Lear*: Cultural Politics and Shakespeare's Art', in G. Ioppolo, ed., *A Routledge Literary Sourcebook on William Shakespeare's King Lear*. London: Routledge, 2003, 59–60, p. 59.

133. Ibid.

134. Friedrich Nietzsche, *The Birth of Tragedy*. Francis Golffing. Trans. New York: Doubleday, p. 142.

135. Ibid., p. 145.

136. Palfrey quotes the director Grigori Kozintsez: in 'Shakespeare's world … nothing perishes without trace, and death is answered by birth, and when the darkness reaches its utmost limits, an almost invisible spark already begins to burn, and the darkness loses its power in comparison with this tiny fragment of light': *Tom*, p. 139, n.6.

137. Badiou, *Paul*, p. 66.

138. Young, p. 253.

139. Meisel, p. 127.

140. Kahan, p. 1.

141. Shaw, p. 115.

142. Badiou, *Century*, p. 140.

143. Bradley, *Shakespearean*, p. 304.

144. Badiou, *Century*, pp. 140–141.

145. Ibid., p. 142.

146. Ibid., p. 140.

Afterword

1. Hazlitt, *Poets*, p. 276.

2. Walter Pater, *Walter Pater: Three Major Texts*. William E. Buckler. Ed. New York: New York University Press, 1986, p. 165.

3. Badiou, *Being*, p. 162.

4. Badiou, *Paul*, p. 77.

5. Nietzsche, *Birth*, p. 142.

6. Nancy, *Finite*, p. 229.

7. Badiou, *Being*, p. 192.

Works Cited

Agamben, G., *The Time That Remains: A Commentary on the Letter to the Romans*. Patricia Dailey. Trans. Stanford: Stanford University Press, 2005.

Aristotle, *Poetics*, in D. A. Russell and M. Winterbottom, eds., *Ancient Literary Criticism*. Oxford: Clarendon, 1972.

Bacon, F., *The Major Works*. Oxford: Oxford University Press, 2002.

Badiou, A., *Being and Event*. Oliver Feltham. Trans. London: Continuum, 2005.

Badiou, A., *Deleuze: The Clamor of Being*. Louise Burchill. Trans. Minneapolis: University of Minnesota Press, 2000.

Badiou, A., *Ethics: An Essay on the Understanding of Evil*. Peter Hallward. Trans. London: Verso, 2001.

Badiou, A., *In Praise of Love*. Peter Bush. Trans. London: Serpent's Tail, 2012.

Badiou, A., *Logic of Worlds*. Alberto Toscano. Trans. London: Continuum, 2009.

Badiou, A., *Saint Paul: The Foundation for Universalism*. Ray Brassie. Trans. Stanford: Stanford University Press, 2003.

Badiou, A., *The Century*. Alberto Toscano. Trans. Cambridge: Polity, 2007.

Badiou, A., *Theory of the Subject*. Bruno Bosteels. Trans. London: Continuum, 2009.

Belsey, C., 'The Name of the Rose in Romeo and Juliet', in White, 47–67.

Belsey, C., *The Subject of Tragedy: Identity and Difference in Renaissance Drama*. London: Routledge, 1985.

Benjamin, B., *Illuminations*. Harry Zohn. Trans. London: Fontana, 1992.

Benjamin, W., *The Origin of German Tragic Drama*. John Osborne. Trans. London: New Left Books, 1977.

Berger Jr, H., *Making Trifles of Terrors: Redistributing Complicities in Shakespeare*. Stanford: Stanford University Press, 1997.

Bergson, H., *Creative Evolution*. Arthur Mitchell. Trans. London: Macmillan, 1911.

Bergson, H., *Matter and Memory*. Nancy Margaret Paul. Trans. New York: Zone, 1988.

Bergson, H., *Time and Free Will: An Essay on the Immediate Data of Consciousness*. F. L. Pogson. Trans. London: George Allen, 1912.

Blanchot, M., *The Writing of Disaster*. Ann Smock. Trans. Lincoln: University of Nebraska Press, 1986.

Bloom, H., *Hamlet: Poem Unlimited*. New York: Riverhead, 2003.

Bloom, H., *Shakespeare: The Invention of the Human*. London: Fourth Estate, 1999.

Bradley, A. C., *Oxford Lectures on Poetry*. London: Macmillan, 1926.

Bradley, A. C., *Shakespearean Tragedy: Lectures on* Hamlet, Othello, King Lear, Macbeth. Second Edition. Macmillan: London, 1932.

Broke, A., *Romeus and Iuliet*. Amsterdam: Da Capo, 1969.

Cavell, S., *Disowning Knowledge in Seven Plays of Shakespeare*. Updated Edition. Cambridge: Cambridge University Press, 2003.

Cefalu, P., *Tragic Cognition in Shakespeare's* Othello*: Beyond the Neural Sublime*. London: Bloomsbury, 2015.

Charney, M., *Shakespeare on Love and Lust*. New York: Columbia University Press, 2000.

Cinthio, G., *Hecatommithi*. J. E. Taylor. Trans. http://shakespeare-navigators.co m/othello/Osource.html. Visited 26 April 2017.

Cixous, H., 'The Laugh of the Medusa', in V. B. Leitch, ed., *The Norton Anthology of Theory and Criticism*. New York: Norton, 2010, 1942–59.

Coleridge, S. T., *Coleridge's Criticism of Shakespeare*. R. A. Foakes. Ed. London: Athlone, 1989.

Coleridge, S. T., *Coleridge on Shakespeare*. T. Hawkes. Ed. Harmondsworth: Penguin, 1959.

Davis, L., '"Death-Marked Love": Desire and Presence in *Romeo and Juliet*', *Shakespeare Survey* 49 (1996), 57–67.

Davis, P., *Shakespeare Thinking*. London: Continuum, 2007.

Davis, P., *Sudden Shakespeare: The Shaping of Shakespeare's Creative Thought*. London: Athlone, 1996.

De Grazia, M., Hamlet *Without Hamlet*. Cambridge: Cambridge University Press, 2007.

Deleuze, G., and F. Guattari, *Anti-Oedipus: Capitalism and Schizophrenia*. Robert Hurley, M. Seem, and H. R. Lane. Trans. London: Athlone, 1984.

Derrida, J., *Acts of Literature*. Derek Attridge. Ed. New York: Routledge, 1992.

Derrida, J., *Politics of Friendship*. George Collins. Trans. London: Verso, 1997.

Derrida, J., *Spectres of Marx: The State of the Debt, the Work of Mourning, and the New International*. Peggy Kamuf. Trans. New York: Routledge, 1994.

Derrida, J., 'Structure, Sign and Play in the Discourse of the Human Sciences', in P. Rice and P. Waugh, eds., *Modern Literary Theory: A Reader*. London: Edward Arnold, 1989, 149–65.

Dollimore, J., *Radical Tragedy: Religion, Ideology and Power in the Drama of Shakespeare and his Contemporaries*. Third Edition. Basingstoke: Palgrave Macmillan, 2004.

Eagleton, T., *The Ideology of the Aesthetic*. Oxford: Basil Blackwell, 1990.

Eagleton, T., *William Shakespeare*. Oxford: Basil Blackwell, 1986.

Elam, K., *The Semiotics of Theatre and Drama*. Second Edition. London: Routledge, 2002.

Eliot, T. S., *On Poetry and Poets*. London: Faber, 1957.

Eliot, T. S., *Selected Essays*. London: Faber, 1932.

Empson, W., *Essays on Shakespeare*. Cambridge: Cambridge University Press, 1986.

Empson, W., *Some Versions of Pastoral*. Third Impression. London: Chatto, 1968.

Fernie, E., ed., *Spiritual Shakespeares*. London: Routledge, 2005.

Fernie, E., *The Demonic: Literature and Experience*. London: Routledge, 2013.

Fernie, E., 'The Last Act: Presentism, Spirituality and the Politics of Hamlet', in Fernie, Spiritual, 186–2011.

Foakes, R. A., 'French Leave, or Lear and the King of France', *Shakespeare Survey* 49 (1996), 217–23.

Foakes, R. A., '*Hamlet* versus *Lear*: Cultural Politics and Shakespeare's Art', in G. Ioppolo, ed., *A Routledge Literary Sourcebook on William Shakespeare's* King Lear. London: Routledge, 2003, 59–60.

Foakes, R. A., 'The Reshaping of *King Lear*', in Kahan, 104–123.

Gallagher, L., 'Waiting for Gobbo', in Fernie, *Spiritual*, 73–93.

Garner Jr, S. B., *Bodied Spaces: Phenomenology and Performance in Contemporary Drama*. Ithaca: Cornell University Press, 1994.

Gibbons, B., ed., *Romeo and Juliet*. Arden Shakespeare. London: Methuen, 1980.

Gibson, A., *Beckett and Badiou: The Pathos of Intermittency*. Oxford: Oxford University Press, 2006.

Gillies, J., 'The Question of Original Sin in *Hamlet*', *Shakespeare Quarterly* 64.4 (2013), 396–424.

Girard, R., *A Theater of Envy*. New York: Oxford University Press, 1991.

Goldberg, J., 'Romeo and Juliet's Open Rs', in White, 194–212.

Grady, H., *Shakespeare and Impure Aesthetics*. Cambridge: Cambridge University Press, 2009.

Grady, H., *Shakespeare's Universal Wolf: Studies in Early Modern Reification*. Oxford: Clarendon, 1996.

Grady, H., 'Theory "After Theory": Christopher Pye's Reading of *Othello*', *Shakespeare Quarterly* 60.4 (2009), 453–459.

Greenblatt, S., *Hamlet in Purgatory*. Princeton: Princeton University Press, 2001.

Gurr, A., and M. Ichikawa, *Staging in Shakespeare's Theatres*. Oxford: Oxford University Press, 2000.

Hazlitt, W., *Characters of Shakespear's Plays and Lectures on The English Poets*. London: Macmillan, 1903.

Heffernan, J. J., *Shakespeare's Extremes: Wild Man, Monster, Beast*. Hampshire: Palgrave Macmillan, 2015.

Hegel, G. W. F., *Aesthetics: Lectures on Fine Art*. In two vols. T. M. Knox. Trans. Oxford: Clarendon, 1988.

Hegel, G. W. F., *Introductory Lectures on Aesthetics*. Bernard Bosanquet. Trans. London: Penguin, 1993.

Hegel, G. W. F., *The Hegel Reader*. Stephen Houlgate. Ed. Oxford: Blackwell, 1988.

Hegel, G. W. F., *The Phenomenology of Mind*. J. B. Baillie. Trans. Second Edition. London: George Allen & Unwin, 1961.

Hill, G., *Collected Critical Writings*. Kenneth Haynes. Ed. Oxford: Oxford University Press, 2008.

Holbrook, P., *Shakespeare's Individualism*. Cambridge: Cambridge University Press, 2010.

Holinshed, R., *Chronicles of England, Scotland and Ireland*. Text of 1587. www.cems.ox.ac.uk/holinshed/. The Holinshed Project, 2008–2010. Visited 26 April 2017.

Holmer, J. O., 'The Poetics of Paradox: Shakespeare's Versus Zeffirelli's Cultures of Violence', *Shakespeare Survey* 49 (1996), 163–179.

Holy Bible. King James Version. New Jersey: Thomas Nelson, 1972.

Hutson, L., *The Invention of Suspicion: Law and Mimesis in Shakespeare and Renaissance Drama*. Oxford: Oxford University Press, 2007.

Jackson, K., and A. F. Marotti, 'The Turn to Religion in Early Modern English Studies', *Criticism* 46 (2004), 167–190.

Jones, E., *Scenic Form in Shakespeare*. Oxford: Clarendon, 1971.

Kahan, J., ed., King Lear: *New Critical Essays*. New York: Routledge, 2008.

Kermode, F., *The Sense of an Ending: Studies in the Theory of Fiction*. New York: Oxford University Press, 1967.

Kierkegaard, S., *Fear and Trembling*. Alastair Hannay. Trans. London: Penguin, 1985.

Kierkegaard, S., *Fear and Trembling and The Sickness Unto Death*. Walter Lowrie. Trans. Princeton: Princeton University Press, 1970.

Kierkegaard, S., *Repetition: An Essay in Experimental Psychology*. Walter Lowrie. Trans. London: Oxford University Press, 1942.

Kierkegaard, S., *The Concept of Anxiety: A Simple Psychologically Orienting Deliberation on the Dogmatic Issue of Hereditary Sin*. Reidar Thomte and A. B. Anderson. Trans. Princeton: Princeton University Press, 1980.

Kierkegaard, S., *Works of Love*. David F. Swenson. Trans. Princeton: Princeton University Press, 1946.

Knight, G. W., 'The Othello Music', in Wain, 72–95.

Knowles, R., 'Carnival and Death in *Romeo and Juliet*: A Bakhtinian Reading', *Shakespeare Survey* 49 (1996), 69–85.

Ko, Y. J., and M. W. Shurgot, eds., *Shakespeare's Sense of Character: On the Page and From the Stage*. Farnham: Ashgate, 2012.

Kottman, P. A., *A Politics of Scene*. Stanford: Stanford University Press, 2008.

Kottman, P. A., 'Defying the Stars: Tragic Love as the Struggle for Freedom in *Romeo and Juliet*', *Shakespeare Quarterly* 63.1 (2012), 1–38.

Kottman, P. A., *Tragic Conditions in Shakespeare: Disinheriting the Globe*. Baltimore: Johns Hopkins University Press, 2009.

Kristeva, J., *Tales of Love*. Leon S. Roudiez. Trans. New York: Columbia University Press, 1987.

Kuzner, J., *Shakespeare as a Way of Life: Skeptical Practice and the Politics of Weakness*. New York: Fordham University Press, 2016.

Kyd, T., *The Spanish Tragedy*, in K. E. Maus, ed., *Four Revenge Tragedies*. Oxford: Oxford, University Press, 2008, 1–91.

Latour, B., *Pandora's Hope: Essays on the Reality of Science Studies*. Cambridge, Mass.: Harvard University Press, 1999.

Leavis, F. R., 'Diabolic Intellect and the Noble Hero', in Wain, 120–140.

Lee, J., *Shakespeare's* Hamlet *and the Controversies of Self.* Oxford: Clarendon, 2000.

Levao, R., *Renaissance Minds and Their Fictions.* Berkeley: University of California Press, 1985.

Levinas, E., *Entre Nous: Thinking-of-the-Other.* Michael B. Smith and B. Harshav. Trans. London: Continuum, 2006.

Locke, J., *An Essay Concerning Human Understanding.* London: J. M. Dent, 1961.

Lupton, J. R., *Thinking with Shakespeare: Essays on Politics and Life.* Chicago: University of Chicago Press, 2011.

Luther, M., *Martin Luther's Basic Theological Writings.* Second Edition. Timothy F. Lull. Ed. Minneapolis: Fortress, 2005.

Maguire, L., '*Othello*, Theatre Boundaries, and Audience Cognition', in L. C. Orlin, ed., Othello*: The State of Play.* London: Bloomsbury, 2014, 17–43.

Marion, J., *The Crossing of the Visible.* James K. A. Smith. Trans. Stanford: Stanford University Press, 2004.

Mauss, M., *The Gift: The Form and Reason for Exchange in Archaic Societies.* W. D. Halls. Trans. London: Routledge, 1990.

Meisel, M., *How Plays Work: Reading and Performance.* Oxford: Oxford University Press, 2007.

Montaigne, M., *Essays.* In three vols. John Florio. Trans. London: Dent, 1980.

Nancy, J., *A Finite Thinking.* Simon Sparks. Ed. Stanford: Stanford University Press, 2003.

Nancy, J., *The Ground of the Image.* Jeff Fort. Trans. New York: Fordham University Press, 2005.

Nietzsche, F., *The Birth of Tragedy and The Genealogy of Morals.* Francis Golffing. Trans. New York: Doubleday, 1956.

Nietzsche, F., *Untimely Meditations.* R. J. Hollingdale. Trans. Cambridge: Cambridge University Press, 1983.

Palfrey, S., *Poor Tom: Living* King Lear. Chicago: University of Chicago Press, 2014.

Palfrey, S., *Shakespeare's Possible Worlds.* Cambridge: Cambridge University Press, 2014.

Palfrey, S. and T. Stern, *Shakespeare in Parts.* Oxford: Oxford University Press, 2007.

Pater, W., *Walter Pater: Three Major Texts.* William E. Buckler. Ed. New York: New York University Press, 1986.

Pechter, E., 'Character Criticism, the Cognitive Turn, and the Problem of Shakespeare Studies', *Shakespeare Studies* 42 (2014), 196–228.

Petrarch, *Petrarch's Lyric Poems: The* Rime Sparse *and Other Lyrics.* Robert M. Durling. Ed. Cambridge, Mass.: Harvard University Press, 1976.

Ponech, T., 'The Reality of Fictive Cinematic Characters', in Yachnin and Slights, 41–61.

Potter, N., *Othello.* London: Continuum, 2008.

Pye, C., '"To throw out our eyes for brave Othello": Shakespeare and Aesthetic Ideology', *Shakespeare Quarterly* 60.4 (2009), 425–447.

Reynolds, B., *Transversal Enterprises in the Drama of Shakespeare and his Contemporaries*. Basingstoke: Palgrave Macmillan, 2006.

Roche, Jr, T. P., '"Nothing Almost Sees Miracles": Tragic Knowledge in *King Lear*', in J. L. Halio, ed., *Critical Essays on Shakespeare's* King Lear. New York: G. K. Hall, 1996, 149–169.

Ruda, F., 'Badiou with Hegel: Preliminary Remarks on A(ny) Contemporary Reading of Hegel', in Vernon and Calcagno, 105–121.

Ryan, M., *Literary Theory: A Practical Introduction*. Malden, Mass.: Blackwell, 1999.

Ryan, K., 'The Murdering Word', in White, 116–128.

Sawday, J., *Engines of the Imagination: Renaissance Culture and the Rise of the Machine*. London: Routledge, 2007.

Shakespeare, W., *The Norton Shakespeare*. S. Greenblatt et al. Eds. New York: Norton, 1997.

Shaw, P., *The Sublime*. London: Routledge, 2006.

Shoaf, R. A., *Lucretius and Shakespeare on the Nature of Things*. Newcastle: Cambridge Scholars, 2014.

Smith, S., 'Love, Pity, and Deception in Othello', *Papers on Language and Literature*, 44.1 (2008), 3–51.

Sidney, P., *Astrophil and Stella*, in M. H. Abrams et al., eds., *The Norton Anthology of English Literature*. Seventh Edition. Vol. 1. New York: Norton, 2000.

Sinfield, A., 'From Bradley to Cultural Materialism', *Shakespeare Studies* 34 (2006), 25–34.

Starobinski, J., *Montaigne in Motion*. Arthur Goldhammer. Trans. Chicago: University of Chicago Press, 1985.

Snyder, S., 'Ideology and the Feud in *Romeo and Juliet*', *Shakespeare Survey* 49 (1996), 87–96.

States, B. O., *Great Reckonings in Little Rooms: On the Phenomenology of Theater*. Berkeley: University of California Press, 1985.

States, B. O., *Hamlet and the Concept of Character*. Baltimore: Johns Hopkins University Press, 1992.

Tanner, T., *Prefaces to Shakespeare*. Cambridge, Mass.: Belknap, 2010.

Tate, N., *The History of King Lear*. James Black. Ed. London: Edward Arnold, 1976.

Thomasson, A., *Fiction and Metaphysics*. Cambridge: Cambridge University Press, 1999.

Toscano, A., 'Taming the Furies: Badiou and Hegel on *The Eumenides*', in Vernon and Calcagno, 193–205.

Tribble, E., 'Distributing Cognition in the Globe', *Shakespeare Quarterly* 56.2 (2005), 135–155.

Tribble, E. B., *Cognition in the Globe: Attention and Memory in Shakespeare's Theatre*. New York: Palgrave Macmillan, 2011.

Vernon, J., 'Badiou and Hegel on Love and the Family', in Vernon and Calcagno, 155–176.

Vernon, J., and A. Calcagno, eds., *Badiou and Hegel: Infinity, Dialectics, Subjectivity*. Lanham: Lexington, 2015.

Wain, J., ed., Othello*: A Casebook*. Second Edition. Houndmills: Macmillan, 1994.

Watts, I., 'Alas! And Did My Savious Bleed?' *Hymns and Spiritual Songs*, 1707–9. www.hymntime.com/tch/htm/a/l/a/alasand.htm. Visited on 18 April 2017.

Weimann, R., 'Mimesis in Hamlet', in Patricia Parker and G. Hartman, eds., *Shakespeare and the Question of Theory*. New York: Routledge, 1990, 275–291.

Welsford, E., 'The Fool in *King Lear*', in F. Kermode, ed., King Lear*: A Casebook*. London: Macmillan, 1969, 137–149.

White, R. S., ed., *Romeo and Juliet, William Shakespeare*. Basingstoke: Palgrave, 2001.

Whitehead, A. N., *Adventures of Ideas*. Cambridge: Cambridge University Press, 1933.

Whitehead, A. N., *Process and Reality: An Essay in Cosmology*. Cambridge: Cambridge University Press, 1929.

Witmore, M., *Culture of Accidents: Unexpected Knowledges in Early Modern England*. Stanford: Stanford University Press, 2001.

Witmore, M., *Shakespearean Metaphysics*. London: Continuum, 2008.

Yachnin, P. and M. W. Selkirk, 'Metatheater and the Performance of Character in *The Winter's Tale*', in Yachnin and Slights, 139–157.

Yachnin, P. and J. Slights, eds., *Shakespeare and Character: Theory, History, Performance, and Theatrical Persons*. Basingstoke: Palgrave Macmillan, 2009.

Young, R. V., 'Hope and Despair in *King Lear*: The Gospel and The Crisis of Natural Law', in Kahan, 253–277.

Žižek, S., *In Defense of Lost Causes*. London: Verso, 2008.

Žižek, S., *On Belief*. London: Routledge, 2001.

Žižek, S., *The Fragile Absolute or, Why is the Christian Legacy Worth Fighting For?* London: Verso, 2000.

Žižek, S., *The Metastases of Enjoyment: Six Essays on Woman and Causality*. London: Verso, 1994.

Žižek, S., *The Sublime Object of Ideology*. London: Verso, 1989.

Žižek, S., *The Ticklish Subject: The Absent Centre of Political Ontology*. London: Verso, 1999.

Index

Page numbers *in italics* indicate entries in the footnotes.

adventism, 8–9, 26–29, 53, 194
aesthetics
    characterise the event, 133, 206, *215*
    frame author's view of Shakespeare, 205
    ghostly of *Hamlet*, 132
    and Hegel's xenophobic self-consciousness,
        19, 75
    insufficient for subject's becoming, 130
    new subject not grounded by, 82
    of a work figure its illimitability, 81
Agamben, Giorgio, 27, 128
agency, 18, 76, 80, 129
    Belsey on Hamlet's, 130
    bequeathed, 138, 139
    Bradley on Macbeth's, 149
    impelled by event, 18
    reciprocal, 66
    through readiness, 131
    through submission, 130
Althusser, Louis, 36
Aristotle, 18, 120
arrival, 6, 18
    action precedes intent in, 16
    as creative destructiveness, 169
    delayed, 71, 87, 202
    escapes Badiou's frame, 153, 168, 205
    essentially processive, 6, 65
    essentially transformative, 20, 25, 197
    implies action produces character, 18
    indistinction of, 82, 120, 133, 140
    involves violence, 62, 169
    involves vulnerability, 85, 89, 128
    irruptive, 9
    marked by detail and action, 149
    and the problem of evil, 152
    produces subject, 5, 75, 81
    and readiness, 128, 135
    repositions character, 6, 14
    sublime implicated in, 159, 187

    tenuousness of, 11, 12, 138, 197
    through love, 38, 43, 49, 169, 177, 184, 202
    unachieved potential of, 171, 172, 202
    unpredictable, 135
    void essential to, 117

Bacon, Francis, 175
Badiou, Alain, 30–37
    and adventism, 9, 26, 53
    author's use of, 13
    on contemporary pessimism, 203
    and control, 161
    on courage, 64, 133, 159
    critiques Hegel, 17, 35
    on declaration, 49
    differs from Montaigne, 7, 54
    on the event, 8, 28, 30, 46, 112, 132
    on Evil, 11, 88, 152
    on excess, 34, 145, 204
    on fidelity, 30, 78, 88, 95, 187
    on grace, 65
    on justice, 138
    on love, 42, 44, 48, 55, 59, 64, 84, 86
    and Montaigne on diversity, 7, 31–32
    on poetry, 59, 132–133
    on potential of non-action, 117
    queries how transformation happens, 39
    rebuts Bergson, 23, 114
    on religion, 27
    on repetition and identity, 75, 84
    on the State, 146
    on the subject, 6, 30, 36, 45, 89, 97, 106, 114,
        136, 164, 169
    as thinker of division, 15
    on truth, 31–32
    uninterested in diversity *qua* diversity, 31
    use of set theory, 33–34, 178
    on the void, 158
Barker, Francis, 115

Belsey, Catherine, 48, 50, 65, 115, 130
Benjamin, Walter, 9, 37, 87, 128, 137, 138,
    139, 144
Berger, Harry Jr, 144, 146
Bergson, Henri, 9, 19, 20, 22, 113, 116, 118, 164
    critiqued by Badiou, 23, 114
    as process philosopher, 174
Blanchot, Maurice, 200
Bloom, Harold, 115, 119, *213*
Bradley, A.C., 14–18
    on agency, 18
    on character, 6, 14, 17, 18, 188
    on Cordelia, 179
    and discontinuity, 15, 16
    on division in Macbeth, 155, 162, 168
    on Iago's motivation, *225*
    on justice in *King Lear*, 182, 203
    on Macbeth and agency, 149
    on Macbeth's guilt, 165
    on Othello, 72, 73
    privileges spirit, 200, 201
Breton, André, 203
Broke, Arthur, 43, 51, 63, 65

Cavell, Stanley, 95, 96, 111, 163, 174, 181, 185, 199
Cefalu, Paul, 71, 73, 80, 91, 96, *212*
character, 133
    A.C. Bradley on, 6, 14, 17, 18
    becomes subject, 23, 188
    critical interest in, 1
    in *Macbeth*, 163
    not predictable from circumstances, 20
    not pre-formed, 12, 15, 17, 18, 21
    terminological difficulties of, 6
    transformed by event, 22
Charney, Maurice, *217*
Chaucer, Geoffrey, 20
Cinthio, Giraldi, 81, *225*
Cixous, Hélène, 60
Coleridge, S.T., 39, 114, 173
consecration, 79, 80, 95, 96, 101, 167
    glossed, 77–78
    subject founded on, 90, 91, 102
courage, 63, 64, 102, 164
courtly love. *See* Petrarchism
creativity, 115
    arises from suffering, 203
    can imagine attractive evil, 168, 172
    and character, 5–6
    dispersed in *King Lear*, 184–192
    in *Macbeth*, 153, 170, 171
    in naming, 87
    negative, 93
    releases potential of arrivals, 149
    in *Romeo and Juliet*, 48, 60, 68–69

and terror of the void, 205
    transformative for audience, 203, 207
    and violence, 169
    from the void, 116
cues, actors', 24, 52, 74–75, 84, 108, 141, 147, 150,
    177, 192, 193
    as subject-making event, 21

Davis, Lloyd, 44, 64
Davis, Philip, 21, 24, 118, 163
de Grazia, Margreta, 104, 109, 110, 114, 115
Deleuze, Giles, 23
    critiqued by Badiou, 23
Deleuze, Giles and Félix Guattari, 164, 195
demonic
    evokes both death and hyper-life, 156, 167,
        169, 170
    fidelity in, 166, 167
    as a form of life, 169
    glossed, 91
    and susceptibility, 195–196
Derrida, Jacques, 13, 14, 50–51, 65, 69, 106, 134,
    138, 171
    on difference and absolute justice, 134
    differs from Badiou, 134
    on excess, 138
    on love, 54
    on openness, 134–135
    supplements Badiou on *Hamlet*, 136
Descartes, René, 19, 36, 181, 188
    subject–object divide of, 18
discontinuity, 15, 23, 24, 25, 26, 28, 32, 34, 35, 46,
    76, 85, 87, 117
    as subject-forming, 16
    demanded by adventist tradition, 28
    irruptive, 29
Dollimore, Jonathan, 159, 178

Eagleton, Terry, 130, 143
Eliot, T.S., 10, 49, 50, 71, 102
Empson, William, 40, 168
event, 20, 21, 22, 24
    arises ambiguously, 43, 82, 85, 88, 98, 104, 120,
        133, 141, 168
    Badiou's formulation critiqued, 135
    can coalesce with evil, 168
    enables possibility, 130
    ethics and, 152–153
    glossed, 8, 30, 112
    introduces truth, 32
    involves excess, 27, 34, 47, 63, *91*, 95, 151
    love as, 42–47, 71
    requires fidelity, 59
    requires intervention, 49
    requires wager of faith, 132

as rupture, 8, 89, 103, 112, 183
subject-forming, 17, 18, 32, 38, 82, 88
tenuous aesthetic of, 132
violence and, 98
eventral site, 82, 143, 189
glossed, 152
excess, 22, 112
enables love, 176
of Hamlet, 112, 119
in language, 42, 143
links situation, void and event, 33–34
of Macbeth, 159
as mark of the human, 183
in painting, 131
prompts affirmation from the negative,
137, 204
of the subject, 30, 69, 80, 134
of the void, 78

Feltham, Oliver, 152
Fernie, Ewan, 130, 156, 166, 169, 185, 187, 192, 195,
196, 197
fidelity, 28, 36, 69, 133
as action, 79, 87, 112
affirming immanence, 201
Badiou on, 8, 94
connects situation and void, 78
defined, 30, 36, 95
demonic, 166, 167
destroyers of, 152
to an event, 152
by giving, 61
involves vulnerability, 57, 88, 174
not necessarily heroic, 205
from negatives, 169
to openness, 94, 197
Romeo's failure in, 59, 64
to a simulacrum, 176
unacted, 112, 118, 133, 134, 135, 169
Florio, John, 21
Foakes, R.A., 199, 201
Foucault, Michel, 36, 152, 153
Freud, Sigmund, 36

Gallagher, Lowell, 106
Garner, Stanton B. Jr, *211*
Gibson, Andrew, 135–136
Gillies, John, 107
giving, 53, 60, 68
as authenticity, 52
as fidelity, 59
as grace, 61, 62
as love, 53, 54, 59, 61
and self-discovery, 21
Goethe, Wolfgang, 74

Goldberg, Jonathan, 40, 43
Grady, Hugh, 57, 137, 183, *225*, *239*
Greenblatt, Stephen, 111

Hamlet, 11
contrasted with *The Spanish Tragedy*,
105, 131
event diffused, 138
events are aesthetic and indeterminate, 133
events undecidable, 133
Hamlet compared to Montaigne, 103,
107, 118
Hamlet's interior–exterior divide,
107–114
indistinction in, 120
interiority readings dismissed, 114–116
justice in, 134, 136–140
language in, 110, 118
readiness in, 128–136
Hazlitt, William, 20, 21, 25, 161, *209*
Heffernan, Julián Jiménez, 31, 137
Hegel, Georg, 16, 19, 36, 39, 44, 84, 93, 140
critiqued by Badiou, 17
dialectic sense of character, 14
on experience of art, 155
on the new, 114
privileges spirit, 200
self-consciousness as aesthetic xenophobia,
19, 75
on the subject, 45
on source of action, 17
on Symbolic Art, 73, 83
as thinker of division, 15
on tragedy, 102
on the tragic hero, 102
on truth through the negative, 46, 193
on Unhappy Consciousness, 90, 97
Heidegger, Martin, 135
Heraclitus, 23
Hill, Geoffrey, 69
Hillman, David, *211*
historicism, 10, 30, 31, 106, 160, 168, 206
history, 9, 141, 144
Nietzsche on, 10
paradoxically anachronistic, 9
Holbrook, Peter, 17, 21, 38, 39, *228*
Holinshed's *Chronicles*, 141, 144, 158
Holmer, Joan Ozark, 64
Hutson, Lorna, 17

immanence, 11, 23
and art, 132, 135
exceeds presence, 129, 132
and the future, 136, 174
glossed, 20

immanence (cont.)
  Hegel on, 35, 115
  as promiscuous process, 23
Inwood, Michael, 19

Jackson, Ken and Arthur Marotti, 27
Jones, Emrys, 66, 120, *231*
justice, 134, 145, 149, 171, 182, 193, *See also Hamlet*

Kahan, Jeffrey, 201
Kant, Immanuel, 13
Kierkegaard, Soren, 9, 29, 61, 169, 191
  on the demonic, 91
  on greatness, 167
  on love and deception, 93
  on possibility and necessity, 119–120, 130
  on repentance through despair, 194
King Lear, 11
  Edgar's radical receptivity in, 195–197
  France's arrival, 189
  language in, 190
  Lear's and Othello's rejections compared,
    180, 181
  love in, 174, 175, 176–180
  'nothing' as void, 182–183
Knight, G. Wilson, 72, 74, 100
Knowles, Roland, 40
Knox, T.M., 14
Kottman, Paul, 39, 41, 44–46, 48, 51, 55, 58, 61, 63,
    64, 66, 67
Kozintsez, Grigori, *241*
Kristeva, Julia, 56–57, 62, 67, 68, 88
  on violence and love, 62
Kuzner, James, 30, 58, 73, 83, 85, 86, 87,
    96, *214*
Kyd, Thomas, *The Spanish Tragedy*, 105, 132

Lacan, Jacques, 36, 41
language
  changed by event, 29
  indicates arrival, 56
  and love, 47–48, 49–51, 57, 58, 178
  power of, 182
  silence through, 101
  used pragmatically, 66
Latour, Bruno, 9, 18, 19, 20, 138, 151, 167
Leavis, F.R., 99, 100
Levao, Ronald, 120, 134
Levinas, Emmanuel, 41, 84, 89, 106,
    193, 197
love, 59–61
  as commitment, 77
  as event, 42–47, 71
  forms joint subject, 46–47
  as giving, 53, 54, 61

grace-like, 202
involves excess, 180
involves vulnerability, 175
and language, 47–48, 49–51, 57, 58, 178
Lear and Juliet compared, 175
precedes knowing, 95
Lucretius, 23
Luhrmann, Baz, 43
Lupton, Julia, 67
Luther, Martin, 9, 85, 130
  stresses transformation by grace, 27
  on subjection and rebirth, 194

Macbeth, 2, 11, 23, 34
  changes from source, 141–142, 148,
    157, 158
  coalesces event and evil, 168
  indistinct event in, 141
  language in, 142, 145, 151
  supernatural contrasted with *Hamlet*'s, 142
  weird sisters' role in, 141–143, 144, 149, 154,
    157, 158
Maguire, Laurie, 77
Mallarmé, Stéphane, 134
Marion, Jean-Luc, 43, 106, 153
  on the excess of painting, 131
Marlowe, Christopher, 16
Marx, Karl, 32, 36
Mauss, Marcel, 51
Measure for Measure, 179
Meisel, Martin, 101, 178, 185
Montaigne, Michel de, 3–6, 7, 20, 21, 30, 45, 59,
    88, 92, 93, 170
  and Badiou on diversity, 31–32
  compared to Hamlet, 103, 107, 118
  contrasted with Shakespeare, 4–6, 24–26
  on the Creation, 183
  dislike of multiple voices, 134
  incremental selfhood in, 25
  mocks Petrarchism, 40
  on need for faith, 130
  and the new, 3–4
  values moderation, 160

Nancy, Jean-Luc, 60, 175
new, the, 2, 6, 7, 22, 33, 58, 68, 170
  ambiguous presentation of, 82
  Hegel on, 114
Nietzsche, Friedrich, 9, 10
  on art, 201
  on excess and freedom, 159–160
  on history, 144
  on human autonomy, 175
  on need for limits, 131
nightingales, 68, 69

Othello, 10, 16, 17, 65
   departs from source, 81, *225*
   Iago and Othello contrasted, 91
   indistinct event in, 141
   language in, 72–74, 83, 86, 99, 100, 101
   Lear's and Othello's rejections compared,
      180, 181
   Othello eschews creativity, 75
   pity in, 78–80
   self-narration in, 75–76, 78, 79, 80, 83,
      91, 101

Palfrey, Simon, 21, 23, 38, 46, 196
Palfrey, Simon and Tiffany Stern, 24, 51,
   146, 150
Pascal, Blaise, 95
   Pascal's wager, 29, 35
Pechter, Edward, *208*
Petrarch, 40
Petrarchism, 43, 44, 47, 48, 51, 53, 58, 68, 78
   contrasted with *Romeo and Juliet*, 61
   Romeo's, 5, 10, 38, 40, 42, 44, 46, 47, 65
Pinter, Harold, 101
Ponech, Trevor, 29
postmodernism, 19, 30, 32, 37, 94, 115, 188, 190,
   201, 203
   on the sublime, 202
poststructuralism, 36
Potter, Nicholas, 77
process philosophy, 3, 9, 13, 18–23, 83, 89, 113, 115
Pye, Christopher, 76, 82

readiness, 128–136
   brings beyond and situation together, 163
   glossed, 129, 131
rebellion, 144, 146, 151, 154, 168, 203
relativism, 19, 138
Reynolds, Bryan, *213*
Romeo and Juliet, 10, 22, 38–70
   changes from source, 43, 51, 65
   language in, 43, 46, 47–48, 49–51, 69, 72, 73
   situation in, 39–41
Ryan, Kiernan, 47

Saussure, Ferdinand de, 50
Sawday, Jonathan, 175
Shakespeare, William. *See also* individual plays
   contrasted with Montaigne, 4–6, 24–26
   faith of, 26
   impartiality of, 170
   and the new, 2
   transformative processes in, 8
Shaw, Philip, 202
Shoaf, Richard, 23, *238*
Sidney, Philip, 40, 51, 53, 61

simulacrum, *93*, 152, 153, *176*
   glossed, 176
situation
   absent from early Symbolic Art, 83
   described mathematically, 33–34
   divided by event, 15
   event grounded within, 30
   generates simulacrum, 152
   Iago's role as, 72, 90, 91, 94
   has limiting language, 151
   paralysed in *Macbeth*, 11, 146, 153
   repeated violence of, 117
   in *Romeo and Juliet*, 39–41
   ruptured by event, 6, 8, 22, 30
   as structure, 42
   in vanishing term, 189
Smith, Shawn, 78
Snyder, Susan, *217*, *221*
St Paul, 2, 8, 9
   Badiou on, 28, 30
   contrasted with Montaigne, 27
   as conversion figure, 27, 80, 153
   counsels submitting to grace, 130
   disgust at sinful flesh, 107, 119
   and pity, 79
   and event, 27, 32, 53
   sees charity as loving grace, 79
Starobinski, Jean, 45, *208*
States, Bert O., 7, 16, 39, 70, 72, 104, 155
subject, 9, 26
   as arrival, 6, 36
   bears fidelity, 174
   distinguished from character, 6–7,
      23, 30
   enemies of, 97
   escapes repetition through the event, 164
   founded on consecration, 90, 102
   fragility of, 75
   glossed, 169
   intervenes for event, 35
   involves excess, 9, 80, 106, 140
   irruptive, 30
   as political, 37
   produced by event, 9, 19, 28, 30
sublime, 67, 187, 203
   creative potential of, 203
   postmodernism on, 202
supernatural
   doesn't destroy agency, 18
   event is not, 30
   in *Hamlet* and *Macbeth* contrasted, 142
   in *Macbeth*, 154

Tanner, Tony, 70
Tate, Nahum, 177, 202, *237*

Tempest, The, 11, 172
texts, acting, 24
Thomas Dekker, *The Seuen Deadly Sinnes of London*, 175
Thomasson, Amie L., 22, *211*
Toscano, Alberto, 15
Tribble, Evelyn, *212*
Troilus and Cressida, 58

vanishing term, 173, 189–190
violence, 98, 169
    as event, 62
    in *Hamlet*, 29, 112
    in *King Lear*, 179
    in *Macbeth*, 144, 150, 153, 163, 164, 169
    in *Othello*, 77, 100, 169
    in *Romeo and Juliet*, 57, 62, 63, 64, 67, 169
    repeated, 11, 117, 137
    transformative, 63
void, 35, 36, 82
    glossed, 8, 34, 119, 154, 195
    integral to subject's action, 128
    involves excess, 11, 33, 34, 128
    produces good and evil, 169

Weimann, Robert, 117
Welsford, Enid, 191
Whitehead, Alfred North, 9, 19, 22, 65, 70, 115, 137, 171, 188
Winter's Tale, The, 61
Witmore, Michael, 19, 20, 23, 157, 180

Yachnin, Paul and Myrna Selkirk, 22

Zeffirelli, Franco, 43
Žižek, Slavoj, 9, 28, 32, 68, 85
    on ethics and the event, 152
    on lost causes, 172
    on love, 41, 59, 62, 89, 96
    on possible futures, 139, 198
    on postmodernism, 94
    on the event, 52, 56, 153
    on the sublime, 67, 187
    on trauma, 87

Lightning Source UK Ltd.
Milton Keynes UK
UKHW020737150622
404452UK00019B/324